Media
Warfare

Media Warfare

The Americanization of Language

The Language of Journalism
Volume 3

Melvin J. Lasky

Being a Third Volume,
Wherein the Language of Journalism is Examined,
Its Splendors and Miseries—
including Clichès and Trivia,
Sensationalism and Prurience,
Wit and Witlessness,
Fiction and Faction,
Pseudery and Jabberwocky,
Scoops and Hoaxes,
Racism and Sexism,
Profanity and Obscenity,
Virtue and Reality,
Culture and Anarchy—
and the Abuse of Slang, Style,
and the Habits of Writing Good Prose.

Transaction Publishers
New Brunswick (U.S.A.) and London (U.K.)

First paperback printing 2007
Copyright © 2005 by Transaction Publishers, New Brunswick, New Jersey.

This book is printed on acid-free paper that meets the American National Standard for Permanence of Paper for Printed Library Materials.

Library of Congress Number: 00-034408
ISBN: 978-0-7658-0302-3 (cloth); 978-1-4128-0728-9 (paper)
Printed in the United States of America

Library of Congress Cataloging-in-Publication Data

Lasky, Melvin J.
  The language of journalism / Melvin J. Lasky.
        p. cm.
  Includes bibliographical references and index.
  Contents: v. 1. Newspaper culture.
  ISBN 0-7658-0001-2 (v. 1.: alk. paper)
    1. Newspapers—Language. 2. Journalism—Language. I. Title.

PN4783.L37 2000
070.4'01'4—dc21   00-034408

Contents

Part 1

Intermezzo
Robert Burton's Melancholy Dilemma:
Journalism without Newspapers

*"You do not need to leave your room. Remain
sitting at your table and listen. Do not even
listen, simply wait. Do not even wait, be quite
still and solitary. The world will freely offer itself
to you to be unmasked, it has no choice, it will
roll in ecstasy at your feet."*
—*Franz Kafka,* Reflections on Sin, Pain,
Hope and the True Way *(1917-1919)*

*"What did Burton read in his solitary study? As
far as we can see, everything, absolutely
everything: ancient classics, modern literature,
latin and Greek, French and English,
philosophy, philology, history, politics,
travel, mathematics, astornomy, medicine.
He was a complete humanist scholar, but
he loved the English poets too, and was
up-to-date in all modern subjects. Like
his contemporary, Francis Bacon, he took all
learning for his province....*

*"It [The Anatomy of Melancholy, 1621] has left
traces in our literature for the next two
centuries. We find traces of it in the poetry
of Milton and the prose of Sterne. It was
the only book which could get Dr. Johnson
out of bed two hours early. It inspired Keats.
It was enjoyed by Byron....*

*"Like most interesting men, Burton is not quite
consistent. He preaches the happy mean and
does not practice it....He is as frank as a
pornographer and as mincing as a prude."*
—*Hugh Trevor-Roper,*
Renaissance Essays *(1985)*

1

The Universal Assignment

We have been pursuing the techniques of censorship by punctuation–they are evidently as old as the hills...especially those odious mountainous obstructions, indeed those s———, f-******, and otherwise unmentionable ranges which block our perception of the road ahead and a clear vision of blue sky. Byronesque asterisks, as we have seen, managed to create enough discreet obfuscation to preocccupy searchers for plain-speaking unambiguous evidence on Lord Byron's life and loves for centuries. Burtonesque dashes–to which we will be coming in due time–were even older; and their decipherment is rather more complicated by the suspicion that the ingenious seventeenth-century English essayist was being playful and provocative, and justifiably felt that he had expressed his robust and subversive opinions on important topics of the day with sufficiently outrageous directness. Why, then, the blankety-blank dashes?

Here is Robert Burton, going on in his radical way about his civilization and its discontents, in the second volume of his *Anatomy of Melancholy* (1621).

He poses the question: Who, in point of embarrassing or harassing historical fact, were the great men of power and distinction who constituted the indomitable ruling class of his Elizabethan and Renaissance age? No small dangers lay in this question, especially if it were to be answered candidly and with no sparing of words. After all, acute struggle–between social classes, political clans and their power-hungry kinsmen; among troubled or otherwise discontented souls–has often been held to be historically determined, to be our destiny: "We are sent as so many soldiers into this world, to strive with it, the flesh, the devil; our life is a warfare, and who knows it not?" But Burton also knew that truth had more than one side–an open-mindedness very rare in such parlous times. His beloved Homer was blind, "yet who made more accurate, lively, or better descriptions, with both his eyes?" Perception was all, and the insight obtained therefrom would penetrate whatever blocked the path to truth:

Homer was blind, yet who (saith he) made more accurate, lively, or better descriptions, with both his eyes? Democritus was blind, yet, as Laertius writes of him, he saw more than all Greece besides; as Plato concludes....When our bodily eyes are at worst, generally the eyes of our soul see best. Some philosophers and divines have evirated [emasculated] themselves, and put out their eyes voluntarily, the better to contemplate. Angelus Politianus had a tetter in his nose continually running, fulsome in company, yet no man so eloquent and pleasing in his works. Aesop was crooked, Socrates purblind, long-legged, hairy, Democritus withered, Seneca lean and harsh, ugly to behold; yet show me so many flourishing wits, such divine spirits: Horace a little blear-eyed contemptible fellow, yet who so sententious and wise? Marsilius Ficinus, Faber Stapulensis, a couple of dwarfs, Melancthon a short hard-favoured man, yet of incomparable parts all three. Ignatius Loyola, the founder of the Jesuits, by reason of a hurt he received in his leg at the siege of Pampeluna, the chief town of Navarre in Spain, unfit for wars and less serviceable at court, upon that accident betook himself to his beads, and by those means got more honour than ever he should have done with the use of his limbs and properness of person: a wound hurts not the soul. Galba the emperor was crook-backed, Epictetus lame; that great Alexander a little man of stature, Augustus Caesar of the same pitch; Agesilaus *despicabili forma* [contemptible in appearance]; Boccharis a most deformed prince as ever Egypt had, yet, as Diodorus Siculus records of him, in wisdom and knowledge far beyond his predecessors. *Anno Dom.* 1306, Uladislaus Cubitalis, that pigmy King of Poland, reigned and fought more victorious battles than any of his long-shanked predecessors. Virtue refuseth no stature, and commonly your great vast bodies and fine features are sottish, dull, and leaden spirits. What's in them? What but sheer bulk and stupid insolence?

This was colorful and exuberant; but if Burton would go on (and he would), insolence and worse would be the grievous charges of yet others who felt they were being–as later victims were to cry–slandered, libelled, and calumnied. Burton had no time for those would-be grandees who furtively changed their names, burned down their birthplace ("because nobody should point at it"), bought titles, coats of arms, and by all means "screw themselves into ancient families, falsifying pedigrees, usurping scutcheons, and all because they would not seem to be base." As Burton says, "Of all vanities and fopperies, to brag of gentility is the greatest." It was, for him, "a mere flash, a ceremony, a toy, a thing of naught."

How did such great families of the day begin (i.e., when was the first screw fastened or consummated)? He names the ways: "Oppression, fraud, cozening, usury, knavery, bawdry." Last but not least: "murder, and tyranny."

No revolutionist in history, mounting the barricades as the first step to "change the world," had clenched in his tight little fist so vivid a list of the public enemies which the new society–Burton dreamed of an "excellent commonwealth," organized "for the common good of all"–would never ever miss:

One hath been a blood-sucker, a parricide, the death of so many a silly soul in some unjust quarrels, seditions, made many an orphan and poor widow, and for that he is made a lord or an earl, and his posterity gentlemen for ever after. Another hath been a bawd, a pander to some great men, a parasite, a slave, prostituted himself, his wife, daughter to some lascivious prince, and for that he is exalted. Tiberius preferred many honours in his time, because they were famous whoremasters and sturdy drinkers; many come into this parchment-row by flattery or cozening; search your old families, and you shall scarce find of a multitude…that have not a wicked beginning….For who did not reach their present position through violence or deceit, as that plebeian in Machiavel in a set oration proved to his fellows, that do not rise by knavery, force, foolery, villainy, or such indirect means. They are commonly able that are wealthy; virtue and riches seldom settle on one man: who then sees not the base beginning of nobility? spoils enrich one, usury another, treason a third, witchcraft a fourth, flattery a fifth, lying, stealing, bearing false witness a sixth, adultery the seventh, etc…

It was, in effect, a cascade of curses, which somehow managed by literary skill alone to evade the twin peaks of the cultural dilemma of his time–the theocratic dangers of blasphemy (on the one side, from above) and the secular vulgarities of profanity (on the other, from below). Journalists on the modern scene are well acquainted with this challenge of a semantic tightrope walk; so many falter, lose balance, trip and fall.

Like the happiest of reporters in any epoch he was exclusively interested in the story. "I am not poore, I am not rich, *nihil es nihil deest*. I have little, I want nothing…." On occasions he would, with a conspicuous coyness, insist that he was living "a Monastique life," and in a moment of pique he snapped: "If you like not my writing, go read something else." More than that: privately, at home–living like "a Collegiat Student"–he had "no Wife nor Children, good or bad, to provide for." And yet, and yet–"I heare and see what is done abroad, how others run, ride, turmoile, & macerate [harass, mortify] themselves in Court and Countrey, far from those wrangling Law suits." End effect: "I laugh at [it] all."

Not unlike a few other "Great Intelligencers"* of the day, forerunners of that flowering of the Journalistic Imagination in more enlightened times, Robert Burton lived his life on permanent, universal assignment to cover the world. What later newspapermen (and -women) would call "scoops" he thought of as "*new newes every day*"; and when he summed up his uneventful life and unregistered achievements (no honors, only one book), he linked the kind of "*reporting*" he did to the kind of intellectual imagination which soars as high as history and as far as philosophy. How many glittering prizes for unprecedented excellence would grateful contemporaries have bestowed upon him– if only he had not remained "penned up" in his study (at Christ Church, Oxford)…living "a silent, sedentary, solitary, private life." But he owned some 2,000 volumes, and the resources of the Bodleian Library were only a few steps away. A lonely, quiet man-of-letters is often tempted to play the role of the thunderer:

---

*   I am thinking of such "heroes of history" (in Sidney Hook's phrase) as Pierre Bayle (1647-1706) and Samuel Hartlib (d. 1662), among others, whom I have sketched in my book on *Utopia and Revolution* (1976) – see the portraits in chaps. 9-10, "The Great Intelligencers," pp.. 320-383; and Sidney Hook, *The Hero in History* (1943).

> What is gentry, this parchment nobility then, but…a sanctuary of knavery and naughtiness, a cloak for wickedness and execrable vices, of pride, fraud, contempt, boasting, oppression, dissimulation, lust, gluttony, malice, fornication, adultery, ignorance, impiety?…A nobleman therefore in some likelihood is an atheist, an oppressor, an epicure, a gull [simpleton], a dizzard [blockhead], an illiterate idiot, an outsider, a glow-worm, a proud fool, an arrant ass….They were the first in rank, so also in rottenness.

As I have hinted, there was a sort of journalistic dimension to the Burton literary imagination, and specificities had to be enlisted to give factual and colloquial strength to the airy abstractions in which *idéologues* tend to lose themselves. The author readily succumbed to the temptation to name names, at first only ancestral (and relatively) examples and then current (and usually vindictive) neighbors:

> The nobles of Berry are most part lechers, they of Touraine thieves, they of Narbonne covetous, they of Guienne coiners, they of Provence atheists, they of Rheims superstitious, they of Lyons treacherous, of Normandy proud, of Picardy insolent, etc.; we nay generally conclude, the greater men, the more vicious. In fine…they are most part miserable, sottish, and filthy fellows, like the walls of their houses, fair without, foul within. What dost thou vaunt of now? What dost thou gape and wonder at? admire him for his brave apparel, horses, dogs, fine houses, manors, orchards, gardens, walks? Why, a fool may be possessor of this as well as he; and he that accounts him a better man, a nobelman for having of it, he is a fool himself. Now go and brag of thy gentility.

I have slightly compressed the soaring invective, in order to accentuate the cluster bombs of epithet. For I want to broach again the question of whether in the general history of English political prose–or in "the language of journalism," from detail-padded reportage to inflammatory editorial injunctions–things that needed to be said, in appropriate force and liveliness, could ever be conceived without the shadow of profanity and obscenity, that creative darkness of every great language, lurking on the vulgar periphery of the vernacular.

2

The Journalistic Imagination

My reader is reminded that Burton died in 1640, the opening year of the so-called Puritan Revolution. I suspect that Oliver Cromwell–and even his pamphleteering sidekick John Milton (a.k.a. his Latin secretary)–could not have had any real use for him, despite Burton's belligerent volubility. His views were sharp and radical, if a wee bit overstated, and his temperament openly enthusiastic. But he was constantly warning his readers that his was "an unconstant, unsettled mind." Gods as well as demons were always failing him; his critico-melancholic spirit was not entirely reliable. Propagandists for a new and better society's "*Good Cause*" need to be of sterner stuff.

Still and all, he was in at the beginning of the future's modernity; and his work, conventionally termed "a bridge between medieval and modern thought," is relevant to the dramatic onset of such configurations as *ideology* (which, unlike some illustrious contemporaries like John Milton, Marchamount Nedham, et al., he abhorred) and *utopia* (to which he was fitfully attracted). In fact the whole Western emergence of an intellectual class composed of increasingly independent (or perhaps only free-floating) scribblers–men of high spirits who were committed to shape public opinion for the better (or indeed the very best) on behalf of enlightened human ideals–could scarcely transpire without the development of a journalistic temperament. Burton admitted to a vision, "an Utopia of mine own" (vol. I, p. 97); and whatever it was that he himself thought he was up to, he remained committed to his indefatigable pursuit of "*the new newes*"–from "stealing newes from others"…to curing the human race of its melancholy afflictions…moving closer to some utopian solutions to "those tumults and trobles of the world." His almost endless amassment of telling facts, allusive quotes, sparkling details served to buttress a grand and historic alternative of beneficent human ideals. Implicit in his critique of the ways of the world was a discernible liberal-humanist ideal of good governance.

Scouring every line of Burton's thousand pages, one literary critic found "buried" therein a lively Utopianism–"a Utopia which suggests ([H.G.] Wells"–

7

embracing the author's social and political convictions. It was, in fact, a daunting and beguiling program of innovations and ameliorations. Burton was "revealed" as a humanitarian enemy of war, an advocate of better highways and inland waterways, the reclamation of marshlands, the building of garden villages, and the granting of old-age pensions….To be sure, he was more of a reformer than a revolutionary (that "hard word" was not yet in general usage) but his personal partisan commitment sounded like an absolutist dedication: "I will spend my time and knowledge, which are my greatest fortunes, for the common good of all."[1]

The serious mode of responsibility has had for most utopian intellectuals in history very slippery handles. They slide and fall, and when they get picked up again, the grip is very different, if there is a grasp at all. Here is Burton justifying the grand utopian mission and almost reaching the point at which the Principle "Hope," *das Prinzip Hoffnung* (in yet another philosopher's formula), gives way to *Praxis* Realism or the pragmatism of experience. "…I will yet to satsfie & please myselfe," Burton wrote emphatically, "make an *Utopia* of mine owne, a new *Atlantis*, a poeticall commonwealth of mine owne, in which I will freely domineere, build Cities, make Lawes, Statutes, as I list my selfe. And why may I not?"

The question was rhetorical; he full well knew why not. Thomas More was beheaded in the Tower; and Michael Servetus was burned at the stake in Calvin's Geneva. But before he turned the proposition on its head, "*topsy turvy*" in the "*hurly burly*" (the phrases of the day), he gave the free poetry a good run…before the humdrum prose took over: "I will provide publike schools of all kinds, singing, dancing, &c. especially of Grammar, and Languages, not to bee taught by those tedious precepts ordinarily used, but by use, example, conversation, as travellers learne abroad, and nurses teach their children." There was a footnote here in which Burton paid the obligatory tribute to the "best," then and for centuries thereafter: to Comenius (the Moravian reformer, who was then in England), the father of so-called Progressive Education. And indeed our own John Dewey would have been pleased by the consignment of "tedious precepts" to the dustbin of history. Mankind now had a richly detailed agenda to fulfill.[2]

Among the planks in the platform were: "Hospitals of all kindes for children, orphans, old folkes, sickmen, madmen, souldiers, pesthouses, &c." Conduits for sweet and good water. Opportune market places for all sorts, for corn, meat, cattle, fuel, fish. Engines for quenching of fires. Public walks. Spacious fields for sports. Theaters,. Separate places to bury the dead (but "not in churchyards").

Would the managers in Burton's Utopia be friendly, efficient, and cooperative? The intellectual-in-chief gave his personal guarantee, and we had better believe it. He was evidently thinking of running a one-man Ministry of Full Employment. "As I will have all such places, so will I ordaine publike governours, fit officers to each place....They shall bee subordinate to...Gentlemen." He was peremptory about lurking domestic evils: "I will have no boggs....I will not have a barren acre in all my Territories." He even had a sketch for an up-to-date foreign policy for those second and third worlds just beyond his horizon. "Reforme all distressed states & persons...Cure all manner of diseases...Root out Barbarisme out of America. Finde out the North-East and North-west passages....Irrigate those barren Arabian deserts" (vol. 1, p. 85).

And yet, and yet....The poetical inspiration became exhausted and turned inward on itself; it reversed direction and slowed down into sobriety. Burton's conclusion—which another disappointed generation in another century would be calling "*dialectical*" (because things had a habit of turning into their opposites, with quality not turning into quantity, or into the contrary, or into anything else desirable or useful)—"*Utopian parity is a kinde of government, to be wished for, rather then effected*"—is, as I want to signal to my reader, a kind of jump story which is to be continued on a subsequent page.[3]

The complexities and stubborn difficulties of matching fine human ideals with crude political realities is the stuff of history, and historians since Herodotus have been taking up embattled positions. It is a noble, if predictable and often ineffectual (alas!) enterprise; and it has been going on for a long time now. As I write this, I turn to my morning's copy of the *New York Times* and the (ex-*Manchester*) *Guardian*. The editorial in the former and the leading article in the latter follows on from the "*new newes*" on wars, disasters, and crises about which they have been reporting for days and weeks, if not centuries. The twentieth-century editors have their foreign correspondents in place almost everywhere, and the graphic dispatches they publish offer an interpretation of the causes and consequences of "the tumults and troubles" which kept Robert Burton so busy all those years ago. Great conspiracies have been deviously compounded, and innumerable scandals have regularly stained every walk of life. Youthful reporters can be relied upon to try and "*dig up the dirt*," to "*spill it*"—and to "*tell all*." In turn the older editors go on periodically "*to View with Alarm*," and to suggest (sagely, with a measure of anger, urgency, and self-righteousness) reasonable ways to clean things up. We are all reformers and utopians, now.

Still, Robert Burton in his century enjoyed the cultural infrastructure of a serviceable language which had the strength of glad, confident morning. In the twilight of our own days, neither the words nor the sentences—and hence neither the ideas nor the intellectual communication—seem to be turning up right. Ms. Maureen Dowd will surely be saddened by the whole spectacle, and will resort to writing her "*Oy!*" column, exploiting all the ethnic pidgin from *schmus* to *chutzpah*. Mr. Thomas L. Friedman will offer another of his periodic "Open Letters," this time to Shakespeare, and would share with his *Times*' readers Bardic wisdom on what has gone wrong since Othello—oh so wrongly!—killed Desdemona...or since an indecisive Hamlet failed famously to make up his mind. Mr. Frank Rich will expatiate on the misguided influences on the American language as a result of the takeover by powerful (and sinister) German media moguls of the main Manhattan publishing houses. As for the *Guardian* in London there will be yet another stylish feature story, with analysis "in depth" and snappy interviews, about the dire manipulations of "the Jewish lobby," operating undercover in Washington and New York (and, not unsurprisingly, Tel Aviv).

3

Reporting Murder, Observing the World

But I digress, in a possibly ill-advised effort to span a bridge between distant centuries and resonating parallels. Problematical, too, could be the broad use of professional terms like *reportage*, *news*, and even *journalism*. Nevetheless, my references in this chapter–quotations, actually–to Robert Burton as *"reporter"* are not really an anachronistic play on words; for Burton came very close to the modern usage, i.e., when he offered this couplet to his seventeenth-century readers in the famous "Democritus Junior" preface to his magnum opus:

> *What e're men doe, vowes, fears, in ire, in sport,*
> *Joyes, wandrings, are the summe of my report.*

In the paragraph above and below, Burton has a mélange of quotes from Plutarch to Copernicus, and so an exact ascription as to the author of this little jingle is a bit difficult to decipher. Since Burton invented or freely rewrote so many of his quotations, we need not be overly finicky in ascribing to him so much of the wit and wisdom, so many of the fine lines, original phrases, startling words, that make up his masterpiece–a treasure chest of almost everything that was new (or old) under the sun. Leaving aside philological concerns, the ideas and basic attitudes are uniquely surprising: and in this context the notion of something to which I have referred to as the *Journalistic Imagination* springs out of many of his pages–the Reporter as Historian, the Observer as Philosopher, the Scribbler ("in this scribbling age") as Intellectual...the News-hounds as Prophets of the Times. Burton would have been the ideal staff man, the prolific correspondent, the stimulating leader writer, and (not least) the most understanding of copy editors, improving (by adding to, or subtracting from) edition after edition. He was indeed a precursor of the "Fourth Estate," which only emerged properly in the century of the French Revolution; and he should, I feel, be remembered in every school of journalism:

> as Diogenes went into the Citie, and Democritus to the haven to see fashions, I did for
> my recreation now and then walke abroad, looke into the world, and couild not chuse
> but make some little observation....I did sometime laugh and scoff, satyrically taxe,
> lament....I was much moved to see that abuse which I could not amend.[1]

So many of these "little observations" were large truths, and even some four
centuries later still have a spooky note of pertinence about them. Burton, like
all greatly endowed reporters, is seen holding fast to the entrenched center of
a flourishing vocabulary; in good words was his safety. Without benefit of
Roget (or any other kind of thesaurus), he indicts a whole range of the
Establishment's vices and villains without, as I say, taking in vain the names of
the gods in their heavens or turning for expressive help to the dirty demons of
illicit demotic. No writer who ever lived (except, as Mark Twain is said to have
said, Jane Austen) was above a temptation to the profane and obscene. A number of verbal tricks–puns, and the like–were all available (for Shakespeare, for
Byron) to do the proper camouflage, if necessary. Perhaps, in Burton's case (as
I surmise), there was protection and insurance in the very excess of the forceful
words in robust repetitiveness. It was a strength through synonymity. His words
could never easily be manipulated–or, as we would now say, *spun*–into simple
political slogans. This was at once a source of public tension and personal
sovereign control.

Voluble and grandiloquent though he was, Burton could never have been a
simplistic, serviceable propagandist. His Cromwellian contemporaries were
soon to be caught up in a civil war and indeed in "a revolution" (borrowed
from the Italian *rivuluzione* in the 1640s); and they could come up with a
powerful maxim in defense of combat, mayhem, and political violence, *viz.*
"*Killing No Murder,*" but the catchword would have been for Burton an inad-
missible paradox. At best, it was a political ambiguity according to which the
mass casualties of a new régime's purging of the old order could be defended as "*killing*"–or condemned as "*murder*" as the battlefield victor so
decided. True, even *Ecclesiastes* (3:3, in the King James version) legitimated "*a time to kill*," alternating with "*a time to heal*"; but *Matthew*
(19:18) quotes Jesus as enjoining "*Do not murder.*" Shouldn't the Sixth
Commandment have been retranslated, and simply revised to read "Thou
shalt not *murder*"? After all, the Old Testament is replete with revolts and
rebellions, Armageddons, battles and wars of aggression and defense, all
of which called for killing *en masse*. Burton was too sophisticated to believe
that the crimes of his side were virtues in the name of the good cause, and the
mayhem on the other side was a monstrous sin, base and unforgiveable. He
made no convenient self-serving exceptions; and included in his bill of indictment, in addition to the usual suspects, were "religion, policy, and human
invention, to keep men in obedience, or for profit, invented by priests and
lawgivers to that purpose."

This kind of verbal jugglery is the usual and very practiced ploy to confound means and ends; it is the keen-witted ruse of subtle intellectuals from time immemorial who have dabbled in philosophy and theology, and other rich sources of rationalization, to justify deviltry without seeming to join the party of the Devil. Milton captures one such moment; and Burton, had he known the lines of *Paradise Lost* (iv, 108), would have been deeply disturbed.

So farewell hope, and with hope farewell fear,
Farewell remorse: all good to me is lost;
Evil be thou my good.

The poet was involved in the highest drama and its transcendental stratagems in the great tragedy of human existence; the reporter was only trying to follow the "new newes" as it reached him from every scene in the human comedy.

Still, as one of Burton's twentieth-century admirers (H.R. Trevor-Roper) put it, "Like most interesting men, he is not quite consistent. He preaches the happy mean and does not practice it....He is as frank as a pornographer and as mincing as a prude." Burton himself is almost as self-critical when he admits at the outset: "I have mingled *Sacra prophanis*, but I hope not prophaned." After all, he was a member of the Anglican clergy...and as such paid attention to sins and linguistic lapses, to "swearing" of all kinds. What were those "filthy tunes and tones" he reported on and was shocked to hear? and who uttered them?[6]

Robert Boyle, an Oxford near-contemporary who was troubled by what he thought to be the signs of degeneration of language in his day (and the vile place of "cursing" in the century's public discourse), might well have been satisfied with Burton's evasive efforts.*

---

* See: chapter 28 on "A Curse on Boyle's Law," in this volume.

4

From More to Tyndale to Burton

Burton knew the quarrel that had raged a full century before between Thomas More and William Tyndale–both of whom were, in the end, executed for their singular opinions, with More supporting (even instigating) the Church's bonfire of Tyndale's heretical vanities (1536) by which time King Henry VIII had already ordered More's beheading (1535) for his stubborn Roman orthodoxies. One wonders how much, detail-obsessed as he actually was, of the two tragedies Burton knew.

More's harassment of heretics was, to be sure, well known; and he once wrote to Erasmus (who must have shuddered at the letter) that he wished to be "as hateful to [heretics] as anyone could possibly be." Partisans of Tyndale have gone as far as to write: "More revelled in burnings"; but More did not himself live to see the destruction of "his great enemy" who was judged to be "at the head of the dark galaxy of the Antichrist." News of Tyndale's arrest and imminent destruction (as one Tyndale biographer surmises, on a note of grim sympathy) "would clearly have lightened More's steps to the block."

Deprived in the London Tower of any writing materials (he had been smuggling lengthy manuscripts out of his cell) a last letter to his daughter Meg was "penned" with a piece of coal. A chronicler of More's trial recorded that the jury had only been out for fifteen minutes. And the formal sentence condemned him to be hanged, cut down while still alive, castrated, his entrails cut out and burnt before his eyes, and then beheaded. One English historian notes: "The king in his graciousness commuted this to beheading." Ultimately, the headless corpse reached his daughter for private burial; but before that the head was publicly exhibited on a pole on London Bridge and it had been boiled ("to preserve it and add terror to its demeanor, overboiled in fact, so that it turned black").

More's beheading occurred on 6 July 1535. As for Tyndale, the bishops who served as inquisitor-generals at Tyndale's trial in Antwerp solemnly cursed him for, among other crimes, having "counseled with the Jews." They knew, of course, that the imprisoned heretic had been asking for "Hebrew materials" (I have a facsimile of his letter on my study wall)–and so continued his translation of what, after all, was indubitably the *Hebrew* Bible. But he never got around to the *Psalms* and the *Song of Solomon*. He was executed on 6 October 1536. The executioner strangled Tyndale "moments before" burning him at the stake, a small act of mercy for which he had qualified by the failure of the court to prove that he had been "a relapsed heretic." Still, his soul was "committed to the devil," and the ashes of his incinerated body were disposed of in the "sullen waters" of a local river "so that no trace of the heretic remained to defile the earth."

In the fatal debates the English Bible figured prominently and what was subsequently to be published and revered as "*the Authorized King James version*" was in point of fact Tyndale's magnificent, earlier translation. Utopia and utopianism also played a central role in the mortal controversy, and More's *Confutation of Tyndale's Answer* (1532) was written in a bitter and intolerant mood against "*Luther's pestylent heresyes*"–not, to be sure, against Luther's powerful version of the Bible in German but rather against Tyndale's more dangerous (because closer to home) version in English. As More wrote in his justification of the banning of the English Bible–and that particular version lives today, for Tyndale's words form some 75-85 percent of the classic King James text!–those were the days.... "in which Tyndale hath (God amend him!) with the infection of his contagious heresies, so sore poisoned malicious and new-fangled folks." And hence the repressive decision "for the while to prohibit the scripture of God to be suffered in English tongue among the people's hands, lest evil folke by false drawing of every good thing they read into the colour and maintenance of their own fond fantasies, and turning all honey into poison, might both do deadly hurt unto themselves, and spread also that infection further abroad."[1] Turning honey into poison was only More's domestic-kitchen version of Pascal's more theological formula of turning a would-be paradise on earth into a living hell. Here the father of Utopia made his historic retreat, overtaken by a personal sense of troubled self-consciousness. It prompted, as I have argued before, an intellectual withdrawal which has left a disfiguring question mark on the whole story of simple utopian innocence:

> I say therefore, in these days in which men by their own default misconstrue and take harm of the very scripture of God, until men better amend, if any man would now translate [Erasmus'] *Moria* into English, or some works either that I have myself written ere this, albeit there be no harm therein, folke yet being (as they be) given to take harm of that which is good, I would not only my darling's books [i.e., Erasmus'] but mine own also, help to burn them both with mine own hands, rather than folke should (though through their own fault) take any harm of them, seeing that I see them likely in these days so to do.

More himself was quite prepared to burn his own book on *Utopia* to avoid the deadly hurt of utopian fantasies. It was an extraordinary moment in intellectual history when the utopian became an anti-utopian. His extravagant concern for the ideal future drove him back to a renewed involvement in the real-existing present and its entangling complexities. Second glances cleansed perceptions. Second thoughts forced More to a self-destructive critique of irresponsible and, what's more, untenable social fantasy. Was a "poeticall" exaggeration the root of this grand error in modern culture and civilization? As the poet Hölderlin once put it, "What has always made the state a hell on earth has been precisely that man has tried to make it his heaven." Pascal put it more concisely: "*Qui fait l'ange fait la bête*. (He who plays the angels ends up as the beast)."

5

Euphuistic Euphoria

Robert Burton shared the hopes, doubts, and disenchantments of this first great intellectual class that created the Western words and mental patterns which we, four and five centuries later, still sense as the obsessive impulses in our public discourse. More than others who might take refuge in a revised philosophy, or at worst in a new ideology, Burton's magniloquence tinged itself with a shade of cynicism about the capacities of human effort, which ignobly falls short when the noble creature most extended himself. It was a memorable "*If*," even if it put the reader into a kind of euphuistic* euphoria:

> if princes would do justice, judges be upright, clergymen truly devout, and so live as they teach, if great men would not be so insolent, if soldiers would quietly defend us, the poor would be patient, rich men would be liberal and humble, citizens honest, magistrates meek, superiors would give good example, subjects peaceable, young men would stand in awe: if parents would be kind to their children, and they again obedient to their parents, brethren agree among themselves, enemies be reconciled,

---

* The *Oxford English Dictionary* defines "*euphuism*" as: "the name of a certain type of diction and style which originated in the imitation of Lyly's *Euphues*, and which was fashionable in literature and in the conversation of cultivated society at the end of the 16th and beginning of the 17th century." Hence it is applied to any similar kind of affectation in writing or speech, "and (loosely) to affectedly periphrastic or 'high-flown' language in general." Further:

  "The chief features of 'euphuism' in the proper sense are: the continual recurrence of antithetic clauses in which the antithesis is emphasized by means of alliteration; the frequent introduction of a long string of similes all relating to the same subject, often drawn from the fabulous qualities ascribed to plants, minerals, and animals; and the constant endeavor after subtle refinement of expression." *O.E.D.*, Volume III, *D-E*, pp. 322-323.)

  John Lyly (1554?-1606) was the author of *Euphues, The Anatomy of Wit* (1578) and *Euphues and His England* (1580).

  But why take Lyly as the prose model? Burton had a magnetism all of his own. Charles Lamb, among many others, revered the essayistic style of the "fantastic old great man," so much so that he could – and, on occasion, did – write what has been called "*perfect Burtonese.*"

servants trusty to their masters, virgins chaste, wives modest, husbands would be loving and less jealous: if we could imitate Christ and His apostles, live after God's laws, these mischiefs would not so frequently happen amongst us.

Here we meet the Burton who moans: "*I am ashamed, disgraced, dishonoured, degraded, exploded...*" – and the Burton who complains: "*I have lost my ears, odious, execrable, abhorred.*" He must have lost his eyes as well, our indefatigably perceptive "reporter" who vowed to "*walke abroad, looke into the world,*" all in order to come up, modestly, "*with some little observation.*" He had a full agenda, promising:

you shall see many discontents, common grievances, complaints, poverty, barbarism, beggary, plagues, wars, rebellions, seditions, mutinies, contentions, idleness, riot, epicurism, the land be untilled, waste, full of bogs, fens, deserts, etc., cities decayed, base and poor towns, villages depopulated, the people squalid, ugly, uncivil. (Introduction, p. 79)

It was too much of a muchness. Our observer was overwhelmed, in a fast-forward vision of a future informational overload that was eerie in an olde university common room that had yet to see a single printed newspaper.* When the daily journals began to roll off the presses, cluttering all the kiosks on the world's street-corners, to the cacophonic accompaniment of deafening electronic media and to the flashes of blinding multicolored images in case you could still manage to keep an eye open and an ear alert...one would be forced to pay some more attention to the gruesome clinical pages (which I have neglected). I refer to Burton's pioneering medical venture in describing the sad state of mankind when so many thousands, nay millions, fell under the demonic assaults of dejection and depression, melancholy and madnesse.**

One sorrow drives out another, one passion another, one cloud another, one rumour is expelled by another; every day almost come new news unto our ears, as how the sun was eclipsed, meteors seen i' th' air, monsters born, prodigies, how the Turks were overthrown in Persia, an earthquake in Helvetia, Calabria, Japan, or China, an inundation in Holland, a great plague in Constantinople, a fire at Prague, a dearth in Germany, such a man is made a lord, a bishop, another hanged, deposed, pressed to death, for some murder, treason, rape,

---

*   Robert Darnton reminds us that the first London daily began publication in 1702 – long after the first daily newspaper in Germany (Leipzig, 1660) but long before the first in France (Paris, 1777).
     "Print, talk, and coffee combined to create a powerful new force everywhere in Europe: public opinion took a radical turn in all the great cities...." (Robert Darnton, "A Euro State of Mind," *New York Review of Books*, 28 February 2002.)

**   In our day, Andrew Solomon uses Burton's book effectively in his recent autobiographical "anatomy of depression." See his chapter on "*History*" sandwiched between "*Addiction, Suicide*" and "*Politics, Evolution.*" Solomon, *Noonday Demon: An Anatomy of Depression* (2001), pp. 301-304.

theft, oppression, all which we do hear at first with a kind of admiration, detestation, consternation. (Vol. ii, pp.199-200)

This, for "a reporter" in 1621 who had never caught the 8 o'clock news or the 10-o'clock bulletin of the latest headlines–or indeed scanned the front page's compact index to the important events that happened yesterday–is undeniably prescient. The man had covered all the "*new news*" that would in the next handful of centuries be deemed fit to print on our ever newer machines.[1]

6

In Dreams Begin Irresponsibilities

There are utopians who lose themselves in the dream of a benevolent mankind: in an extravagant hope for universal peace and prosperity, linked to a world order of justice and happiness. It has been, in history, a means of a private escape and, on occasion, a personal spur to such activists and extroverts in the utopian ranks who were prepared to go on heroically from there. The dedication to something revered as *revolution* would transform "*the great globe itself*"–or, at least, one or two corrupt societies spinning thereon–systematically and totally. "*Utterly*" in Yeats' favorite phrase.

In Marxism the relationship between utopia and revolution was taken to be one of "theory" and "practice." In other programs of radical political change, the *Leitmotif* was the general promise of a prospective paradise-on-earth. The image of a golden future was fed by a prayer for a real change in the hearts and minds of an ideal global citizenry. Miraculously, this would transpire at the same time as a corresponding establishment of perfect institutions which, everywhere, would prove to be well-functioning and stable, hence permanent. The revolution–peaceful or violent, in one country or the world over–was thus a utopian means to achieve a utopian end. Intellectuals over recent centuries tried to create an all-embracing "*Sociology*" to help make "Socialism" or any other variety of the Good Society a plausible and reasonable effort–for some, in "*Social Science*," it was an inevitability–controlled by laws of motion. But in the end–probably around 1991, with the Soviet Union's abject collapse–the whole project turned out to be a vacuous form of theology or a specious construct of ideology, with little or no intellectual credentials at all. And yet, it had been an unavoidable intellectual temptation, at once magnificent and embittering, for men of thought and action in the West (and not only there).

In *The Anatomy of Melancholy* (1621) many of these developments were uncannily prefigured. Although Robert Burton was a practicing and believing Christian, attached to the ideas of original sin and of a heavenly, i.e., an otherworldly paradise, he sensed the seductive charms of what twentieth-century scholars Raymond Aron and Jacob Talmon were to call "a secular religion."[1]

23

Burton, like Thomas More in the century before him, had the imaginative power to conceive of an alternative way of life and civilization in times that were so nasty and brutish as to put the ideal of a Good Society–or, at least, a Better Social Order–permanently on the agenda of modern history.

Still and all, there are passages in Burton's seventeenth-century text which have the familiar pathos of an endless number of Western novelists and poets, professors and playwrights, actors and clergymen, and last but not least, editors and journalists, who were tempted by what Immanuel Kant called *"the sweet dream."* They committed themselves to social movements and to political parties and to the whole range of the written word in order to facilitate cultural forces working for that Other and Better World. We might well have to wait a bit for the final conflict; but even in a liberal democracy, power could do a power of good. Masses could be persuaded to vote, the brightest-and-the-best would proselytize for comrades as well as supporters. For, when the opportunity presented itself, militants have been known to become inspired to mount the barricades, to throw bombs, to take the partisan fight into the mountains and forests, all to help inaugurate new social arrangements for which suffering humanity was audibly crying out. Onward, Utopian soldiers! marching as to war....Would the intelligenstia know their sure-footed way around the dimly-lit corridors of power? We were all of us "most worthy" men, but Burton had troubling doubts about our competence to manage for the better the great and desirable changes in the course of history. As he wrote in his second volume, on the subject of characters who turn up running things in his own day:

> It is an ordinary thing in these days to see a base impudent ass, illiterate, unworthy, unsufficient, to be preferred before his betters, because he can put himself forward, because he looks big, can bustle in the world, hath a fair outside, can temporize, collogue [to wheedle, flatter], insinuate, or hath good store of friends and money, whereas a more discreet, modest, and better-deserving man shall lie hid or have a repulse. (Vol. ii, pp. 190-191)

More than that, the "most worthy" failed to make it–and resignation displaced enthusiasm. Where was hope when "'Twas so of old, and ever will be," as the ancient folk wisdom pessimistically warned: "He that hath skill to be a pilot [lacks] a ship, and he that could govern a commonwealth, a world itself, a king in conceit, wants means to exercise his worth, hath not a poor office to manage." The prospect of Robert Burton–who himself rarely left his poor Oxford rooms at Christ Church–as an office manager of Cromwell's revolution to establish a good commonwealth in England's green and pleasant land...is bizarre. A bit of this fantasy lurks between the lines on many of Burton's thousand pages. Of course, he knew it was not to be, for it was all doomed to unavoidable political failure, or at least to a cultural contradiction, leading to a social impasse.

Still, the cultural contradiction was deeply rooted in an intellectual psychology which shaped his basic temperament: an irrepressible attachment to contraries. This mentality had nothing to do with the playful coyness of a clever man who enjoys his slipperiness, and thus evades the various attempts of his critics to crucify him for one heretical (or orthodox) opinion or another. There is a school of enthusiasts who detect his greatness in just such ambiguities and even divided loyalties. Burton's mind had the elements of an enlightened skepticism and self-criticism which prefigured the flowering of an Enlightenment *Weltanschauung* with noble strands of thought from "intellectual heroes" as widely spread as Erasmus and Thomas More and Pierre Bayle.

One Burton scholar praises the inquisitive alertness of the man, and no higher praise could be mustered than that he knew "few of the answers but all of the questions." If all the fanatics in a violent century had hesitated a mite before battling on, with "all the answers," to defend the old order or to help inaugurate a new society, historians would not be having to tally up so many casualties. They would have enjoyed perhaps more books, less bonfires; would have written about more masters and their masterpieces, and fewer martyrs at the stake. Alas, the Western tradition was crowded with dogmatists and ideologues who would trample on corpses in the name of their implacable certainties; we needed much more of such wary Burtonesque tentativeness. For it was indeed not a sign of weak-minded journalistic hesitation to leave complex questions open–but rather a mark of strength, of mental character, in the attachment to what was good in both the new and the old...even thought it all appeared to the innocent reader a "perplexing confusion." *Sanity in Bedlam* was the title of one of the best modern studies of Burton's achievement; and the American author remarked admirably: "If like Robert Burton he [the reader] ahd an inquisitive and receptive mind, he would be inclined to accept the new; if like Burton he felt the respect for authority which was general among the learned, he would be disinclined to reject the old."[2]

In the third volume Burton gets around to contemplating what "daily experience teaches"–"*as anyone will see who reads history*..." (iii, p. 386). He was not destined to be around when the great historic event of his time happened: the Cromwellian insurrection came to power but the Puritan Commonwealth (1649-1660) was relatively short-lived, and King Charles patiently waited in French exile to come back to reclaim the throne....

For Burton this could not have been a surprising story. Decades before, he had written, as the sum of the experience of reading history, that utopian ideals are only social arrangements that may be *wished* for...but are unlikely to be *effected*–and, in certain national crises, *undesirable* to be undertaken. Indeed in the longing for such perfect solutions to complicated and, in the end, intractable human problems, one sets out on a destructive course along which the movement is wildly misled and good causes degenerate.

What wondrous contemporary cures–which Burton might have hailed for the effective pharma-treatment of *"all manner of diseases"*–led to certain risks and side-effects which, sad to narrate, practically nullified a hopeful era's radical medical progress? How many ecological disasters, or how many unexpected tragedies, would have directly followed on the Burton Five-Year Plan to *"irrigate those barren Arabian deserts"*? Was the "genocidal" extermination of the native Red Indian tribes–horrible prospect!–entailed in the high-minded impulse to *"root out Barbarisme out of America"*? And how many goodhearted systems of Welfare for All, from the cradle to the grave, would have to be revised or revamped, reformed and reconstructed before the good and caring society took proper care of its citizenry in a tolerably acceptable fashion?

He was attracted to the flowers of the early utopian literature; and he knew the "witty fictions" of Thomas More, of Campanella and his "City of the Sun" (*Civitas solis*), of Johan Valentin Andreae and his happy German republic; and (last but not least) Francis Bacon's *New Atlantis*: "witty fictions, but mere chimeras" (i, p. 101). He did not have to wait, as did his fellow utopian comrades in the twentieth century, for gods to fail, for noble experiments to disintegrate in bloody fiascos, for the shock of other hard evidence ("noisome or fulsome"), to arrive in the end to the suspicion that in dreams begin irresponsibilities. (Yeats got it wrong; so did Delmore Schwartz.)

I must explain. My reference here is to the William Butler Yeats' epigraph in a book of poems of his in 1914 which was made additionally famous by the short story, *"In Dreams Begin Responsibilities"* (1938) by the young American poet, Delmore Schwartz. It was published originally in the New York literary journal *Partisan Review* (where I read it in the City College library). Its readers happened to include every young student I knew. The well-thumbed magazine (known intimately as *P.R.*) represented at the time an enthusiastic atmosphere of New York Marxism in which Revolution was the dream –and in that dream, we fancied, began our generation's glowing sense of responsibility and dutiful commitments. Our engagement was, presumably, to make a revolution in America…or Russia…(or somewhere). Or so said Leon Trotsky–and now Delmore, echoing Yeats.

The next year we all began reading Freud, and this began giving dreams a dirty name. But it probably was not till the subsequent era of Karl Popper (*Utopia and Violence*, 1963) that every last *P.R.*-nik in Manhattan shed the frayed shreds of his youthful utopianism which had combined with histrionic revolutionism. In my own case it eventually produced a melancholy Burtonesque book, *Utopia and Revolution* (University of Chicago Press and Macmillan/London, 1976). Intellectual styles are subject to change, and I struggle in this digression with the so-called "Overkill in Communication"….That is to say, the glut in the language of journalism, especially when memories begin for every new generation, however journalistically inspired, just the day before yesterday.

7

Secret Expletives

I come, at long last, to those Burtonesque dashes, as printed, corrected and confirmed by the author. Burton was surrounded by rude and outspoken critics, "foul-mouthed senseless railers who cry thee down"–but he would not reply in kind for, as he said archly, "smutty language suits not learned pen." Still, one wonders: did he lapse, even once? Could lewd innuendo be taken to be "smutty" and always deemed "unsuitable" for serious discourse? We have the page proofs, but not the handwritten pages. The missing manuscripts would not be, in many important details, so revealing as are the available proof copies of *The Anatomy*'s various editions. Corrected pages have been preserved, and once on a visit to All Souls, Oxford, on the invitation of the Warden (then John Sparrow), I was shown Burton's proofs and I tried to decipher Burton's own marginal corrections and revisions. One could quite understand how the next edition would be replacing, as often happened, a corrupted quotation with an erratic footnote. As Sparrow pointed out to me at the time (my interest in such cryptic markings was only a beginner's curiosity), that when a note was added as a stop-press correction in 1621–or a new note added to a later edition–the reference symbol was likely to be...either an asterisk (*) or a dagger (†).[1]

Frequently, as the Burton scholar J.B. Bamborough explains, the next edition would re-letter (using the Roman alphabet) the note series. The asterisks and daggers were thus eliminated...and left freely available for subtler subsequent usage, for there would come a time when *cuss-words* would (almost) come into their own. Weaker writers would turn to "stronger" language, or the blue suggestion thereof, to "profane," to break taboos. It could be that asterisks served no real discreet purpose because Burton–so very unlike Lord Byron– had nothing to hide.[2]

At least one Burton enthusiast over the centuries needs to be rescued from oblivion, and I choose Floyd Dell, an unusual autodidactic figure in the *Melancholy* scholarship.[3]

Floyd Dell (1887-1969) was in his youth famous in the U.S.A. as a socialist campaigner. He helped edit the left-wing *New Masses* with Max Eastman, and he stood trial with John Reed for his anti-war pacifism in 1917, the year President Woodrow Wilson (with the aid of his General Pershing) went to war against the Kaiser's Germany in support of the Anglo-French *Entente*. Before "rediscovering" Robert Burton's seventeenth-century *Anatomy of Melancholy* book he did much, as an influential young literary critic, to publicize new American writing (praising and befriending such notable talents as Sherwood Anderson, Vachel Lindsay, Edgar Lee Masters, Theodore Dreiser, Eugene O'Neill, et al.). For a self-educated high school dropout, Dell was considered by academicians to be "a major force in American literature, becoming a bellwether of literary experimentation."

His political ideals were, of course, built upon the eighteenth-century's optimistic faith in reason–socialism had its roots in "man's reasonableness." But in time and "not without cause," he learned otherwise: from "books" (above all, Shakespeare) and indeed from "life" (above all, wars and tyrannies). The mind-changing lesson was: the passionately unreasonable aspects of human nature. A much-quoted scrap of Dell's verse suggests his "magical"-intuitive connection with the zeitgeist and the ideological hurly-burly of the day:

> 'Neath shifting sands of twice ten thousand years,
> It lies, the lost Atlantis of my youth;
> And this I have to show my sister spheres
> A dead dream, and these lingering tribes uncouth.

This was from his autobiographical *Homecoming* (1933); but in connection with his editorial work on a new American edition of Robert Burton's *Melancholy* he made a passing political remark for which, if for nothing else, he deserves to be remembered. Perhaps he was influenced by his friend on the *New York Times*, John Chamberlain, who called Dell "a walking contradiction" but who himself bade a shortlived *Farewell to Reform* (1932), and embraced "revolution"…only to find that for him too the dream had died. Perhaps, again, he was influenced by Max Eastman who made a masterly translation of Leon Trotsky's *History of the Russian Revolution* and then promptly reevaluated his attachment to "uncouth tribes" and their illiberal customs, that is, he "broke with Stalin's Russia."

As a young journalist in Manhattan, I came to know personally both Eastman and Chamberlain; and, as it happened, both suggested I meet Floyd Dell and promised to arrange for a meeting but, alas, nothing came of it. It could be that Dell, serving at that time as a New Dealer, active in the Washington bureaucracy, was reputed to be a ghostwriter for Mrs. Eleanor Roosevelt…and this, for a youthful New York *idéologue*, eager to interview "heroes of the day," didn't sound very auspicious.

Still, Floyd Dell had come to rethink–and so did I, among thousands of true believers squirming to secure their foothold on the barricades–men and politics and ideas in a self-critical and chastening light, and Robert Burton was one of the outlying stations of the way. Dell's concluding lines to his remarkable edition of the *Melancholy* book deserve, I think, reprinting here.

Burton grew up during the age of Shakespeare. It was an age that was frankly interested in the passionately unreasonable aspects of human nature. Between that time and our own there have intervened two periods, the eighteenth century and the Victorian era, in which a great emphasis was laid upon, and perhaps an undue confidence reposed in, man's reasonableness. Today, again, and not without cause, we are interested in the "unreasonable" part of man's mind. And Burton, who is not the least of the great Elizabethans, can speak to us across the centuries (p. xiv).

8

Across the Centuries

What rare and strange creatures they are, those spirits who can speak to us across the centuries! Their voices sound uncanny, for the messages they resonate appear to remain universally and immutably true, or at least meaningful, yet in a quite inexplicable way. And if those verities persist in their sameness when all other things have changed and have even become unrecognizable, then there must be a core of human life, or a remnant of compelling attitudes, which has an indestructible, timeless constancy. Why should this be so surprising? The old saw seemed to say it as it always is and was: *Plus ça change, plus c'est la même chose*, etc.

I emphasize two themes to be found somewhere in Burton's "message across the centuries." One raises the question of the natural limits of human nature in the quest for agreeable social arrangements; the second follows on with the suspicion that the world's stage is too crowded and too stormy for simple and orderly directives to determine a happy, ethical plot.

1. The central thesis in the Western tradition–ahtough one can trace the intellectual sentiment from ancient Plato and Aristotle to the modern philosophers such as John Dewey, Karl Popper, et al. – is indubitably the eighteenth-century aphorism of Immanuel Kant...who himself went from a utopian optimist in the first days of the French Revolution to a resigned critic of unconscionable violence as well as of imaginative hubris. The chastening words in his famous aphorism have been reiterated innumerable times, in other ways in the centuries before and after: *"From such crooked wood as man is made of, nothing perfectly straight can be built."* It remains as concise and cogent as Burton's long sigh at "new newes," for what did they amount to if not stories of even more crooked imperfections?[14] Here Burton poses the greatest *"iffy question"* (Franklin D. Roosevelt's catchphrase) in political history, and I have already quoted the hypnotic-euphuistic passage: *"if princes would do justice."* If man was all virtue, we would still be in the Garden of Eden. And since when was it "news" that if pigs could fly they could all be angels?

but being most part so irreconcilable as we are, perverse, proud, insolent, factious, and malicious, prone to contention, anger and revenge, of such fiery spirits, so captious, impious, irreligious, so opposite to virtue, void of grace, how should it otherwise be? (ii, pp. 202)

2. Could the haphazard course of human events have been otherwise? (Could have been? should have been?) Even those tragic victims of the Melancholy which Burton was anatomizing as a pioneering therapist were being offered some small prospect of betterment. Even Marx and Engels conceded that the Great Change might not come utterly and all at once, i.e., that peaceful reforms might lead to that happiest of all ends, a brave new world. In the history of Christianity there have been many wise men (and some were duly sainted) who recognized after much cogitation that the old apocalyptic view which expected a sudden cosmic transformation should reasonably have given way to a sense of process, involving stages and periods – for the perfect state could only be the fulfillment of a *development* (Irenaeus, in the second century A.D.). After all, there are many kinds of perfection, even when it comes down to it there is "*relative perfection*" (St. Ambrose, fourth century A.D.). More than that (or less), part of perfection "consists in the recognition of *our imperfection*" (John Calvin quoting Saint Augustine)….The great and good state of (relative) felicity may not come to mankind all-at-once but bit-by-bit; for, as St. Basil said, "It is better to advance a little at a time."

Even this modest jumble which amounts to a doctrine of meliorism, with a prudent note of progress, is fraught with difficulties when one actually looks at the record of achievement between hope and compromise. All historic movements are surprisingly subject to the winds of distraction and disorientation. The lurid newspaper file of the last few centuries can well be read as a chronicle of interference, natural and unnatural, in the path of man's purposefulness. For the pious the unexpected difficulties represented the mysterious ways of the Divine Controller. For the impious all those miserable "unintended consequences" constitute what the amiable cynics have called Murphy's Law. As for the rest of us, we have comforted ourselves by paying attention to the twist-and-turns of "dialectics" or to other fashionable forms of confronting, minimizing, and evading the troublesome problems.

For example: unburdening oneself of the so-called Information Overload. It is perhaps Robert Burton's most astonishing contribution that he appears to be the first to underscore a factor in the communications equation of progress and failure which was thought to have emerged only in our very own time as we moved from a newspaper print culture to globalized media. This factor in the history of intellectual moods and climates of opinion is a *variable* since it is weighed differently in every epoch. But it is a *constant* in that the overload, however measured, is always felt to be an intolerable burden. One man's cacophany is another man's quiet contemplative opportunity. Another man's wide intellectual horizon, with adequate sources of news and no end of incisive news analysis, may well be the cause of confusion and misperception. Somewhere along the way we have, in Burton's phrase, "lost our eyes and ears." The passage I have included above – *"one sorrow drives out another"* (vol. II, p. 199) – is unjustly neglected in the Western canon. When does suchlike become, if ever, old news? Burton, without a printed newspaper page ever having soiled his hands, registers acutely the headlines and the stop-press stories in brief:

> All which we do hear at first with a kind of admiration, detestation, consternation, but by and by they are buried in silence: thy father's dead, thy brother robbed, wife runs mad, neighbor hath killed himself; 'tis heavy, ghastly, fearful news at first, in every man's mouth, table talk; but after a while who speaks or thinks of it? It will be so with thee. (Vol. II, p. 200)

Late and soon, the world has always been too much with us.

9

Mentioning the Unmentionable

My final quotation from Burton's *Anatomy* (1621) does not provide an answer to many open questions I have posed; it only prompts another question. But it does move the problem a few centuries back from where it usually crops up in the accounts of "Bowdlerization" or the later disquisitions on shame and sex and language in an expressive culture. Even Burton, a Shakespearean master in his day of striking phrases and fine distinctions, senses in the end a need for a demotic unmentionable–perhaps a shocking word of Chauceresque earthiness; or an unusual reference to a personal malpractice; possibly a scatological phrase which could give final persuasiveness to a virtuous campaign for the true, good, and beautiful; even a polite omission. These tempting verbal lapses generally occurred when he had to confront "*erotick*" details of which he found certain aspects distasteful. As one of his modern editors remarks, he "could not bring himself to deal with [them] in English; and indeed to one such passage–in safe and sound Latin–he appended a footnote, '*Good Master Schoolmaster, do not English this.*'"

But the American editors of the "All-English" edition had no compunctions about "Englishing" the difficult matters, since "the matters...are not nowadays so frightful." Nowadays was the year 1927–and all hail to that enlightened, post-frightful turning point! No need to apologize for the text or for the author who was, after all, "a 'melancholy' bachelor whose acquaintance with the other sex"–and doubtless with his own!–"was gained chiefly from his books."

What was the nature of the frightfulness? The fearful reader, or editor/publisher, intimidated or upset by the details or possibly the very language (Latin was reputed to be subtler, or discreeter), could skip the indelicate passages. But their indelicacy was not actually a matter of what Burton once referred to as "smutty language." The context here was a discussion of the role of hereditary factors in the causation of melancholic illness. Burton was summing up the contemporary state of knowledge (which was very limited for the time and rather anachronistic for the present day reader) about inherited characteristics. The whole problem was "much defaced with hereditary infirmities which by our lust and intemperance we had contracted" (i, p. 213). "Lust" was more like it, but even that element of sensuality or bawdiness would not necessarily force Burton's dramatic recourse to Latin to camouflage any obscene usages. No, it was essentially a decision to avoid a queasy factor of indelicacy, or bad taste, or a mix of slight modesty and slightly more embarrassment. All in all, Burton steered a characteristically middle course. He put in Latin–and refrained from the perils of "Englishing"–what he had to say about the tragic onset of melancholy and "the particulars of sexual uncleanliness" (especially during the menstrual period); and he observes that "the Jews bitterly inveigh against this foul and filthy coupling amongst Christians...who are so often leprous, raving, debilitated, scabby" (i, p. 186).

When it came to the fairly innocuous "dietary" factors, such as eating garlic or onions or "fasting overmuch"–or the engaging biological paradoxes of the subject, namely "wise men begetting fools" (and indeed Erasmus' repartee about fools begetting wise men)–then he turned to English which was good enough to get on with the story. How pithy the language became when it was not plagued and hindered by the "confusion of hereditary diseases" and the sad turth that "our generation is corrupt...with crazed families...*parentes peremptores* (our parents are our ruin)." "Our fathers were bad," he concluded with an obvious touch of contagious melancholy, "and we were like to be worse."[1]

Burton was, to be sure, "self-censoring"–not unlike Gibbon a century later–by taking refuge in evasive Latin versions of what he wanted to say (and without embarrassing or upsetting his readership). The text in question was not unusual in its vocabulary; flourishing, as far as I can make out, no lewd word or salacious phrase. At the end of the long insertion (from *Intemperantia veneris* to *menstruis* [*i*, pp. 213-214]) he smoothly shifted his linguistic gears with a curt, dry remark: "I spare to English this which I have said." In an explanatory footnote of their own, the American editor of the all-English edition confessed to "some reluctance in doing what was against Burton's desire"; and they added that "they feel what might have seemed blushworthy to a frocked bachelor of the Seventeenth Century is but a commonplace in this day of psycho-analytic literature." Perhaps Freud's work was not the right reference; James Joyce, D.H. Lawrence, and Henry Miller might have been more apt. Writing today, editors would have been tempted to drop the names of Monica Lewinsky and President Clinton (not to mention Judge Kenneth Starr, their ruthless inquisitorial and faithful word-for-word "publisher").[2]

The case against modern up-to-the-minute "Englishing" is not merely an aesthetic matter of preserving an archaic tang, or protecting discreetly a private meaning. It is rather an intellectual issue involving the reading of history with a bifocal attention to past and present. It should not be just a concern, worthy that it is, so that Burton's book "may be read easily for its own sake." It also touches on the *experiencing* of history in the double meaning of the word, and which entails going in for that kind of exercise in what Hegel thought of as *Aufarbeitung* and *aufheben* with all their dialectical subtleties. History is worked through or raised up, elevated and recaptured, being an unalterably old story yet always freshly read and renewed.

Still and all: classic translators, estimable as they may be, often lose their bearings by failing in a consistent and timely way to adjust their clocks or watches to the zeitgeist, moving them forward (or backward!) as the case may be. They try to be up-to-date when they should be old-fashioned, and remain trapped in archaisms when a word or simile needs (to coin a phrase) a shot-in-the-arm. I have read vivid Latin American novels about guerrilla warfare among the peasants in the Andes wherein an altercation among terrorists or partisans is resolved by an expostulation like: *"Take that, you rats!"* Even high Roman generals in Caesar's armies *"rat"* on each other (in Dr. H.V. Rieu's willful Penguin translations from the ancient Latin).

In re: Burton's translators (i.e., of the non-English passages, mostly Latin), one *Melancholy* editor–Holbrooke Jackson, in 1932–is so solicitous of the need for "clarity and agreableness" (p. xvii, Everyman edition) to serve the "present-day reader," that he finds no other way to render a bit of Burtonesque skepticism about unbelievable tales–*credat Judaeus apella*–but with: "[*tell it to the Marines*]" (Everyman edition, iii, p. 379). As for Floyd Dell, memorable pacifist as he was with a very conscientious objection to Marines or any other war-making troop, he had Burton going on to say: "let he who likes believe" (p. 425).

In contemporary journalism, the foreign correspondents abroad and their foreign-editors in the home office seem even more oblivious to the problem. Warlords in Afghanistan or tribal terrorists in the Sudan are quoted as saying newsworthy things (as published in the *Washington Post* and the *New York Times* and throughout the country in the regional press) which they never could have said, at least in that accent, inflection, style, or vocabulary. The quotations are concocted from the rough pidgin commanded by the mostly non-English-speaking protagonists being interviewed, plus the "G.I. lingo" that some locally recruited native interpreter (if available) may have picked up by hanging around Americans. Thus: we get up-to-the-minute Yankee slang and pop-world buzzwords emanating as from Kabul and Kigali. It's all clear and agreeable foreign policy information for our East Coast readership: Gee, they talk just like us!* (iii, pp. 248-9).

---

*   Aside to the editors of *The Library Journal* (August 2000): In their hostile review of my first volume (*The Language of Journalism*, 1999) they accused me of writing "one long sneer" at the writing in American newspapers. The reviewer suggested that such specialized U.S. libraries that may think they need to stock my book on their shelves should keep it in a glass bookcase under lock and key!...Well, I am not sneering. I am only recommending that Editors edit – and that they cut out the fun-and-games that journalists have with quotations from foreigners – from Afro-Asian warlords as well as Argentinian footballers and Russian tennis players. These guys just happen to speak funny...like because their English isn't so great....

Accordingly, words failed Robert Burton occasionally. What might Burton have been trying to communicate by those mystifying dashes?

> Now may it please your good worship, your lordship, who was the first founder of your family? The poet answered: He was either a shepherd or something which I prefer not to mention....

> Thy great-great-great-grandfather was a rich citizen, and then in all likelihood a usurer, a lawyer, and then a ——, a courtier, and then a ——, a country gentleman, and then hee scraped it out of sheepe, etc...[3]

Whatever sheep scrapings might have comprised or symbolized, the Burton scholars who have pored over every word in each and every edition (in the absence of Burton's manuscripts) conceded his claim to be "'a loose, plaine, rude writer', [who] calls a spade a spade....I respect matter, not words."[4]

There are many words and elongated sentences about "passionate adultery...obscene actions...brutish lust" as well as "scurrile talk...homely embraces...meretricious kisses"; but practically nothing that transgresses the contemporary lines of taboo, at least knowingly. Elizabethans were playful punsters, and perhaps Burton was in a teasing mode when he quoted an ancient doctor who shrank from marriage and rejoiced in the freedom of a single life...although he was "a rambler"...*erraticus ac volaticus amator*...and (to use his own words) "*per multiplices amores discurrebam*, I took a snatch where I could get it."*

Burton reports here and there about "the swearing and cursing" that was going on; but he quotes nothing directly in English, going as far as he thinks he can go in discussions of "adultery and fornication" and the wanton influence of "bawds and whoremasters." The abbess in one Gloucestershire nunnery is simply "*deflowered*"; but the young lover in Burton's story stayed on with the nuns in the convent and "in short space he got up most of their bellies" (iii, p. 117).

There was, again, much report of "lascivious talk" as well as "monstrous gestures...wanton tunes..."–and, in a burst of editorial prudence, "*that which is not to be named*"; but what, pray, did he himself hear or, even less likely, see?

---

* Some modern etymologists include *snatch* as a fairly recent taboo word for "a woman's crotch...the vagina," and one notes that it was "Common since c. 1935." This is dubious, since I myself heard it many years earlier as a youngster on the streets of New York! "*Snatch*" is listed (by Jonothan Green in his *Dictionary of Slang*, p. 487) as a late seventeenth-century term for sexual intercourse ("esp. quick or illicit or with a prostitute"). Astonishing is the oversight by Wentwirth/Flexner in their *Dictionary of American Slang* (p. 495)—attributing the *taboo* meanings to the 1930s! –wherein Eric Partridge's research is ignored and even his reference to Burton overlooked. Partridge gives: "A hasty or illicit or mercenary copulation, C. 17-20...." (*Dictionary of Slang and Unconventional English*, 3rd ed., 1949), p. 791.

Was he in any way a witness to what he called "*the spur of lust*" (from Petrarch's *incitamentum libidinis*)? Did he actually *overhear* or just *hear about* the various melancholy "allurements" with which he was exhaustively engaged in the clinical parts of his diagnosis?

If, on balance, Burton managed the unmentionables within the bounds of contemporary discretion, he knew that the very mention of the carnal follies–"buggery" and the like–would (and did) subject him to the charge of positively disseminating the news about sin, vice, ruin, and corruption. Even straight news can be so suggestive.

Hemingway once remarked about the delights of love that to talk about them was to lose them. For Burton to write about the melancholy vices of sex (among other passionate human activities, such as corrupt politics, mercantile greed, ruinous wars, etc.) was to spread them; or so his critics charged in his day (and as they would today). Even the favorite authors in his own library–among them: Erasmus, Thomas More–seemed to be warning him of intellectual hubris…of the unintended consequences of "phantastical" literary ambitions…and in the case of "love-melancholy," taken up in explicitly "amorous discourse," the grievous outcome being: "the very name of love has become odious to chaste ears" (iii. p. 3).

Whereby we are plainly catapulted over the centuries into the loose language of modern rudeness; wherein an innocent n-word ambiguity can cause a race riot. When did a spade become an ethnic epithet and cease being a handyman's instrument or a cardsharp's metaphor for straight talking? An English contemporary, who listened to Burton's torrential conversation, noted that he was, for a diagnostician of melancholy, "very merry, facet[ious] and juvenile"; his talk was "lively" but "very innocent." Wherein lay his juvenile innocence, and where his rude reportorial realism? Were there secret expletives that needed to be omitted? As we have seen, things haven't changed inordinately in roughly four centuries, and an asterisk or a dash/slash or a modest hyphen is still a helpful crutch to hobble over certain obstacles which continue, for one dark reason or another, to present some "frightful" human difficulty.

Burton's was a melancholy dilemma. Words matter; meanings matter more. It was a time when one could not risk one's neck by putting a foot wrong. The times would come again, and again…in the form of dangerous thoughts, blue imagery, dissident aberrations, and the like.

Part 2

The Orgasm that Failed

"Why is my verse so barren of new pride,
So far from variation or quick change?
Why, with the time, do I not glance aside
To new-found methods and to com-
pounds strange?...

So all my best is dressing old words new,
Spending again what is already spent."
—William Shakespeare, Sonnets (76)

"Space is what prevents everything from
being in the same place.
Language is what prevents everything from
meaning the same thing."
—Jean Baudrillard, Cool Memories (1987)

"Good authors, too, who once used
better words now only use four-
letter words writing prose.
Anything goes."
—Cole Porter (1934)

10

The Swinging Pendulum

I have already called attention to the pattern of unequal bluntness; and when coyness comes into it, newspapers are coy when they do, and coy when they don't. House-style rules and recommendations are rarely as inflexible as they were at the *New York Times* when an editor named Theodore M. Bernstein was the unquestionable authority on what the paper should be printing. (He was a much-admired fanatic on the subject of "syntax sinners.")*

It would be enough, according to the strict constructionists, for a sports story reporting, say, the outbursts of temperament on a Wimbledon or (Forest Hills/Flushing Meadows) championship match for the telling detail to say that rude or coarse language was used, promptly censured, and duly fined by the Lawn-Tennis Association. This was the general practice in the heyday of John McEnroe's fits of temper, from his famous *"You're the pits!"*–unsportsmanlike, but harmless enough–to whatever coarser expletives he hurled at the referee, at the linesmen (and ladies), or at some noisy spectator or photographer, none of which were ever documented.

As I write, a morning newspaper reports from Rome at the Italian Open that André Agassi was fined "one quarter of a one per cent of Agassi's prize money this year" (respectively, £1,602 and £655,807). Exactly what verbal outrage he had committed was not spelled out in corresponding detail. He had been defeated ignominiously in the quarterfinals, and had been booed by the crowd. We learned only that "Agassi, the world No. 1, hurled four-letter abuse at the fan who had cried out, 'What a waste of money! You cheated us!'"

As for loose constructionists in the matter of journalistic style, they argue that this Victorian kind of discretion has long since gone out of fashion. More than that: by maintaining prudish silence, journalists were guilty of withholding information and obstructing the course of true speech. The leftover constructionists in between–sometimes strict, often loose, but generally

---

* See his books, *Watch Your Language* (1958); *The Careful Writer: A Modern Guide to English Usage* (1965).

pragmatic–often base their editorial decision on the "effing frequency coefficient." On a day when, on the finance pages, staid London executive officers are denouncing "b**l-s**t" and a famous actress, storming out of a New York theater, is quoted on the arts pages as to exactly where the director and his moneyed backers could "stuff it," then it behooves André Agassi to emerge on the sports pages with a mere fine around his neck and no f-word on his lips. Even the most investigative of newspapers can have too much of a good thing.

The pendulum, swinging from coarseness to modesty, does not necessarily reflect the actual flavors of "true speech" out there in the real world of newsworthy characters. A high churchman's lapse into low language will be cited directly. A philologist's excursion into the history of profane words, astonishing in its lexicographical discoveries, will be reported with diffident reserve. Thus, in a front-page British story on the new dictionary of Welsh expletives, translated for the first time into English, there was nary an example to suggest what a pioneering scholarly effort it was.

But the bishop of Edinburgh, who is the head of the Anglican Church in Scotland, seemed to be stepping beyond the mark by saying that God had given human "promiscuous genes"; and thereby he (and perhaps the deity too) appeared to be condoning adultery. There was a storm of controversy. The Rt. Reverend Richard Holloway admitted that he liked to "shoot from the lip," which flat joke only made the flipness worse. Churchgoers felt he was betraying the "sacred monogamous family." Even adulterers felt they were being robbed of their free libidinous will. The Bishop said that the whole incident had been "hell on wheels" for him, which also didn't seem doctrinally quite correct. He says he likes taking notes, but that he should have foreseen the headlines, "Bishop Says Let's Play Whoopee" (which dates him a bit). In the end, as the *Daily Telegraph* reported (18 May 1995) he had realized "the effect of his off-the-cuff remarks only when he arrived in Lincoln on Tuesday night": "There was a message from my secretary saying 'the shit has hit the fan.'" Whether scatology can make good for theology we will leave for the elders of the church to decide. At the moment the bishop has only been risking his soul.

Much more is at risk when in the business community and its "new culture of capitalism," chief executive officers of large prospering enterprises opt, in a similar spirit of liberty and license, for "the color blue." I want to turn a little later to those copywriters who do advertising texts which, from time to time, in our newspaper culture, emulate the new verve in journalistic prose: "shooting from the lip."

Shy and Wry, Coy and Twee*

In what might be called the post-Tynan era in vernacular straight talking, the English who have lived (and loved) with this problem the longest–at least

---

* "Twee (adj.): Br E, infml: too delicate, unpleasantly dainty." *Longman's Dictionary of Contemporary English* (1978), p. 1192.

in our shared language, from rude Chaucer to the directness of D. H. Lawrence and James Joyce–have, in their high-quality journalistic products, almost perfected the technique to a flawless method.

It has a long form, and a short one. In the long form, a special writer– preferably an academic, or perhaps the paper's by now resident sexologist–is assigned a theme for a lengthy article or two on some grave matter of social relations.

It is undeniably worthy of exploration and research. Possibly, the challenging assignment is the state of prostitution today (after some recent piece of new legislation or a revised instruction to the police); or its related scandal of bi-sexual child-prostitutes. Or: the homosexual situation before and after AIDS (with some excursions into the actual scene in Manhattan bathhouses or Piccadilly lavatories). Or: the new style of pornographic literature (and its photography) based on what the Customs authorities have been confiscating in the steady exports from Copenhagen and Casablanca. Or: the shameful bureaucratic difficulties that gay or lesbian couples have been having in order to get some semblance of official recognition for their "marriages" or, worse yet, for their attempts to adopt children and establish a family. Or: what's happening to big-city street-walking and curb-crawling?

Everyday life, and you had better believe it, is in contemporary society full of suggestive points of departure. The journalist busies himself with the story for a week or two and then turns up with riveting copy. He (or, more and more, she) spots a trend or two, and offers some relevant and illuminating sociological data. Official misdemeanors and injustices on the part of the Establishment are viewed with alarm; and the whole narrative exudes a moral atmosphere which authenticates thus the pride that our newspaper culture is so alert, so conscientious, and in tune with the ways and words of the world. At least half of my documentation of the history of the f-word and other obscenities comes from this species of worthy reportage.*

The other half comes from the short version. A reviewer or a columnist is taking high-minded exception to the offensive language in certain new films

---

*   I know whereof I speak, having worked on the pioneering piece which proved to be one of the most controversial documents of the day—Wayland Young's article on London's street-walkers, entitled "Sitting on a Fortune: the Prostitute in London." I published it, not without legal entanglements, in *Encounter* (May 1959), pp. 19-31.

Lord Kennet, as he is today, went on in the libertarian absolutism of those years to develop a misguided sexology in his notorious book, *Eros Denied: Sex in Western Society* (1964). It still, however, remains useful as a guide to the illusions about pornography and literature, enriched by f-word eloquence, as entertained by the generations in the 1960s. An absolute verbal candor was part of their utopian revolution that would "utterly change" this sex-sick world. "Let it all hang out..." was a popular phrase of the day. I have always thought of it as a somewhat more sophisticated form of the ideal of "total nakedness" which gripped the Dukhobor sects (and whose fetish of nudity has so fascinated Canadian anthropologists).

or novels, and doesn't hesitate to offer some evidence. An interviewer wants to indicate that the successful businessman, or the prominent politician, or the romantic show-biz star, is not all sugar-and-spice and everything nice, but a real man or woman for all that, using he-man cuss words like the rest of us. Whether asterisks or hyphens are used or not in some cases when there's no fooling around, no beating around the bush, the offensive references have an aloof touch of objectivity about them–*others* are saying them...*we* are only transmitting honest knowledge of the external world.

This rationalization on the part of the newspapermen, heirs to a grand tradition of hard drinking and foul talking, breaks down when journalists succumb, as they always do, to bouts of playfulness. For example, a charming writer named Patrick Connor reviewed a Brighton exhibition of memorabilia in the hometown of the greatest British music hall comedians of yesteryear, that "Cheekie Chappie" called Max Miller. In his heyday of the 1930s he could never be broadcast on the BBC because he was "too *risqué*." None of his scripts for the theater were found objectionable by the Lord Chamberlain, at the time the government's official censor; but then Max Miller never followed his scripts, improvising saucily as he was carried along to the sounds of raucous laughter from the lads in the back. The writer has always a sharp eye for the lurking paradox in the lives of clowns, and we are assured that he was quite strait-laced off-stage: "he hated swearing or any bad language." Before his death in 1963 Max Miller had made tapes of his best acts, capturing "the saltiness of the air in his multi-layered *double-entendres*."

I would have thought by now the reader would have had his appetite whetted for at least a grain of the sea salt, or otherwise have to rush down to the Brighton Festival and catch the tapes on the Exhibition earphones. But no. As the *Daily Telegraph* writer explains, "I wish I could end with one of Miller's jokes, but even today many of them would seem inappropriate in a family newspaper. Better go and hear for yourself."[1] When they're shy they're wry, and when they're coy they're twee. In some weeks the same newspaper's TV critic, Hugh Massingberd, is having a frightful time of it, keeping his eyes and ears open. "'*Bugger all*' this week, '*Old farts*' last week, what further vernacular threats do they have in store?" (12 May 1995). This was on a Friday, and on the next Monday he was registering a mild, but respectful objection to a strong woman TV character who happens to be a governor of a high-security prison: "a tousle-haired, saucer-eyed psychology graduate, an expert in 'prison suicide awareness' in her early thirties who says 's***'" (15 May 1995). And he can't wait till the Tuesday when he musters up enough courage to give vent to his full, honest-to-goodness dismay at yet another powerful TV woman, this time a chief inspector of a Midlands police constabulary: "My only grouse is that these tough telly career women's tendency to say 's***' at regular intervals (about every 20 minutes according to my reckoning) is becoming a bit of a bore. The same epithet also cropped up...*etc. etc.*" (16 May 1995) According to my reckoning, the same epithet cropped up every twenty-four hours, which is par for the course for a hard-driving, professional newspaper reporter.

From Bonk to Shag

A New York magazine recently published a radical critique of U.S. journalism's coverage of the Vietnam War. It was based on a two-volume anthology which was mostly devoted to the celebrated antiwar crusaders (from David Halberstam to Michael Herr) and their indictment of Washington's wrongful and tragic military participation and, more than that, the culpable "war crimes" committed against the Vietnamese people. Was this indictment simplistic, or biased, or perhaps sentimental and pacifistic at its blue-eyed wide-eyed best? Was this body of journalism knowledgeable or naïve, unable (or unwilling) to distinguish between the hellishness of all wars and the excesses of a particular case? Were American writers, in the eternal national recurrence, yet again Innocents Abroad?

> One sometimes wishes that American innocence were some purely literary notion, a quaint confection out of Henry James. Instead, it is a perhaps ineradicable trait of our national character, one that appears to be renewed with every generation and that affects the cynical no less than it does the truly innocent.[2]

Of the American resistance to the crucial Tet offensive against Saigon in 1968, Michael Herr writes, he and some colleagues complained about "how *terrible* it was": "A correspondent who had been covering wars since the 1930s laughed at them: 'What the fuck did you think it was?'" Try, dear reader, camouflaging the f-word, or editing the sovereign contemptuous remark, at once angry and piteous, to "What the hell—...," "What-in-God's-name...," or omitting the expletive altogether. The judgment becomes toothless. It has no more bite than repeating General Sherman's *War-is-hell* aphorism or General McAuliffe's *"Nuts!"* There is some life yet to the f-word when it is given a rare chance to crawl out on its own power from under the rock of the taboo and out of the shadow of ritualistic taboo-breakers.*

---

*   The association of war and profanity is, of course, an old story. In a 17th-century book which I had collected for my work on *Utopia and Revolution* (1976), I find a passage on an English Civil War battle describing the forces under the command of Sir Thomas Fairfax and the King's Forces under the command of the Lord Hopton. Recounting the hand-to-hand fighting "in the lanes near Squire Rolls' estate," and in the streets of the town of Torrington, the author notes:
"...and so faced each other for about two hours, within half a musket shot, exchanging course [*sic*] Language and Bullets now and then."
(John Rushworth, *A True Relation concerning the late Fight at Torrington* [1645-6])
Modern reporters tend to neglect "Language and Bullets," the former being too "coarse" for newspaper publication, the latter ("now and then") being too occasional to be included in an important news story.

Readers who have cultivated a certain alertness to words and meanings sense a difference in the post-puritanical coyness in the mainstream American press–for there is a twee distinction between the journalism that tip-toes up to the outer limit of the conventional and the world-weary professional sort that reluctantly accepts this messy world of unhappy compromise. The latter is best represented by William Safire who, even after "the Lewinsky year" sorely tried the souls at the *New York Times*, still goes by the latest edition of the house-style book and sedulously avoids "dirty realism." In a sharp commentary on the testimony of Vernon Jordan in the Clinton impeachment trial he cast doubt on the statements that were offered to the Senate about the confidential intimacies that had been exchanged by the president and his best friend. But Safire thought it the more valorous side of modesty to clinch the argument by merely writing, "When asked what he talks to the president about, Vernon has replied frequently and famously with a single feline noun." (*Newsweek* in its sketch at the time of the "palsy-walsy" Clinton-Jordan relationship quoted that "*single feline noun*" to be: "*Pussy*.")

The self-employed journalistic restraint, whether intended to be witty or safely tactical, always hovers between euphemism and periphrasis. Synonyms and alternative phrasings are in demand. Even one of the most solemn of commentators on *The Washington Post*, E. J. Dionne, Jr., finds himself having to wink broadly at his readers when approaching the blue limits of permissible vulgarity. In one of his *Post* columns, he is writing, with much sentimentalism, of "a distinguished old language known as cablese."* This was invented by foreign correspondents in the days before fax machines and computer satellite systems. Telegraphic communications were expensive, and to save a word or two in a cabled message was to save money. Dionne enjoys telling a number of famous old stories by colleagues who succinctly told their editors their whereabouts: EYE EXJOBURGING NAIROBIWARD; or they imparted the latest Palace news: QUEEN DAUGHTERED. These are today useless, even cryptic messages, but such were the tricks of olden times. One other usage is tossed in for good measure: "A famous angry cable from a reporter to an editor began: 'UPSTICK JOB' and then suggested where the job be stuck, using the -ward formulation after the anatomical reference." I find it unclear whether telling it straight out–the "-*ward formulation*" is, presumably, ASSWARD–would spoil the joke nowadays by exposing its witlessness and hoary unoriginality...or whether the humor is in the circumlocution. Why use a soiled cliché where a genteel roundaboutness will do very nicely? You wouldn't tell it that way to

---

*   There was a fairly innocent time, and not so long ago, when newspapermen told innocuous stories of such verbal trickery. Robert Graves relates of an evening newspaper (when they were still around) injudiciously printing a letter to the editor without paying attention to the signature: which was *R. Supward*. In those days, as Graves adds, "the edition had to be destroyed at a cost of thousands...." (See Graves, *Lars Porsena*, (1927), pp. 76-77.)

the boys in the backroom or to the gents at the bar. But in the *Post* (and its syndicated associated papers) it does appear to fit agreeably into the general blur.

The latest edition (1989) of the *Washington Post*'s style-book lists a number of painless do's-and-don'ts under "profane and vulgar language"; and its sage advice ends up, as does the *New York Times* in similar circumstances, by cannily recommending the Big Indian Chief solution (always turn to Sitting Bull, wisely puffing on his pipe of peace): "Bowdlerized words may be put between brackets. *"They're all [messed] up,"* he said. Do not use initial letters with dashes or ellipses: s— etc. When in doubt, consult the managing editor or the executive editor." But who–or whom, or what–do those two redoubtable braves consult when things still get to be all [m——d] up?

That this kind of editorial guidance is evasive, to say the least, needs no documentation. But, as it happens, a story in the *Sunday Telegraph* emphasizes as I write the transatlantic difference between prissy American self-censorship and the addiction of British editors to teasing camouflage. The *Telegraph* reports an "ugly scene" between two Tory politicians in which one "stuck his face right up against mine and snarled, 'Don't you f***ing mess with me.'" Qualifying the mess, in or out of brackets, makes it even messier.[3]

H. L. Mencken was "brought up with a start" when he registered the word in a British pre-War advertisement for a popular brand of smoking tobacco (*News of the World*, 19 June 1938, p. 15): *"Want a good shag?"* Mencken tended to think that obscenities that filled so large a part in the American vulgate would–with overuse (e.g. "hell" as in "the hell you say!," "Hell, yes!," "colder than hell," etc.)–wear themselves out in a few years. The h-word is no longer taboo and hence not very popular; the f-word still shows remarkable energy....Although (as we have seen) it has been fast approaching zero-meaningfulness in its pop-culture proliferation. There are sensitive and dramatic occasions where it is unavoidable, indeed indispensable–as in a number of rude cases I have cited in this volume (Chaplin, Crosland, Cassius Clay, et al.) when its rough intrusion in a remark is vitally necessary to the full triumphalist impact.[4]

It is surprising and altogether instructive that a good generation ago there was the feeling abroad in the land that the end to profanity as-we-have-known-it was at hand. Henry Louis Mencken, in his classic work on *The American Language* (first published 1919, several times revised afterwards), accepted the conventional wisdom of the day that "profanity is now in one of its periods of waning." No less a literary figure than Robert Graves devoted a whole book to "the Future of Swearing and Improper Language" and believed, in the face of their steady decline (at least since the age of Queen Elizabeth I!), future there was none. Language experts were reporting from Ireland that even the Irish were no longer swearing much, resorting mostly "to some harmless imitation of a curse."

It could be that they were all listening out for traditional imprecations and ancient accursed maledictions; and with the decline of theology in a secular century they found their notebooks increasingly bare. Mencken himself had his eye peeled out for "true oaths" and not mere "ugly words" which might have descended from true religious oaths but were now "merely dirty." He wanted to register what was considered in that day "full-blooded expletives"; but, as one of his sources instructed him, "all the surviving English expletives, save only *bloody*, had been reduced to a pansy-like insignificance, and were quite devoid of either zip or wow."

American profanity was deemed to be no less "feeble," and was "fast losing its punch." *Time* magazine in 1944 caused a mild sensation by quoting an angry President Roosevelt in front of a defective voting machine (it was November and presumably he was casting his ballot on behalf of his own fourth term in the White House), expostulating: "The *goddamned* thing won't work!" On other heated occasions, at best *gosh* would be varied to include *gosh-darn* and *gosh-almighty*, relieving the over-used *golly* (for God) and *What the Sam Hill* (the devil, in Hell).

At the time, to be sure, there obtained what one European traveller to these shores termed "the extraordinary prudishness of the American newspapers." And when in a public lecture the observer in question ventured to remark that "American grammar is fast going to hell," a New York newspaper (it was Hearst's *Journal-American*) printed only...h—l. (A Boston paper, the *Globe*, as Mencken rushed valiantly to record, actually spelled out the word.[5])

Swearing may be the curse of language, but the larger nemesis lies elsewhere. D. H. Lawrence grasped at and came to depend on a linguistic trick that could not disguise the deficiencies of his basic conception: low language illicitly wedded to high romance. The notion was heady: grafting the f-word on to the heart of true love. But in the end it was too weak, too thin, perhaps not for Lady Chatterley, but for (as literary critics have not failed to point out) Emma Bovary or Anna Karenina among so many others who confined themselves to mainstream manners and conventions in their private lives. That other school of liberationists, the "dirty realists," rely on a quasi-ideological faith that all words are free, and are equal to the humane tasks that we set them. This related notion of a semantic utopia—words old or new, obsolete or obscure, high or low, can be effectively conscripted into the struggle for a better life, an ideal society—was similarly delusional. In the sturdy American hands of a Norman Mailer or Tom Wolfe it hinted at a robust way forward from traditional repression. But it quietly bogged down in the general inflation of obscene usages wherein no individuation, surely the pride of prose masters, could be detectable.

There is a third school in the newspaper culture which bears upon the zigzag course of the four-letterization we are trying to chart. This is the journalistic search for an *ersatz*, for a usable vocabulary of profanity: that is to say, for the substitution or replacement or evasion of taboo obscenities with more or less virile circumlocutions. Few writers of real-existing conversation truly believe that even their most ingenious verbal inventions would ever amount to a scatological or copulative equivalent. Euphemisms in a traditional religious context soon lose their relevance (from "*bloody*" to "*gee whiz*"); and a newspaper critic recently wondered how the most famous Hollywood expletive of its day–Clark Gable's mildly scandalous "Frankly, my dear, I don't give a damn" in *Gone with the Wind* (1939)–could ever have elicited so much agitated discussion. Hell and damnation used to seem so real. Circumlocutions in the centuries of blue-stocking censorship when a vowel or a consonant would be transposed (from Mark Twain's "*aw, sh...ucks*" to Mailer's "*fr*ggn* '")–and proper Christian names given to improper Anglo-Saxon references (from "willy" to "percy" and "nellie")–become obsolete stratagems, and are abandoned as soon as the real thing is generally lawful and widely acceptable. As Robert Graves once pointed out, "It may be that 'bastard,' and similar words, may gradually creep into legitimate speech, but only because obscener equivalents have been found." The pattern of obsolescence, or falling out-of-fashion, obtains even among authentically obscene expressions and not merely among circumlocutions (from "gor'blimey" to "Jeepers-creepers"). Even the f-word has been giving way a little to the onslaught of the "obscener" m-f-word.[6]

Still, there is a measure of self-consciousness in the new liberated style of usage; and we have seen serious newspapers defend the plethora of fruity words in their columns, pleading reasonable moderation in publishing "only" (the statistics here are not very reliable) 565 f-words and 398 s-words as against 145 p- and c-words...per annum, that is.

Only a handful of utopians, as I say, entertain the prospect of creating a virile lingo which would carry such a burden of emotion and repression, of daring and even deviltry, as the immemorial "dirty talk" once did. Our enlightened millennium has almost completely laundered the unmentionables into whiter-than-white, fluttering openly on the wash-line in the sun.

For most journalists and men of letters the invention of synonyms is of provisional tactical duration. A word or phrase is insinuated into the language, serves salaciously for a season–like "to bonk" or to be "engaged in Ugandan activities"–and the search is on for yet another fresh equivalent for the old stale one. Following "bonking" came in the late 1990s a season of "shagging."

Perhaps the high point was reached with the popularity of the British film made by Mike Myers entitled *The Spy Who Shagged Me* (1999). Its distribution in the USA caused only minor problems although one movie critic ejaculated (as he put it), "You can't call a film *that*!" But it developed–such are the variations in the common language–that you can...in America. One American English dictionary was quoted to convincing effect that "to shag" is *to dance*...or to hit practice baseballs for fielders to catch (*shagging fly balls*). Put away the thought that the film, it follows, could just as easily have been called "The Spy Who Hit Baseballs for Fielders to Catch." The "shagger" has become a cult figure although there are some that the entire "shagtastic" incident amounts only to a cheap publicity stunt. But even stunts have a literary life of their own: and if by their words shall ye know them we might sometime devote a moment to Mark Ravenhill's international hit play which would have been entitled in a more benighted time, "*Shopping and–Shagging*...or *Bonking* (or *Sleeping Around*, or, perhaps, *Going to Bed*) to use recent circumlocutions. But there is no point to reviving the exhausted euphemisms of yesteryear.[7]

Young writers of talent, even if they are addicted to shock tactics, are not permanently wedded to the f-word, at least not in their plays. For Mark Ravenhill's next stage work, for instance, he turned to a phrase which drama critics thought inscrutable: *Some Explicit Polaroids* (1999, New Ambassador Theater, London). But a sigh of relief went up from ticket agents and the like who had to deal for years with Mark Ravenhill's unutterable success. The new play, if equally successful, would only be carrying an extra plug for a film-and-camera company that may or may not value such free-ride publicity. Perhaps the obscenity-by-association would prove too much; for even the sympathetic reviewer in the *Times*, the forward-looking and backward-leaning Benedict Nightingale, took the precaution of warning the shockable that "at one weird moment a Russian gay man masturbates the corpse of the youthful sugar daddy who has just died of Aids." Ravenhill's earlier message reflected the unprintable title by expressing the writer's "dismay at a society where consumption and copulation seemed to be the highest virtues." The youthful author's views had taken in the ensuing years a sharp intellectual-ideological turn. They constituted now, in Nightingale's words, "a nostalgic lament for the end of the class struggle and the triumph of the 'chaos' of the market." Given such familiar and friendly discoveries of revolutionary insight, some newspaper commentators were heartfully grateful that the "vulgar realism" of old-fashioned Marxism was now, just before the new Millennium, diverting for a moment the crude onslaught of four-letterization. Characters are utterly defined by their economic circumstances: Capitalism is the root cause of human misery. What else is new? No matter....The simple-minded vulgarisms of yesterday's agit-prop are a welcome turn away from the tidal wave of the obscene future.[8]

If one sets this development in a more innocent context of conventional profanization and the general coarsening of conventional communication almost everywhere, it loses its strategic deviousness and becomes (as a newspaper columnist put it) "the common denominator of those cultures which have not yet come to terms with sex." This may, alas, include most of the known world. One woman writer (and fairly young mother) falls back on her family experience and reports on the reaction of her teen-age son to that "hilariously subtle nod to Sheridan" by dubbing characters "Felicity Shagwell" and "Ivana Humpalot": "To my son, the decision to use in a film title a word that he, correctly, regards as obscene is just a pathetic example of would-be hip adults trying to impress the young with how laddish they are, and getting it wrong. I am glad he is old enough to see it that way."[9] Still, if the inadequate sexual culture falls short of true standards of maturity, what has gone wrong in a cool bit of pubertarian fun? Perhaps it is not the words that are obscene but the "laddishness" to want to be seen to be sly, almost breaking a taboo, and adding a wily nod, nudge and a wink. The ruse adds a small codicil to my old law of participatory obscenity. Here the salacity is not truly shared by the two crossworders–he disguises the acrostic, you have to puzzle it out. Here the indelicacy lies almost entirely in the eye of the beholder. The public is seduced into substituting one or two immodest synonyms, and you've brought the offense and the offensiveness upon yourself. I myself happen to be a latecomer to the current usages of to *shag* and to *bonk*; and thus I have to work a bit harder to participate fully in the profanity. To others, more knowledgeable about such things, the blush comes easier. As Ms. Tyrer writes, "Even when I was a child, 'shag' was one of the dirtiest in the canon of dirty words and it now marks a distinct step down from the ghastly 'bonk,' which was coined for polite people to use." And so were, in her collection, the whole series of car stickers and T-shirt messages which exhibit in the millions a cunning measure of suggestiveness.

"Honk if you had it last night."

"You are the most beautiful girl in the world [read the shirt front in the Notting Hill film scene, and in the back:] Fancy a ——— (no dashes in the original)."

"When I die, bury me upside down so that the whole world can kiss my ——."

I merely excerpt; the reporter and her newspaper editors are more than eager to oblige with a full documentation, hampered only by the fact that bawdy words are not as vivid as erotic pictures: "In an episode I watched recently with my 16-year-old daughter we were treated to a scene, lovingly filmed…[and] in circumstances I cannot describe in a family newspaper the heroine mistakes a dollop of male body fluid on her boyfriend's shoulder for hair mousse." Short of being asked to come with her (or his) DNA so that some incriminating match could be made, the reader is coming away from all this grief more lightly than Ms. Monica L. did in unloving circumstances rather more grave.

Tom Wolfe's "Bleepo's"

Such circumlocutions turn out to be short-lived strategies of evasion. As we have seen, the opportunistic attempts to offer the reader an acceptable alternative to a taboo word–which has enjoyed centuries of notoriety in the shadows of enlightened speech–lack a certain tensile strength to survive. One or two make it on the disputed frontiers of profanity and acceptable communication, that is, to *sleep with...or to lay* (or be *laid*), etc. Some others fade quickly from wink-and-nudge popularity because the conceits are too outlandish to weather too much repetition ("Ugandan practices," and the like). In general, the analogies are thin, anemic, and in the end bloodless. ("He had her" or "they became intimate" or, even, they "exchanged carnal knowledge.") However, in the electronic age, moving surrealistically far away from hand-held blue-pencil editing of racy manuscripts, there are additional possibilities for telling the dirty truth by daring to suggest what one might have said if one were utterly free to say it. It is, mostly, a cynical ploy; but, on occasion, it can score its point effectively, for whatever it is worth. Here is one illustration of this literal buzzword phenomenon.

In the furious polemics that every new work by Tom Wolfe stimulates, there is a semantic element that casts its shadow over the language of journalism with which the putative father of "the New Journalism" is inextricably involved. I myself think that the undeniable power and persuasiveness of Tom Wolfe's first novel–*The Bonfire of Vanities* (1987)–could have benefited by the author (or by a friendly line-by-line editor at his publishing house) eliminating some hundreds of s-words and thus heighten...rather than diminish...the scatological fury of his hatred of what New York City life has become. In his defense of his second novel– *A Man in Full* (1998)–Wolfe counter-attacked three of his major American critics–"rival" novelists: John Updike, Norman Mailer, John Irving–under the curious title, "My Three Stooges."* Some newspapers excerpted his *apologia pro vita sua*; others smuggled dainty bits of gossip into their columns devoted to such "rows in the celebrity culture." For our purposes there was in Wolfe's essay a notable example of circumlocution. It illustrated the electronic possibility of taboo evasion by the ingenious use of onomatopoeia.

It is, as is well-known, an old and standard practice in radio and television to "bleep" out–a buzzing cancellation on the sound tape of some inappropriate word or phrase–what the TV Channel Censor would not permit to soil the transcription. In the case of Tom Wolfe vs. John Irving (and vice versa),** the following was documented. Wolfe had explained that Irving had been in Toronto, and then when the literary chitchat turned to Wolfe's new novel:

---

*   Tom Wolfe, "My Three Stooges," in his collection called *Hooking Up* (2000), pp. 145-171. In England *The Guardian* was happy to pre-publish the whole chapter, not least because it did not add to the hand-count of f-word expletives which, in its annual confession, it tells its readers it was bold enough to print without any discreet or cowardly typographical camouflage. *The Guardian*, "My Three Stooges," 28 October 2000 (Saturday review), pp. 1, 3.

**   John Irving (b. 1942 -) author of *The World According to Garp* (1978), *Hotel New Hampshire* (1981), *A Prayer for Owen Meany* (1989), among other well-known novels.

"Irving threw a temper tantrum on television...Irving's face turned red. His sexagenarian jowls shuddered. He began bleeping." *Bleeping* here is a synonym for cursing or getting into profanities or, in this case, simply uttering the f-word. And Wolfe was pleased to surmise, when he saw the videotape imported from Canada, that "It was all the show's technicians could do to hit the bleep button fast enough":

> Wolfe's problem is, he can't bleeping *write*! He's not a *writer*! Just crack one of his bleeping books! Try to read one bleeping sentence! You'll gag before you can finish it! He doesn't even write literature–he writes...*yak*! He doesn't write *novels*–he writes journalistic hyperbole! You couldn't teach that bleeping bleep to bleeping freshmen in a bleeping freshman English class!

The reaction in the local media was, not unexpectedly, a slightly embarrassed enthusiasm; for the interviewer was seen on the TV screen alternately smiling (you can still have a tingle with the f-word) and covering his face with his hand (the proverbial monkey-like gesture for seeing-and-hearing-no-evil). John Irving had spoken his mind, even at the price of "the old coot" having made "a spectacle of himself." In the final reckoning the cultural course of four-letterization had been moved forward–"but, wow, it's wonderful television!" Mind you, a *wow!* will always win out against an *ugh!* As Wolfe goes on to explain the mode: "It was spellbinding. I don't pretend to be a lip reader, but it took no particular expertise to de-code bleepos that began with such bitterly lower-lip-bitten *f*s." What little expertise it did take involved the correct and speedy identification of the profane expletive which the *bleepos* noisily tried to bleep out. This linguistic knack comprises the rapid mental exclusion of all other expletives that could possibly match the visible, if inaudible, hard lip-biting plosive. All in all, considering what we have been going through, it represents one of the great certifiable triumphs of the phenomenon we have called participatory obscenity.

The Wolfe-Irving fracas signalled the fresh involvement of tens of thousands of new viewers in the visual, if not aural, enjoyment of a titillation that necessarily had escaped old listeners, and even old readers. The sharp-eyed viewer was treated to a new dimension in a long history of oaths and curses: secret sounds, silent articulations, furtive fury. Now, at long last, what you saw on the little screen–with a modicum of witting experience and mental gymnastics–is what you got. Wow! Ugh.

Dahl's Nudity

There are engaging differences as well as rough similarities between the politics of profanity and the commercial ventures into blue enticements in the consumer marketplace. One is afraid of losing votes, and hesitates to alienate a sensitive minority, or indeed any sizeable political group of citizens prepared to protest and withhold crucial electoral support at the next polling date. The other is fearful of losing customers and sacrificing bottom-line profits.

In the academic-intellectual debate over "democratic choice" in a capitalist democracy where the voter chooses in the polling station and the consumer chooses in a competitive marketplace, Professor Milton Friedman used to insist that the consumer and the voter are interchangeable. In a free market and deregulated society both register their individual choices, one for an attractive political candidate (their "sort of guy") and the other for a shop-window's pretty chiffon blouse or a pseudo-shabby pair of flared trousers which suggest convincingly that the ready-to-wear items are *chic* or *in, cool* or *with it*.

Alas, both are subject to suspicions and pressures. In the case of the young Tory attempt to try out obscenity by anagram, the alert conservative controlling elements were too strong for the daring young men on their flying trapeze. It was difficult enough to rally a right-of-center majority without the streetwise kids trying out dirty words. As for the innovators of *The French Connection*, would they be able to get away with it? It is, I know, a cynical way of putting it, but it is not mine; it's the media experts who watch warily the interpenetration of language-styles between on-line journalists and off-color copywriters.

Whether–or not–the *F.C.U.K.* company would indeed be able to "get away with it" became in the first year of the new century a local spectator sport, with a good deal of betting going both ways. I would have lost my own wager. When I heard in London (it was the summer of the year 2000) that a "storm of controversy" would be coming up when the Advertising Standards Authority would be coming out against a "sexy" ad on behalf of the Yves Saint-Laurent's Opium perfume, I sensed a breakthrough, a new-century turning point.

The Saint-Laurent advertising people–there was no text to read so "copywriters" could not have been involved–risked identifying their product with total nudity. The *Opium* advert chose the shapely figure of twenty-three-year-old Sophie Dahl (an off-spring of a famous storyteller [Roald Dahl] and a celebrated actress [Patricia Neal]). The final photograph was a rather idealized, or touched-up, snap of a youthful beauty lying flat on her back, enjoying a moment of aromatic ecstasy. They had made a relatively safe choice–for, as has been reported, there had been even more "explicit" photos of Sophie Dahl taken during the photo-shoot in America. (As one news-item reported, "One of them shows a man's head between her legs.") Indeed the final photo choice almost represented conservative caution. After all, a recent Gucci ad–for a perfume called *"Envy…for men and women"*–caused the Standards Authority "no concern," although in the pictorial mélange of lovemaking flesh there was an open-mouthed suggestion of oral sex (which since the Clinton-Lewinsky affair can, arguably, be termed to be "not sexual").

The Dahl case must have constituted a special stress on the standards of the Authority. The directors, new and old, were always insisting–flaunting their correctness on the issue of "prudity"–that "We're not a fuddy-duddy organization wanting to ban nipples." In addition to that, the Authority's offices were "staffed largely with young women"; and in the backwash of the older feminist movement many young women are not overly concerned with flashing female nudity which some still see as "a sign of empowerment."

Unpredictably, the empowerment structure collapsed or, at least, flip-flopped. There was a surprising backlash against Sophie Dahl's naked body which was already to be seen on giant billboards throughout the country. For one reason or another there ensued an avalanche of protests, mostly (it was reported) from young women, to the effect that the ad was intolerably "offensive." Was the prohibition a return to the familiar prudery which sought to protect a society and its macho stalwarts from "the display of female pleasure"? Could it be that photos were failing where words had already succeeded? Was the taboo on the blue picture stronger than the off-color words pertaining thereto? For a moment I was regaled by the spectacle of highly paid curvaceous models being consigned to unemployment on the hoary old charge of "sexploitation."

So-called empowerment is a short-lived delusion. It never refers to a real or true "seizure of power," but amounts only to a stylish buzzword which serves to disguise its flimsy relationship to fashionable attitudes of the moment. Perhaps this is the fate of all, in Flaubert's phrase, "*idées reçues*." Gone today, here again (maybe) tomorrow.

As one English female columnist recently confessed in one melancholy Sunday edition: "Oh dear. One of the many punishments of getting older is having to watch the pendulum of fashionable ideas swing needlessly, wastefully back and forth."[10]

Our newspaper culture is subjected here, as in most other instances, to two contradictory impulses. On the one hand, there is the long-term and persistent drive to permit what was once forbidden, to "out" without fear or favor, the privacies and intimacies of sex life. On the other, there is the still strong feminist tendency–in its extreme expressions perhaps of only temporary enthusiasm–to defend the "dignity" of women and resist any and all macho attempts to exploit gender for hoary sex-object purposes. Thus, in the latest altercation which I have recorded, one newspaper headline reported:

SOPHIE DAHL POSTER
TOPS ADVERTISING COMPLAINTS

The "wimmin's movement" was especially provoked by the poster which featured the model reclining naked on a bed except for a pair of high heels and a diamond necklace–diamonds being, as is well known, a girl's best friend, if she's out for such friendships. A London daily recorded that it was the most complained-about advertisement "in the last five years." Did the Yves Saint Laurent advertising and marketing executives appreciate the formidable records in quasi-obscenity that they had broken? Against a competition–which, like

The French Connection, played with antediluvian literacy and fiddled with alphabetical f-word combinations–they had effectively relied on the power of wordless emblems, graphic images, and pre-literate symbols that went to the heart of desire under the elms. The ensuing provocation attested to its targetry; but the consequences were also deemed inevitable and unwelcome. The poster was withdrawn. The grounds were that it was "offensive and degrading to women."

I must add that sex is not always the main theme of the guardians of our emotive integrity. The Advertising Standards Authority tabulated the tens of thousands of complaints that it had received in the year 2000 and listed as second on the list a campaign for a gas supplier (*Npower*, to be precise) which featured, of all things, a picture of a ginger-haired family bearing the slogan in slightly puzzling words: "*There are some things in life you can't choose.*" They had intended to defend their superior product in the energy market, but had they really been "offensive to redheads"? The ASA disagreed with the thousands who, out of some hirsute pride and unmodified genetic dignity, had registered their protests. The board said that a complaint was not justified.

But sex reared its head again in the race for the third place. The campaign for a species of women's underwear named *Gossard's* showed a naked woman lying on a bed above the caption: "*Bring him to his knees.*" This was judged by the authorities, confident in their expertise about the role of position and posture in sensitive near-sexual situations, "to be likely to cause serious or widespread offense." What standards were these watch-dogs defending? Old- and new-fashioned puritanism was surely not involved. The days of censors armed with the whip of "blue laws" are over almost everywhere. The men in Hollywood's famous Hays Office are, in these days of extensive sexual simulation on the silver screen, perpetually spinning in their graves. Even in stuffy old Britain nary a soul remembers the fearful days of a Lord Chamberlain–who made the life of Sir Laurence Olivier so bothersome in his last days in London's National Theater, and who put the fear of God and his prim-and-proper commandments into would-be publishers of the doings of Lady Chatterley or Humbert Humbert.

No, nowadays our guardians seem to be more of a bemused lot. Why are such curious pictures and estranging messages coming at us with such abandon? Why don't entrepreneurs, who are so eager to peddle their wares, remain loyal to the commercial spirit of the capitalist marketplace? Shouldn't they, in the very nature of things, try to refrain from offending their customers–even if only 10 percent of them, whose alienation can lead to bottom-line disasters? "It still seems to happen," said a spokesman for the Advertising Standards Authority, trying hard to be objective (and even, as the cool ideal of classic sociologists had it, *wertfrei*): "but advertisers are starting to realize that the short-term benefit of publicity may be outweighed by the long-term damage to their reputation."[11] This is one of those perceptions which may be misperceived. Some resounding benefits of scandalizing publicity may well be long-term–and even in the short-term, a surge in salesmanship may make some of us happy millionaires. As for a spotless repute, blue chips have in our day, from Wall Street to Hollywood, turned out to be (in George Eliot's phrase) "the large home of ruined reputations." There is much melancholy evidence to suggest that it pays to be tasteless.

It is only to be expected that the self-regulatory agencies will be inconsistent in their decision-making, with the print-press being more–or, as the case may be, less–daring and even militant...and looking hesitantly over their shoulder as to what the television people are doing with the self-same texts (accompanied, naturally, by tantalizing pictures in motion). There was a note of triumphalism, in London, when both the Independent Television Commission and the Advertising Standards Agency came down hard on one of the telecom giants, Vodaphone.

Two advertisements featuring embracing couples were banned for being "explicit and gratuitous." Both pictures–erotically moving (in one), suggestively static (in the other)–were accompanied by the caption "*Get the flirting over with before you get home.*" There were many complaints, but it was not divulged whether the complainants, very often middle-class family-oriented stalwarts, objected also to the discrimination against "*the home*" as a site for normal lovemaking procedures. In any case the obvious recommendation for a "quickie" seemed to many to be coarse or incorrect, or both.

In its defense, Vodafone said it believed the advertisements "reflected the real mobile behavior of the target audience of younger people." They would say that, wouldn't they. Vodaphone, after having bought Mannesmann in Germany, is in fierce worldwide competition with the Swedish Nokia in the sale of *mobiles*, which the Swedes call..."*cell-ponnes*" and the Germans call "*handys.*" But Mo–il–ty is what they are both after.[12]

From "Bleepos" to "Typos"

Where do we go from here? The main connection to the last stop–at which our questing modern culture might find, hopefully, the grail of a usable profanity–defies all maps and time-tables. One way through is via *abstraction*–whereby the four-letter words are stripped of their alphabetical character and emerge as squiggly emblems which have a blankety-blank power but no real relation to the immemorial vitality of dirty realism. A recent article in *Newsweek* took this route and was appropriately headlined:

IN DEFENSE OF
*$##@&$%#

The other route is rather more direct and time-saving–not emblematic but anagrammatic, whereby a letter or two is transposed and the full Monty is there for all to see...almost...but unadorned enough to mark a new century's valiant attempt to let it all hang out.

I have already chronicled the zigzag hesitations in the British campaign for FCUK, the logo of the multi-national textile firm *French Connection United Kingdom*; but in the latest newspaper reports (October 2000) they have taken another and perhaps definitive turn. Media experts of faint heart suspected that the FCUK people, in dishonorable timidity, might have gotten cold feet...a bottom-line-chill...the conventional commercial anxiety and marketing fears that traditional custom could be lost. Would they risk offending customers who still belong somehow to families with family values? (After all, they had dared to connect themselves with being "French," which, as is well known, is still a naughty come-on in all red-light districts.) Or would they be true, like enterprising entrepreneurs who know that frontiers are here to be transgressed and taboos there to be broken, loyal to the *now* urge "to be with it"? In our culture of compromise who nowadays will have the courage of their countercultural convictions?

With millennial dash the FCUK people put paid to the old prevarications and stormed ahead to an *admass* language (as J. B. Priestley used to call it) where no mainstream corporation had ever ventured, reaching the parts and particles that no other copywriter had ever reached. Their fulsome advertising campaign consisted of full newspaper pages in jet-black with slogans and texts gleaming out in white: white and pure as the driven snow. I reproduce without any further ado one such ad in its entirety (although its selling point is now the shop on London's Oxford Street rather than the one on Chelsea King's Road which I have been following):

WORLD'S
BIGGEST
FCUK

Tomorrow sees the arrival of the fcuk of your dreams.
fcuk Oxford Street is an fcuk like no other. Womenswear, menswear and the new fc bar. Experience a different kind of fcuk altogether. And enter the free prize draw which could bag you £2,000 worth of fcuk stuff.* fcuk Oxford Street. One humungus fcuk.

I omit the asterisked footnote at the bottom of the ad which merely refers to some of the conditions for entering "the free prize drawing"; it specifically excludes "employees of the French Connection Group and their families"...all other families being eligible to enter and, with f****** luck, to win some of the "*fcuk*/stuff" on offer.[13]

As for "humungus," a curious English newspaper-reader will be puzzled to find it unlisted in any standard dictionary (*Longmans, Oxford, Websters, Ran-*

dom House, etc.). It presumably has its origins in American 1960s usage. Spell it, therefore, as you like it. Green's Cassell/*Slang* (p. 264), gives it as "homongous…humungous" and defines it as "huge/monstrous/tremendous." Lighter's *American Slang* (vol. 2, pp. 193-94) also prefers the *-ous* ending, and quotes more than a dozen demotic usages, the earliest being 1968. Thus, the combination of the f-word and the h-word may be taken by the *fcuk* people as a happy Anglo-American marriage of the old and the new. They must have had a sides-splitting kick, bordering on the orgasmic, thinking up in their *fcuk* frenzy such commercial four-letter come-ons.

Swearing by the Ad-Man's Prose

There is, thus, an obvious and, on occasion, irresistible temptation for an adventurous entrepreneur to try and cash in on the indelicate temper of the times. (I am not thinking, at the moment, of the panderers who manufacture colored and flavored condoms and a whole assortment of soft- and hard-porn video cassettes.) They may all be honorable men, albeit with high cultural ambitions: not unlike trendy bishops and other fellow travellers of the zeitgeist in the fashionable pop world. They still want, above all, to sell such wares or services as they offer in the open market. But can they not, at the same time, cultivate a public persona, give their companies a new imagery, talk to their customers out there in up-to-the-minute language, with a fresh message and even a slightly frivolous formula? They can–but they are putting their profits and indeed their capital solvency on the line…just as the illustrious poet vowed that he would wager his immortal reputation on his composing, on inspired demand, an incomparable couplet–quite oblivious to the danger of doggerel consigning him to oblivion.

In recent years, the most sensational impact in the advertising world was made by the audacious efforts of the Italian firm of Benetton, foremost in stylish textiles. Its international campaign featured on all continents full-page ads in newspapers, billboards, and kiosks, whereon (at least when it didn't run into difficulties with the censors) a message of universal good will for a multiracial, cross-cultural society was daringly presented. There were eye-stopping photographs, fashionably done by the best studios in Milan, of men and women of all races and colors hand-cuffed to each other; of a black priest kissing a white nun; of a ripped pair of blue-jeans revealing an AIDS stamp on a rump, etc. etc. There were a dozen or so vivacious scenes, reflecting the idealism and the joyous optimism of the Benetton family (and its flamboyant advertising director) for a brave new world of health and happiness. The global slogan sang out at us in every language–*"LET'S COME TOGETHER!"* Whether there was a deliberate double-entendre for the coming orgasmic get-togethers is arguable. In any case good sex is part of the good society, and surely what's coming is also an erotic utopia.

Some thought the double-entendre sly and daring; but it already had, in the decade before Benetton identified with it, a singular and explicit history. It is recorded that the phrase was popularized–if not exactly coined (for the pun was obvious and old)–by the sexologist Timothy Leary as a slogan for his planned campaign against Ronald Reagan for the governorship of California in 1969. Leary appealed to John Lennon to write him a campaign song. The ditty was duly composed, but the psychedelic master didn't get to sing it. Governor Reagan took the opportunity to deny Leary bail on a marijuana charge, and the togetherness man sat the campaign out alone in his cell in an Orange County jail. Nevertheless, the Beatles launched the Lennon-McCartney song, *"Come Together,"* in that same year; and the historian of their recordings writes, "With its sex-political title, *Come Together* constitutes the last of Lennon's espousals of the counterculture." The influences at the time were "partly *LSD*-enhanced" and partly "the prevailing countercultural atmosphere as defined by pundits as diverse as Marshall McLuhan [of *The Gutenberg Galaxy* and its "the Medium is the Message"], Arthur Janov [of *The Primal Scream*], R.D. Laing [of *The Divided Self*], and Herbert Marcuse [of *One Dimensional Man*]." They were all "hippie sages of the day," along with "a bewildering guru/shaman modeled on Timothy Leary, Ken Kesey [of *One Flew Over the Cuckoo's Nest*], Carlos Castaneda [of *The Teachings of Don Juan* and *Journey to Ixtlan*], et al.* Most had gone on record with a friendly espousal of a doctrine of "coming together," and some libertarians even advocated a free and wider form of orgasmic collectivism.

But for now there were too many grumblers and dissenters for Benetton's business interests to escape with impunity. There was a retailer backlash, even a customer boycott, and Benetton could persist if only they would be prepared to reckon with substantial losses. And persist they did, even to the extent of attracting a few famous imitators.

Copycat corporations are too mindlessly unwieldy to decide sharply whether other people's businesses are making money or only gathering notoriety (which may still be, as I have suggested, a shady way of maximalizing profit). For nothing succeeds like excess. One adventurous wordsmith may go a bit too far

---

*   Ian Macdonald, *Revolution in the Head: the Beatles' Records and the 60s* (1995), p. 287.

   This book is plugged as "the finest piece of fabs [the fabulous four, i.e. the Beatles] scholarship ever published"; and it is very useful for details of dates and recordings, but also for remarks which can go straight into the pompous punditry of *Pseud's Corner*:

   "Enthusiastically received in campus and underground circles, *Come Together* is the key song of the turn of the decade, embodying a pivotal moment when the free world's coming generation rejected established wisdom, knowledge, ethics, and behaviour for a drug-inspired relativism which has since undermined the intellectual foundations of Western culture" (p. 288).

but, in the trade, the marketing coup may well impress more timid and medio-cre souls who adjust and adapt to whatever detritus the extremism had left behind. Department stores advertised their wares in the new hope that their goods and their customers would be "coming together"; and some high-fash-ion boutiques ventured to picture young and nude lovers embracing their offer of "Complete Customer Satisfaction Guaranteed." Outsized vast multi-national companies tried to warm up to their clientele in a more intimate way by organizing *"Come Together"* assignations.

As I write this (Spring 2001) I have an invitation from the Mercedes-Chrysler management to attend a local shareholders meeting. I happen to have only a handful of shares, and this apparently entitled me to attend a grand reception in the deluxe Esplanade Hotel in the heart of new Berlin. The German invita-tion is up-to-the-minute in its Americanized accents–Mercedes-Daimler has recently taken over Chrysler and is now also a powerful player. It is fulsome in inviting me to their *"Come-Together Party,"* and nobody could be nicer than the host who lists himself as *"Leiter der Kommunikation"* with a Stuttgart rank of *"Senior Vice President"* (in English, of course). I declined but found time to remind Mercedes' head office of the Benetton and Beatles history of coming together: that it was a slightly obscene euphemism in coarse usage. Wouldn't "a *Get-Together Abend"* have been good and proper? While I was being cur-mudgeonly I added that he might safely insert a hyphen (a *Bindestrich* in German punctuation) in his official title–as in the vice president of the USA, Mr. Dick Cheney–otherwise the Vice Squad might be inquiring what exactly were the Senior Vices he was presiding over? (A small joke, not to get too heavy about it all.)[14]

Of course, what I have referred to as "orgasmic collectivism" was far from the minds of the Mercedes executives; and certainly they did not intend to be sexological (as John Lennon) or countercultural (as Timothy Leary)...nor in-deed to make a contribution to the undermining of "the intellectual founda-tions of Western culture." It was just that everybody felt that "coming together" was a pretty good thing.

With rather more wit and insouciant abandon was the advertising campaign of Heineken's Beer which promised, in an endless series of witty, if mildly salacious, cartoons all illustrating the point: a potent drink that "would reach the parts that other beers cannot reach." What exactly the Dutch brewers had in mind, other than maximizing attention and sales, is neither here-nor-there; it was suggestive, even (to use the old-fashioned word, still popular in some circles of *louche* Amsterdam) risqué. But it was never intended earnestly enough to be misleading, since all beer-drinkers the world over were painfully aware of the relation between alcohol and impotence and/or incontinence. If those were the parts the Heineken people were promising to reach, it would be Closing Time, Gentlemen, for the lusty lads in all the corner pubs of the Western world.

My third and final example of the coyness which dares not speak its name was a recent campaign, and the results are not yet in. That staple diet of all slimmers, *Ryvita Crispbread*, decided a few years ago to change its image. Obviously the calculations of whether there is a large profitable market among the people who eat more than among the slimmers who are resolved to eat less, has given them to think. How could they ever convert the millions of women customers who had been swearing by their dietary doctrine?

As the papers reported (in May 1995), it was "a shocking change of image." Instead of the snack that helps dieters, mainly women, win what is called "the Inch War," or "the Battle of the Bulge," the new message is that it can be eaten with anything, however fattening! The blunt slogan (which has the usual built-in discretion for family diners who read family newspapers) is:

"Forget your *F*-Plan
Go for the F-it Plan"

Was there–unusual in jingles targeted for the mass millions–a certain willful obscurity intended here? Was it supposed to be a pun on the word *"Fit"*? Reporters, quick to suspect a double-entendre from their long practice, pressed the matter; and the Ryvita spokesman (it *was* a man) confirmed that the f- and the -*it* were meant to be pronounced separately. "Tasteless," snapped the *Daily Mail* in a crisp pun of its own, castigating an "unsubtle message." And it reproduced, in appetizing color, the Ryvita poster showing a woman covered in whipped cream and strawberries, sandwiched between two slices of her favorite slimming bread. A further bit of good advice added: *"The war's over. Enjoy the liberation."*

It all sounded like (if the calorie-rich word is not misunderstood) a lot of waffle; and the advertising experts went on waffling in a style not quite seen since the Ford Motor Company promised an Automotive Revolution with a new, ill-starred model called the Edsel.

> Diets like the *F*-Plan are out. We are in the age of the F-it Plan. Women are taking control of their lives and are not prepared to take orders about what they eat. They are fed up being told they have to look a certain way to please people.
>
> The super-waif look is out, and we are encouraging people to eat what they like if that's what they want. It is a bold campaign, but I think a lot of women are feeling bold about the subject.

What this is supposed to mean is that, in an age of prospering feminist revolution, Ryvita wants to live off the fat of the land.

The Health-Food lobby was the first to complain since, obviously, the million-dollar campaign encourages unhealthy eating. Then came the even graver tones of the Advertising Standards Authority. These guardians of the ad man's integrity and the copywriter's prose were not against "taking on a new identity" or even being "hard-hitting" and "causing a fuss." But wasn't it likely to cause *offence*? Wasn't it patently *rude*? "Saying *F-it* doesn't really leave much to the imagination."

Among the more unimaginative aspects of the whole affair was the wild punning it induced; and one tabloid buttered up its readers with this smear on a lofty campaign which, after all, would encourage calories to be getting (or "coming") together, with crackers that promise to reach the parts that other biscuits cannot reach.

> *"In two crisp words,*
> *a crudely-bred Ryvita."*

By my reckoning, crisp words there were three, almost four; but no matter. The signs were clear that dieters in their millions, as one indignant reader wrote to her favorite newspaper, would be "swearing back" and "swearing off." This was the kind of wordplay on the part of paying customers that could spell out the loss of serious money.

Benetton took risks when a million-dollar company committed itself to "shock ads," quite apart from the consumer goods they were peddling, on the controversial subjects of AIDS, abortion, racism, and the like. But it apparently didn't hurt business when the Italian clothing group over the eighteen years of controversy went to its high in worldwide sales amounting to some nine billion dollars. Still, a dramatic announcement from its Treviso headquarters, made in April 2000, gave news of Oliviero Toscani's departure and it quickly described the split as a "friendly separation." All the usual p.r. euphemisms were circulated to the effect that the company only wanted its corporate advertising to personify a team spirit rather than a talented individual.

To be sure, there had always been a distressed or outraged public response to almost all of Benetton's deliberate provocations, from the huge billboards of black-African and Caucasian nuns (in full habit) kissing each other...to the most recent "shock" of Oliviero Toscani's photographs of convicted American murderers–who, after all, believes in Yankee justice?–who have been waiting so long on Death Row for their capital punishment, for the death penalty. There was a storm of indignation, and Luciano Benetton, the founder and patriarch of the northern Italian family-controlled enterprise, was forced in one recent incident to apologize to the families of the prisoners' victims as well as to his company's U.S. sponsors.

The financial press in Italy as well as abroad always referred to Toscani as an "advertising guru" and affirmed that Benetton had shocked its way to a "unique international image" and to "a global brand" by means of Toscani's series of original advertisements. They had become "classics in the marketing world." What was it, then, that convinced the company that it was time for "a new approach...for a new style"? What will a global audience do when it will have to forego regular politically correct instruction in the most sensitive issues of social and moral concern? Compared to his imaginative images and tendentious propaganda the strongly opinionated editorials in our newspapers and magazines are models of prudence and chronically fair comment. The corporation might well want to win back a few alienated retailers. Sears, for one, the department store chain which had decided to ban Benetton products. Costly and nasty legal actions had been launched in many places. The Midwest U.S. state of Missouri took court action against the idea of "miscegenative breast-feeding" which supported the "united colors of Benetton" and which had first made the pink and purple knitwear famous.

Who would give the self-styled "Pasolini of publicity" a new platform? One could think, if one put one's mind to it, of dozens of social problems in our societies which called for adventurous taboo-breaking shock treatment. But would the master also want to be seen selling fast food which is now part of the "diversification" plan of Benetton in the new millennium? Meanwhile, from California came the news that Oliviero Toscani who had been recently advising the new U.S. magazine *Talk*. He would now be going to work for its chief executive officer, Ms. Tina Brown, the former editor of the *New Yorker*, who is a proven expert in her own right in shock-tactics which alienate old customers.[15]

There is, to be sure, an extremist school in newspaper-reading circles which suspects that a certain "foreign" element, brash and new to the indigenous cultural community and its linguistic manners, is largely responsible for certain current excesses. (The Italian Benetton's advertising campaign is the prime example–as if English publicists were bereft of their own native roots in profanity, going back to Chaucer!) A further example is one I have already mentioned. It concerns a multi-national textile company oddly named *The French Connection* which, wittingly or no, tries to take some advantage from the sexual connotation of *French* among its English customers. Thus, its flagship shop on the King's Road in Chelsea once covered its windows with the good news of its commercial establishment in the United Kingdom (hereafter known, fatefully, as the UK). The acronym was gleefully plastered all over the shop...namely, FCUK.

For some it was a schoolboy prank, rather unworthy of a serious commercial establishment, even if it happened to be happily called (in full) *French Connection UK*. All newspapers reported it, some with the standard wink-eyed comment, "*Goddit?*" Someone–the local advertising manager himself, or an alert customer or passer-by?–suspected it was indeed a devious double-entendre, in fact an anagram of the f-word, nudging the funny-bone of the connected "*French*" world. Could it possibly help sell macho men's jeans or hippie ladies' skirts? Might it not upset, offend, or otherwise alienate a large class of prospective customers?

It did. The F.C. (UK) company's directors announced–presumably covering up some staff whippersnapper's attempt at a blue joke–that the f-word had been far from their minds, that it appeared to them to be only "a good *logo*," and it did not in the least imply that their clothes, stylish though they were, were somehow "sexier" than the worthy competition which could only feature dry puritanical English connections. Walking by on Chelsea's Kings Road I noted that the *French Connection* logo had disappeared from the window dressing. It was the only setback the f-word had suffered on the streets of London in many years. But the four-letterization of our culture would not be denied, and *FCUK* snatched victory from the jaws of defeat.

Connecting with the French Crossroads

I return to one of the starting points of modern porn jargon, the medically disguised sexual secret of the venereal mishap known for several generations as "*French 'flu.*" Presumably it enabled a whole host of unfortunate young lovers to mention an unmentionable of the day, namely, syphilis. In a dozen other variations (e.g., *French letters* [condoms]; ...*love* [fellatio]...*kiss* [tongue reinforcing lips]; ...*photography* [homosexual snapshots]; ...*postcards* [erotic poses]; ...*tickler* [contraceptive sheath with extra protrusions]...etc., etc.) How infectious was the French 'flu? how contagious was the general eroticism, based on half-suggestive synonyms, or fully explicit anagrams? how catchy the love-style and its titillating vernacular?

I can't imagine a way of determining realistic estimates of such soft-porn practices where most of the evidence was confined until only yesterday to hushed, embarrassed whispers. In our more forthcoming era we have more useful, realistic benchmarks. Books brought back from a long weekend in Paris can be calculated and tabulated (and Booker Prizes in London have been famously given to novels which broke existing records of f-words per hundred steamy pages). Innovative sex shops have vied for custom in the sales of relevant instrumentalities, in rubber or plastic. Libertarian legislative commissions explored the nightlife from Cannes to Copenhagen (most notoriously, by the late Lord Longford, a.k.a. Lord Porn), scoured the midnight shows and simulations for possible guidelines to a more permissive enlightenment governing consensual intimacies.

Be that as it may, in the case of our French Connection (as below), it would seem to have had a contagious effect on modern corporations, large and small, eager to promote their products in popular contexts, ranging from "playing together" (smoking, drinking, sunbathing) to "coming together" (multilingual details of orgasms as yet unavailable, but the sound effects are joyful noises). The newspaper and television ads to illustrate these pitches are too well known to need any further documentation here.

A radical breakthrough in the mainstream image-making can be recorded for the winter of the year 2001-2002, when the contemporary automobile industries–from Detroit to Tokyo–were desperately trying to make new connections, evidently not excluding the French one. At least there was a suggestion of a breakthrough in this direction when a Toyota *Yaris* ad (or was it a Ford *Ka*?) played with pictures of a man "gazing longingly" and then was interrupted by an image (as one newspaper meticulously reported) "of the shape of a pair of buttocks worn into the wall." Whose buttocks? what wall?

The Coca Cola campaigns on behalf of "Diet Coke" were not far behind. The new themes are illustrated by photos which, in turn, are somewhat cryptically captioned "*French Toast.*" Having hinted, mouthwateringly, at something delicious to come, they go on to explain: "love fizzes over a Diet Coke as repressed Brits are urged to 'taste the moment.'"[16]

Advertising editors on their media pages reminded us of the long way we have already come with the Diet Coke campaigners–"remember the 11 o'clock moment when the office women gathered to watch the hunk take his shirt off–focused exclusively on women.'" This, we are told, was an American ad distributed globally. But the new campaign which is "designed to appeal to men and women," both sexes evidently subject to roughly the same urgent bouts of thirst, is announced to "signal a shift in emphasis."

This is "what happens" in a so-called French Revolution of advertising upheaval, which is signalling a whole new world era, that is, if enough thirsts need to be quenched in the globalized coming together: "A young woman is registering evening class attendees. A young man arrives for the French class. She asks, 'French literature...French polishing...or French...?' and reaches forward to kiss him...'A plus tard' she says as he goes to the class. 'Taste the moment,' says the endline." What is being timed here? Female initiatives? France's clocks (which, notoriously, tick differently)? What we also need to know is that, like all multi-national advertisers, "Coke is torn between producing global ads and bowing to local market conditions." At unusual times in turbulent historic events, such as the collapse of the Soviet Union (1917-1991) the great dilemma for a company whose marketing is devoted to the color of blazing red is to persist with a color which, alas, is eliciting popular antipathies–or switch to another hue when the eternal competition (Pepsi-Cola) is currying favor among the ex-Soviet masses by flashing the color blue. The new–or old–color you identify with can be (don't forget it) a whole new culture!

The latest news is: "At the moment the pendulum is swinging." This might mean that the swing could be back to centralized U.S. control in Atlanta, Georgia, where experts will be determining globewise how far the kissing flirtation can go in non- or *anti*-"French" marketing areas. In London the million dollar decision appears to be easy. The English reporter approves the starting point which is "the British sense of reserve," and Coke is only "encouraging us to let go." Other places around the globe may have deep-seated impulses *to hold fast* rather than *to let go*. The ideal of coming together has its complications. It all depends on what you mean by "*French...?.*"

At any rate, the large implications of the trivia we have been considering in the language of journalism, caught between the hucksters of commercial sloganeering and the titillation of literary libertinism, are not to be denied.

Looking back on the half-century which has been preoccupying us, we should be astonished to find that we are precisely at the crossroads of two great traffic-laden cultural convoys. One is the old highway which in all the years of the Cold War (in a campaign sustained by the insistent editors of Hubert Beuve-Méry's *Le Monde*) haunted the NATO alliance and its protagonists– namely, what the French called the *"Coca-Colonisation de tout le Monde."* The second is the new road over which we have been hurtling; namely the *four-letterization* of the everyday vernacular which we all (most of us) speak and write.

Now we have reached the point when Coca Cola itself meets, in a tasteful if dramatic moment, the f-word…with French echoes to boot (and, especially, the robust melodies from the *Moulin Rouge* soundtrack). It must all mean some-thing.

There are only a limited number of combinations, as any scrabble-scarred player will testify, in which a four-letter word can be arranged to be relevant to a company's commercial interests. The *French Connection* (U.K.) may well still be undecided as to whether or not to abandon its *FCUK* logo–under pressure of offended customers, always a powerful lobby affecting a shop-owner's mentality. Still, there is a factor of copycat commination which is at work here. The competitive concern that a blue or any other off-color anagram might generate for a hard-pressed business enterprise an element of publicity, or new sales, or newspaper notoriety, make it likely that the celebrated exple-tive (a mere four letters out of the twenty-six) could be recycled to someone else's advantage. Suddenly on the defensive, the executives of *F.C. (U.K.)* took a dim view of the latest new logo which was insinuating itself into the public prints. When a rival anagram, with a slightly different form of back-rhyme orthography, appeared blatantly on the scene, it announced to the press that it was "considering action."[17]

A London broadsheet daily, the *Telegraph*, found the impending "culture war" so newsworthy that it featured the new logo of the political organization of Young Conservatives–after all, Walpole and Pitt were fairly young when they became illustrious Tory Prime Ministers–on its front page, and in living color.

CFUK
Conservative Future United Kingdom

In fact the Tory newspaper was playing both sides of the street in its cover-age. On the one side, it was helping the Young Tories (of whom they approve) "to try to improve their image"–and, on the other, demonstrating the validity of its usual editorial stand against so-called progress and change, that is, amelioration means deterioration. Party stalwarts were reported to be enraged.

The *French Connection*, as mentioned, worked itself up into a wrath, and mobilized its lawyers for possible legal action against some infringement of its rights: since CFUK had a striking resemblance to FCUK, and both were relatively equidistant from the magic word holding corporate culturists in thrall. But the Young Tories, uneasy for a long time with their "stuffy image," defended their decision to use the initials on posters, leaflets, and tea mugs as a "marketing tool." If the bills for the heavy costs of printing had not been already incurred, suspicion might be justified that the whole affair was really an adolescent prank, what in schools like Eton and Winchester are called "cads' tricks." However, the unrepentant chairman of *Conservative Future* insisted that "These are the *1990s!*" and he was on to new ways "to market politics to young people."

Middle-aged middle-class Tory neo-Conservatives thought of the new slogan as reflecting "the puny perverse pull" of child's play. On occasion in Westminster or in Chelsea I did hear them utter, loud and clear, the fearful de-anagrammized word–but "privately," not for printing even in scrambled form. But, as they insisted, there is a *private* aspect to profanity, and it was too serious a matter to be left to public-school boys. "Kids"–the Americanism is now spreading in the U.K.–tend to want to hold fast in their prehensile way to the first dirty little secrets they had been exposed to, clenching something infantile in their tiny little fists....The f-word was once a battle-cry for a whole generation in collegiate revolt. In the post-militant era of prospering consumer capitalism they now re-label their badge of immaturity as "a marketing tool."

The Advertising Standards Authority which had criticized the *French Connection* in 1998 was reluctant to make up its mind and possibly establish a copyright precedent for piggy-back porn, that is to say, whether the initials *FC* and *CF* could be reversed with impunity, allowing an ad campaign to ride free on the back of another. One conservative advertising expert played it safe by venturing the thought that "it was unlikely that 'cfuk' would cause offense in the same way as 'fcuk.'" This would all depend, obviously, on the way each was being pronounced. Some phonetic experts dared to call attention to the unprintable fact that whatever the differences in orthography and possible lexic shadings the two words were intimately related in a common f-word family of rude sounds and spellings. Once again lips were pursed to try out the aural variations, especially the plosive resonance when the "*c*" is hard or soft, sibilated or altogether silent. (My preference was for a strong and broad *u:* together with a slightly aspirated *k*.)

In any case, rarely has what we have called the law of participatory obscenity created a field of noise which sounded so suspiciously coarse.

In the light of all this, what importance can we assign to the little linguistic fun-and-games that our young conservatives have been having with that titillating anagram of the f-word? We left them, a few pages back, with a rising wave of protest as if they were effete Proustian aristocrats dreaming of virility or Molly Bloom streaming her consciousness of the futilities in life.

The latest news about the incident closed the whole affair with a twist as if it had been a scene in the theater of the absurd.

HAGUE DROPS CFUK LOGO

London.—William Hague has agreed to scrap the attempt by young Conservatives to brighten their image with the logo Cfuk....The Conservative Party agreed not to distribute any more merchandise bearing what had been hoped would be a true-blue slogan for youth....The young Tories had planned a big recruitment campaign at universities with the Cfuk slogan.

This appeared to be yet another instance of youth being deprived of the richness of its true-blue inheritance. Not even a scramble of letters...only four in number...signifying nothing but a knowing naughtiness with which they might just scandalize and enjoy a winning moment of popularity. But it was not to be.

The sinister forces–in part Scrooge, in part Uriah Heep–stood foursquare in the way. Profanity had nothing, or little, to do with it. The lawyers of *The French Connection p/c* had made it clear that "the company was extremely concerned when they learned about the use of the logo by Conservative Future." It was a trademark clash; and they happened to make their mark first. The law–protective of copyright...in a spirit of economic liberty...all were on their side. Court proceedings were initiated for breach of all of these...and Hague's Party decided to settle out of court. *The French Connection*, after all, had been using their f-word logo since 1997. The company was given a number of undertakings with which it was "satisfied." The f-word, and its scrabble or scramble, belonged to them. (Saatchi, who had helped elect Mrs. Thatcher, has had it easier with his *"Sensations"* although he may well yet land up in court.)

Nobody had a right to play with obscenities when the "French" got there first. The English defeat represented the supreme irony of the loss of a rich subculture of obscenities: the profane promise of a thousand years, with tribal taboos and cultural wars and lyrical hope. But the word or its desirable variation now turned out to be just not available. It belonged to somebody else. No wonder Proudhon came to the conclusion that property was theft. No wonder young people always rediscover the idea, combining two great impulses, that an effing revolution was on the historical agenda of the day.[18]

11

Searching for an Immoral Equivalent

Word Count

There is, as we have seen, a severely competitive aspect to the arithmetics of the f-word, and not merely between the voluble cavaliers for whom the more the merrier (and they'll carry their righteous case up to the Supreme Court in the name of freedom of expression)…and the thin-lipped puritans who tot up the instances of sin, ruin, vice and corruption (and go on to lobby for censorship). We learn that the latest (and posthumous) television script of the prolific Dennis Potter uses the f-word forty-one times in an hour! But surely this straightforward kind of content analysis, especially if the arithmetic is done by computerized search, tends to a significant margin of error.

In point of fact, I came up with a slightly different sum, and I listened carefully to the BBC and the Channel 4 versions of Potter's *Karaoke*. It is all about an ailing, dying TV writer (namely, himself) who confesses instructively about his last scribblings: "It's not just marks on a page. It's not just words in other people's mouths. I make them do things. I even let them screw each other or lie to each other or kill each other. Yes! Kill! Kill!" One would, even as a loose constructionist, have to adjust the counters. For one of the star characters is given the task of constantly uttering Spoonerisms: and how, in the conventional table of bad language, does one register *"Kucking Faraoke"?* Even the TV critic of the *Sunday Telegraph* thought it worth puzzling over. Other observers counted it in; he gave it a miss.[1]

In the Pop and Hollywood world the exploitation of the speech defect of poor old Dr. Spooner * would appear to be a far too subtle device for maximizing what since "gangsta rap"–and even the ordinary rap of Elmore Leonard's gangsters (in, say, the 1996 film version of *Get Shorty!)*–has been calculated

---

* **"Spoonerism**....after Reverend W.A. Spooner, English scholar (died 1930) reputed to make such errors, 'You hissed my mystery lectures'. The accidental or deliberate transposition of initial letters of two or more words." *Concise Oxford Dictionary* (1988), p. 1026.

by the entertainment moguls as the sine qua non of saleable salacity. This liberty, or license, was generally interpreted to be the point at issue between the giant Sony Corporation and the meteoric George Michael in which bitter altercation the latter won his "artistic freedom" from the former in a settlement costing millions. And none too cheap for striking a blow for the rights of the individual! Expletives must (and do, with the help of Dolby's system) come over loud and clear, with no static or music up-and-under to interfere with the obligations of "dirty realism." The '68 movement of student protesters in Berkeley was very much in tune with history, at least on the Hollywood coast, when the demonstrators carried their f-word banners proclaiming F for "free speech."

Imagine, then, the surprise which was conspicuously tinged with disappointment when some half-dozen years later the new George Michael album, obviously entitled *Older*, was brought out by nobody less than the Virgin people and it was found to be lacking (as one critic put it) "the zest and bravado that made him a global pin-up." Above all: "There is nothing here that Sony could possibly have objected to." What, not an f-word, not even spoonerized? No, the "older" George Michael has now become relentlessly inoffensive. Well, with one very small exception, as one newspaper critic reported as a result of his investigative *akribie*: :Admittedly, he utters one obscenity, but it is buried so far in the mix you wouldn't noticed it at all if it were not for tell-tale asterisks in the lyric sheet."[2]

We have reached the point now where the telltale asterisk, once the fig-leaf of literary discretion, or the leafy camouflage of the avant garde, treacherously reveals all. What is even more culpable is the context which sensitive newspaper reviewers found to be a touch immoral (even worse: politically incorrect). And we are given the scandalizing details about "the multi-millionaire ranting against whining stars": "Michael sings 'Who gives a f*** about your problems, darling/when you can pay the rent?'" What has possibly gone wrong? A rare case of a pop star gone straight? Or had the years involved in the court case against the battery of Sony attorneys taken their toll on his sense of language? One newspaper's theory was poignant: "In his absence from the music scene throughout the Nineties, an entire decade of trends appears to have passed him by. Perhaps he was too busy consulting lawyers to pay attention to the trip-hop or acid jazz which might have lent his excursion into easy listening a more contemporary sheen." This evidently was the tragedy of "the Eighties biggest Britpop star." It is all the more heart wrenching when you consider that the 1990s were only half over when the whole decade was being pronounced upon, and the years that the poor young man had missed out on took him from twenty-seven to thirty-two years of age. The teenage guardians of the youth-culture sheen are almost heartless: "At 32 the golden boy may be starting to show a few wrinkles." If you have young eyes to see, you sure can spot them. Even more: "He yearns to be taken seriously, even going so far as to cut off his enormous mane of blow-dried hair and grow the kind of peculiar goatee young bohemians used to stroke in poetry clubs."

If you have sharp ears to hear, you can listen for the whine, loud and clear even in the mix. It discloses telltale f-words for which poets and songsters, as is well known, have so much trouble finding good rhymes to give their lyrics a proper contemporary sheen.

For some intellectual editors on serious daily newspapers, the enlightened ones, say, on the liberal-left *Guardian*, the current *"attitude"** is to feign a certain blasé unknowingness about the hard etymology and semantic significance of what they recognize as "the most popular four-letter word." In one leading article in the *Guardian* an editor writes, "Just why this word retains such a power to shock–unlike its synonym 'bonk'–is a bit of a mystery." The paper is well aware that the word can trace its literary origins deep down in the past centuries, and concedes that Shakespeare and Fletcher were classically content to use synonyms. Indeed for over 100 Victorian years it was even too shocking to be included in slang dictionaries (until "outed" by Lawrence, Joyce and, more recently, the poet Philip Larkin whose racy verses brought it within sight of England's syllabus for A-level graduates). Why, after all, should it shock a generation brought up on Hollywood thrillers, late-night TV exhibitionism, gangsta rap hit-songs, or, indeed, even playground primary-school talk? But they like to be convinced that newspapers, like television, "reflect new realities."

And these, inevitably, have a quantitative message. In the year 1991 the number of f-word usages (and they counted them all, whatever the bowdlerized form) was 125 a year, combining the files of both the *Guardian* and the *Independent*, now under one business–and shock-control–management. And five years later? In April 1996, standing at 328, "it is now more than twice as high." Does this statistic signify more freedom? Less shock? Growing reader indifference? The *Guardian* editor waxes philosophical.

Historians may find it curious that in the age of deregulation, the Government has not seen it fit to deregulate language. Maybe we have a deep psychological need for one or two words that dare not speak their name. If the floodgates opened then, perish the thought, a word that had taken so may centuries to become unspeakable would soon become a boring cliché. What would we do then?

For now, at the very least, it can be rationed and used sparingly; counting in the low hundreds it certainly lasted out the century and postponed the onset of boredom and exasperation.

---

*   I put this in quotes since it is the current buzz-word for opinion which has a strong and approved quasi-ideological flavor. Current pop-cult favorites all have *"attitude,"* and this ranges from outlandish social prejudices to currently improper argot.

They have, I surmise, a little list, registering all the taboos that never would be missed. Since a taboo is by definition coercive/repressive and hence reactionary, it is the better part of liberal, enlightened valor to set about breaking them, one by one, willy-nilly. In British television a fourth program-maker emerged, rivaling the private commercial ITV and the two public BBC channels; and Channel 4 was nothing if not iconoclastic.

In the ideological 1980s it was the first to break the taboo which had obtained in the British conflict with the IRA terrorists. The Government of the day disallowed interviews with IRA spokesmen, at least not to broadcast their own voices (actors summed up their replies to journalists' questions). Sir Jeremy Isaacs was then in control, and dramatically broke the official ban. Liberty and tolerance demanded that even spokesmen for terrorists should be allowed their own voice to sound off as they pleased (short of flagrant incitement to violence). One could now hear the bombsters in their own accent, authentic lilt, personal singsong.

Political targets gave way in the sexy 1990s to aiming at destroying the last restrictions on obscenities as well as on full-frontal soft pornography. Channel 4's managing director, Mr. Michael Grade, scion of a famed show business London family, had a successful flair for filmable bawdry. Bashfulness was abolished; horizons were extended.

As I write, Channel 4 is continuing its historic demolition job on what straight, conventional British society used to think were "standards" below which outrageous and offensive bad taste ruled. The channel's latest programs, evoking the usual protests, were (as one newspaper reported, September 1999): "considered to have broken one of the last taboos, tackling a subject never before explored on British television." Complaints were made on the charge that "bestiality" is illegal, and therefore Channel 4 should not have covered the subject–with which argument, formally speaking, the protesters were on very weak ground. Making a program about illegal practices–on murder? kidnapping? bank robbery?–surely did not constitute a breach of any existing code of conduct. Stronger arguments were put on the basis of the breaching of "Taste and Decency" guidelines.

In any case the latest installment of Channel 4's "*Hidden Love*" series was filmed in the USA, mainly in the backwaters of Missouri where, it is held, "sex with animals"–experts referred to the subjects' "sexual orientation" as "zoophilia"–was not found to be illegal. Entitled *Animal Passions*, one of the TV-films focused chiefly on (according to the dry report in the *Times*) "a man who had sex with his pony and a woman who had sex with her Labrador-cross dog." This was saying *boo!* to the taboo with a vengeance.[3] This constitutes, for some, to be "as far as you can go." Surely not. Any medieval bestiary or modern aviary will suggest further associated themes to take Channel 4 and their taboo-breakers far into the new millennium. Other hidden passions of animal love are presumably already on their little list. Watch their milky screen for yet another blow being struck for human freedom as one more taboo bites the dust.

The end in any case is not nigh. For American usages, freshly renewed with every incoming generation (which often gets it wrong), we can generously reckon with a margin of error of a decade or two, perhaps in some cases even half-a-century. In a mass culture where *My Fair Lady* is an evergreen, and hence the Shavian difficulties with the Victorian *"bloody"* are ever-present, real-existing English nuances from Chaucer to Philip Larkin cross the Atlantic with seasick delay. Recently one U.S. writer actually wrote about the power of the f-word–and its English counterpart which was, he explained: "in Britain, *'bloody'.*" If he can believe that he can believe anything; and he does. Convinced that the peculiar power of four-letter words in a certain vocabulary (as in *Pygmalion*, perhaps, but he quotes the Russian theorist Bakhtin) resides in its "incorporation of other people's words," our young American commentator concludes in a study of this kind of linguistic "outsiderhood": "In the end, saying 'fuck' and 'bloody' turns out to be more like contemplating the depth of the ocean, the height of the air, or the uncomprehending sunlight than anyone but Larkin would have guessed" (Stephen Burt, "High Windows and Four-Letter Words: a Note on Philip Larkin," *Boston Review*, October-November 1996, pp. 18-19). Whatever that means it does not spell the end of the f-word as we know it.

Larkin's literary contribution–as our critic writes–veers between "Radiant high windows and high diction on the one hand, fucking and four-letter words on the other." One is struck by a note of misanthropy tempered by a weary recourse to the low language of common folk, of all our "mums and dads" who, in the classic Larkin pun, generate and ruin you–

> They fuck you up, your mum and dad,
> They may not mean to, but they do.
> They fill you with the faults they had
> And add some extra, just for you.
>
> .   .   .   .
>
> Man hands on misery to man.
> It deepens like a coastal shelf.
> Get out as early as you can.
> And don't have any kids yourself.

Can these be the lines of doggerel that presaged a new literary canon? Does our newspaper culture, envious of the unfettered independence of élite spirits, long for the taking of such liberties, and duly trust in the coming of an f-word utopia? We may all be waiting for the one little word–four letters away from the revolution–that will finally straighten us out.[4]

And so, in the meantime, the *Guardian* will try to keep the body count under some control. It will explore all the ways of taking the stylebook sting out of using borderline phrases in full orthography, without over-working those putatively demure asterisks and hyphens. There could be a skilfully placed highbrow adjective (say, "*unmitigated*") or a respectable cautionary qualifier ("*reportedly*" will do, although it begs the question who in fact reported it). Here is a candid interview with a hard-driving BBC personality who explains why his deceptively friendly chat-show style is for his interviews to begin and open out rather slowly: "You know you are going to get unmitigated bullshit for the first four or five minutes, so you let them go [on]...and let them say it" (the *Guardian*, interview with John Humphrys, 18 July 1994, pp. 8-9). In one of its own stylish interviews–with a rough-and-tumble U.S. TV executive whose momentary fame is based on being "the mogul's mogul" (Barry Diller of *QVC*, the home-shopping cable-TV channel)–it takes no circumlocutions from the man or the sources around him: "He has the obligatory pit-bull manner and reportedly calls his employees 'fuckheads' when they fall short of his high expectations." The language was grainy with sea-salt as the *Guardian*'s reporter lived up to high expectations in delineating the kind of Yankee brusquerie that treats any rival and competitor as "less than scum." In fact "[he] basically wanted to rip out his eyes and piss in his skull."

It happened to be a slow blue Monday, and this may account for the fact that the loyal and careful reader found explicit sexual references few and far between. Indeed, the *Guardian* turned unprecedentedly prim, for it could still come up with this closet cliché: "There is constant speculation about his sexual orientation." This may be, for the moment, approved PC, but by their own post-Shakespearean standards wildly incorrect. This is the kind of un-mitigated pre-AIDS evasiveness up with which *Guardian* readers should not put. Towards what sex might the chap be oriented? We need to have specifics. Out with them, man.

And, on the same day, there was published an uplifting account of how a group of troubled Cambridge female college students put out a restriction (on the obvious grounds of "sexual harassment") in order to silence the building workers on a nearby construction site. The navvies had been indulging themselves in their traditional "wolf whistles." The militant feminist, a Ms. Caron Freebourn, told the *Guardian*'s Patricia McBride how they stopped all that. Since Lucy Cavendish Women's College is the employer, and the prohibition was now written specifically into its revised building contract, and the stratagem was "working very well" to keep the animals quiet. No wolf whistles from the scaffolders, not even any *"me luvs"* or *"me old beauty"* from the bricklayers. As Ms. Freebourn, enjoying her own unblushing sense of liberation, was quoted as saying, "The good thing about having this policy is that we don't feel we have to blush or say F— off."* The latest word from the Lucy Cavendish building site is that the wolves are cunning enough to be demanding their animal rights; and this has, especially for the *Guardian*, the makings of tragedy: a conflict of liberal entitlements in a clash between two cultures in Cambridge.

In cosmopolitan London the perilous situation between the whistling wolves and the harassed maidens has evidently long since been clarified. It appears that the strategic wisdom, belated in provincial Cambridge, is conventional knowledge in the capital. Indeed it is already incorporated in a much-praised TV serial (which "shows life in the capital the way it really is, not the usual chirpy Cockney version"). As the party-girl Claire confidently revealed to a newspaper reporter, "the two words you need to survive in London are 'F***' and 'off.'" The f-word in its command voice tone is now a standard item in the Londoner's survival kit. Legal phrases written into paper contracts will hardly deter predators. But, whether or not a rude, manly two-word remark will provide sufficient protection for the endangered female of the species in our asphalt jungles–and in unruly neighborhoods positively ringing with expletives!—is another and more questionable matter. Safe profanity, like safe sex, doesn't always work.[5]

By and large, there are precious few fundamental differences on the Anglo-American scene although, as we have noted, there are significant variations in the post-Puritanical style. What we have in common ranges from frankness in transatlantic dictionary-making to low-life dialogue in the cinema (if not always in made-for-TV films)–from scabrous street-hep speech to the titillating circumlocutions in the newspaper press. In the latter the London usages appear to be a shade more daring, and indeed, cynical while the American dailies usually try to maintain a decent respect for the proprieties of mankind. Thus, it may be no mere coincidence that where the f-word has had its rude breakthrough in the New York press it is more often than not in the company of some Olde Worlde English connection.

The *New York Observer*, a weekly broadsheet newspaper, has the distinction of regularly publishing its art criticism on its front-page–elegant and argumentative notices by the celebrated culture critic, Hilton Kramer. It is also printed on pale pink paper which had been the previously unique hallmark of London's *Financial Times*. In the matter of rude discourse it surely outdistances its English cousins, even the London *Observer* on a long raunchy weekend. It prefers to have no part in the camouflaging of anyone's expletives. In an interview with a rich visiting publisher, the *New York Observer* intro-

---

*   *The Guardian*, "Pursed Lips at a Site for Sore Guys," 18 July 1994, p. 12. It could be that I have been reading this story wrong, and the punning in the headline (and not the effing in the text) was the whole point of the journalistic exercise. Reporters have been known to go even further for a good gag...always a sight for sore eyes.

duces him thus: "Felix Dennis, British multi-millionaire, international playboy and self-described 'mad fucker,' whirled back into the living room of his
East 49th Street apartment...etc." Evidently he was about to launch his Lon-
don-based men's magazine, called *Maxim*, into the U.S.A. market, and it would
be featuring "cleavage on every cover and sex and money advice on the pages
inside." A newspaperwoman, improbably named Lorne Manly, regales us with
some gossip about Mr. Dennis' career, public and private. This included his
early notoriety with the pornography trial involving *Oz* in London (in the
whirling 1970s); also the still current rumors of his "bedroom prowess" (and
there exist, we are told, photographs of "the girls clenching their fucking
things together").[6] Apparently obscenities are easier to do when a Brit comes
to town; the words come off more trippingly from the tongue. The arrival of yet
another English celebrity offered yet another opportunity to salt the paper
properly. He was Mark Birley, the noted London owner in Mayfair of Annabel's
night-club (among many other bars and fashionable dives), and he was good
for an off-color anecdote or two, including this one recounted in full in the
New York Observer:

> Mr. Birley told a joke. An English gentleman is riding the Tube in London when a
> punk, with spiked hair dyed bluer than a peacock's feathers and music banging from
> the headphones of a cassette player, sits across from him. "What the hell are you
> staring at?" the punk asks the gentleman. "Ain't you never done nothing that's not
> conventional?"
> "Actually, yes," the gentleman responds. "I once fucked a parrot and I wonder if
> you might be my son."
> Mr. Birley and his guests rose from the luncheon table, laughing.[7]

I may, I readily confess, be tearing this passage from the *Observer*'s "Style
Diary" out of context for my f-word chronicle. The journalism of this kind of
anecdotal evidence tends to be vaguely allusive and indiscreetly ambivalent.
It could be more relevant either to the latest Manhattan Anglophilia–just
adoring Britain's contemporary gentlemen who are capable of putting down
surly Manhattan punks–or to the quirky twists of the current English sense of
humor. Editors—and their feel for the hidden tastes of the readers—should not
be underestimated.

Media critics have emerged in most Western cultural communities, and
they often function to explain and exculpate, to apologize and rationalize the
extent (as one put it) to which "vulgarity has encroached upon the media." If
it is true that "now the air is nightly blue with irreverence," let us begin
counting the words and dividing the sum in the full context of a newspaper's
(or a radio and TV station's) output to establish how far the process has gone.
The result will, inevitably, prove to be miniscule. Weather reports and stock
market tabulations remain squeakily clean, and the whole of the rest of "the
news" tips the balance to the formal honor of the free press.

This is, of course, deceptive or illusory. Neither "content-analysis" nor any other form of quantification, those hoary old methods of sociological analysis, can be relied upon to estimate the four-letterization of our general culture. One half-way serious London tabloid–itself one of the major players in the deleterious f-word games–thought it might be fun to divert attention from its own libertinism towards its competition, the serious mainstream broadsheets. It feigned alarm and, alternatively, encouragement that "the four-letter f-word has become so routine on screen that it is gradually being supplanted by an altogether more obscene rival: the c-word." How convenient, at least for writers looking for a nice fast quote, that the c-word should also have four letters, fitting the empty space to a dot and a dash. What, then, of the hard measurable facts?

The *Standard* carried out "thorough electronic research" to establish how widespread the use of swear words is, at least on the British (perhaps only London) scene. Recall that H.L. Mencken, in his studies for *The American Language*, often took his cues from what was happening to the English language abroad. However, the reader must be warned that "thorough" research can mean in such contexts anything from "superficial" to "non-existent." But the claim, as published, read:

> It [the research] shows that *The Daily Telegraph*, *Daily Mail*, *The Express* and *The Times* have kept almost completely clear of profanity in the last twelve months. The same is true of their Sunday counterparts and, I hasten to add, the *Evening Standard*–even though Jon Ronson's feature this week about Lennox Lewis' boxing fans (embittered by the "draw" decision in the Madison Square Garden's championship fight) was liberally sprinkled with F****** this and f****** that.[8]

The "almost completely clear" hides, as we have pointed out, a multitude of blue transgressions, and it disguises as well its hidden presupposition that its conservative contemporaries speak more daintily than the foul-mouthed liberals, held to be so loquacious in their permissiveness.

> In fact the only heavy duty exponents of profanity are the liberal broadsheets–the *Guardian, Observer*, and *Independent*. More than 400 articles have appeared in *The Guardian* with f*** or f***ing in the year up to 1 March [1999], while there have been 34 references to the *c*-word. In this field, *The Guardian* leads the world.

Characteristically embarrassed at the prospect of something English being a world-wide winner at anything, the London editors of the *Guardian* are reported to have promised that "things would be tightened up a bit." In fact the editor of the paper (Alan Rusbridger) sent an internal message to all writers "to remember the reader." He offered the suspicion that even the *Guardian*'s readers "might find [four-letter words] as offensive as we [the enlightened editors and staff] might find the words '*nigger*' and '*poof*.'" And the moral of the story? "All viewpoints deserve respect. And respect demands that we should not casually use words that are likely to offend."

But the *Guardian*-watchers in the self-styled respectable camp offered these damaging statistics: "Since that statement three months ago, the *c*-count has gone up by 72 per cent, while the *f*-count has stayed stable, with 147 *f*-rated stories appearing since 1 November [1998]." An additional bit of thorough research suggests that since "the dilemma with *** after the letter *f*" is that it simply looks "too genteel" for serious-minded liberators. They have been freeing themselves from the old, conventional hang-ups, and there has been a turn to a new stock-in-trade, namely to double-entendres—. This ingenuity for double-talk has led to the invention of a vocabulary of "dirty babytalk" (words like "bonk" and "shag") to protect the sensibility of their readers. The obscenities are now being "packaged"; a thin sheet of glistening cellophane provides a shield for what used to be rough, raw slabs of language. The *Standard*'s media critic, Mark Porter, apparently approves the turn which made the circumlocution come full circle...for he concludes with "I rest my effing case," whatever that case might have been.

I admit that I do not know as a matter of fact that there is a daily ration of sauce or naughtiness for newspaper editors in London; but even a cursory reading of those quality broadsheets, the *Times* and the *Telegraph*, reveals the rhythm of systematic usage; and they rarely "miss out." Many of the tricks of the trade by which the quota is fulfilled have emerged in the various items I have cited, the cheapest of which is the repetition of an item previously published. As we have seen, no excuse is flimsy enough not to serve as a cover. Indignant readers will get more of the same, for protests ought to be self-explanatory and so the outraged letter-writer has to recap the outrage. Quick readers will not get away with slipshod oversight, for the week-end edition will be quick to reprint the tell-tale paragraph that failed the first time around to catch your eye. Thus, the resident porno-scribe at the *Sunday Telegraph* can always round out his editorial-page feature, *"Spirits of the Age,"* with an f-word filler like this one requoted from the daily edition of only a few days earlier: "A juror took the law into his own hands yesterday and told a defendant: 'Why don't you plead guilty? You are ——ing guilty.' Shane Smyth's outburst at Luton Crown Court halted the trial of a man accused of supplying crack cocaine and earned him a ticking-off from Judge Alan Wilkie, QC.—*The Daily Telegraph*."[9] Who is there so prudish as to tick off a newspaper editor with an eye for a good quote (and in his own paper yet)?

On the Legal Front

When Jack Kerouac died in 1969 the writer's estate amounted to $91. Now it is worth something like $10 million (not yet adjusted for inflation), and his family (according to the latest reports) are "at daggers drawn."

Francis Ford Coppola was busy producing a film of Kerouac's famous bestseller, *On the Road*, and there are new editions of every scrap of his writing that can be found, including his *Selected Letters*. This last volume was assembled by Ann Charters who is siding with the family of Kerouac's third wife, Stella Sampras, against daughter Jan, who with the support of biographer, Gerald Nicosia, is mounting a courtroom challenge to the old will. Jack's deceased mother had been named as the sole beneficiary. But there was for a long time no benefits. As such legendary cases always go, when Kerouac died at forty-seven, a "sorry, drunken, and untimely death," his reputation was as much on the skids as he was....Now he is an icon of hippie culture. As a Sunday newspaper in London tries to explain to non-Americans ("Jack *who*?"), the revival of interest in his life and work is extraordinary, both "as a lodestone for postwar American literature and as a fanciful antidote to the homogenised conformity of American life." Kerouac never knew he was on the road to a fortune.

One sentence in a last Kerouac letter provides the central disputatious point in the whole affair. It is given twice in the *Sunday Telegraph* features. Once in the photo-reproduction of the typescript with three letters of one of Kerouac's favorite expletives squarely blacked out (presumably by the editors of the family newspaper, since the unexpurgated original will be a crucial courtroom document in the family war). The second time it is inoffensively reproduced in the text of the article with the usual light and airy dashes. The intention, whether it is admissible evidence or not, is clear. The man wanted to leave whatever he was worth to "someone directly connected with the last remaining drop of my direct blood line": "and not to leave a dingblasted f— ing goddamn thing to my wife's own hundred Greek relatives" (*Sunday Telegraph*, 30 April 1995).

It could be that the context of obscene racialist abuse will play a role in evaluating the legitimacy of the original sentiment. You can't nowadays go around cutting anybody off without a cent in that kind of language. Then there is the curious matter of that half-deleted or bowdlerized expletive. Looks like a forgery, says one lawyer paid to be skeptical about tampered exhibits. It could be that Kerouac liked to use asterisks, but surely not in one of his choice cuss-words.

I am confident that the court in Florida, under the patient glare of the Miami television cameras, will have time to straighten out that one. Prose and its punctuation may well have a genetic code, and either word-processing computers or slide-reading geneticists can be relied upon to make a final dingblasted determination.

As an afterthought, it is of interest to note that the coinage of "*beat/beat-nik*" and all its variations has usually been attributed to Kerouac's mentor, a writer-friend who on the occasion of his recent death (June 1996) at the age of eighty-one, was described in one obituary as "thief, liar, drug addict, rent boy, and jailbird."

Beat was used by Herbert Huncke merely to indicate his perpetual physical exhaustion from days and nights of street walking, sexual activity, and drug abuse. But the Columbia-University-educated Kerouac saw in it a good tag for a dropout literary movement, and was not indifferent to the punning suggestion that their "alternative" existence had "beatific" qualities. Huncke's friends insist that it was he (through his Times Square dealer contacts) who brought the novelist William Burroughs into the "beat" circle as he did the poet Allen Ginsberg. He conducted "field research" for Professor Alfred Kinsey, and some of his experiences–mostly cruising 42nd Street bars with the famed sexologist–provided material for the "Kinsey Report" on *Sexual Behavior in the Human Male* (1948). Huncke called his role "pimping for Kinsey," and he thought rather less of it than his youthful years during the Prohibition era as a legman for Al Capone's gang in Chicago.[10]

From [Deletions] to *Italics*

If the vulgate, which incorporates elements of sexual aggression (a not unknown factor in international relations), became an ever-present source of diplomatic language in its roughest and most insulting mode, it also domesticated itself into maxims of home politics. Especially in the Clinton White House of the 1990s, young advisors to the President (and even the relatively youthful President himself) spoke naturally in the language of common men, faction-fighting for favorable positions to whisper a special message in the ears of power. In time the vocabulary became cruder, meaner and altogether less discreet. One close advisor (George Stephanopoulos), in sharp conflict with a despised rival (Dick Morris), recorded, "Dick had me cornered there. 'Screw with me,' he was saying, 'and I'll screw with you.'" Even the president, in the privacy of confidential policymaking, took advantage of resourceful profanity to put one point or another robustly on the agenda of U.S. foreign policy. Talking in the private sitting room between the White House kitchen and the presidential bedroom, Bill Clinton tried to formulate an appropriate response to the military casualties at Mogadishu in 1994 which led to a humiliating withdrawal of U.S. troops from Somalia:"'We're not inflicting pain on these fuckers,' Clinton said, softly at first. 'When people kill us, they should be killed in greater numbers.' Then, with his face reddening, his voice rising, and his fist pounding his thigh....'I believe in killing people who try to hurt you, and I can't believe we're being pushed around by these two-bit pricks.'"[11]

President Nixon's tape-recorded expletives were mostly confined to his personal bigotry, phrased in the conventional obscenities of racial and religious prejudice. Now the four-letterization of our political discourse–or, at least, the conversation in the corridors of power (and in some adjacent rooms)– had advanced into ideology. It had penetrated the vocabulary of high decisions of state...just before, that is, their final formulation in laundered words after the speechwriters and spin doctors had cleaned up the act.

Here is more low-down from one close Clinton associate in the White House. The foreign-policy issues from Somalia to Bosnia had estranged Dick Morris and George Stephanopoulos, and the domestic issues–from the unbalanced budget to a possible Cabinet re-shuffle (notably the planned firing of Attorney General Janet Reno)–put their relations in the White House at dagger's point. George describes his impressions of Dick at a first meeting in Washington, D.C., and they are printed in his White House memoirs in *italics*, representing his innermost thoughts, previously unspoken and hitherto unknown.

> *Where is the cocksucker?...*
> When he returned from the phone, I got my first look at Dick. He was a small sausage of a man encased in a green suit with wide lapels, a wide floral tie, and a wide-collared shirt. His blow-dried pompadour and shiny leather brief-case gave him the look of a B-movie mob lawyer, circa 1975–the kind of guy who gets brained with a baseball bat for double-crossing his boss....
> *Spare me the unctuous bullshit, you insincere prick. You've been trying to get me fired for months..How can Clinton even listen to this guy? He wants us to abandon our promises and piss on our friends.*[12]

Of "a solid Greek immigrant family" (and son of an Orthodox missionary priest), Stephanopoulos subtitled his White House memoir "*A Political Education.*" But his book doesn't attest conspicuously to the merits of his previous education, particularly the course on "Culture & Civilization" in the *studium generale* which Columbia College affected to be teaching young undergraduates in those years. One shudders to think what the "prose input" amounted to in his drafts of Presidential speeches during four White House years. Still, there is some evidence that he read "Great Books" in Columbia's "distinctive core curriculum." Evidently what he took from whatever was assigned in the semester course devoted to James Joyce (and Virginia Woolf and even, perhaps, Dorothy Richardson) was the avant-garde notion of "stream of consciousness." His italicized passages–and I have already quoted several–represent his collegiate notion of an "*interior dialogue,*" a literary breakthrough in its day; and it is still serviceable for journalistic purposes, questing for that extra little bit of highbrow something which smacks of candor and authenticity.

Stephanopoulos, thus, was making a significant contribution to American political culture. He deleted no expletives. Not even as courtesy or respect to the most august national figures does he edit a rude word once spoken, or censor an angry oath or a foul derogatory expostulation. As for his own deepest feelings and repressed remarks, now it all can be told...and he lets it all hang out. Historians of the language of politics in America may well be crediting him, if journalism keeps pace with the "dirty realism" in the corridors of power, with a significant step forward in the four-letterization process and its brusque outing. Can this be the way they think (and mutter under their breath) in the highest places in the land? We know about Lyndon; now we know about Bill.

There was, to be sure, something of a prim and even proper backlash in the Anglo-American book reviews which may delay Stephanopoulos' recognition as a minor pioneer. In the *New York Post* (23 March 1999, p. 25), Brent Bozell emphasized the factor of money (millions of dollars in advance royalties) which facilitated the "airing of all the dirty laundry, and some people just think that's sorta gross."

English critics have affected that they already knew it all. And even in London's *Sunday Times*, which published excerpts for many weeks running, a reviewer complained that this was emphatically not a book for those seeking fresh titillation. But there were, he conceded, triumphal aspects to this presidential reportage, especially "the literary device of italicizing his inner voice" which is taken to be "witty and hip." London literati always show themselves grateful when they discover an American politico who claims to have read a couple of books.[13]

But nothing more than that. The four-letterization of American political culture "from Nixon to Clinton" which I have been describing doesn't seem to engage English critics. So what if young George Stephanopoulos read the opening pages of Virginia Woolf's *Mrs. Dalloway* (1925) and Molly Bloom's reflections in the closing pages of Joyce's *Ulysses* (1922)? Oxonian critics wearily noted, "Stream of consciousness... interior monologue...taboo language." They've been there already, and done that. But really now: do we know what dirty names Winston Churchill called Joseph V. Stalin in Casablanca and Yalta? (We don't even have the "inner voice" of his son Randolph, and he was a straight-talking newspaperman!) There's some way to go yet before we, on both sides of the Atlantic, read it–with or without italics–like-it-was....The Potsdam papers of 1945 do, as I have previously noted, document the personal antipathy between Stalin and Truman. When the President of the United States referred to the *Vozhd* of all the Russians as a "son-of-a-bitch" and conceded that Stalin thought as much of him, acute students of "the culture of profanity" could have dated the outbreak of the Cold War then and there. It might take another half-century, and even more, for expletives to insinuate themselves into more public formal declarations of hostilities. But the four-letter words were already pushing ahead, getting there.[14]

Home politics, as in foreign affairs, has become a free-for-all. Nobody is exempt, not even the wife of the President, the so-called First Lady who is, in certain tense moments, defined by the c-word, full of the b-s-word, put beyond the pale by the f-word. At one stormy White House altercation, where Hillary Rodham Clinton broke down in tears at the untoward way things were going, she threatened the president's staff, "If you don't believe in us, you should *leave.*" Listen to one victim who did leave the room, and subsequently would leave the team for good, recording his thoughts: "How could she say that? Nobody's fought harder for them....I went out there every day...and would get killed, just humiliated. People would laugh at what I would say....Fuck her: I'm arguing for what's best–for her, for him, for all of us and everything we're fighting for: Fuck her"(Stephanopoulos, *All Too Human*, p. 232). Perhaps some imperial courtiers throughout modern history have had similar sentiments in such private executive altercations. We don't know exactly what was said or "intimately thought" when Bismarck went out through the door and down the ladder in the Kaiser's "dropping the pilot" drama in nineteenth-century Berlin–nor what hissing expletives were hurled at Madame Pompadour or Marie Antoinette at certain steamy moments in the heated history of the Bourbon monarchy. Since profanities still differ from language to language, expletives in translation may lose in obscene content from crisis to crisis, country to country, where the books get written and re-written. As a consequence, First Ladies in foreign lands may be spared some American measure of coarse hostility. Hillary Rodham Clinton has taken her full share, and as time goes on it seems that no expletive will ever be deleted from the record. We will be getting to have them all. Hanging out.

The general question of whether the language of historical personalities in dramatic and decisive situations is–or is not–precisely rendered and transcribed by creditable witnesses is a thorny one. More than that, when the quotations that are ascribed to presidents and their close advisors involve the controversial taboos on profanity and obscenity, the so-called anecdotal evidence becomes sheer hearsay, often tempered (and tampered with) by lapses of clear, unabashed memory and by added rhetorical flourishes. One American writer about the Clinton scandals has rushed into print with the results of his researches which obviously consisted in locating "new witnesses" who could say something fresh and possibly true about what had happened, interviewing several dozen more men and women (and indeed children...when the tale touched upon young Chelsea Clinton and her schoolmates, all trying to cope with the embarrassments).

In Christopher Anderson's first reports–in advance of the publication of his book by Little, Brown–there was little or none of the steamy language which made a bestseller of the Starr Report. Either the interviewees had cleaned up their anecdotes (in an exercise of unusual discretion) in talking to a journalist avid to get the juiciest version of what actually happened–or the journalist refrained from repeating the salty and salacious bits in a formidable act of self-censorship; for he had come to suspect that, like in all good, lusty, scandalizing stories, expletives are additives. In an early version one impressive witness reports that the high-ranking visitor was told rudely to "*get lost,*" or to *get-the-hell-out-of-here*–in a later account it becomes the blunter, more virulent dismissal "*to piss off*" or even to "f—— *off!*" What the actual discursive phrase actually was would not make very much difference in the long perspective of serious things–if we were not addressing the important issue of the language of politics and the possibly grave deterioration of its vocabulary. In this context the adjective or adverb, the way it was actually expostulated, is indeed of concern. A raunchy raconteur would insert his own kind of vehement verbs and verbiage; a soft-spoken (or perhaps more conscientious) diplomat on the scene might paraphrase smoothly to sanitizing effect. In offering his portrait of a troubled marriage between Bill and Hillary Clinton, Anderson at one point writes quietly, with deceptive reserve:

"Furious quarrels and outbursts of blue language were commonplace between them."

For a story that was advertised to be "sensational," this kind of historical writing resembles what Veblen playfully called "sabotage" or the conscientious withdrawal of efficiency. But this was only for starters; the laundered sentence appeared in the first installment of Anderson's book as pre-published in the British *Daily Mail*. By the third installment, some two days and three thousand words later, the author was obviously warming to the task. Out of the innumerable jottings made on the stories told to him by persons who claimed to be in-the-know–or were within earshot, or happened to be near enough to see something...or, as life would have it, were told of the blow-by-blow events soon after in shared confidences–a more robust version is fashioned. Then the historico-journalistic account becomes: "Many were shocked by the frequency and intensity with which both Clintons employed choice Anglo-Saxonisms. 'Everything was **** this or **** that,' said one ex-White House employee. 'They talked like that in front of congressmen, senators, even Chelsea.'" The style was evidently infectious, and as a consequence: "The First Couple's lack of self-control was quickly mimicked by staff members. After one prickly White House news briefing, Press Secretary Dee Dee Myers wheeled around and shouted at reporters: 'Eat **** and die!'"[15] The historiography of the future, as we fondly hope, will be able to sort the wheat from the chaff in this type of off-the-cuff investigation of the lurid personal crises that overtook the Presidency in William Jefferson Clinton's second term in the White House.

But what was believed to have been said and done in these years, in the varying and vivacious accounts published at the time, had an inevitable and independent influence of its own on a parallel historical and contemporaneous process. It had a conditioning effect on, as I suggest, the changing language of public discourse; on the popular awareness of the loosening limits of verbal improprieties; and, in the special case of the U.S.A. as the greatest arena of "Anglo-Saxonisms," on what we have been referring to as the four-letterization of the national culture.

The intermingling of high and low modes of political discourse has, obviously, intensified with private memories and personal secrets going public. In the end, as in the White House story in the Monica Lewinsky scandal, one cannot blame the newspaper reader for not recalling precisely whether the President took consistent refuge in the fineness of the language ("It depends on what the meaning of the word '*is*' is...") or actually, as in the Lewinsky-Tripp tapes, used "inappropriate" language for inappropriate behavior. In any event, from a strict historiographical point of view, one can rarely confirm the verbal accuracy of anecdotal evidence, especially when a spicy or important incident is repeated, retold, and willy-nilly rephrased by second and third parties–and, finally, by the reporter who tells it "like it was" or, in many notorious instances, like his literary agent or his magazine or book editors like it to be. A veteran English correspondent has recently disclosed (*Sunday Times*, 20 June 1999) the witting and, to be kind, unwitting literary restyling of reportorial evidence. Peter Millar writes, "And I have never yet come across a journalist who will not admit to having, on occasion, improved a quote." Did Bob Woodward (of *Washington Post* "Deep Throat" fame) improve some of the quotations in his lively portraits of five U.S. presidents in his book of 1999? One suspects that some of the obscenities, spelled out in full (but sparely asterisked in newspaper excerpts), are touched up–some, I suspect, are touched down. We know from other sources how often the erotic demotic cropped up in the conversation of those Washington pals, Bill Clinton and Vernon Jordan. Now from Woodward we presumably learn with what unembarrassed directness the President was confronted when Jordan, early on in the Lewinsky troubles, popped the crucial if vulgar question: "Jordan gave Clinton his best and most dramatic, level-with-me gaze, staring him in the eye. 'You aren't boffing this kid, are you?' Jordan asked."[16] "No way," said the president, "absolutely not." Addicted to lexical ambiguities, he took advantage of the many-layered meanings of the four-letter word vocabulary. Did Jordan's boffo question imply "to score" or "making out with" or "sleeping with" or "going to bed with" or even "screwing"? With these still-standard euphemisms there would have been ample room in the circumlocution and indeed its literal denotation of posture to deny "absolutely" that such words truly pointed to the "inappropriate behavior" which at that time he persistently refused to admit. "Boffing"– as well as *bonking* or *shagging* or *having it on*–was indeed spacious enough to be comfortable with. As one recent (1998) *Dictionary of Slang* records: "*boff*:....a strong blow...an act of sexual intercourse...a laugh, a joke...to hit, to assault...to copulate...to masturbate..."*

The president could have maintained his cool comfort even with the real thing, for he was no blushing flower in the presence of f-words, giving as good as he got in the verbal horse-play with his back-room boys. I have not seen any one of Woodward's passages excerpted in a U.S. mainstream paper, not even in the Paris (France) edition of the *International Herald-Tribune*. (My asterisked quotes came from London's *Sunday Times*, which is an eagle-eyed sharpshooter in such matters.) But they are worth collecting as further evidence of the four-letterization of the political vocabulary. Their use in the context of war and peace (and other grave issues) are wrapped in the same ambiguities and imprecision which prevents an honest straight word, or an accurate or incisive or even clear thought, from breaking through. On the same morning of the mili-

---

*   *The Cassell Dictionary of Slang* (ed. Jonathon Green, 1998), p. 122. See also J.E. Lighter's *Historical Dictionary*, vol. I, p. 218.

tary order to bomb targets in Afghanistan and Sudan (used as bases by Osama Bin Laden's terrorist organization), the President tallied up the sad reckoning of his dissembling habits and the cruel backlash of the Starr-chamber inquisitors: "'I f***ed it up,' the president said. 'I was mad. You won't believe the questions they asked me....A f***ing witch-hunt.'" Despondent and brooding...but was he in a state of denial? "'Goddamn it, I'm not in a state of denial. I got my ass kicked. There's no denial here.'" Still, modish "denial" or no, would he with all his legal training persist in denying something that he knew to be true and would, in one way or another (shamefully, it came with the DNA-analysis of a semen-stained dress), emerge in full embarrassment? His lawyer at this time was Bob Bennett who offered him this advice: "'I've been doing this s*** for 30 years....The key is, don't go in and perjure yourself.'" Between the low obscenities there was a clean, dizzying sense of high drama: "'If...' Bennett said, stopping for effect. 'You are dead. You are dead!' 'I hear you,' the president said." All this is in the past, and some say that the prim and proper rhetoric of the Senate's high-falutin' impeachment oratory has almost wiped the slate clean. The subsequent flurry of memoirs of the "salad days" of the Clinton administration–with Woodward's characteristic revelations of well-researched "inside stories" adding on to the first-person account of George Stephanopoulos–has now been re-establishing the reputation of William Jefferson Clinton as a master of profane political parlance in a league, and possibly even in the same ballpark, with presidents Johnson and Nixon.

> "Those f***ers, one of their goals," Clinton told one of his close White House aides, "is to get me to lose it, to blow it, to lose my cool, to lose my mind."
> It was a victory, the president said, he was not going to let "those f***ers" ever achieve.

Still, each day in a nightmarish impeachment year brought its setbacks, even if in the end there was acquittal–some say a Pyrrhic victory. One day in September 1998 was especially cruel with a mounting sense of family tragedy. He was aghast that his daughter Chelsea had read the Starr report with all its prurient detail–and he was now uncertain that his wife Hillary would remain loyal and forgiving. Woodward quotes the President memorably: "'Goddamn, f*** it,' Clinton told one friend that night. He said nobody could conceivably understand how he was suffering." Nor is it likely that anybody ever would...unless, in the near future when a favorable opportunity arrives in the new millennium for the forty-second president of the United States (with the literary assistance of an esteemed ghostwriter) to tell this tortured, painful part of his turbulent story. Would it conceivably rise to the occasion by resorting to the usage of an expanded, enriched, and elevated vocabulary? There are, it is well known, great resources in the English language for the expression of anger and hostility, of shame and suffering, beyond the simple expletives. Before the low course of four-letterized culture commands all the heights of our communication, these assets might be brought into play.

The impact of journalistic style, hobbling along with the help of asterisks, is very limited. But the prose doesn't need to rise to the level of poetry. Great and meaningful stories–and this is certainly the faith informing the writing of this book–can be prosaically told with a clean, lively concision and a dramatic dignity. Even by Presidents. Even in newspapers.[17]

Mistresses as well as wives of public figures are well-known objects of coarseness and contempt. On indiscreet occasions they themselves turn out to be even more candid sources for the semantics of statesmanship, given the contemporary impulse to transfer all private lives on to the public record. Monica Lewinsky's personal tapes, and hence Judge Starr's published transcripts, were replete with her (and those of her confidant at the time, Mrs. Linda Tripp) youthful expletives. But self-obsessed as she exhibited herself, most of the flippant chatter was revelatory of what "I-said-and-then-she-said" intimacies, and little–except for a few choice items–about the President's sentiments on political issues and Washington personalities. Other recent accounts of affairs of men in high places have been more fruitful.

Take Ireland. No *taoiseach* (Irish premier) in the history of the modern Irish republic has been so scandal-ridden as the career of Charles Haughey; and his acceptance of gifts, bribes and pay-offs were not the least of it. One recent newspaper report made an additional summing-up of his "brazen lifestyle": "gun-running charges, the acquisition of a sumptuous mansion, a yacht and a private island, not to mention a £1.3 million gift to fund his opulent lifestyle." He had served long years as Ireland's prime minister (many terms in the 1970s and 1980s), and presided over the new Irish prosperity as a new member of the European Community. He also figured in the early attempts at a "peace process" with the British, and they always seemed, for some reason or other, to break down execrably. IRA terrorism persisted, and the Anglo-Irish hatefulness raged on.

But it appears that one chapter of Haughey's secret life had escaped public scrutiny–"the story of his fiery concubine," and it was promptly told when Mrs. Terry Keane "revealed all" on a Dublin television show in order to forfend the sensation of a new and indiscreet book by several of her colleagues. Insiders, or so it was reported, had expressed surprise that an open secret had taken so long to come to light. Little of the tempestuous relationship which lasted some twenty-seven years (and it was still on) is of relevance to the pages of this book but one item may well be of interest to analysts of Irish-British relations who are keen to write "total history," that is, with nothing being left out.

Their standard explanation of "the Troubles" is conventional and well known–Oliver Cromwell's attempted "genocide" in the seventeenth century left the Irish survivors as implacable enemies to this day. "Ethnic cleansing" (including the manipulation of a sinister famine) amounted to a humanitarian catastrophe, and hundreds of years of exploitation and poverty inflicted deep political scars. Even "Irish jokes," staple slurs of generations of English stand-up comics whose favorite butts were the sons-of-Erin, kept open wounds festering.[18]

What words could suffice to be adequately expressive? Many of the violent political passions, mostly among the IRA bombsters, were of Bonapartist proportions. As Mrs. Terry Keane wrote of Ireland's former *taoiseach* or leader of the Gaelic/Celtic tribe, "Haughey was obsessed with Napoleon and expressed paranoid hatred for the English." She added: "'The English,' he'd say. 'F***ers.'" The recourse to obscenity–which, I suspect, is in this context the ultimate term of tribal antipathy, replete with curse and contempt–may not be new or infrequent but its outing is in keeping with the times. As Mrs. Keane (English by birth and accent) tells the tale of their first meeting in London's Mirabelle Restaurant, Haughey had lived up to his reputation as "Champagne Charley." He had ordered the best *Roederer* (presumably "*Cristal*") for his table, and when another diner touched his bottle to inspect the impressive label, Charlie exploded, "Who's that f***er and what's he doing with my champagne?" As she recalls, "I couldn't stop laughing: the facade of sophistication demolished at a stroke. But that's Charlie. I think I fell in love with him at that moment....It was a moment of deep bonding." It remains to be said, perhaps gratuitously, that as in this documentation the f-word is curiously close at hand in all affairs of heart...and of State. Haughey's reputation "as a politician of mercurial genius and rogue" is not unique in contemporary politics. But it was he who inspired *Private Eye* to identify "the favorite pastime of Dublin's chattering classes" for whom sex and political intrigue merged. The phrase was: "horizontal jogging."[19]

We are becoming accustomed to monosyllabic declarations of war–or, at least, ethnic enmity–which are increasingly supplanting complex and long-winded explanations of nationalistic aspirations or irredentist claims. The classic expletive is an all-expressive mindfull (if not exactly a mouthful), serving to take the place of mainstream ideologies. Four plosive letters–not unlike, or unrelated to, General McCauliffe's famous "*Nuts!*" as a reply to General von Rundstedt in the Bastogne Battle of the Bulge (1944)–is quite enough...and the street-corner concision of pop diplomacy has therewith triumphed over old-time palaver about *démarche* or a *casus belli*.

I have referred to, and illustrated, the growing role of profanity in the maxims of governance.

Still, the conditions of its semantic acceptance necessarily depend on the vagaries of political mood in the highest places. In many crises of governmental policy there is a macho indicator, that is, a telltale coarsening of language. Sometimes it is associated with (and these occasional cases are simple to read) a psychic-compulsive need to demonstrate a sign of strength, to exhibit a certain masculine virility. One or two audible obscenities may well do the trick. In wartime much depends on whether the enemy is listening, and gets the unmistakable message. (Who interpreted "nuts" in the German *Hauptquartier?*) In peacetime things may be more simple.

The only complexity in the use of expletives in the White House from Lyndon Johnson to Richard Nixon was whereas in LBJ's Texas drawl it all seemed ordinary and even natural–in Nixon's Quaker-dry speechifying it struck political friends and foes alike to be unexpected and rather surprising. With Bill Clinton there was, as so often in simple American country boys, an extra complication. The elation which comes with good news from the home and foreign front as well as the despair and indecisiveness coming from bad news are mediated by the public approval ratings which he incessantly consults as to whether the victory or the defeat is really to be taken seriously. One Washington observer–"a Democratic strategist who is influential at the White House" (*Washington Post*)–remarked that to the American electorate, foreign policy for the President is like snow removal for a big-city mayor: You get little credit when things work well but are punished when they don't....Thus, you can never tell.

On the night of May 7th (1999) President Clinton was on a political trip to Texas, and he was informed of the embarrassing news from the Kosovo bombing campaign: one raid in error had hit the Chinese Embassy in Belgrade. It was reported that the President was "angry," was "upset" and "baffled by how it happened." But, as one correspondent percipiently reported, "But Mr. Clinton's storm may have been as noteworthy for what it was not." The story was the non-story. As in Sherlock Holmes' case of the barking dog (which didn't bark), what did not happen was the unusual clue: a non-event. What it *was* constituted only a minor blip in the diplomacy and seventy-eight days and nights of bombing raids which were to lead to victory, peace, and a UN resolution. What it was *not* appeared to be yet another private occasion to "whine" and curse his fate. As John F. Harris reported in the *Washington Post*, "The errant bombing was the kind of event that in an earlier time might have triggered profanity and blame-casting, followed by self-pity and self-doubt, according to many past and current Clinton advisers and friends."[20] Many of these, in turn, are not selling profanity short nor any of the other temperamental constants. You can't win or lose them all–it isn't for nothing that the man has been called "the come-back kid"....The four-letter words will return. They are now conspicuous even by their absence.

A last item before the deadline.

It could be, as some newspaper editors have argued, that as younger men (and their nubile women) ascend into the higher corridors of power, more sexual allusions are bound to penetrate the accounts of politics and the activities of statesmen at play. In the 1940s nobody looked for nor did they find–at least at that time–the "playboy" stories which might humanize and/or scandalize the aged giants of the day–Winston Churchill, President Franklin D.

(and Mrs. Eleanor) Roosevelt, General Charles de Gaulle, Dr. Konrad Adenauer, and their likes. "Love affairs" appeared to be unlikely, and when evidence of furtive liaisons did surface the mainstream journalism of the day deemed it non-news, unnecessary to print. Nowadays, in the strong currents of four-letterization of the language and the raunchy expectations of dirty little secrets, all politics profanes and power politics profanes scabrously.

In the autumn of 1999 the official announcement was made in Westminster that the prime minister's wife would be giving birth to a child early in the next year. The tabloids promptly speculated as to the moment of conception, and whether it could have been (if gynecological calculations were correct) in the high summertime of Tony and Cherie Blair's holiday in Tuscany. More serious newspapers informed their readers of the more medical aspects of pregnancies in women over forty, as well as the logistics of bringing up a baby in the relatively small rooms of 10 Downing Street. Lobby correspondents in Parliament sounded out members of the House of Commons on the party-political implications of this rare and life-enhancing development. One response dovetailed with the journalistic phenomenon we have been following.

Ms. Mo Mowlam had been recently retired from her post in the Cabinet as the minister who dealt with the efforts at peacemaking in Northern Ireland, torn with violence from terrorists on many sides. She still had some Cabinet responsibilities but was known to be writing a book of memoirs that would "tell all," that is, the "inside story" of Ulster's violent sectarianism. A columnist for the *Sunday Times*, mindful of his paper's commitment to conservative family values and the like, expressed the pious hope: "Let's hope it's not as vulgar as Mowlam's off-stage comment about Cherie Blair's pregnancy: 'Imagine being f***** by Tony Blair,' she said."[21] A quasi-discreet element of porn is being systematically added to the political imagination in our days.

Beyond Raunchy Synonyms

No such uninhibited prospects of progress are likely to be reversed or soon exhausted; the word will out, come what may. One stratagem shrewdly avoids the danger of losing the f-word in the general field of noise, or sacrificing its immemorial virility by sheathing it in some vapid synonym. But a word by any other name is not, semantically speaking, an immoral equivalent. Other tacticians put it into the title, thus guaranteeing desirable repetition with every advertisement or announcement.

Thus, the reports about the new offerings in a forthcoming London theater season (1996-1997), mention a Royal Court and/or West End production of a play by a new young writer, Mark Ravenhill, who entitles his "splendidly filthy" play *Shopping and F—ing*. It is referred to by one newspaper critic, who has evidently enjoyed the script in advance, as "a feisty addition to the jobless-urban-young-gays genre." This all sounds decent enough; and, with some more praise from the reviewers, the title and all should fit nicely into the little squares of the daily newspaper theatrical ads. But how would a playgoer ask for his tickets at the box office? How does one pronounce, or enunciate, the feisty Ravenhill masterpiece? One thinks with concern about an epidemic of stammering along Shaftesbury Avenue, if not on Sloane Square–the nervous Englishman's stutter indeed which almost stopped brash Kenneth Tynan from outing the f-f-f-word on that historic BBC occasion. Evidently the producer of Ravenhill's play did consider changing the title; but all other versions were rejected, including *Shopping and...that F-Word*. As Max Stafford-Clark (who runs the theatrical company involved, called "Out of Joint") defends it, "The title isn't gratuitous and it accurately announces the play's main activities" (*Sunday Telegraph*, interview with Max Stafford-Clark, "the once hirsute, critic-eating leftie," 5 May 1996, Sunday Review, Arts, p.8). Whether his application for an official Arts Council grant to help fund his production might or might not cause "palpitations and mental asterisks," he remains true to his "young audience out there," who are "hungry for contemporary work which reflects their own experience"–true to that "good market for minority plays" which continues the Royal Court traditional commitment to "reflecting our contemporary society, especially the bad bits."

What is meant by the "bad bits" is located roughly in that urban frontier area of our inner cities where social injustice expresses itself pungently in correspondingly bad language. This zone, and its neighboring middle-class and even gentrified boroughs, is often exploited by writers and film-makers who are eager to establish for themselves a reputation for quality pornographers, what are called "noble nasties," where violence meets rape, exploitation includes sexual harassment and interrupted coitus, strip tease steps into full frontal nudity, and brutality merges with sado-masochism. Indeed in one of the recent Cannes film festivals, as one correspondent tells us (*Sunday Times*, 19 May 1996, p. 14): "No longer hidden away under plain wrappers, porn movies now overshadow mainstream cinema....A hundred porn exhibitors have been setting up stalls of explicit, hard-core erotica." Its producers hold daily press conferences and proudly present their buxom starlets (with muscle-bulging consorts); and they insist that they now "make quality films with strong story lines." One of the most successful of these is a porn adaptation of *Hamlet* which (according to the *Sunday Times*) is entitled, with a credit to the Bard's famous soliloquy, *"To F*** or Not to F***."* The Italian producers have no effing problem with its English enunciation–nor the *Times* report with its conventional spelling (although lexicographical purists would insist on a footnote to the effect that the asterisks were in the original). What was in the original text of Ravenhill?

London critics, unfailingly to a man sympathetic to new writing and the next wave of a possible avant-garde renaissance, thought the young playwright "a writer to watch"–if only, as one qualified it, "from behind eyes half-closed to the nightmares he stages." These nightmares included "the despair of junkie drifters...a terrible kind of Ecstasy-induced alienation...simulated male buggery" and assorted other attacks on "the susceptibilites" of the audience. For the rest, as Sheridan Morley noted in his review of *"Shopping and..."*: the full title is unprintable. [The play] is at times as sensationally shocking as its name which is giving typesetters and broadcasters headaches all over London." What was painful for the American-owned *Herald Tribune* was slightly less so for the enlightened band of headstrong English typesetters who did manage to cope a little more fully with the aid of a handful of asterisks. And any excuse to give the Royal Court production an additional bit of publicity suited the tabloid stylists who have, as is well known, their daily *pensum* to fill. Thus, I find in *The Sun* a follow-up item of theatrical news which is typical of the way *les extrèmes se touchent*–at a pop point, namely where the arrière-garde catches up with the avant-garde.

BARELY HONEST

When asked to appear naked on stage for a few seconds in a new play, actress Kate Ashfield said no.

She says, "I refused because it is not necessary to the plot. If it was important to the play then I would consider it."

Admirable, Kate, but there's one eensy weensy problem here. The play is called *Shopping And F*****g.*"[22]

Fully enrolled Chatterleyites would, in turn, have an "eensy weensy" problem with the ill-starred orthographic restraint–just as American veterans of Hugh Hefner's *Playboy* pull-out nudity would feel deprived at the modestly touched-up G-string strip of the *Sun*'s page-three beauty-models. You can't win them all.

Other small problems remain, from which the highbrow men of the theater may well learn. How explicit do you have to be in order to be explicit? How much erotica do "the bad bits" of porn-eroticism have to contain? These are elastic concepts. One American producer who has been in the business for thirty years warns that "the only way to stay on top is to be ever more explicit." The trick of defying the law of diminishing explicitness is a mise en scène in itself. As he explains, "There is no foreplay or eroticism in adult movies now. It is all bestiality, anal sex, S&M and hard-core. A lot of it is very sick." In the porn-*Hamlet* it is the lack of foreplay that catches the conscience of the King; and, worse than that (the *Times* calls it "ominous"), the absence of the use of condoms frightens the actress who plays the hapless Ophelia who is regularly tested for AIDS. She explains: "Directors won't shoot you if you use condoms because it ruins the fantasy." The f-word here helps to bridge the gap between the new fantasy, which is more explicit in every montage, and the old dirty realism.[23]

On the American side of the commitment to "reflect reality," the sheen is also brighter in the language of feature films and decidedly less so in the world of newspaper prose. The closest the *New York Times*' columns come to reflecting "bad bits" is in the etymological pursuits of its enterprising "Language" columnist, William Safire. And even there, and even he, is hard-pressed to be at once precise and entertaining, to come on as coy, discreet, and grammatically correct, all at the same time. Thus, in a discussion of the increasing States-side use of *naff*, usually denoting *"tatty, tacky,"* the *New York Times*' resident semanticist ventures to tell us rather more: *Naffing* was an RAF euphemism for an adjective-verb-gerund originally denoting copulation."* And it was even re-popularized recently when Princess Anne angrily told harrassing journalists at the Badminton Horse Trials to *"naff off."*

Again, in a bout of research into the usages of *"same old same old,"* as explored in various dictionaries (*Merriam-Webster, Random House*), the repetition is traced to origins in an unrepeated state: the derogatory U.S. Army expression, S.O.S., which is cited in an off-hand, self-critical way: "[it] referred not only to the initialized derogation of creamed chipped beef on toast, but also to *same old stuff* (a bowdlerized form)."

As for the persistence of *Bowdlerization*, old-fashioned and almost obsolete as the nineteenth-century practice has become, it has gradually lost its ethical, puritanical spirit. It is largely, as we have seen, a stylistic strategy or a verbal maneuver which leaves the suggestion of salacity virtually intact. Shakespeare's deviltry, some say, has something to do with it; and it may be the Bard's revenge (for Thomas Bowdler's fame was as the expurgator of Shakespeare's works). A recent newspaper item reports on the changing requirements in U.S. university courses where, in the *"Literature"* syllabus, authors like Chaucer, Milton, and the Bard have been increasingly dropped from the curriculum. The "dumbing down of America" is signalized, it adds, by the emergence of up-to-date Literature Courses in *"Hard-Boiled Detective Fiction"* and *"Representing Sexualities in Words and Image."* Thus, the bawdy language of an Elmore Leonard, mostly a soft-boiled product of his own verbal ingenuity, is available for recycling into the *In*-lingo of other would-be street-smart generations. Indeed, all of the world's art, literature, and poetry can be ransacked for "words and images," in old and new combinations, to give added gloss to the sheen we need and expect of our sexuality representations.[24]

THE strenuous efforts, at least on the part of pioneering British journalists, to find a usable all-purpose printable *ersatz* for the f-word is inevitably limited by the parameters of such linguistic inventiveness.

On the one hand: If the coinage is new it will have a hard time before it is instantly and universally recognizable. Who now remembers *Private Eye*'s gossip about celebrities who were reputed to be "indulging in Ugandan practices"? (In the Ugandan spirit of the late Idi Amin these activities *could* range from sexual orgies to grand larceny.)

---

* *New York Times/IHT*, 13 May 1996.

On the other hand: The would-be alternative expletive, adapted from the already existing stock of four-letter words, is handicapped by previous unerotic usages and other non-sexual meanings which only serve to dilute its saltiness. To *bonk* is thus weakened by all those eccentrics (like those idiosyncratic Lords, that is, Frank Pakenham and Quinton Hogg) who have been called "bonkers." To *shag* has a copulatory suggestiveness which was blurred even for H. L. Mencken by the advertisements for a popular smoking tobacco ("Want a good shag?"). As for *shag*'s twin trope *to slag*, it is similarly spoiled by an older bit of slang used by sharp-penned Fleet Street critics who are good at "slagging off" hapless victims or indeed "slags" (in the sense of "generally unacceptable persons"): "The drama critic of *The Observer* [wrote] a furious attack on the incompetence of West End theatre publicists....Sue Hyman must have been gratified to escape, while all her rivals were so comprehensively slagged off."[25]

A lonely newspaper critic here and there may raise a dissenting voice, especially against films in the genre of *Things to Do in Denver When You're Dead* (1996), which is to say against the excesses of Hollywood's aggressive resourcefulness in peddling the demotic: "We're introduced to an arcane low-life vocabulary: *mammy-rammer, fico-freak, dokey-fist* and, especially, *buckweeds* [sic]. I don't know what they all mean, but I have a feeling that if I did I wouldn't be allowed to write them in a family newspaper. The argot of *Denver* sounds like Damon Runyon gargling in the sewer."[26] Some unreconstructed spirits refuse to believe–in Philip Larkin's quip, marking the D. H. Lawrence revolution–that sexual intercourse "began in 1963" (or whenever else it was). They manage, at least in the press, to keep their distance from the raging erotomania and its dialogue. Even the sacred text itself, *Lady Chatterley's Lover*, the fountainhead of our literary profanity, is given the supercilious treatment, as in this press notice of an adaptation of the novel for the London stage: "the plot is paper thin, the language priapically bloated, and the characters little more than ciphers for the author's kooky quasi-religious beliefs about sex and class...with some of the silliest dialogue known to English literature: 'We fucked a flame into being and for me it is the only thing on Earth' (and the audience sniggered)."[27] How to escape from silliness or from the snigger?

The search for immoral equivalence is on, with useful synonyms for the f-word calculated to earn large popular rewards. Satirists in *Private Eye*, employing lusty circumlocutions like "Ugandan activities," pioneered some ways to suggest sin without incurring punishable libel; but they seemed to be less penetrating than evasive, disclosing less than they conceal. Best-selling novelists have put into circulation a variety of verbs and adverbs, to avoid carrying the f-word burden into being unoriginal, or boring, or alienating, or all three at once. "*Shagging*" has come and gone. At this writing Ms. Jilly Cooper is the leading spokeswoman for "*bonking*" as is repetitiously clear from her latest romantic novel about jockeys and musicians, *Apassionata* (1996):

True to Cooper form [writes a critic in the *Sunday Times*], whenever sex scene is scented, the prose starts to whinny and snicker. But what ensues–all hooting bounciness– is about as erotic as a session on a trampoline. Cooper's favorite four-letter word begins with *b*, and–"bonk...bonk...bonk"–it reverberates through her chapters like tired old bedsprings.

The word gets over-stimulated into sessions of "*mega bonking*," and other couplings become facetious romps (such as the "*bonking bonanzas*" that the members of the orchestra are regularly pushed into). Another novelist, the M.P. Edwina Currie, formerly a minister in Mrs. Thatcher's cabinet, has also stirred interest with inventive sex scenes; and her fellow M.P. (and another ex-minister) Philip Oppenheim, has followed on with a best-selling novel featuring gossipy affairs, secret adulteries, intra-parliamentary beddings (including "sex with handcuffs" and other lascivious doings). On the day of its publication the *Sunday Times* gave it the headline:

MPs TWITCH AS MINISTER PENS 'BONKBUSTER'

Thus, the raunchy synonym becomes adulterated (if that's the suitable word). It appears to be too weak, too pale and wan for proper shock effect, even in *ersatz*. No, this will not do; its critical reception has been a case of bonk debunked, and we will need in order to compete with our tired old f-word an expletive of some sturdier Anglo-Saxon provenance. The quest for an immoral equivalent is still on.[28]

Safe Sex, or a Shield for Protected Profanity

Yet for the time being the strategies of evasiveness, with all the "tricks of the trade" from suggestive orthography and circumlocution to explicit suggestiveness, dominate the editorial way of life. Every day there are enough "sex stories" to be getting on with in the newsrooms of alert papers, and journalistic devices for extracting enough passing pleasure to satisfy the desires of the day. To be sure, the story can be salty without the explicit insertion of profanity at all.

A New York newspaper persistently pursued the scandal in Hollywood involving the British actor Hugh Grant (and in the wings, his even more famous mistress, the model, Elizabeth Hurley). Their reward was a tangy interview with a lady of the streets, "hooker-turned-celebrity" Divine Brown, whose notorious rendezvous with Hugh Grant on the front seat in a parked car had been making headlines. A *Post* reporter's questions prompted the professional prostitute to ponder the meaning of sexual relationships: It was all for the edification of readers who were still interested in the personal-erotic difficulties of Mr. Grant and Miss Hurley. Their celebrated attachment had been troubled by the half-hour affair with Divine Brown, embarrassingly interrupted by the Los Angeles police ("oral sex" in a public place is a bookable offense). The

New York Post reported: "You wanna hold your man, you have to know how to entertain him," she said. "That's the reason that Hugh Grant did what he did. 'Cause he wasn't getting it at home...It wasn't no satisfaction there. And for him to be such a sexy man?"

But she cautioned, if she had been Hurley and Grant was her boyfriend, he wouldn't have had such an easy reconciliation: "Forget it, baby. If I caught his ass doing me like he did her, he's history. O.K.?" she said. "Gotta go pal. You did it once, you'll do it again, that's it."[29] Apart from Divine's contribution to the strengthening of fidelity in heterosexual relationships–why take Divine when you have divinity at home?—the vigor of the recorded speech may be a blow on behalf of "Black English." (What other dialect can juggle so deftly "it" and "doing it" and still remain quotable in a family newspaper?) It serves surely as a bridge for interracial activities.

For an English actor who catapulted to fame in one film (*Four Weddings and a Funeral*, 1994) with its opening machine-gun repetition of the f-word in its first scenes, it all came to a relatively happy end. Another English actor's melodrama in London, where happiness is not so relentlessly pursued, cast more shadows in the press. The star of a new Simon Gray play, Stephen Fry, walked out mysteriously and caused consternation in the theater, where (according to a London press report) it was announced: "We're all f****d. Stephen's done a runner." The paper's headline, "*And still no sign of a happy ending*" (*London Standard*, 4 August 1995, pp. 12-13), belied the actual news that Fry had not committed suicide, as had been feared. He had after a few tense days "run back"–and the show, as it must, went on, but only just. The transatlantic difference here, if it is relevant, is that Hugh Grant was reported to be fond of quoting W. H. Auden, Stephen Fry was famous for playing P. G. Wodehouse characters. High art has its rewards.

At bottom (which is, in English usage, also a tricky trope) the London press does, in contrast to the metropolitan papers in the U.S.A., show elements of a weary indifference to the raciness of language, even if there are still the traces of illicit hedonism in the breaking of old puritanical taboos and of more recent schoolboy prohibitions. In a recent Reith lecture on the BBC, an academic linguist tried to explain (according to *The Times*): "*F*-words swarm like bees in some recent literature....Yet today's swear-words are undergoing a bleaching process, a fading of meaning that happens in all semantic change." Just as oaths using the name of God were widely disapproved of in the last century, but have now lost their power to shock, "these days *F*-words and s-words no longer horrify so many people." Their meaning has clearly weakened as their original connection with sex and excrement fades.[30]

Why this should be so becomes clear from many of the classical texts of anthropology, especially Mircea Eliade on *The Sacred and the Profane* (1957) and Mary Douglas, *Purity and Danger* (1966). The profanation of the sacred in our modernizing world proceeds apace; and what was once held to be dangerously impure is no longer so. One anthropologist (Meyer Fortes) records in his tribal studies the one annual chink in the armor of the all-powerful paramount African chief–a single seasonal opportunity for the witchdoctor or medicine-man to hurl imprecations at the autocrat on the golden stool. This singular outburst of protest and dissent is formally ritualised, i.e., is accepted, or forgiven, or ignored, as the case may be. What happens after a thousand years when this kind of ritual has broken down utterly, and dangerous and profane words have long since undermined what were once stable acceptances? We are faced with dissidence, opposition, mayhem, and possibly worse.

Perhaps for this reason it is still necessary to offer the improper signals when an illicit transgression is threatened or indeed a foul deed is to be done. Here is a recent newspaper account of a local political quarrel that was angrily slipping beyond bounds: "Mr. Hepburn took exception to a page of jokes that the Councillor Iain Malcolm had written on a sheet of paper. He held him in a headlock, hit him across the head and shouted: 'I am going to f****** kill you'"[31] There is, one senses, an unnatural emphasis to the expletive, here half-deleted but still darkly resonant and revealing. Bad deeds need bad words; victims at least get strong advance warnings.

I have made passing reference to the erratic "misspellings" of an already Bowdlerized vocabulary, thus preventing stable house-styles for permissible obscenities to be established.

Obviously there is a discrepancy of intention as well as effect between the sonority (however accented) of the expletive, spoken in full phonetic clarity, and the various newspaper stratagems of quoting it without losing, in the camouflage, its explicit reference or recognizable identity. Nonetheless, when the quote is repeated or otherwise recycled with dashes or asterisks or whatever, it should be gotten right. Varying the set conventions does not, of course, affect the reader's participatory lip-reading but it does add to the violations of a certain prose rectitude to which serious journalism originally committed itself. The quote is correct or it is defective; and tampering with it may have unknown dangers.

For the expletive adjusted is like safe sex; it is a form of protected profanity, mediating sexual contact with the benefit of a thin shield. Should these precautionary practices be reformed or revised? Should the f-words be universally and totally outed? Special cases are being made on behalf of major literary works which have earned a new, reprinted edition and the f-words in question are to be transliterated into the modern style of full-frontal orthography. The idea of liberated publishers is to strip the various fig-leaves and indeed go on to restore, for one thing, Hemingway's self-censored "bad words" and expurgate, for another, Norman Mailer's quasi-onomatopoeia by which the expletives in his early novels sounded almost like the rude words were meant to sound (friggin,' etc.).

Still, there is a school of sexual correctness which finds the evasive euphemisms of yesteryear to be sacrosanct or, at the very least, historically preservable. And if editors leave well enough alone, the f-word will live on, in all its virginal variety, untouched, untouchable.

From Crosland to Aldrin, Chaplin and Muhammad Ali

I want, first, to give an additional example which suggests the extra-emphatic power of the f-word and how its usage–and its recorded report in the public prints–discloses an essential profane truth about the role of radical ideas in politics and society which would otherwise go unappreciated. And there follows, secondly, several other illustrations where the use of an obscenity is so revealingly essential to a true story that one can very much regret its bowdlerization on the altar of conventional prissiness.

During the early 1960s I was, as the new American editor of *Encounter* magazine in London, rather close to the leading figures of the British Labour Party, especially Hugh Gaitskell and C. A. R. Crosland who were inspiring an intellectual campaign to rewrite, or up-date or modernize–to "revise" was what the revisionist activity was then called–the Party's old socialist doctrine. *Encounter* published many articles criticizing the statist dogma of the old Left which was committed to a total nationalization of the economy (and the Party's leader, Hugh Gaitskell, struggled before his premature death to revise the fundamentalistic "Clause Four"). I was at the time a Social Democratic sympathizer from the journalistic circles of the *New Leader* in New York; and, as a matter of fact, I had participated in Berlin as the editor of *Der Monat* in a related campaign of "revisionism" together with Social Democrats like Ernst Reuter and Willy Brandt. In London I had frequent editorial meetings with Tony Crosland whose chapters in his influential book *The Future of Socialism* (1956; rev. ed. 1964) were pre-published in the pages of *Encounter*, stimulating wide controversy.

Crosland was an elegant writer and a cool theoretician, and we were in substantial agreement on every piece he submitted–except one. When he came to outlining his views on "education in the new Britain," the public-schoolboy and conscience-stricken Oxonian graduate lost his cool. For my own part, I had been impressed with the academic record of the famous Manchester Grammar School, and found the views of its then principal, Lord James, not only progressive but sound. (In fact he seemed to be elated when I remarked that his school reminded me of my own–the then excellent DeWitt Clinton High School in the Bronx.) But for Crosland, the grammar school system was damnably élitist and privileged; and like those awful private (i.e., "public" in British English) educational institutions which he and other, innumerable upper-class socialists had attended, they were to be destroyed root-and-branch and give way utterly to democratized equalized homogenized comprehensive institutions. No exceptions allowed.

Tony Crosland vowed there would be "no exceptions" in his radical purge of the British educational system. Yet in the complex realities of British governance there were always "exceptions" being made, with associated inconsistencies, embarrassment, and prevarication. Britain's current Labour prime minister, Tony Blair, who had himself attended Fettes, an exclusive English public (i.e., private) school as well as a college in Oxford, declined to educate his children in the "educationally correct" manner. He sent his sons to an "élitist" or "old school tie" institution called the London Oratory.

In yet another round of rhetorical polemic against "class-biased education" the Labour Chancellor, Gordon Brown, stirred up a press controversy in the summer of the year 2000 by renewing the Old Left offensive against Oxbridge "élitism." His colleague Baroness Jay, the Leader of the House of Lords, re-wrote her personal history by defending her years at Blackheath High School by saying "I went to Oxford from a pretty standard grammar school...." This inaccuracy was exposed with glee by the Tory press as "whitewash" and "hypocrisy"–Lady Jay's Blackheath school evidently was never part of the state system and had never been called a grammar. She had conveniently forgotten or hastily covered up.

But, then again, the British élite neurotic complex about a politically incorrect education is not confined these days to a left-of-center ideology ("We are all guilty" as Dr. Heinz Kiosk sued to say). Douglas Hurd, former foreign minister in the Conservative administration of the 1990s, dismayed admirers during a Tory leadership contest by appearing embarrassed at having been a scholar at Eton. But in the 1960s the novelist C. P. Snow, then a minister in Harold Wilson's cabinet, had outraged his Labour Party supporters by insisting on sending his sons to...Eton.

Small wonder that in this turmoil of inconsistencies, exploited by "Fleet Street" (as it once was known) to the last hypocritical detail, Englishmen (and -women) have turned to expletives to make their various meanings clear enough to cover the outrage and embarrassment on all sides.[32]

I demurred, and subsequently published the dissenting views of Crosland's own assistant, the economist John Vaizey (elevated later into the House of Lords by Prime Minister Thatcher). When Labour came to power in 1964, Crosland held fast in government to the "Comprehensive Revolution in Education"; his close ally, Mrs. Shirley Williams, was instrumental, when she succeeded Crosland as minister of education in Harold Wilson's Labour cabinet, in the wholesale abolition of all of England's estimable grammar schools. It is generally agreed that an unfortunate and disgraceful decline in a whole society's educational and cultural standards was to follow.

Why the uncharacteristic zealotry in otherwise mild and reasonable exponents of left-liberal gradualist reform? An analysis of the elements of class self-hatred in the circles of Britain's upper-class idealists–privileged products so often of Eton and Westminster and Winchester, and then "Oxbridge"–would take us too far afield into the wilder reaches of political neurosis and self-destructive intellectual obsessions. Not only Crosland and Baroness Williams (as she is today) would be involved; similarly disputatious were many other friends and *Encounter* contributors like Richard Crossman, Roy Jenkins, John Strachey, Roy Hattersley, et al., all worthy characters who were named by Anthony Sampson in the first 1962 edition of his *Anatomy of Britain* as members of "the *Encounter* group" in the Labour Party.) For now I am only interested in a word, the f-word: its relevance to the understanding of one important event and its controversial "outing" in the public prints. In the long perspective of decades, it appears to loom as a historic English counterpart to *le mot de Cambronne* and *das Götz-von-Berlichingen Wort*.

The primary source–although all of us who knew him could add a gaggle of footnotes to the phrasing of Tony Crosland's resonating remark–was the candid memoir of American-born Mrs. Crosland (who, under her own name, Susan Barnes, had made a bright mark in the journalism of the day). The *Times*, in quoting it recently–with large radiant asterisks that almost dared to speak their name–called it "the most notorious remark in our education history." Here was no titillation, no pubertarian foreplay, no Laurentian allures, no journalistic tease. This was a defining moment of political passion, with a ritualized cry that suggested danger and abandon. No one who had heard it, in one version or another on various occasions in the lively company of Tony Crosland, would ever want to tamper with its homely revelation. Mrs. Crosland records:

> "If it's the last thing I do, I'm going to destroy every f*****g grammar school in England," he said. "And Wales. And Northern Ireland."
> "Why not Scotland?" I asked out of pure curiosity.
> "Because their schools come under the Secretary of State for Scotland." He began to laugh at his inability to destroy their grammar schools."[33]

Here is the f-word fulfilling its traditional extra-sexual semantic function, a profane signal for an angry transgression, an illicit assault. Impassioned and overwhelming, it is an excessive cry of radical protest, as if the old anarchist's delusion of destruction being an act of creation were really true. The f-word in its destructive element has no immoral equivalent. Once said, and deeply felt, it is inescapable.[34]

Unfortunately, it is also true for the epigones who deal with it in a kind of black-market of expletives. Once a dealer, always a dealer; and they even develop an ethos of under-the-counter transactions which passes for honorable straight-talking. The Crosland incident which I have cited is widely known and is chronically repeated again and again with no better excuse than a bit of strong language on a slow day in the editorial office. But the style also has its loyalties, with (in Boyle's phrase in his seventeenth-century pamphlet on swear-words) "a propensity to repetition."

I return again, in the next example of an f-word loyalist, to Perry Worsthorne who, true to the spirit of the Godfather–the reader will recall my previous pages on the second of my portraits of "Godfathers of the *F*-Word"–remains reliable in his *omerta* to the very end. He proves himself to be a stalwart defender of the f-word, and returns bravely to the scene of his earlier embarrassments. Some twenty years ago he almost ruined his career by pioneering the public use of profanity, thus offending the conservative, old-fashioned owners of his Tory newspaper, Lord Hartwell and Lady Pamela Berry. In time they forgave him. But when many years later he was abruptly forced into retirement by a youthful representative of a newer journalistic generation (Dominic Lawson), oblivious to the notoriety of yesterday, Worsthorne took his anger and his outraged tale of protest to a rival Sunday newspaper. He told all. The curious result was that his old paper rehired him, if only for the daily edition and not "the Sunday" where he had his years of glory. Before long he was back to the shocking habits to which some streak in his dedicated character had remained loyal.

There must be, as I suspect, something of a Godfatherly honor to the f-word, and to the devotion of writers to its serious usage either to shock or to underline a remark of some intended gravity. Sir Peregrine Worsthorne had sworn off, and promised many times to reform. And yet when the latest occasion presented itself, he rose to it. His "Saturday Essay" on the op-ed page of the *Daily Telegraph* (22 March 1997) was on the subject of one of his favorite theses: *"Our Elite Lacks Class."* And in the course of his argument he returned, once again, to one of his favorite villains, C. A. R. Crosland, socialist intellectual and a decisive Minister of Education in a Labour Government. It was he who, at a fateful moment in the history of the contemporary élite, had said the infamous word. His widow, Mrs. Susan Crosland, has preserved it for us, and Sir Peregrine would not, yet again, hesitate to quote it directly: "In her memoir of Tony Crosland, the socialist sage and statesman, his widow quotes him as saying, in the privacy of four walls: 'If it's the last thing I do I'm going to destroy every f—ing grammar school in England. And Wales, and Northern Ireland.'" Crosland's passionate outburst has set the reporter's dilemma–to use, or not to use, the f-word in the morning paper? Worsthorne uses it but safely classifies the whole sense as "ignorant and mindless abuse." But Worsthorne's dilemma is real: for how else would he be persuasively documenting one of the great turning points in the decline of his country's cultural élite? Would anything less than an expletive do?[35]

Thus, our f-word can be seen to have two special rhetorical qualities; and if they are contradictory they do not appear to be incompatible. In its loose, meaningless form it tends to be something of a compulsive-repetitive disorder, as exemplified in what is known to obscenity-watchers as the Australian syndrome (currently popular with Hollywood scriptwriters). The f-word here runs amok. In its tight, meaningful form it fits snugly into an anecdotal rhythm;

and, again, once is never enough, for it seems over years to bear endless repetition, if only in single file, one at a time.

As I read these proofs (spring 2001), yet another British debate about the nature of class *versus* mass education has erupted. Now, within Prime Minister Blair's Labour administration, the old history of Tony Crosland's perfervid campaign in the 1960s against public schools and in favor of "comprehensives" has become topical. Crosland's American widow is re-interviewed to tell how it was in the old days when the abolitionist spirit raged. Decades have gone by, but she must still be good for at least one good quotable anecdote.

Accordingly, the *Daily Telegraph* announces on its front page: *SUSAN CROSLAND, Why my husband tried to abolish grammar schools (News Page 12)*. And there it is, on page 12, filling half a broadsheet (with picture), although the inevitable anecdote must have been too much for Susan Barnes Crosland, a stylish writer herself. It was consigned to be retold in the adjoining story by the paper's education editor (a Ms. Liz Lightfoot) who could be relied upon to get the number of asterisks right whilst giving the piece the proper Tory slant.

The loyal widow still maintains the old ideological pieties. But even Prime Minister Blair has had second thoughts about the alleged uselessness of "élite education" and the social consequences of what in his cabinet has been called derisively "the bog* standard of comprehensive schools."

Crosland's coarse gloss on the fateful Circular 10/65 which was the pride of Prime Minister Harold Wilson's administration was quick to hand: "If it's the last thing I do, I'm going to destroy every f****** grammar school in England and Wales and in Northern Ireland," Crosland famously remarked.[36] This may not exactly be news any more, but echoes of obscenity do give a certain depth to the perspectives of history. This particular bowdlerized f-word–has the new, current generation of newspaper readers ever seen Crosland's expletive in its orthographic fullness?–is kept in a special place in the journalistic archive. Digital morgues facilitate instant retrieval. I have heard hardboiled reporters in nearby ("Fleet Street") pubs compare such precious items to works of art by Damien Hirst or Chris Ofili wherein a single turd is memorably preserved in a full jar of clear formaldehyde. It floats freely forever, a tribute (so say friends of the avant-garde) to the principle of fertility–or of organic fertilizers–in our good earth. Dung is indubitably creative.

Repetitiveness does not preclude little variations. The quote itself gets touched up a bit; and each new context shifts associations and implications.

If in the 1960s a coarse element in political vocabulary still added to the strength of ideological commitment, in the 1990s and after it was more often judged by the different standards of prevailing political correctness. c- and p-words (especially with ethnic or gay twists) become electorally untenable,

---

*   "Bog" – "outhouse; lavatory; defiled with excrement...." Green, *Slang*, p. 123.

although the f-word is generally taken to be neutral...and hence acceptable (even among feminists with robust vocabularies).

On the matter of *"bog,"* local London experts on *"Oirish"* controversies were outraged–not because of Crosland's old educational extremism but because (even older) Oliver Cromwell, so hated for his military cruelty in Ireland, had famously used the phrase *"bog-trotters"* as a triumphant English anti-Gaelicism. Presumably the word stemmed from the Gaelic *"bogach"*–"meaning something soft and green emanating from the nasal cavity." Suddenly newspaper writers who thought of themselves as true sons-of-Limerick (or daughters-of-Derry) were demanding apologies for centuries of snide and snotty *"bog standards"*–indeed even derisive nose-picking gestures–all slurs that should be banished forthwith from the language and public discourse.

Thus, Tony Crosland's liberal-left sentiments were now catapulted into a changed context. When the Labour spokesman in the Blair administration (Alastair Campbell) dismissed classless, socialized comprehensive schools with their odoriferous "bog standards," he was carelessly re-introducing–to the outrage of an ethnic minority–"an imperialist, colonialist racist epithet."

"Bog" is likely to replace *"Bugger Bognor,"* that Edwardian favorite in quotable rude remarks; a three-letter word may yet prove to be a more efficient tagline, slightly more compact in its coarseness.[37]

Obviously most of what gets said confidentially to journalists, or within their hearing, is considered to be inviolable, off-the-record. More and more it can be used but "without ascription" and quoted "on conditions of anonymity"; and even on the highest level of party leadership, both Tory and New Labour, alternating the roles of government and opposition, there were more good pickings this time around than ever before. Among the militant men on the Left there have been especially raw feelings which have favored a field-day for expletives. Since the victory of the modernizing revisionist, Tony Blair, socialists have been speaking another ideological language with the dogmatic edges of yesteryear almost completely polished off. David Blunkett, the newly appointed minister of education in the Blair cabinet, is a special target for Old Labour resentment. He was once an *idéologue*, is now a moderate. Once he would have been called, tellingly, a *renegade*, a *traitor.* Even religious analogies and Christian metaphorics served to vent bruised feelings and a sense of betrayal (*for a handful of silver he left us...*). Today the embittered message is briefer, simpler, nastier, more brutish. A profile of Blunkett in the first week of New Labour's taking office manages to record: "[He] is not the first politician to learn that when you leave one side for the other you risk being trusted by neither. His name so rankles with one fellow minister that he reaches for the vocabulary of old Labour. 'David Blunkett? He's a c—...'"

Old Tories and even Old Labour, in similar circumstances, would have reached for the s— word; and perhaps that augurs revealingly for the shape of the parliamentary contest to come, the furious struggle between the loyalists of the c-word (macho Americans tend to favor the p-word) versus the partisans of the s-word, hurling imprecations across the House of Commons and, perhaps, still feeling enough compunctions to clean up the text for official publication in *Hansard*. Either way, as pundits of profanity predict, things may well be coming to a dirty end.[38]

The increasing use of political profanity in our public discourse is not, as it once was, a personal and idiosyncratic function of singularly personal style. One man swears, another man doesn't. Over time the cuss words get laundered out of the speech of one class (*viz.,* prim and proper phraseology in working-class aspirants to establishment gentility)–and they turn up in another (e.g., taboo-busting expletives among middle-class intellectuals who find it *chic* to be vulgar). What Nixon says on tape in Washington is unlikely to pass over the lips of a Winston Churchill who found the riches of the English language inexhaustible for his every purpose. De Gaulle referred to the unruly youth of the '68 generation in Paris as "*chien-lit* [dog-shit]" in an unusual lapse from his lofty French rhetoric.

But when political passions are running high a reversion to old earthiness can be as dramatic and purposeful as the occasional intrusion of a hasty expletive quickly deleted in the official record. In the case of Mrs. Susan Crosland, remembering the f-word that resounded through the whole of the British educational world, she has been led to searching in the wrong social class. The generation of middle-class socialists after C.A.R. Crosland–Prime Minister Tony Blair and Chancellor of the Exchequer Gordon Brown are today the leading British representatives–no longer feel the need to speak with a crude affinity to their proletarian comrades. They have been wooing (and successfully so) the political and social center, offering reassurances to the middle classes not the least of which are the niceties of language. As for their rough and tough brothers on the Left in the party, they have reluctantly cleaned up their act but are being more and more driven to radical discontent. They surely did not join the movement to accept so many leftovers of the old bourgeois society–the profit motive, private property, monarchical mummery, a House full of geriatric lords. They are even having to face a new constitutional system of proportional representation which would only help the class enemies in a smaller, third party. One faction comes from a genteel world where fair is fair; another where the surly f-word was always there to go down on the record as being an earthy sign of bloody opposition.

In this light, journalists have been well assigned to cover the British Deputy Prime Minister, an eloquent man of the people who usually says what he thinks and usually thinks in simple *yea-yea, nay-nay* terms. It was John Prescott, lowbrow to Tony Crosland's highbrow, who felt called upon to save the traditional honor of the movement; and he rallied to shore up at least one old ideological commitment with the force of no-nonsense expressiveness. While the prime minister was nice and fair enough to appoint the Liberal Leader to a

Cabinet committee in the prelude to some kind of arrangement for Proportional Representation., the deputy prime minister spoke his mind or, as he would prefer, shot his mouth off: "John Prescott's instinctive position on proportional representation was summed up by an uncharacteristically lucid remark to one campaigner for constitutional change: 'I'm not in f—ing favour of f—ing PR of anything.'"[39] Was not the f-word here, as in the Labour Party's debate over education, indispensable for the elucidation of an authentic and deeply felt political sentiment? How better to suggest that a true believer, alarmed at the erosion of most of his articles of faith, must in the end hold on to something?

This eminently quotable anecdote has been proving to be a hardy perennial in journalistic annals. It is not especially felicitous but it remains apt. Lady Chatterley's love affair is dated, even obsolete. But the Crosland cry has retained a certain pertinence which facilitates its regular recycling whenever, every several years or so, an "educational crisis" turns up. What to do with a "mixed school system" wherein the millions of British schoolchildren attend state-supported "comprehensive" institutions and the thousands "opt out" and are educated in independent private so-called public schools (symbolized by Churchill's Harrow and Crosland's Eton and, across the line, even Lord James of Manchester Grammar)? The Labour Party in government has never had sufficient energy and solidarity to "put paid" or otherwise destroy the public school *alma mater* which has consistently provided the élitarian half of the Party's leadership. And Conservative administrations were never courageous enough to defend the old traditions or to decide definitively what the balance should be.

Thus, when yet another "school crisis" began to boil over during the early months of the year 2000 it was time to dust off the aging f-word of yesteryear. This is how the *Sunday Telegraph*, elated by the turnabout by Prime Minister Blair's Education Secretary, moved that old bit of profanity from the yellowing clippings in the morgue to the gravity of a leading article's opening lines: "If it's the last thing I do," said Anthony Crosland in 1965, "I'm going to destroy every f—ing grammar school in England." Thirty-five years later another Labour Education Secretary, David Blunkett, has finally undertaken to bury this poisonous commitment once and for all." In an interview with the paper's correspondent, the cabinet minister gave reassurances that the government is not "hunting grammar schools" and that he would feel "vindicated" if the remaining 164 now survive. In some circles the promise would have been more convincing had Blunkett thrown in an f-word or two to counter-balance old Crosland's impassioned profanity. Who believes anyone any more unless the vow is sealed with relevant raunchiness? Not in marriages and weddings, and surely not on the hustings.[40]

She might have been "present at the creation" of yet another outing of the historic expletive. It might have been the semantic "double first" for the books.

Susan Barnes Crosland was given by the *Sunday Times* the journalistic assignment to do the first interview with the new Chancellor of the Exchequer, Gordon Brown, a Scotsman of much dark intensity and the theoretician of Britain's so-called socialist revolution of 1 May 1997. She duly did the good feature piece under the eight-column banner headline: *"My Burning Passion."* Thus, some decades after the Labour government of Wilson and Callaghan, in which her husband Tony Crosland had played such a tone-giving role, she had the opportunity–more by calculation, I suspect, than by coincidence–to record (possibly…hopefully) another resounding use of the f-word. The *Times* had already reported that the Blair cynics were dubbing Brown's headquarters *"Planet F***"* (because there everything is supposed "to get f—ed up"). What would he, in the first flush of power and passion, want to do with all his heart-and-soul? What would he want to expunge from the *ancien régime?* Mrs. Crosland pressed on with the persistence of a *tricoteuse.* She noted that when Gordon Brown spoke of his "applying basic convictions" he clenches his right hand in a fist. But he already missed the chance to smash that citadel of finance capitalism, the Bank of England. (On his first day in office he prudently privatized it and made it cleanly independent of governmental, including his own, interference.) Wasn't there some *infâme*, comparable to those hated élite schools of Tony Crosland's fury, that he would want to *écraser?* She hoped he would throw "his thunderbolt." As Mrs. Crosland wrote, "The workaholic I knew best was driven by a tension between his puritanism and hedonism. What drives Brown?" She copied down everything he said, but there was little flash and no fury. He was being prim and proper as befitted the dour son of a Church of Scotland minister. She sought, in vain, for his "emotional core." She was almost exasperated: "What else drives this workaholic?" After all, he might have said: "the passion to drive all the f****** money-changers out of the temple, and in Wales and Scotland too!"

The next day Gordon Brown would refuse to wear a tuxedo at a formal City dinner of bankers and financiers. It surprised and even outraged many. He might have justified his break with tradition by quotably saying that he "just doesn't go in for this kind of sartorial s—t." But he didn't; history's thunderbolts don't strike twice. His quoted words were in explanation, safely enough, of news fit to print anywhere (Susan Crosland on Gordon Brown, "My Burning Passion: Susan Crosland talks to him about his policy goals and lifestyle," *Sunday Times*, 11 May 1997, p. 13).

The verbal excesses in the excitement of winning a British national election and moving into London's Downing Street (if only No. 11) stamped Gordon Brown as a legitimate plain-talker. He had some roots, as any authentic representative of the working-class should, in the way the working-class really spoke. More important, at least for the observer of the language of journalism, he was now officially accredited as a reliable, dependable source who dared to speak the name-of-the-game "like it was"; and thus the British newspapers and their Parliamentary correspondents could maintain and fur-tively continue the f-word tradition in regular turns on a variety of political occasions. It was never again "the full Monty," especially after a brief gallant truce to mark Fleet Street's gratitude for the story of the Chancellor of the Exchequer's old-fashioned marriage ceremony at the age of fifty to Ms. Sarah Macauley, and other nuptial niceties, while still in office.

Six years into the Exchequer, with recurring rumors of difficulties with Prime Minister Tony Blair (who but Gordon Brown was there to succeed him?), and what began in a basic power struggle against the Tories is right on track, whatever the race. Expletives may become more important than experts, or even invisible imports. Chancellor Brown's Budget for the year 2002 was reported to be playing a decisive role in the internecine rivalries of national and Labour Party politics. Could the possible successes of these new tax and health-service policies be credited to one or to the other in the highest places of power? A well-informed press knows about such things. It was, accordingly, reliably reported that some two years previously, "on Sir David Frost's sofa," Tony Blair had already publicly announced the stirring new program. As a result, "By doing so, he forced Mr. Brown's hand–'You've stolen my f***ing Budget,' the Chancellor is said to have raged the next day."[41] The f-word had established itself solidly in the speech patterns of men in the highest places; nothing (or very little) can be thought about, discussed, formulated...from the structure of British secondary education (and the future of the Public Schools) to the intricacies of Taxation and the National Health...without the touch of salt whose tang represents the sharpness of the commitment of high-minded poli-ticians to earthy policies. In English circles where Karl Marx and, more re-cently, the ascetic Sir Stafford Cripps and the aesthetic Lord (John Maynard) Keynes set the tone of household discourse, the four-letterization of a nation's finance is a notable event.

None of the above is a final or exhaustive record of what might be consid-ered as profanity *in extremis*. Most human language (who knows the excep-tions?) have betrayed a tension between approved usages of vocabulary in non-casual communication and the occasional outburst of unapproved words on which tradition has put a taboo. In our own time there is also an extraterres-trial aspect to the phenomenon. The exploration of outer space and its atten-dant dangers to the American astronauts traveling in areas and spaces "where no man has ventured before" gives our problem a kind of cosmic context, in which, as in all mortal efforts to express rage, fear, or desperation, the old earthy expletives appear to be even more touching and significant. On the historic *Apollo 11* flight (July 1969) which finally landed three U.S. astronauts on the moon–to establish "Camp Tranquility" on the so-called Sea of Tran-quility–something had gone wrong. A defect had developed. "Buzz" Aldrin first noted this, and said a resounding: "*Son-of-a-bitch!*" His co-astronaut shared the alarm and the disappointment and said noisily "*Aw, shit!*" It is not reported what Neil Armstrong audibly, in his turn, said, nor how the engineering team back at Cape Canaveral verbally responded.

In the *Apollo* memoirs subsequently published there was a little more leeway for heroes who alone among millions had, as Tom Wolfe has written, "the Right Stuff" to make the grade. Their books, almost always ghost-written after extensive (and highly edited) tape recordings, tried to do justice to their every move, emotion, and scrap of conversation. To be sure, they were All-American boys and behaved appropriately. They would tell candidly the full story of how an apparently spontaneous phrase was, as we had surmised, carefully prepared and typed out on cue cards. Nothing would be left to chance, not even a "*Gosh!*" or a "*Wow!*"–certainly not the noble evocation of light and darkness in the recitation from *Genesis*–or the cool registration of small and giant steps for men on the moon or for mankind, respectively. In the vast and profound silences that the astronauts were penetrating were also broken at some point by street-corner expletives, so small on the great scale of extraterrestrial things; but I am not aware that any newspaper felt obliged, by the very gritty humanity of the drama, to publish them. They first became an official part of cosmic discourse, as far as I can determine, when the BBC decided a quarter-of-century later, to dramatize the Aldrin story (broadcast in January 2000). For the documentary was based on the astronaut's memoirs of 1973, and sent out the obscene words into the ether whence they came. It was a galactic moment of great reverberation.

One thought, for a moment, how these much-disputed taboo phrases got so far into the stratosphere. Would Hemingway have quarrelled with his publisher over retaining expostulations halfway to the moon that "get it right"? Would Lawrence have felt an element of galactic tenderness in the combination of terrestrial terms with a climax of pure big-bang nothingness? Surely Tom Wolfe, delineating the right stuff, would have known to accommodate low language to high endeavor? Arty, fanciful questions. Neither literature nor journalism have an absolutely satisfactory answer.

Language was the least of the concerns troubling the *Mercury* and *Apollo* astronauts; they were training to go into orbit and subsequently to be the first humans to land on the moon; and, accordingly, they were saddled with a thousand gadgets. Still, they knew that their every word in space, accidental or premeditated, would be reported and were likely to "echo forever" in the world's media. None of them had ever been touched by the talents of a man of letters; and they accepted, if grudgingly, editorial and intellectual advice from their betters. Even President Nixon was inspired enough to tinker with a word– it was in the text of the patriotic plaque which would be left on the moon. A tense was changed, with the astronaut's approval, in "*We come in the spirit of peace for all mankind*" which now became "*We came...*"The past tense was a bit better. Their touchdown had been historic, and this surely would be their first and last visit to Camp Tranquility. Still, armed as they were with "the right stuff" which included a sense of *can-do* superiority, they were touchy about what they were being told to think and say. The NASA bureaucrats were, in effect, being told off by our intrepid explorers: *"Did Queen Isabella tell Christopher Columbus what to say?"* Well, as a matter of fact, Columbus knew his Bible thoroughly, as well as the pious royals; and he extracted hope (and sometimes geographical error) from divine or heavenly sources; his diary is, accordingly, full of apparently apt scriptural references. The astronauts on *Apollo 8* concurred in the suggestion that a wondrous passage from *Genesis* should be read out.

One cannot but be fascinated by the spectacle of ghost writing in outer space, and in one case we can feel the grip of the long arm of censorship. Buzz Aldrin disclosed in his memoirs that he had wanted to take communion on the moon by reciting the traditional ceremonial passage from the Book of John. This was vetoed by NASA, for the Space Agency was already involved in a legal wrangle with elated churchmen and outraged secularists "over the *Apollo 8* crew reading from '*Genesis*' while orbiting the moon over Christmas...."* Aldrin compromised. The first extraterrestrial communion had to be privatized. In his "Personal-Preference Kit" (every astronaut was allowed one) he included a phial of wine, a tiny wafer, a mini-chalice, and a small cue-card from which he read out –silently, to himself–the scriptural text.[42]

Apart from the few examples of U.S. Army expletives which have been recorded in the astronautical literature, with the various authors on their best linguistic behavior, there is little to link these dramatic American experiences to the culture of profanity we have been studying. In the loquacious 1960s we hear the obscenities of the battle-weary G.I.s in Korea and Vietnam–of the revolting students trying to outrage their teachers on their college campuses and their parents in their comfy homes–even of foul-mouthed Presidents in the quasi-privacy of the White House....But with our astronauts, culled as an élite from old WASP America, we seem to be left behind in a nineteenth-century culture lag. Theirs are the families that read and revere "family newspapers"; espouse traditional "family values" (although they lapse and relax in the usual adulterous side-play); drink and carouse in moderation (except, perhaps, for one inebriated binge a year). Their offspring could be easily identified anywhere as All-American boys. Even all the reportorial new-journalistic talents of Tom Wolfe couldn't drag them cursing into a four-letterizing century. In his documentary novels of life in New York and in Atlanta, Wolfe's ears were alert to the obscenities which dominated human communication in the real-effing world around him. In his ambitious and much praised reportage of the first dangerous missions into space, he tries to pin-point *the right stuff*–"an

---

*   The credit for choosing this quote is usually given to my old friend, Simon Bourgin (ex-*Time*, ex-*Newsweek*, then Washington's "scientific adviser" to the astronauts). When I asked Bourgin (15 January 2000) for confirmation, he said, "Tricky bit of theology, that. You'd better credit the quote to Moses...."

amalgam of stamina, guts, fast neural synapses and old-fashioned hell-rais-
ing." But the scabrous vocabulary which the rest of America has increasingly
felt to be indispensable to play and purpose, ambition and achievement–as
well as anger and audacity, love and rivalry, fear and anxiety–appears to be
missing in action. Not even the literary energies of the father of "New Journalism" could drive the dialogue over the thin blue line.

I should conclude with a post-script of sympathy for journalists and editors
who suffer such setbacks in the quest for the scabrous with social significance,
for (if you will) a profound profanity. They have convinced themselves that a
properly liberated political vocabulary–even when it is trimmed at the edges
to make it acceptable to conventional audiences–would add in its authenticity to the quality of democratic debate and the honesty of the public philosophy. This aspiration is not necessarily utopian. Inch by inch the beast slouches
to Bethlehem. The progress towards what we have referred to as full and frontal
obscenity has been, so far as the serious press has been concerned, acceptably
incremental. Bit by bit the editors think they are "getting there," with old
Bowdler on his way to becoming an obsolescent memory.

But at times it is a hard slog. A new Chancellor of the Exchequer doesn't
come through with the thunderbolt, disappoints the American interviewer...and
leaves the *Sunday Times* with long paragraphs of uneventful prose.

Another effort was launched a Sunday or two later, this time with a local
male correspondent interviewing an influential female politician, close to the
European Union's effing power structure. He was one of the paper's star investigative reporters, Simon Sebag Montefiore, and she was Emma Bonino, a
well-known (and attractive) Italian high commissioner of the EU in Brussels.
The assignment came at a time of most serious political crisis which had
involved the integration of Europe in almost half-a-century. The paper rose to
the occasion with an interview entitled

A DANCE WITH THE RACIEST DEVIL IN BRUSSELS

It was, as S.S. Montefiore confessed at the outset, "a day of bureaucracy
and bawdiness." He told us that this "thin, formidable bird-like blonde" had
"nonchalant raffish devilry," and that he admired her legs. He questioned her
closely as to "Blair's sex appeal" and her own love life, especially the illegal
abortion she had when she was twenty-seven (which was not so very long ago).
He brought up, persistently, "sex, drugs, and rock 'n' roll" and tried to establish
exactly when Signora Bonino, who holds the European portfolio for fisheries,
food safety and humanitarian aid, lost her virginity ("at twenty-seven"?). She, in
her turn, played along with the young man, who was taking notes furiously and
hoping against hope that she would come up with an unmentionable word,
some bawdy response to his prurient probing, maybe one of those historic
expletives which would then echo through the corridors of power in *Europa.*

Nothing doing. Simon Sebag Montefiore was getting nowhere. She turned down his offer to dance with her in her commissioner's office ("waltz, mazurka, tango, twist, rock"?) and she hedged her answer to his questions about what her choice would be if she had to choose "between sex and politics": "This strange mix of political correctness and outrageous Rabelaisian merriment looks at her watch....*Ciao.*" The reporter went back to London with his story, such as it was, titillating if not bawdy, suggestive if not off-color, raunchy if not Rabelaisian–but for an f-word *aficionado* there were no prizes for the four-letter words the lady didn't say. For the *Sunday Times* Euro-salacity is still, alas, an undeveloped area. These foreigners don't speak English so good. Still, until the following weekend, there'll be time enough to launch the quest for the next outburst of profanity, trailing clouds of social significance.

It is far from my intention to mount an elaborate campaign on behalf of a change in existing newspaper house-style handbooks which would allow, encourage, embolden, empower and perhaps actually help institutionalize the naked publication of the full range of profanities and obscenities. Nor have I been, as the foregoing has tried to make abundantly clear to the reader, defending the ungainly and indeed even sleazy compromises which so-called frank and fearless newspaper prose has been dispensing. If all self-imposed restrictiveness went out of fashion, the replacement would be, as I suspect, the Australian syndrome running amok, effing wildly all the way to Babel. Overused and oversexed, the f-word with all its related unclad phraseology would then be incapable of ever serving as a meaningful quote–on such rare and memorable occasions as arise when they appear necessary and indispensable, when nothing else would do. What would we be left with when someone, somewhere, is in global readiness with the sound-bite and the off-color filler? When everything is profane and obscene, then nothing is.

In short, I have only been illustrating the wisdom of an old proverb made up by Mark Twain (for *Pudd'nhead Wilson's Calender*, 1894): "When angry, count to four; when very angry, swear." The quality of the anger involved, and its effectiveness and general impact, depends on the state of the language and its indelicate permissiveness: to which subject I have devoted so many pages in this book. But before I leave this theme I want to add two additional illustrations of two high usages of the low demotic. They can be registered on the pages of books and of magazines but draw only blanks in almost all serious daily newspapers of record. They involve Charlie Chaplin and Muhammad Ali (Cassius Clay), neither of whom are usually associated with the "bad language" which is routine talk in their respective professions.

Claire Bloom had starred in one of Chaplin's last films, *Limelight* (1952), and she spent some time with him when he flew from Hollywood to London to attend the world premiere at the Empire Theatre, Leicester Square. They took walks around Covent Garden (where he had played as a boy); and he was worried in England whether he would be allowed to return to his California residence, to his Hollywood film studio and, for all the disagreeable troubles with the American authorities, to his adopted homeland. Would the "McCarthyite witch-hunters" be able to prevent the return of an "un-American undesirable alien"? Would the Internal Revenue inspectors finally relent and tell him that his tax affairs were now in order? On both counts, the ideological and the financial, he had made things especially difficult for himself, particularly with his so-called "progressive politics" which followed what was thought at the time to echo perniciously the fellow-traveler slogans of Soviet Russian propaganda. Still, that was not reason enough to harass the man, the beloved and immortal Little Tramp of classic American cinema. He remained for long years (he died in 1977) an embittered exile. Claire Bloom always found him in melancholy and despair.

Times always changed, and things had picked up for the better for Charlie. In 1971, when he was eighty-two, he left his "exile" on Lake Geneva to fly back to Hollywood and accept an honorary Oscar award from the American Academy of Motion Pictures. Claire Bloom says that "it had come to him many decades too late." There was little joy–and much vindictiveness–on the occasion. How would Charlie react? He was now recognized as a genius but was scarcely any more the genial soul of his greatest heart-warming comedies. We owe to Claire Bloom the incident of the f-word which "made history," at least in these pages, but it was the shot that was definitely not heard around the world: "Privately he told me that, as he took his bows, at each courtly obeisance he would murmur, 'Fuck you and fuck you and fuck you.' And who could blame him for that?" Not exactly the sweet and silent Charlie Chaplin of all our childhood affections, but an affecting historic expletive for all that.

In the newspaper culture outside the USA this has been printed (following on from the publication of Miss Bloom's book of memoirs, *Leaving the Doll's House* in 1996); and so has the following, coming as it did uncharacteristically from Muhammad Ali's lips. But the sports pages have it easier, and they are replete with "dirty words" from street-smart ghetto-eloquent black athletes.

Sportswriters everywhere waxed lyrical when they recalled the occasion on which an aging Muhammad Ali, past his prime, recovered his world heavyweight championship title. He surprised and elated the world by knocking out George Foreman in the "epic bout" which took place in the African country once called Zaire. A documentary feature film, Leon Gast's *When We Were Kings*, was put together in 1997, and was given an Oscar award. The remembrance of the whole legendary occasion was studded with superlatives. "A marvelous demonstration of modern film's capacity to grant us a glimpse of immortality," wrote one newspaper; and another had a columnist confessing that "after 40 years of stealing a living as a sports writer, no single moment will ever match that of Ali's African dawn; I doubt if one ever will."

What of the champ himself? Would he brag to the gods that he had, once again, flown like a butterfly and stung like a bee? Would he summon up the

muses and compose an appropriate verse, a quotable one-liner or a witty qua-
train? Might he wave and flourish, in the continent of his ancestors, a tribal
root or two and twit his American compatriots (as he had done during the
Vietnam War)?

A flash flood postponed the denouément. A reporter recalled: "As if in a
thunderclap of applause, the heavens opened up over Kinshasa and the most
spectacular electrical storm cascaded down upon the stadium. Within minutes
seats, telephones and cables were being swept away in a raging torrent." Hours
later, Ali lounged in an armchair in his villa overlooking the grassy, swollen
banks of what used to be the River Congo. He rambled on quietly in a subdued
monologue. Nobody was there to make notes and preserve the great man's
words about his African triumph and its implications. But the camera-eye
caught the scene, and the sound track gave us this: "Ah kicked a lot of asses...and
ah done fucked up a lot of minds." The *Observer* writer, Hugh McIlvanney,
who had been there in Kinshasa added the comment that this was Muhammad
Ali's "accurate, if uncharacteristically crude, assessment." Assessment? This is
a bookkeeper's sort of word. It was, as I like to keep on suggesting, in its way
an historic expletive. Journalists have been known to go to absurd and ridicu-
lous lengths to come back with a quotable bit of profanity to salt otherwise
tasteless paragraphs...and here was one offered up in lonely grandeur, not with a
roar but gently shaken out of the Lion King's mane itself. It was, in the chronicles
of crude demotic, a moving and even majestic *mot;* for what is being recaptured
is a moment of truth, a shibboleth of dignity and pride, dredged out of the
netherworld of language to give words to a supreme highlight of an heroic
life....These are responses that seemed to come from so far inside them that the
words appeared to have a special, vibrant life-force of their own.

Yet in the end, the champ himself, a skilful wordsmith would want to have
it recorded that, by and large over a stormy career, he–a remarkable colored
man, a Negro, a black–had poked and prodded a lot of people and *stimulated*
a lot of minds; *upset* them, *changed* them, *broadened* them. The f-word was for
such special occasions.[43]

On Wearing Brown, or Brooklyn Strikes Back

In the emergence of what I have called a usable profanity for a profane
society, no problem is more difficult than this evaluation of the specific gravity of expletives. The weightiness ranges, as we have seen, from the expressiveness of a heartbreak to the mechanical manipulation of obscenities for
post-taboo ostentation. At times in these semantic tribulations the salacity
seems to reside in the eye of the beholder, or in the ear of the auditor. There
appear to be no objective standards. Obscene is what works as obscene (offending or titillating as the case may be). One person's swear word is another's
breakthrough to truth and authenticity. Specific gravities fluctuate according
to cultural context.

My last problematical usage concerns the wife of the thirty-fifth president of the United States. John F. Kennedy had been assassinated, and in the years to come his young widow and sometime First Lady, Jackie Kennedy, tried to relocate herself in the literary world of New York publishing. Who better to guide her through Manhattan–its tortuous community of argumentative intellectuals, the "in" writers and the "out" journalists, the Jews and Gentiles, liberal leftists and neo-conservatives–than Norman Podhoretz, once the radical editor of the reputable monthly magazine *Commentary* which had, with the years and a changing zeitgeist, been moving to the respectable right? He had been recommended by aging members of yesteryear's youthful Camelot in her husband's White House as a knowledgeable neo-con Cicerone to the cultural landscape, e.g., negotiating on the one side, the divide between patrician William F. Buckley, Jr., and Midge Decter (Podhoretz's vigorously anti-feminist spouse) as against the iconoclastic nihilists like Norman Mailer (whose articles about the Kennedy family had offended her)...and, say, on the other, Dwight Macdonald (a Trotskyite revolutionary whose *Esquire* movie reviews made him into an exotic Manhattan cult figure). Norman Podhoretz proved to be a useful guide. He also became a good friend to the tragic New England girl who, truth to tell, would have been better suited for the sparkling aristocratic life of some Georgian court in eighteenth-century England.

One encounter (it was not their first meeting) has, I submit, a certain historic piquancy. I heard him tell it, with the memorable verve of all Manhattan gossip; and he has recorded it in his latest volume of memoirs entitled *Ex-Friends* (1999). A former Kennedy aide, Richard Goodwin, dropped Podhoretz's name, and Jacqueline picked it up for her next dinner party in her elegant Fifth Avenue apartment. The few previous encounters of the two for tea (or drinks) had served only as hors d'oeuvres–she had relished his "lowdown" on "who was good, who was overrated, who was amusing, who was really brilliant." And now Norman, who tabulated such rungs on his success ladder as giant steps forward for mankind–all registered in his youthful first volume of memoirs, *Making It* (1967)–was ready for a coming-out Kennedy dinner party. He arrived on time. But evidently that did not encompass all that was proper and pleasing. He had forgotten to ask what the dress was for the occasion. Such weekday events were rarely very formal (the youthful Kennedys were also, after all, of the blue-jean generation). Still, there was a residual Anglo-Saxon prejudice against "*come-as-you-are*" casualness, especially against "Manchester brown." Norman P., who had been born in Brooklyn but had pursued his literary studies abroad in Cambridge University, might have observed the aristo-Oxbridge contempt for the local *declassé* sartorial style of tradesmen, shopkeepers and other lower orders. Only the vulgar favored brown.

Whatever he had learned in England (and when he had learned it), on the evening in question Norman came as he was. He rang the bell. Jackie answered and, as he tells it, she greeted her guest (which must be the first time in generations that a Bouvier hostess came personally to open the door). The historic incident happened thus:"I arrived from the West Side [the "East Side" had long since displaced it as the *chic* Manhattan neighborhood] in what Jackie considered improper attire, and as she ran her big eyes up and down from my head and toes, she smiled sweetly and said, 'Oh, so you scooted across the park in your little brown suit and your big brown shoes.'" To which he made a historic reply which deserved to be registered in the history of the f-word culture, not unworthy to rank with *le mot de Cambronne* in the military category and *das Götz von Berlichingen-Wort* in the political class (both rather earthier, and indeed more scatological, than is proper for Fifth Avenue): "To which the Brooklyn boy still alive in me replied, 'Fuck you, Jackie!'" This is, I suspect, a high point in the American sub-section of profane usages. Imagine if you can a number of alternative replies, still consonant with lively Brooklyn repartee, ringing through the Fifth Avenue doorway–"*Go to hell, lady!*" or "How *dare* you say that, and in the presence of my wife!" or even (a shade less euphemistically), "*Screw you, Madame!*" One can also conceive–a mite more cumbersome, perhaps, but a rude indecency for all that–"You can take your fancy dinner party, kiddo, *and shove it!*" In these alternative cases, the repartee would have remained private and with no distinctive (or quotable) semantic significance. Here, as it happened with its crisp four-letter concision, it has (as I have been trying to argue) a touch of authenticity, a historic note of gross necessity. Whole lessons in our national history can be read from this pithy exchange–from the lofty WASP tones of the Daughters of the American Revolution to Ellis Island greenhorns arriving, speechless in steerage, from *shtetl*-ghettoes beyond the pale.

Two other implications suggest themselves for mention. The singular epithet or a single-issue expletive can aspire to immortality or, at least, historicity (in my documentation: Chaplin, Crosland, Podhoretz, Jacqueline du Pré) whereas addiction to repetitiveness and association with low verbal habits–or overloaded purposefulness (D. H. Lawrence, Hubert Selby, Henry Miller, Tom Wolfe, Quentin Tarantino)–only manufactures *ennui*. Secondly, there is an apodictic character to the expostulation that renders it indifferent to whatever consequences ensued. *Le mot* on the battlefield of Cambronne may have induced a measure of French pacifism; the *Götz* phrase in Goethe's Berlichingen play did not exactly promote polite relations in high German places. No matter.

Nor did the exchange on Fifth Avenue result in anything untoward. The mark of such profanity is that it is sufficient unto itself. The four-letter word in such semantic situations is not an instrument of reflection but (as Bronislaw Malinowski reminded us) "a primitive usage…a mode of action…a piece of human behavior." On occasion it can, one must concede, cause bad blood, lead to fisticuffs or riots, or even to a small war. But its secret strength is social candor, individual surprise, a non-violent breath-taking flabbergastedness…as with Jacqueline and Norman whose ultimate reconciliation was presided over and indeed blessed by the f-word, here exhibiting unsuspected reserves of affection. He records, after hurling his expletive: "She liked that so much that I realized how tired she was of the sycophancy with which every one treated her and how hungry she had become for people who would stand up to her even though she was the most famous and admired woman in the world. And so we became even faster friends than we already were."[44] The four-letterization of our culture may well call for a cosmic semantic despair, but one sees that on some social occasions it can have a happy end. The moral of this story of a hurled expletive may well be to keep it short, don't say it again, and wear brown.

The Two Mohameds

Who knows how many American decisions were accompanied by a similar four-letter coarseness, rough and uncontrollable and, when recorded, seen to be profoundly revealing? This was certainly the case in President Richard Nixon's White House, where the tapes secretly recorded "rude and unprintable" language. We learned of his crude anti-Semitism when the president's expletives were not completely deleted and his anger against "the Jewish hecklers" in "Hymietown" led him to cancel in the national budget all federal projects for the benefit of New York City.

In the case of recorded Australian incidents, it is of course a motivational mélange wherein some impassioned political outbursts are only a matter of saying what comes naturally. As Andrew Neil reveals in his "autobiography of a newspaper editor" (i.e., Britain's *Sunday Times*), Mohamed Al-Fayed–who is the affluent and disputatious owner of the famous Harrods store in London–threatened to withdraw £3 million of advertising from Neil's Sunday paper. He was demanding of Neil and his publisher, the Australian (now American) press tycoon, Rupert Murdoch, a retraction of a story critical of the Knightsbridge storeowner–and an apology. It had criticized the way that Al-Fayed was renovating the luxurious villa in Paris once occupied by the Duke and Duchess of Windsor. Neil robustly refused, and he recounts how Rupert Murdoch, armed with good old Australian invective, stood firmly behind him. When Murdoch telephoned from New York, he asked about the amount that Harrods was spending on advertising in the *Times* newspapers. As Neil tells the story –

"About £3 million," I said nervously. There was silence at the other end of the line. I contemplated whether it would be better to back down or resign....
"F—— him if he thinks we can be bought for £3 million," he said, and hung up.*[45]

---

*   This is substantially the way that Dominic Lawson quoted the exchange in the *Sunday Telegraph*: only the F-word had, for the benefit of his own paper's housestyle, three small hyphens rather than the long dash as in Neil's book. The change had some obscure motivation but I can hardly imagine it was somehow significant.

There have been, if I may say so, more ringing pronouncements in the history of the struggle for a free press from John Peter Zenger (1735 in New York) to Hugh Cudlipp (*Publish and Be Damned!* in London, 1953). But, undeniably, it strikes a piquant note of its own; and one wonders whether it would have been worth recording and quoting if it had been put, in all sober propriety, as "Tell the scoundrel in question that we will never accede to his threats or blandishments!" Concision can create cogency.

Some ten years later another Mohamed turns up on the scene, and there is another transatlantic telephone call with Murdoch (and his f-word decisiveness) on the line to the *Sunday Times*: "'It's the great Andrew Neil,' Rupert bellowed down the phone one afternoon in mid-March 1994. 'Not content with taking on one f——g prime minister you have to take on two.' He was referring to the fact that the *Sunday Times* was at war with the British and the Malaysian prime ministers." The altercation with Malaysia involved the scandalous "linkage" between British aid to build up a hydroelectric dam there and a billion-pound contract for the Malaysians to buy British arms. "Sweeteners" were supposed to have been paid to the Malaysian leader, Mahathir Mohammed.

An exasperated Murdoch thought the muckraking stories with some new investigative sensation week-after-week were all pretty boring. Nobody really cared about South East Asia. They were all corrupt out there. It was just "too much"; and "It has to stop." Neil knew that he was in trouble when "the most bad-tempered telephone call I ever had from him" was ended. He knew his situation was precarious when he mulled over "what was really riling" his boss and surmised that it was his "satellite television interests in the Far East." There was, he sensed, "a clear conflict."

Was it time for thinking about "a new, less troublesome editor at the *Sunday Times*"? It was. A new editor was appointed, and Andrew Neil was "exiled" to the United States, with a prospect of "making big money in New York" in Murdoch's television empire...now cleared to expand, mellifluously in South East Asia. He could be "earning real money"–but still he quotes a dear friend as saying to him, "It's a f——g insult." Sealing deals with a kiss or a handshake is no longer in fashion. f-words mark the beginning and end of an affair.

As Dominic Lawson, chief editor of the *Sunday Times'* London rival, the *Sunday Telegraph*, reads the moral of the tale: "Mr. Murdoch was very anxious to sell his Far Eastern satellite television service, Star TV, to the teeming Malaysian millions....The editorial independence of *The Sunday Times* could be bought after all. Mr. Fayed's only mistake was to underbid." Lawson's charge is awesome and devastating in its implications for the future of a free press in a globalized world-economy. One wonders if he would be writing about his own publisher Conrad Black, an energetic and equally globalized Canadian press mogul, in a similar vein in similar circumstances. Andrew Neil's final word on Murdoch and Malaysia: "he wanted to placate Mahathir and send a signal to the rest of Asia that *The Sunday Times* was not a loose cannon that would soon be exposing business practices they would rather keep hidden. Murdoch and Mahathir came to an understanding."

The lesson of Kuala Lampur is a fundamental one for what the papers are *not* saying. How much more grubby are the crude realities than even the most vulgar sociological theory of economic materialism! Neil quotes, with a coolness as if this was acceptable normality in a deceitful world only nominally devoted to civilized ideals, the sordid "understanding" as it was also grasped by a British Minister and the U.K. High Commissioner in Malaysia: "The Malaysian Prime Minister made it clear that Murdoch would never do business in his country as long as Andrew Neil was editor of *The Sunday Times*....Neil had to go. Murdoch obliged." This time money talked, and eight or nine-figure sums spoke louder than even the rudest of four-letter words.[46]

The B-Word Down Under

There are schools of cultural history which try to explain the fluctuations in the fortunes of certain expressive phrases in our vulgar vocabulary–of our everyday language and its *"in"*-lingo, of our changing taboos in literary usage. It is usually ascribed to the shaping influences of the hard-core environment of life. We speak the way we live and love and die. Old expletives get deleted, new obscenities sneak in. Words are in the super-structure, basic etymological causes are in the earthy realities. In this perspective, obscenities are taken to be a kind of cultural onomatopoeia. Would we ever expect a tribe in the Sahara to come up with an image of a burbling brook? or an Eskimo people to come up with a conceit about a sizzling summer day?

Just so are Chaucer's kind of excremental metaphors typical of societies and centuries when peoples lived very close to an old ordure of things. But, then, in a world of white-tiled sanitation, ubiquitous hygiene and toilet training, would the s-word still retain its force as an expletive that had actually outlived its odoriferous relevance? Apparently it has. Is it only a scatological lag?

In an era when the representations of sexual intercourse, pre-marital or post-prandial, are practically a universal occurrence, with a salty soundtrack provided permissively by film and fiction as a taboo-breaking accompaniment, can the f-word survive in its thousand-year-old virility?

I suspect that Australian speech abroad is self-censored and cleaned-up; and, having never ever been to Australia myself, I am not in a position to judge whether the f-word extremism varies among the various classes in the country or how it is reflected (if at all), with proper retouching, in the press Down Under. In England the London newspapers keep the lustiness of the Australo-English language ever-present, and there are innumerable anecdotes available to make a day's filler. Here is another...from Philip Knightley's journalistic memoir (*A Hack's Progress*, 1997), culled by the *Sunday Times* to suggest an

Australian writer's robust apprenticeship. It began with an interview with a rebarbative Melbourne newspaper-owner who "snarled" at him: "Listen sonny. If you want to get on in my effing papers you don't go around giving effing Masonic handshakes. All I want is effing reporters. Is that effing well clear?"[47]

As I have already suggested, here the Australians have been true pioneers. The word has become everyday and commonplace (hence meaningless); fortunately, euphemisms move in to fulfill the old functions of dirty words which have become limp or obsolescent. More than that, when the private parts have been treated to a wholesale rehabilitation, from unmentionables in a blushing reticence to terms of physiological pride when they figure "orgasmically" in what Dr. Alex Comfort decreed was to be "the Joy of Sex," what future can there be for the genital insults, the p-word and the c-word, which were once favored expletives of male contempt?

These are small, if piquant, contradictions in the relationships between words and realities, and it is arguable that what we say (and how we say it) can long survive those naturalistic reasons why we originally were inspired to say them. Survivable words accommodate themselves to new and different meanings; but many are buried, dead as a dodo.

Consider the case of bastardy. Ever since the plaintive cry in *King Lear*– from, naturally, the "bastard son Edmund," who protested hopefully to the heavens: "Now, gods, stand up for bastards!" (I, ii., 21)–there has been a movement for the legitimation of illegitimacy. "Why bastard?" Shakespeare asked. "Wherefore base?" Centuries have worked against the traditional stigma of baseness. Contemporary legislation in many Western nations has put children born out of wedlock on a legal parity with their siblings (at least as far as name-bearing, inheritance, family support, etc. are concerned). More than that, the increase in divorce, the instability and increasing unfashionableness of marriage rites, have led everywhere to an increase of "natural offspring" and indeed to single parenthood. For example, the 1997 figures released by the Australian Bureau of Statistics show that one in three Australian children is now born out of wedlock (almost 70,000 a year), representing a 70 percent increase in the last decade. A newspaper in Sydney was moved to describe Australia as:

"A NATION OF BASTARDS"

In point of fact, excepting parts of the United States, Australia now has the highest rate of illegitimacy in the developed world.

Down under, evidently, Adam no longer delved nor Eve span–who, then, could ever pride himself on being a gentleman? Thus, in this future shock, the b-word in transition–upwardly mobile from its lowly base–has become what a newspaper headline referred to as *"a warm word of abuse."* A Sydney editor reports: "Bastard is a strangely ambiguous Antipodean noun. In one usage,

'G'day, you old bastard,' it is a term of great affection. But when, as I grew up in Queensland, my fellow northerners referred to our longest-serving prime minister as 'that old bastard Bob Menzies' it had a very different meaning."[48] That very difference is the process we have been examining: in part it is an adventurous excursion into low language, in part a safe flaunting of an almost rehabilitated expletive. A recent electoral campaign featured a major Australian party putting up a leading candidate who ran on the slogan: "Keep the bastards honest!" One of Australia's serious national newspapers published a magazine cover story on U.K. Prime Minister Tony Blair which suggested that he was "a Nice Sort of a Bastard." Mind you, even if he were a nasty sort of bastard that wouldn't necessarily make him into a bad chap. It is, as the reader must understand, a comfortable new *macho* distinction just among males. It's no longer a fighting word which, if you dared to say it again, fists flew and blows landed; but it is still a reminder of when men were men, and were all mean critters. As Australians will gallantly inform one, no women are–for the moment–bastards; only men can hold the title, but now "warmly," proudly.

The bastard son in *Lear* would have been happy at "the lusty stealth of nature," positively pleased at the progress the gods had vouchsafed him. They did finally stand up.

Germaine Greer Rethinks

One should not be tempted to niggle about the shortcomings in the feminine approach to profane usages. These are, still, early days yet. These fields have been ploughed and harvested by men for a thousand years, and only in very recent time spots has there been an opportunity for rambunctious women reporters to show that they can compete with the gentlemen of the press in most un-lady-like ways. It could also be that with all taboos off, and no holds barred, it will be productive of only short-lived careers. The bravura will soon be wearing thin; many of the expletives have already had their day, inside or outside their brackets.

Consider the dilemma and ensuing verbal gyrations of Germaine Greer twenty and thirty years on from the Town Hall debates with Norman Mailer which I attended in Manhattan. Mailer has gone on to (among other things) theological hermeneutics, and has been trying–as in one of his latest books, *The Gospel According to the Son* (1997)–to tell the story of Christ in his (and His) own words. Ms. Greer is still trying to shock and to claim equal rights among the swearing and cursing classes by referring to a "fellow journalist" whose gaudy attire betrays her feminist purpose (in addition to which she wears "f***-me-shoes"). How many scabrous put-downs can even a verbally gifted journalist think of in a long, prolific, polemical career? Greer, like so many feminist writers who spent half a literary lifetime staking out their equal claims to a macho vocabulary, may be reaching the point where one senses that the Klondike is over. Or an embittered suspicion that what they have been coming up with is only fool's gold. Here is the most recent (as I write, 1999) effort to come to grips with new challenges. Where Mailer wrestles with the Bible story, Germaine Greer struggles with the challenge of Viagra and the pharmacological distortion of the old war between the sexes as she knew it and fought it (and indeed won a few famous victories on behalf of the "female eunuchs").

The radical Sunday newspaper in Britain, the *Observer* (now owned by the *Guardian*, and both mastheads give every liberal statement an impressive imprimatur) has published Germaine Greer's thoughts on life and love, as of now.[49] The occasion was the popular demand for Pfizer's "wonder drug" which all serious humanitarians (i.e., most doctors and welfare workers serving in the National Health Service) want to have freely prescribed for the millions of male sufferers from sexual impotence: "our society's victims of stress, exhaustion, drink, and old age." But for the feminists, curiously enough, a Viagra pill is seen as a secret weapon in the gender wars. It also appears to be a very regrettable factor in the pre-coital crises which signalled so much feminist triumphalism in the contemporary post-Pill epoch.

No, for Greer Viagra is only a "recreational drug," and its users (capable, effective partners at long last) turn out to be mere figures of fun and, even worse, contempt. An additional oddity is that her five-column piece in the *Observer* (24 January 1999, p. 26) does not sport a single f-word in it, which is unprecedented in the prose style of one of the most flamboyant mistresses of the f-word vocabulary. She prefers to be coy and witty: *priapism* serving for the p-word, periphrasis doing duty for the dirty realism which had become a hallmark. Could it be that the new zeitgeist is calling for *euphemisms*? "When you can have a whole week end of synthetic priapism, what red-blooded male would settle for anything less? Viagra weekends could vanquish football as we know it. Even angling might register a serious fall in popularity once the Viagra culture kicks in [*kick in? Penetrates* would have been her old-time double entendre]." Either sex is too important to be shared with the local druggist, or the lady is developing a new-fangled fancy for the "guy who would prefer to walk and talk, cuddle and kiss his significant other." What we have here could be, in the long run, what Tin Pan Alley used to call "that funny little thing called Love." Suddenly an odd tone of blue-stocking mistressliness has come into fashion: "A good seeing-to is all very well in its place but those legendary multiple female orgasms come from somewhere else." *A good seeing-to*? D.H. Lawrence, that explicit poet of ineffable sexual harmony, would have had a nightmare featuring Jane Austen. Henry Miller, that tribune of *Sexus* and *Nexus*, might have felt himself assaulted by a fierce regiment of *Ladies Home Journal* subscribers. I suspect that the Greer/*Observer* manifesto against Viagra might be the only piece of feminist prose of the dying century on the subject of sexual congress that does not even pretend to be "telling it like it is": "Many a woman who is 'seen to' with unfailing and unsparing regularity is longing for a little love. A man whose penis lets him down and must make love in other ways, penile penetration is only symbolic of the union that is built between people by the interpenetration of minds." Once again, we are surprised at the still, sad note of the music of romantic humanity– of love and of the mind and of "the heart" (her uneasy quotation marks).

And this could be the requiem of the f-word when all is said and done, this revolution which gave so many signs of being irresistible and so permanent. Revolutionary theoreticians might detect here all the symptoms of "a *Thermidor*," a backsliding, a turning-away from the shocking new which had become, alas, the boring old. What has happened to the f-word excitement of only yesterday? For Germaine Greer it has become only "couple therapy," laboratory-assisted, and never to be confounded with the ideal transports of Romeo and Juliet. Who was it, after all, who proclaimed penetration to be a measure of human intimacy? (A thousand articles in the women's magazines of the Western world which had taken their erratic cues from Greer & Associates will now head for shredding.): "It is not beyond the wit of women to learn that a tremulous erection is often more truly moved and more truly responsive than a hard-on of the more mechanical variety. Viagra works mechanically." As if, she adds, "he [the lover] had no language"–for it is language which now appears to be "the real vehicle of love and erector of wit and fancy."

To the extent that Germaine Greer was the spokesperson of an historic forward thrust of the feminist movement, she can be taken to be the grand nullifier of old impassioned Victorian silences as well as their loud replacements; this was the high point of the Lawrentian vocabulary of taboo-breaking hard words. This was (as she famously insisted to Kenneth Tynan and Sir Laurence Olivier)–for a short while, a few fast-talking decades, suspiciously identical with the period of her mechanically active youth and mature years– noisily proclaimed to be necessary and proper. The sound track has been re-spliced again: new dialogue…different background music…up and under.

If this be a disturbing retreat from the imperatives of profanity and obscenity that have seemed in our account of modern newspaper culture to be inescapable, that is, if this reaction persists, then we will be witnessing yet another counter-cultural revolution. We will be on the move again; and, as Kolakowski's phrase about his trolley-car conductor's command to the new incoming passengers, we shall be stepping "forward to the rear." Is it too much to see this all to be foreboding a renaissance of the euphemism? Perhaps even, as the paradigms change (as is their wont) leading to a post-profane period of periphrasis? More than that, for these are only words and verbal signals…it could presage a chastened change in the way that mature men and women choose to think, write, and report on the way they live and love.[50]

Part 3

The Perception of American Words

*"As words become exclusively
emotional they cease to be words
and therefore of course cease to
perform any strictly linguistic function.
They operate as growls or barks or tears.
'Exclusively' is an important adverb here.
They die as words not because there is too
much emotionin them but because there
is too little – and finally nothing at all
– of anything else."*
—C.S. Lewis, *"Studies in Words" (1960)*

*"I do not argue that only demonstrable facts
are news. There are times and occasions when
rumor is almost as important as the truth –
when a newspaper's duty to its readers requires
it to tell them not only what has happened,
but also what is reported, what is threatened,
what is merely said.
What I contend is simply that such quasi-news,
such half-baked and dubious news should be
printed for exactly what it is....If it were done
they [newspaper editors] would have to throw
off their present affectation of omniscience, but
they would gain a new name for honesty and
candor; they would begin to seem more reliable
when they failed than they now seem when they
succeed....It would throw no unbearable
burden upon the journalistic mind; it would
simply make it more cautious and alert. Best of
it, it would increase the dignity of journalism
without recourse to flapdoodlish and unen-
forceable codes of ethics, by Mush out of Tosh."*
—H.L. Mencken, *1925*

12

Feisty to Funky to Flaky

In New York I usually buy my copies of the London papers at the Algonquin Hotel whose lobby is crowded with Englishmen struggling with the *New York Times*, and with Americans indulging their Anglo-Saxon nostalgia with air-mail editions of the British press. Under the headline "*Concise Johnson Dictionary of Current Americanese*" I note in the *Daily Telegraph* that my friend Paul Johnson, at the end of a year's residence in the U.S.A., "under-goes the trauma of decompressing the on-going wordshops of America with the Old World niceties of his empathetic support-function."

We all have our troubles; and perhaps he, fastidious Johnsonian stylist that he is, has had more than most. Friends of his in Washington had role-reversals in order to provide full support functions for their wives' writing activities. He was never sure what was right or wrong, good or bad, about someone who was being called *feisty* or *funky* or *flaky*. Nor was he the only one. Bill Clinton is another. In one of his unfortunate attempts to be inspirational and prophetic, the president suggested that the American people were not quite up to the challenges for change which he was presenting; and he confessed that he was "trying to get people out of their funk." Well, nothing is so unhappy, so ill-starred, as the temptation of a populist–"the president, dressed down in blue jeans and cowboy boots, held forth for nearly an hour," the *Washington Post* reported–to blame the people. If it was a passing slip, then he could claim indulgence (even sharp-shooting cowboys sometimes miss). But his youthful hard-riding advisors were, as always, intellectually over-eager–"He's been thinking about these things all year" (said George Stephanopoulos in the White House), "and his thinking has crystallized."[2]

The crystal lost its glint in the next days. When controversial reactions induced the White House to withdraw from this kind of accusatory thinking, it was explained that the President had not intended to mean that the great American public was "*funky*" about anything. I would like to think of this mishap of an incident (in September 1995) as the feisty attempt to elucidate funk which proved to be flaky. Slugging it out in slang doesn't help your batting average. Try some old-fashioned speech used by old-time presidents who wore ties and had a sharp crease in their trousers.

Twists in the new-fashioned lingo incensed Paul Johnson even more. He didn't like a vice president of the United States predicting more *"fomentation of hegemony in Africa,"* or a famous columnist trying to "diffuse" tension by "wading into this thicket of emotions." But he should really have known the difference between snooty and snotty; and some womanizer in Washington might well have told him what was being referred to in the reference to a "ditsy bimbo."

On my quick coast-to-coast trip I found myself having more linguistic and stylistic diffi-culties than ever before. I stared at whole sentences in the newspapers from New York to Los Angeles and wondered when I had begun to lose contact with the American language. I simply was not sure at the time that I knew what Flora Lewis meant when, in a dispatch from Paris, she reported on some French politician: "He dumps on everybody, left and right." Nor was I any clearer about the same day's *New York Times* story of how Huntington Hartford returned to Columbus Circle: "The former owner was there, looking pleased to see his old building gussied up." Dumping, I imagine, is something bad. Was being "gussied up" something good, or was H. H. pleased to see his old mansion in dirty decline? And was it very small or very large sums of cash that were involved in the Philadelphia Abscam case when the congressman accepted a brown paper bag full of "walking-around money."?

I have been collecting such phraseology for many years now, have indeed envelopes full of tattered clippings which I have never dared to send on to R. W. Burchfield to assist his researches for the new volumes of the *O.E.D.* For one thing it might reinforce his well-known and controversial thesis of how the American and English languages are swerving apart at an accelerating pace and that in another generation or two they will need to be translated in-to each other. (I find this a distressing prospect.*) For another, fast-moving American speech hurtles from innovative slang to obsolescent cliché without ever having sufficient time to make a useful entry in the dictionary.

The Wonderland fact of the matter is that Americans, in their vaunted devotion to freedom and rugged individualism, like to make words mean whatever they want to mean, and like Humpty Dumpty are quite prepared to pay extra for the liberty. What, for example, would have happened to the Cold War meaning of "to deter" when, after having failed to deter the USSR, the U.S. Air Force would have been called in to make a strike? "A Defense Department spokesman agreed that the US could not prevent a surprise Soviet missile attack on Persian Gulf oilfields but added, 'We could inflict substantial damage on them in revenge. That's our real deterrent.'" (*N.Y. Daily News*, 1 December 1980, p. 25). Well, that's a "deterrent" that might well have cost the Pentagon an extra billion.

---

*   See R.W. Burchfield, "On That Other Great Dictionary," in *Encounter*, May 1977, and in *Unlocking The English Language* (1989).

But surely this is not quite comparable to the costs in anguish to the publisher of the *Washington Post* and *Newsweek Magazine* who has usually registered her satisfaction at the passing of the militant mood of the '68 generation (which, in one of its last outbursts, caused a wholesale destruction of Mrs. Graham's printing presses). For anguish it will be, if words actually mean what they say, as in this presumably moderate and middle-of-the-way editorial in *Newsweek*: "Young people seem to be losing ... joy and hope. The saddest thing for our children is that none of their thrashing, lazing or suffering is dignified by words like struggle, organize, reform, overthrow."[3] Overthrow? After all, even Martin Luther King who had "a Dream" only wanted to "overcome."

Sometimes a string of Yankee syllables gets dispatched for consumption which appears to be comprehensible, but, alas, no one can say exactly what its significance is. During the 1996 presidential primaries I came across the following utterance by one potential candidate. It was a campaign statement by Steve Forbes, the millionaire publisher, against several of the other candidates and their charges against his magazines: "We've beaten them competitively for the last 10 years. We've really cleaned their clocks and so they're hitting back the only way they know how" (Associated Press dispatch, *IHT*, 16 January 1996).

The fetish of *comfort*, the importance of being "comfortable" with policies and positions in politics and public life, has been fine-tuned in Washington into various "degrees" of snugness and different "levels" of congenialities. When Admiral Bobby Inman was proposed by the Clinton administration as the new Secretary of Defense (in December 1994), he would agree only after reaching "*a level of comfort*" with the president. He evidently reached it, and had accepted the post when charges of "homosexuality" began to plague the Admiral's candidacy. One Clinton advisor was worried about Inman's membership in an exclusive, all-male club (named the Bohemian Grove) and, as he unhappily put it, the prospect of the Admiral's having to "face some prickly questions" during Congress' confirmation hearing–and indeed from the gay community in Washington (still smarting from Army and Navy discrimination against gay servicemen). After the admiral gave a "mesmerizing and manic" press conference, his nomination to high office was withdrawn. Everyone felt, alternatively, relieved and discomfited. Perhaps the media's popularization of comfort as a category of political effectiveness is gradually proving useful. Looking pained, awkward, and uncomfortable never won votes in any election. Particularly military and former nautical persons need to be able to stand "at ease."[4]

On the other hand: at its best, especially if the sentence doesn't get too long, the tempo of American linguistic verve makes for fast quips, those epigrammatic one-liners made immortal by the collected wisecracks of Groucho

Marx and W. C. Fields. Everyday, and everywhere, one would be confronted with that special kind of wit and wisdom which is a hallmark of the American language. Someone quoted Sgt. Bilko to me: "The race is not always to the swift, nor the battle to the strong, but that's the way to bet."

A sage old New York judge wearily remarked: "There is nothing so bad that it can't get worse." A politician's apt explanation for the disastrous end of President Jimmy Carter's reform years (and it was apt again a decade later, when Mr. and Mrs. Clinton were similarly mired down) recalled H. L. Mencken: "For every human problem there is a neat, plain solution — and it is always wrong." Nor are the illusions of progress any less vulnerable: "I had a terrible dream last night. I dreamed that the man who invented Muzak invented something else."

Finally, those irreverent one-liners of Mae (*Diamond Lil*) West, so reverently collected by the obituary writers when she died, aged eighty-seven.

"Too much of a good thing can be wonderful."
"Between two evils I always pick the one I never tried before."
"I hadn't started out to collect diamonds, but somehow they piled up on me."

But, as I say, the danger point is reached when one ventures beyond the one-liner, and then all of America is endangered by the confrontation with a long paragraph. Words begin to slip, phrases break and leak, an impenetrable fog seeps over meanings and implications.

A few years ago, when I did a little local shopping in Manhattan, I could scarcely find anything that wasn't overpriced with the "Gourmet" label. Well, gourmet is now out—and everything is "Homemade." In Los Angeles, Cal., as in Providence, R.I., I found myself buying and eating cookies, brownies, cakes and breads, all presumably made by Mom and Pop in the shop's backroom. Actually, they were all the same mass-production concoctions, effi-ciently distributed from coast to coast, sometimes with an extra merchandising gim-mick of a little flour-machine or a shiny baker's knife or an aromatic choco-late-melter to give the *trompe d'œil* its ultimate touch of sight and smell.

"Homemade," to be sure–if the factory is a home. The ingredients for all the fancy foods, so faddish in the new national infatuation with the personalized and the handcrafted, are the same ready-mix standard emulsifiers and stabiliz-ers and artificial coloring that go into the supermarket's pre-packaged pasta, ice cream, and soft-centered chocolates.

I am glad to note that, despite all this, the sturdy Yankee character shines through; and I read in today's *Times* an interview with a Mr. Joseph Giordano, one of the giants of the homemade ribbon pasta industry, who told Ms. Mimi Sheraton: "I tell store-owners that our pasta should be cut in the store in front of the customers. It at least doubles the sales. All they have to do is to cut it in front of the customers. They don't have to say it's home-made. They don't even have to lie."

Let's not quibble about the lie already being built-in. Few Americans appear to be truly fooled by such extravagant and basically harmless coups of inventive salesmanship. But the man who invented Muzak may well have invented something else, and the dream is some-thing of a nightmare. The *Wall Street Journal*, which watches all technological innovations like a hawk, discovered a new item called "*Dr. Becker's Black Box.*" It was manufactured in Louisiana by the Behavioral Engineering Corp., and its president, Hal C. Becker, went "dormant" for a while after the Orwellian storm over subliminal advertising twenty-odd years ago. Now, evidently when 1984 has come and gone and no longer holds any vague terrors, his new machine sells briskly for $9,810 (or leases for $4,800 a year). Thus, in a New Orleans supermarket, under a cloak of background music, a subliminal message is beamed to shoppers and employees, and the subconscious is supposed to pick up the in-audible words, "I will not steal. If I steal, I will go to jail."

The supermarket owner is pleased with his machine, and says that pilferage used to cost him $50,000 every six months and now it's down to $13,000. (Even cash shortages have dropped to less than $10 weekly from $125.)

As for a real-estate management concern in Buffalo, N.Y., salesmen hear tapes saying, "I love my job" and "I am the greatest salesman"; and the company president reports that revenue has risen 31 percent.

Before my readers on the Left begin to fulminate against the latest excesses of the acquisitive instinct under late capitalism, I hasten to note that what Dr. Becker calls "human re-source potentiation" is also coming to the aid of Health & Welfare. In Gladstone, Mo., patients at the McDonagh Medical Clinic, waiting for a special type of intravenous therapy that takes up to four hours, are told subliminally *not to be anxious*. A doctor reports: Fainting spells used to be a problem for many awaiting treatment, but the messages have now solved the clinic's problem.

Once again, Europeans need never despair of the resilient elements in the stalwart American character. I have been reliably informed that the American Civil Liberties Union is preparing to attack and sue and picket. "It's tantamount to brainwashing," they say, "and ought to be prohibited by legislation."

The quixotic transformations which the military performs on words and their meanings gets printed in the newspapers, adding further to the distress. It is probably too late for a finger, or a whole hand, to stop up the hole in the dam wall; the incoming tides have become very unruly. Words and their usages have become arbitrary, and when wilfulness does not accent ambiguities and imprecision, a sloppiness which has turned into second semantic nature does the rest of the damage.

One morning came the news of the American punitive strike against Iraq, and the second bombardment a day later was, as a U.S. Army general who was the Pentagon spokesman officially explained, launched for "the *suppression* of Iraq's air defenses" (and thus buttressing the U.N.'s "no fly" exclusion zone). *"To complete the suppression"* is a characteristically unfortunate phrase. It represents an insensitivity to nuances of meaning and suggestiveness which is stolid even for the Pentagon. The U.S. military gave us such self-defeating tags as (in Vietnam) "Operation *Crazy Horse"*–famous in tourist circles as an ill-famed strip-tease joint in Paris (not to mention a tragic Indian figure destroyed by "genocidal" fighters on the wild frontier). It could have been worse (think of "Operation Mad Cow"). *"Suppression,"* after all, is one of the constant pejoratives in mankind's vocabulary of politics. The BBC, announcing the news from Washington (2-3 September 1996) was obviously discomfited, quoted the unhappy Pentagon phrase, and went on to explain by using adequate synonyms like "to attack...eliminate...neutralize...to destroy."

I am reminded of a military incident in the last days of World War II. I was visiting, in my capacity as a U.S. combat historian, an American Army division which had crossed the southern Bavarian border into Austria, always in hot pursuit of a phantom Nazi resistance in the so-called "Alpine Redoubt." The U.S. artillery headquarters was sitting on top of the mountain plateau overlooking the undestroyed city of Innsbruck, glistening in the Maytime sun. A band of Austrian anti-Nazis, led by Karl Gruber (later to become foreign minister), was reported to have arrested the local *Gauleiter* in the Tyrol, and they were heard on the radio announcing that Innsbruck was now in the hands of the Resistance. Whereupon the U.S. Army general growled, *"Resistance,* huh! Let's show them what we do with resistance" and ordered the heavy pieces to zero in on the town in the Inn valley. It took a few very tense minutes until clarification came–namely, that the Resistance movement was *not* against us, but *for* us. The locals were on *our* side, *resisting them,* our enemies....More than fifty years later the military mind has not enriched its vocabulary enough to make for precise political understanding how words can fight with *Us* or with *Them.*

Linguistic influences crossed both ways over the Atlantic–going westwards, with upright standards from old England governing (and controlling) Yankee demotic–or, going eastwards, with imports of catchy or useful vulgarities from the new world coming into continental circulation. In the eighteenth and nineteenth centuries these things happened in slow motion.

In our own day, owing to the major presence everywhere of Hollywood films and the increasing overseas power of New York publishers (not least because most of them had been bought out by European media giants), the outward reach of Americanisms is almost instantaneous. A White House slogan, a Broadway joke, a California quip, a Madison-Avenue adman's tag-line–all sorts of variations on a best-selling book-title–are suddenly on everybody's lips and inescapable in European, especially British, newspapers. Cognoscenti people the scene. Instant expertise on these subjects accumulates; and one notes the growth of a small cottage industry of "wise guys" who specialize in knowing better. Woe unto the hapless Continental translator of a Saul Bellow or Philip Roth novel if his work fell into the hands of knowledgeable critics like Marcel Reich-Ranicki who would find (and, in fact, did) a hundred errors and egregious, sometimes hilarious, misunderstandings. Their newspaper readers were regaled by innumerable scandalous examples.[5]

In England there were, to begin with, a handful of scholars who from the groves of academe did their pedantic sharp-shooting at careless journalists and half-baked punditry. (I mention here, in a splendid if bygone generation, only Sir Denis W. Brogan in Cambridge; Professors Malcolm Bradbury and Frank Thistlewaite in Norwich; Marcus Cunliffe who established "American Studies" in Manchester.) At its best the rambunctious pedantry elevated the standards of accuracy and interpretation in transatlantic writing. With the addition of the manpower of U.S. kibitzers residing abroad, the reportage of things American was, more often than not, knowledgeable to the point of captiousness. They sounded like know-it-alls, but they did know certain things better.

Here is what a *Guardian* book reviewer does with a new novel by Sebastian Faulks who moved on from his popular French trilogy (*The Girl at the Lion d'Or*, etc.) to a shift of novelistic scene with a plot based unfortunately in the good old U.S. of A. The two-column headline gives away the catastrophic thesis –

SEBASTIAN FAULKS GOES TO THE U.S., BUT HE CAN'T DO THE LINGO

Well, he can be excused for alleged misquotations, for his extracts from the poetry of Wallace Stevens and Emily Dickinson were supposed to be, plotwise, fake. But, then, a leading Faulks character is given an "accent from the urban midwest." Where, pray–and what–is that? The *Guardian* critic flourishes his *épée*: "I'm an American, married to a woman from the urban midwest, but I would not recognize such an accent." Be that as it may–and one could ask whether our happily married expert was ever in James T. Farrell's Southside Chicago or in Saul Bellow's midwestern nooks and crannies–but more was to come. For the critic becomes so obsessed with his finicky erudition, so distracted by minor errors that he begins to doubt whether any of the book-full of details could be right. Did the analgesic pill exist at the time the novel's heroine was "gulping Tylenols"? Not on your Nellie. And then again did John Kennedy ever go to law school (as did his brothers Robert and Ted)? As for the man who moderated the Nixon-Kennedy debates in 1960, he was always referred to as Howard K. Smith–and without the *K.* (Faulks' fatal omission) the famous television presenter is said to become a nobody. "I'm not being petty," we are reassured, "but to call him Howard Smith is like referring to FDR as FR...." Even worse was to come. Faulks is describing a scene of a racist killing in the Deep South: "Old boys in straw hats sitting on the verandah had shot-guns across their knees....He saw more than one pearl-handle sticking out from a straining waistband." *Old boys*? As our smiler-with-a-knife asks, with another flourish of his blade, "What's wrong with this?" Well, "old boys" are (in the English context) Old Etonians–armed Alabama verandah-sitters are "good old boys." As for the pearl handles they, "seem better suited to a Western film." The honor of the Deep South is now evidently saved from page-after-page the errors of the furriners.

To be sure, newspapers commit their own ration of errors, and the *Guardian*–painfully satirized enough by "*Private Eye*" as *The Graudian* because of its innumerable typos–now published a paperback edition of its *Corrections & Clarifications* ("a selection of the funnier corrections," price £6.99). What matters, then, these kind of "parodic" slip-ups, especially in the ambitious attempts to reproduce American vernacular? Phrases lose their rhythm, words drop a letter or two.

Faulks' protagonist asks a couple of Americans what they are drinking. They reply "Martini." (That's a label-name of vermouth!) Wouldn't they have said, as every Manhattan cocktail devotee knows, "Martinis"? The *Guardian* does not appear to be upset by this tiny-minded pedantry, vacuously arguing thus: "This is small stuff, but novels are made of small stuff like this. Faulks obviously needs to spend more time watching American television shows." This, surely, is a classic case of driving out the Devil with Beelzebub. The vapidities of bar-counter patter recorded in New York TV soap operas will, if you have time enough for them, save our souls...in the singular or the plural, as the case may be.[6]

13

Godperson and Other Funny Talk

One might well hope so, but then brainwashing is obviously easier to deal with than language-washing. The efforts of educated British churchmen to launder the Bible (and associated hymns and services) are as drops of water, or simple soapsuds, compared to the homemade efforts of their American brethren. In Britain the changes are essentially motivated, foolish and misguided as they may be, by the fear that the word of God may not be comprehended, grasped, cottoned-on-to. Consequently, plain, drab, understandable words are preferred to beautiful old hard ones. In America the cosmetic enterprise is, inevitably, reinforced by so much ideology and sociology that even theology doesn't rear its divine head.

Consider the whole nationwide drive to purge sexism from all (but the private) parts of home and country. In that spirit how can the Church in America still go on about "God the Father"? The National Council of Churches voted to abolish "sexist" references to God, Jesus, and the Holy Spirit (and/or Ghost) by adopting–"a style of language which expresses inclusiveness with regard to human beings and which attempts to expand the range of images beyond the masculine to assist the church in understanding the full nature of God." This presumably should appease those radical women's groups which combine atheism with a caring concern about a "masculine cultural bias" both in the Bible and in Church services. Language dealing with God is to be cleaned up: "It is possible to minimize the use of He for God and accept a distinct theological style where one refrains from pronouns. In such an observation lies the basic theological stance from which we ought to approach the translation of the words for and about God."

All this is intended to apply to Catholics and Jews as well as Protestants, and the new translators will surely have their inter-faith hands full trying to get the *papa* out of the Papacy in Rome or to strike a new bargain between the Grand Rabbi and his *rebbetzin* in Jerusalem. A little theology (*O.E.D.*: "science of religion, study of God, His nature, attributes and relations with man.")

might help the churchmen, but even that might be tarnished by its embarrassing masculinity. "Strictly and theologically speaking," it is conceded,

> no statement about God as Lord, King, Father or He expresses a male reality over against a female reality. The sense of God as Father has no meaning of fa-therhood as over against motherhood.
>
> We would like to overcome the undesired suggestions that the incarnation makes Christ's maleness crucial in such a way as to overshadow the primary im-port of the word having become flesh and the divine having become human.

But there is little point in "strict speaking" in a trend-ridden age. "God the Father" is sched-uled to become "God the Creator"—except, to be sure, in those Judaeo-Christian languages where creativity just might have masculine or feminine articles or endings. One is condemned to go back to "the beginning" which was the word, including its orthography, phonetic peculiarities (the Greek *logos* carried so much philosophical baggage), and its various grammatical usages. Sartre had insisted on the plural, *les mots*, words.

I am trying to be as fair as I can about the fate of words in our American language. When in America you hear a new word, *run!* If it is strung along into a single sentence, *enjoy* the one-liner—but stretched out into a whole paragraph (argumentative, descriptive or prescrip-tive), *leave* the country quickly for foreign parts. And if, the Creator forfend, a text is ever for any purposes whatsoever electronically transcribed to be broadcast (whether on a Black Box or a TV box), then *pray* for your soul.

I am grateful to Jack Smith of the *Los Angeles Times* for calling my attention to what has happened to the word *beau*. Some California lady made some passing reference to a social engagement involving one of her *"beaus."* The old folk present were pleased with the deco-rous language; the young crowd were puzzled, for what did *beau* mean—lover? intimate friend? concert-going companion? roommate? acquaintance? what? They thought it was a funny word to use. The others thought it a perfect word to use, saying just enough about the relationship: not too much, not more than they wanted to know or had a right to know.

Is it merely that the words come and go, and *beau* should now really be "live-in boyfriend"? But what used to be called, for a brief season, "togetherness" is referred to at this point in time (previously known as "now") as "integrative familiar tendencies." Educators refer to a school–where plain English is supposed to be taught–as "a venue for learning systems served by a professional infrastructure."

In a recent book* there is a sharp analysis of *"The Principle of Unnecessary Specification"* by which writers conveniently pad out what they have to say, making the obvious seem profound, the simple complicated, the trivial im-

---

*   Richard Mitchell, *Less than Words Can Say* (Little, Brown, 1980).

portant, projecting an atmosphere or an aroma of insight and expertness: "It is the incense of incantatory prose, and a few deep whiffs can transport the intoxicated worshipper into what grant-seekers of all persuasions would surely call 'new levels of awareness.'"

At its most innocent the fate of simple words and clear meanings is a matter of changing generations; at its most corrupt it is a rebarbative process in which elevators (or lifts to those new levels) become, as they are in fact called in official documents, "integrated single-module vertical transportation systems."

The gobbledygook is, according to Jack Smith, "poisoning our institutions and choking dis-course between them and the people they are supposed to serve"; and he thinks he knows when it began, namely with the fashion of using a "scientific" word instead of a simple word that had long been in use. No wonder he is transported into a nostalgia for the day when iceboxes were not yet electric and were not called refrigerators. He is distressed by the notion that old folk talk funny. Since he has written, all of us have grown ludicrously older.

14

Perception Uncleansed

Funny or not, I cannot escape the impression that "new folk" talk nonsense, and sometimes something worse. The estimable William Safire has now added a half-dozen volumes to his classic study of the political usages of language in America,* and it only reminds us of what a pleasant pastime—for on a serious level, it is a lost cause—"word purism" has become. (A despairing journalist gave me the other day an old, useless badge for my lapel, on which was printed long ago: "*Rock Against the Misuse Of 'Hopefully.'*")

What is the nature of the infection, contagion or mimesis which spreads the hateful, hope-less word like wildfire? Right on. Can it be in the essence of man's speech to resort habitually to primitive grunt-like signals? A rip-off. Is it that people feel better when they speak worse? No way.

As my old Marxist friends use to say, there are deeper social reasons, comrade; and there always are. Why did *perception* become such a modish word, so much so that in one recent fortnight of my travels in the U.S.A. I marked it a total of 215 times in my newspapers and periodicals (not counting the TV news and commentaries)? Sometimes it stood in for (as in "Moscow's perception of Western policy" or "the Administration's perception of inflation") *attitude, view- or standpoint*—often for *notion* of—occasionally for *interpretation* or *idea* of—usually for *understanding, comprehension,* and *cognizance.*

The deeper social explanation is (as I sit at the airport clipping my last American newspaper of the trip, awaiting my plane to London) ready to hand. In an age of mounting superficiality only the visible surface becomes important. Optics are all. A pseudo-Berkeleyanism has run triumphant: only what is seen is really *out there*; and *everything* that is seen must necessarily be real. No matter that you can perceive a *mirage*, or a *face in the clouds*, and that through Aldous Huxley's notorious *Doors of Perception* lay the spectral realms of illusion and fan-tasy. No matter that you may well be forced to confront ap-

---

* William Safire, *On Language* (Times Books, 1980); *The New Language of Politics* (1968).

palling and dangerous realities which you *do not see* and may *never* lay eyes on. The older prayer enjoins us to "both perceive and know," and even William Blake worried about *perception "uncleansed."*

I will be dealing with the racial chromatics in another chapter, but this one example belongs here. A *New York Times'* front-page story is entitled:

Perception Growing Among Blacks
That Violent Incidents Are Linked

Now the various killings and kidnappings of Black persons in some half-dozen different U.S. states in the 1980s were appalling enough; if they were indeed linked in some organized conspira-torial connection it would have been horrendous. But this has nothing to do with "perception"; it has everything to do with *evidence* and *proof*, with hard facts, collected and corroborated, analyzed, pondered, and interpreted. "But," says Mr. Drew Days 3d, who was at the time the assistant attorney general for civil rights, "the more incidents, the more the perception." Yet he only meant the more the suspicion and uneasy alarm—and what of hard evidence?

The *Times* reports: "There is no compelling evidence of a conspiracy even though violence against Blacks appears to be increasing." Compelling or not, *how much* evidence is there of a conspiracy? "The perception that one exists is widespread and growing....The latest murder in Youngstown, Ohio, illustrates how the perception grows, by rumor." One black spokesman is quoted as saying: "There could be a link." The Rev. Jesse Jackson states: "There is almost a hysteria in Black communities because of the belief that there is a conspiracy....Without question there is a psychological conspiracy."

Thus *perception* comes to signify not a piece of reality observed, a real situation seen, but a feeling, an emotion, a suspicion, a fear. Although Mr. Jackson was quite convinced that "this country has taken a definite swing toward fascism," he admitted that he "could offer no evidence to support his assertion."

The careless phrasing of mindless journalism here only exacerbates the wild imprecision which is running amok. Is *"compelling evidence"* supposed to suggest at least some, if not completely conclusive and persuasive, hard facts? To report that the civil rights leaders "say they do not *necessarily* believe that there is a national conspiracy" is to leave one with the "perception" that we are not seeing what we perceive and not believing what we say.

Only the next day was there an adjustment in the direction of sobriety and accuracy when Vernon Jordan, the black leader of the Urban League who was himself badly wounded by a sniper in Fort Wayne, Indiana, asserted that he did *not* believe there was in point of fact "a national conspiracy of violence."[1]

But this appeared to be a rather lonely and isolated example of plain speaking (and plain English) in the land. The discussion returned to the conventional irrationality which still marks the talk of the '68 generation—anything-is-true-if-you-feel-you-think-it-to-be-so—when the head of the leading organization of black Americans, Mr. Benjamin Hooks of the NAACP, put the argument this way: "In my book, perceptions are as important as reality." Whatever one thinks of this as a philosophical proposition, the jumble of words, sentences and paragraphs in America is surely playing a tragic role in the mounting mess. Gibberish coarsens public life, and nonsense can turn out to be an accomplice of murder. There are none so blind as those who only perceive.

The major strand in the web of conspiracy theories involving this black-white tension is the recurring belief in "African-American" circles (i.e., in both Africa and the U.S.A.) that the AIDS disease was deliberately created and spread by white America for the purpose of committing genocide on blacks everywhere. This also belongs to the "perceptions" which are indeed misperceptions that have no real basis in medical or political fact. In the 1980s it was widely reported in the newspapers for its qualities as a wild, lurid surmise; in more recent years the rumor has been "dormant"; and the world's press, having exhausted the story, no longer finds its perfervid repetition newsworthy, unless it comes up with a topical variation (*viz.*, crack in California), or a raging epidemic in central Africa.[2]

Evidently racial tensions on a certain level of argument and polemic remain troublesome enough to maintain a steady reserve of suspicion about every untoward event. In the 1990s there was a momentary flurry of "genocidal" accusations again, launched by a small California newspaper based on reports of the CIA involvement in the local drug trade in crack.

When the CIA-crack-connection story faded there still remained the "perception" that racial hostilities were involved in the spate of torchings of black churches that swept the South. The Rev. Jesse Jackson had described the attacks as "a cultural conspiracy." President Clinton was moved to recall "vivid and painful memories of black churches being burnt in my own state when I was a child." There was little or no evidence that racist groups like Aryan Nation or the Ku Klux Klan were involved. But then readers–often puzzled, confused, and hesitating to make their minds up–were battered by another series of reports and comments to the effect that such evidence (as in the O. J. Simpson case, no?) would be tampered with, wouldn't it? Even the Presidential Task Force registered "significant fears about an increase in racially motivated crime." Yet it had quietly revealed that it had found no evidence of a racist supremacist conspiracy, and noted that white churches had been burnt down at many times the rate of black churches. Was the "epidemic" color-blind? Who would believe that old wooden buildings had been burned down by "accident," or victimized by bored youths, would-be satanists, or burglars attempting to cover their tracks? Public opinion on such questions is hardly guided by hard facts and cool analysis. Even foreign papers often get into the heated argumentation, with the Left offering anti-American scare stories of "a Yankee holocaust," and the Right emphasizing the radical ultra-sensitivity of ethnic protest lobbies. A headline in the Tory *Daily Telegraph* (15 June 1997) reported,

CHURCH ARSON CONSPIRACY IS DEBUNKED

Its New York correspondent even debunked the president, and insisted that "inquiries could find no case of a black church ever being burnt by racists in Arkansas." It was obviously the British journalist's "perception" that the White House had been making things up, just telling a little "white lie" in the good cause of protecting the Black American citizenry from "the rash of crimes that hearken back to a dark era of our nation's history."[3]

"Perception" is also on the verge–the reader may recall my previous remarks on "*Janus*-words" or *contranyms*–of becoming an equivalent for misperception, emerging as one of those rare and striking identities of synonym and antonym, besting some, worsting others. It suggests optical faults, ranging from visual distortions, astigmatism and other eye diseases and even to, indeed, blindness: for clearly, there are no perceptions so unreal as things nearly perceived. The word buzzes from front-page politics to the entertainment supplements to the financial columns.

A mere blur in perception causes slight harm, a misunderstanding perhaps or a passing prejudice. As the *OECD* agency argues against critics of the third or so-called developing world, things are *not* as they appear: Afro-Asia is *not* "stealing jobs," for "the popular perception that the multinationals are moving production to low-wage countries is misleading."[4] More grievous is the imperceptiveness in greater matters of vast profit-and-loss. How else to account for the fact that some of the most sharp-eyed financiers in Wall Street and in the City of London "saw it wrong" and went bust? Barings collapsed because they couldn't see as far as Singapore where a young dealer was losing millions for them in "derivatives" (which obscurantist word has no visible, meaningful derivation). From bankrupt junk-bondsters to old-fashioned risk-takers on margin, the giants stumbled "eyeless in Gaza." It was worse than "misperception," sadder even than being "visually challenged." A well-known American investment banker summed it up with a revealing one-liner: "Markets are now governed by perceptions, not logic."[5] Since logic, by some awkward syllogism of high finance, is imperceptible to even the most discerning, this really means: No point being perceptive and incisive, or reasonable and logical–just trust to the hunches of blind luck...that's the way to make billions. (A man named Soros has, and did.)[6]

One American journalist, writing in Britain about European diplomacy, has been on the trail of this connection between perception and deception, of "unacceptable words" which function only deliberately to delude. She put together from all the briefings she attended a nebulous vocabulary which represented the victory of semantic spin over what had actually transpired. As Anne Applebaum (formerly with the *Economist* and *Spectator*, later a columnist for the *Evening Standard* and the *Sunday Telegraph*) wrote in an article entitled "A triumph, if you say so": "In European affairs, perception is reality. Words matter more than actions. If the French say they have achieved a historic compromise by issuing a jobs statement and planning a jobs summit, then so they have." What you get to see and hear, you'd better believe.[7]

The p-word moves on strongly from myopia to astigmatism and beyond. To see, or not to see, that is the question; and perceptive answer there was none. The BBC, in an otherwise unexceptionable news-review of the major topics of the day (as of 30 May 2002), highlighted an especially grave and contentious issue by asking, "Are we grappling with a real problem, or only with our perception of one?"[8] This is a good question. An even better one would be whether the perceived real problem constitutes a truly real perception? And/or whether we are actually grappling with it or just thinking that we are? Newspresenters, reciting from the clipboard or text-cue screen the headlines of fast-breaking stories on the world scene, sometimes talk prose without knowing it; and, more than that, think philosophy (especially the metaphysics of knowledge-of-the-external-world) in fits of absent-mindedness.

Not very far beneath the surface of these superficial confusions lie the strands of old and classical intellectual disputation. The wayward journey could take us from Plato and Bishop Berkeley to Bertrand Russell and Wittgenstein. Flotsam and jetsam about objectivity and subjectivity, confounded with bits of nominalism and idealism, might float into view. A reference to I.A. Richards would turn up; after all he had pondered *The Meaning of Meaning*. Almost as unavoidable and inevitable: a quote from Sir A. J. ("Freddie") Ayer who, in his day, had popularized the message from Vienna of "Logical Positivism": its illogical negativism made incorrigible skeptics of a whole Anglo-Saxon generation raised in doubt as to whether words in even the most simple of sentences meant anything at all. The aforementioned world service of news and its correct interpretation (BBC, 1 June 2002) instructed its listeners who might well have been auditing rather than perceiving: "Perception is more important than fact." If perceptions are illusions and facts can be faked, where does this leave us?

In the end–and, hopefully, we are nearing it, if imperceptibly–perceptions have left the field of 20/20 vision and its optical clarities. Perception has become a weapon of argument in which what *you* see is real and true and actually out there, and what the *other* perceiver *mis*perceives is as unreal as a mirage, as untrue as an error, as insubstantial as non-existent connections. A widespread mistake is, thus, taken to be based on shared or common perceptions; and nothing could be more commendable than mounting a campaign against it (and them). Who perceived that the new *New Yorker*, under the innovative editorship of a flashy English editor, Ms. Tina Brown, would prove to be a journalistic as well as commercial success? In August 1996 she announced that not only circulation but advertising as well had increased; and after four years of a "new editorial formula," the famous weekly was well on its way to becoming profitable for its owners. It had been a time that had tried her soul. As the *New Yorker*'s president, a man named Florio, remarked: "many people in this industry treated Tina a bit like a schoolgirl." Well, she was now graduating with honors, and upsetting the critics who had been living sentimentally in the past with Harold Ross, S. J. Perelman, Frank Sullivan, A. J. Liebling, Edmund Wilson, James Thurber, and other greats of by-gone days. She remained faithful, as she put it, to "the cerebral material" and won a new readership at the same time. She was proud of going up-market and down-market at the same time. "It does go against common perception, I know, but who cares about common perception anyway." It was indeed a common misperception, and perhaps that is what she meant to say; but no matter, "cerebral" readers would have gotten the message, whatever the orthography. In any case, her days at the *New Yorker* were numbered when the perceived profits were now seen to be losses.

The only real solution to the problem of perceptions which are seen to be misperceptions, or anything else optically arguable, is for them to become...imperceptible; and then all of us can go on to take a fresh look. Thus, in the quarrel between the tennis players and the U.S. Open authorities in the summer of 1996, the seedings seemed to be tampered with and the manipulation was discernible. One top player (Thomas Muster of Austria) charged that "It's like cheating!," and the sportswriter added, "That perception is what irritated others too." He thought there could be reconciliation by going back to the system whereby players were seeded according to their official world rankings: "All anyone wanted is for the tournament to be conducted by the luck of the draw, not by any perceived plan. That's why the U.S. Tennis Association opted for a re-draw."[9]

If "to best" and "to worst" can mean the same thing–and "hot jazz" can be *cool, man*–why cannot perception also mean its opposite, *misperception?* As a consequence of the synonymity of antonyms, the clear sighting of things becomes astigmatic, blurred almost to the point of delusiveness.

On the occasion of the Atlanta Olympics there was some surprise and dismay at the extent of the commercialization of athletics due to the exclusive funding of the games *via* business sponsors (Coca Cola, IBM, et al.). This led, as the *New York Times* reported, to "a mad scramble to find ways of standing out amid that advertising overload." The trade publication *Advertising Age* declared the "biggest and most lavishly sponsored Olympiad" to be "the marketing event of the century." Certainly it was a field day for advertisers and salesmen, and among other triumphs they successfully figured out "how to fend off the so-called ambush marketers that exploit Olympic and athletic imagery to create perceptions among consumers of official ties that do not exist."[10]

If Olympic shoppers misperceive non-existent messages it costs only spending money; rather more troubling are the misperceptions involved in race relations where whole peoples can be short-changed in highly charged situations. In Argentina, for example, there has been a resurgence of old-time anti-Semitism, and its Jewish citizens have been recently in much danger. Some blame was put on the former minister of justice who had belonged in his youth to a pro-Hitler fascist organization. In a dispatch from Buenos Aires, the *Washington Post* correspondent described how he saw the matter: "The minister, Rodolfo Barra, dismissed his association as a youthful indiscretion. While he eventually resigned, the perception that he was 'forced out by the Jews' produced a new volley of anti-Semitic attacks." Well, was he or wasn't he "forced out"? And who perceived it so? A newspaper reader's elementary curiosity demands a little more information on the subject: for if it was indeed a misperception, then the proper reading of the events includes the familiar and tell-tale stereotype of blaming the Jews for everything. It is all rather less sinister if Señor Barra had been dropped in a normal governmental cabinet re-shuffle. How did the *Post*'s man in Buenos Aires really and truly perceive the matter?

The construction of the sentence and the use of inverted commas suggest that there, once again, perception means misperception. Or could it be (in the phrase used, on the same day, by a liberal London newspaper) that the "retributive Jewish lobby" had struck again? As I say, none are so myopic who only get to see perceptions.[11]

The unfortunate phrase about a "Jewish lobby" was also used by that otherwise unexceptionable stalwart of the *Evening Standard*, Alexander Walker, writing about the "Nazi" films of Leni Riefenstahl. I imagine he didn't intend it pejoratively but only wanted to suggest that he agreed with "the Jews" in thinking that those famous Third *Reich* documentaries were more propaganda than art.[12]

I have been illustrating what happens when "*perception*" becomes fashionable, and turns into a fancy vogue word. It becomes widely serviceable in a continuous play of distortion, in a kind of a game of blind man's bluff. Another example of a perceptive remark by a Pacific-rim banker on the precarious financial situation in a Hong Kong about to be taken over by the mainland Chinese, casting a shadow over loans, mortgages, investment capital: "People don't trust going to the mainland. You have a perception of guarantees here. You don't have guarantees really, but there is that perception."[13] Perception, then–from Hong Kong to Atlanta, from London to Buenos Aires–is about what isn't there; and being perceptive, *nolens volens*, is tantamount to being gullible, foolish, credulous if not duplicitous. For when erratic illusion is reality, then self-deception is something palpable and straightforward, with perception willfully transforming everything in sight.

The phrase received its "last communion" recently at a Mafia funeral when the Italo-American community in New York was wracked by argument–what was myth and what was reality in the vast literary industry of telling Godfather stories in print and in film? Peter Maas, a well-informed crime reporter in New York before he turned to writing a half-dozen books on the subject, argued that the fictional *Godfather* was "myth-making at its most compelling." It was a saga which contained everything that concerned and excited us: "family, romance, betrayal, power, lust, greed, legitimacy, even salvation." As a chronicler of that saga he does not function as a critical historian, skeptical of old anecdotes, disdainful of new embellishments. He is less concerned with the truth about the crimes than with what the criminals thought (and said) they were doing as they played out the melodrama of money and murder. As Maas writes in one of his latest portraits of a Mafia hero and renegade (*Underboss*, 1997, p. 342), "Never mind that loyalty and honor played no part in the actual Cosa Nostra. Perceived reality was what mattered." *Perceived reality*–if it never existed it could not have been perceived; if it did not happen to be real, or what had really happened, then it could have had no part of reality, perceived or not. Alas for the poor phrase...it still had, when last heard of, a lot of life in it.

Two writers in the *New York Times* tried to give it a proper burial. They were professional lexicographers and had compiled and annotated *The American Heritage Dictionary of American Quotations* (1997). And they also collected what they call *"anti-quotations"*–aphorisms, quips, comments and phrases that elicit such derision that they can never be used seriously again. For example, President Clinton's laconic explanation of one of the White House's financial scandals: "*Mistakes were made.*" So "passive-evasive" nobody will dare to be again.

Pride of place in the *Times*' collection of such anti-quotes–how wise and witty a newspaper can be in moments of self-criticism!–is given to the reply it recorded which was made by the FBI when it was asked why the Bureau had spent so much time and so much money refuting rumors about the TWA Flight 800 which had crashed off Long Island. Had it been "downed"? Had a mysterious missile sent it exploding in flames into the waters of the North Atlantic? The G-man said: "Perception is reality."[14] Were the FBI principle ever to catch on in all police inquiries, most of the world's detective work would be devoted to such "perceived realities," that is, murders that were never committed, robberies that never took place, arson that never saw a flame. It would be a surreal world of the blind pursuing the invisible and the mute speaking up for the deaf. Any old gun would do for incriminating evidence so long as it was not perceived smoking.

Readers are, I surmise, perceptibly being wearied. I will file-and-forget my archive of "entries" in all these decades and land briefly in our mid-1990s for a quick look. Perception is still marching on; it continues to have its say, "*filling the air* [to borrow a Miltonic phrase] *with barbaric dissonance.*"

In a particularly confused column in the *Washington Post* in January 1995 (*IHT*, 7-8 January 1995), Stephen Rosenfeld does a 700-word post-mortem on Cold War Intelligence. It was, as he can now reveal, only a game between Their Spooks and Our Spooks. All the players are rated as politically defi-cient in a kind of amoral sub-IQ equivalence of America's CIA and Russia's KGB. They manipulated, and we bluffed; we pretended, and they huffed and puffed. But, in the end, Rosenfeld quotes an authority to the effect that the KGB threw more boomerangs, claiming that "the games of deception, disinformation and distraction designed by the *KGB* masterminds had a deleterious effect on global stability. They certainly contributed to the perception in Washington of expansive Soviet ambitions." Once again we are thrust into the basic se-mantic quandary: Did Washington perceive a genuine threat of totalitarian expansion? Or was it only a perception of pretense in a looking-glass war, a blurred glimpse of a great game? I am afraid that the historians of the Cold War will have to be holding their breath until the doors of uncleansed perception are pushed wide open.

Abroad, the "blur" is often spotted by foreign correspondents, but since the English share a common language the elusive American usage tends to get away, to spread and scatter quickly. In Los Angeles, the correspondent for the *Daily Telegraph* in London, writing about the forlorn comeback of O. J. Simpson (trying to mix "news and entertainment" and trade in on his notori-ety), observes that "L.A. is a town where perception is often mistaken for reality."[15] And London is a town where the local dictionary, Longman's, still defines perception as "keen natural understanding...something quickly no-ticed and understood" (*Longman's Dictionary of Contemporary English*, 1978, p. 805). Reality is longing to be perceived; and if mistakes are made, how much of the error can be blamed on a word?

"Perception" here–even among English journalists–becomes shorthand for faulty perception, and covers any error from an astigmatic blur to a political prejudice. The *Telegraph* report from Los Angeles suggested that both the public's perception of O. J. Simpson and O. J.'s perception of the public were both imperceptible to keen observers who "notice and understand": He is totally living in a land of make-believe if he thinks the public perceives him as they did before....After the verdict, blacks celebrated, the majority seeing Simpson as a hero. But that perception seems no longer to be so widely held."

It could, of course, only be that I have grown out of touch with my own language. I never understood what my old friend Jimmy Baldwin really meant when he tried to justify "the Fire Next Time" with the prediction that the whites were "preparing a genocide" of the blacks. Nor did I understand a word of what Amiri Baraka (a.k.a. LeRoi Jones), sitting next to the late James Baldwin at a Columbia University forum, was trying to say. (It was November 1980, and Reagan had just been elected president.)

When I was writing *"Kill white people, kill white people, kill white people"*–and I wrote a lot of poems like that—everybody here read my poems. I wrote a lot of "Kill-white-people-immediately-right-now" poems: "Do not pass, go kill 'em at once." Now, I'll tell you something interesting. I had less trouble getting published then. But when I said that the ruling class of this country consists of six-tenths of one per cent, you know, and they are white, then I began to have difficulty.

The crisis is this: "White" does not any longer mean what it meant when I was born 56 years ago. Neither does the word "black" mean what it meant then. The principal underlying vocabulary was vanished. If England is no longer the centre of the world, it is no longer important to be white. The vocabulary that I'm speaking of comes for us, we the black Americans, comes out of that extraordinary holocaust, that diaspora. Despised till today by history, despised by the Western world, despised by people who think they are white, but that voyage across all those oceans has created not only a new black person, but a new white person, too.

I will tell you this, my friends: The present Administration in Washington is a symptom of the end of the white world as we have known it.[16]

The usual prizes for any funky or feisty explication of this flaky text, or indeed any home-made perception supportive of what it all really means. Etymology rules, ok?

A decade later there were, as I have mentioned, the same constituent elements of a confusion-worse-confounded with a "conspiracy" (1) to inflict a "genocide" in California (by the CIA's allegedly spreading crack-cocaine in the black ghettoes); (2) to burn down black community churches in the Deep South; and (3) generally to maintain the traditional bias of white discrimination in American society. In the 1990s only the names and incidents have changed. The suspicion of a vast and sinister racial conspiracy remains endemic, and neither nationwide skepticism nor denial from high government officials and in most of the media seem to provide an effective antidote. A highly charged vocabulary continues to distort characteristically the whole "communication crisis" on this explosive issue. As an etymological emblem the usage of the word *"perception,"* as I have been documenting, can be found unfailingly close to the heart of the matter.

Aspects of the California crack story lingered on, since the connection between drug-sale profits and CIA-funded military operations in Nicaragua in the 1980s had *some* evidence to support it (and might have more, after future research). But the U.S. press' counter-reaction–in part, to be sure, mixed with the chagrin of not having paid sufficient attention to what was happening on their beat–did subvert the ghastly notion that the California black community had been deliberately targeted for harm and, in some nightmares, for genocide. The original story with its sinister implications had reverberated throughout the African-American communities from extremist Farrakhan *Nation Islam* followers to moderate black commentators.* One of the latter, Carl T. Rowan,

---

*   For an analysis of the *San Jose Mercury News'* "journalistic scoop" in which a
     knowledgeable media critic contends (convincingly, I think) that the paper's sensa-
     tional stories about Nicaraguan drug dealers in a CIA plot were "wildly exaggerated"

speculated: "If this is true, then millions of black lives have been ruined and America's jails and prisons are now clogged with young African-Americans because of a cynical plot." It was not true. Still, the ruin was real...even if there was no plot, only the tragic drama of vice, greed, and a scourge of medical consequences. For a minority that had just taken an apology from the U.S. President for the grisly medical experiments on Negroes in the 1930s (the "Tuskegee" affair in which black V.D. (venereal disease) patients were injected "experimentally" with a variety of drugs, often fatally), the conviction that the crack epidemic in California was a calculated assault on its racial existence would die hard, would never go away.[17]

Gary Webb of the *Mercury News* had won a Journalist-of-the-Year prize for his "Dark Alliance" series which swept like wild fire through the U.S. media– until the counter-critique in the *New York Times*, the *Washington Post*, the *Boston Globe* and other "mainstream" newspapers damped it out. There were, subsequently, even angry moves in the newspaper world to "strip" Webb of his award as had happened in the Janet Cooke case (see my "Janet Cooke & the Color of Truth," above). Most major U.S. newspapers tried their belated best to follow up on the "genocidal" implications but found them groundless.

In reporting recent (1996) incidents of racially-biased discrimination in the "corporate culture" the *New York Times* touches upon the problem but hardly moves it forward": To deal with discrimination you have to recognize it. For many people perception is reality. If you are perceived to be discriminatory in your practices, in effect you are."[18] For many other observers perceptions are also *sounds*; and presumably what you see you can also *hear* (and, probably, *feel*), thus making a proper mishmash out of almost all of our sensory powers– as in the definition of SPLAT: "the approximate sound perceived upon stopping a wet snowball with one's ear."[19]

Between audible feelings and palpable illusions falls an ominous splat over the complex of comprehending racial conflicts. The necessarily difficult path to objectivity and a true picture is befogged by a nebulous vocabulary which persists in clouding over the difference between perception and misperception, between astigmatism and accurate sighting, between delusions and demonstrable truths.[20]

The nature of the misdemeanor and the general malpractice here is not merely confined to the ken of grammarians and, say, authors of "guides to modern usage" like the late Sir Kingsley Amis. In his posthumous book, *The King's English* (1997), he reminds us that the Latin roots of *perceive* indicate that it meant to *grasp thoroughly.* Although, as he knew, Latin roots of English

---

– that "the weight of the evidence was over-stated" and did "not provide conclusive proof for the sweeping conclusions" – see Peter Kornbluh, "Anatomy of a Story: Crack, the Contras, and the CIA: The Storm over 'Dark Alliance,'" *Columbia Journalism Review*, January-February 1997, pp. 33-39, and its follow-up, *CJR*, May-June 1997, pp. 8-9.

words are notoriously often bad guides to meaning, not seldom, as here, they may "remind the user of what the English word once unequivocally meant."

> To perceive something, or that something is so, used to mean simply to *take in* with the senses of the mind; you would perceive a tree on the horizon or the importance of heredity. The word is almost a synonym for *see*, except that a degree of special effort or special ability is implied. But whatever you *perceived* was understood to be really there.

Amis sensed that the new meaning began creeping in during the 1970s. What was perceived no longer had to be really there. I can recall one lunchtime at the Garrick Club bar, one corner of which was presided over by Sir Kingsley, his exploding when he overheard another barfly going about about "perceptions of the Labour Party." This was not only wrong, but "uneven," "temporary," "wishy-washy," none of which (as he reminds us) could have been intended by the great Samuel Johnson when he said to an acquaintance, "Sir, I perceive you are a vile Whig." The other chap *was* what he was perceived to be. Vile. Truly depraved. Everybody could (and should) know it.

Contrast this with what a member of President Clinton's first-term cabinet did, or did not, perceive in an agitated session at a 1995 Congressional hearing. The secretary of labor's competence in economics was being rudely challenged; his accuracy was impugned with offensive challenges to produce "Evidence! Evidence!" It was an altogether unruly affair, and Robert Reich described it all in his memoir, *Locked in the Cabinet* (1996). But one reviewer took the trouble to check the details in the transcript of the Congressional hearing in question. Unfortunately, "the heck of a scene" just never happened. The videotape showed the interrogation to be very decorous and polite, with no angry words or other agitations transpiring: "Reich appears to have fabricated much of this episode for dramatic effect....He has replaced a dull, earnestly wonkish hearing with a Hollywood script in which a mean Republican hammers a decent Democrat." So ran the reading, or the sighting, of the actual film. But Robert Reich had heard it and seen it differently, defending himself thus: "It's a memoir. It's not investigative journalism. I'm not a journalist. As I said on the first page, these are my perceptions. This is the way I experienced it." In the old days, such experience would be related to *traumatic nightmares* or at least to *fantasies*. Such perceptions would, as ocular phenomena, be swiftly put (as we have) into the same optical class (as we have) as myopia, astigmatism, and indeed delusional hallucinations.

This is, clearly, more than the "muddle" that Kingsley Amis was afraid of: as a melancholy Englishman dismayed by transatlantic buzz-phrases, saddened by "the departure of a once-useful word." It has to do with the relativization of objective truth: it is about the democratic legitimacy of all viewpoints ranging from simple prejudices to sheer phantasmagoria. What it amounts to is the absolutization of everybody's right to "tell it like it is" even if it ain't.[21]

15

Hillary, and Getting the Perception Right

The ultimate victim of the blindness which is mere perception was, at the moment, the wife of the president of the United States, and probably (at this proof-reading) the newly elected Senator from New York.

With her instinct for the verbal follies of the day, the president's wife verges on a kind of acrobatic splitting of infinitives, as in this remark she made to the press in Australia (November 1996): "'There's really no way to escape the politics of one's time if you're in that position than to just totally withdraw,' she said. 'Perhaps have a bag over your head when you come out into public'" ("Amid Fun in Sydney, Clintons Show Strain," *NYT/IHT*, 22 November 1996, p. 6). A small bag of ungrammatical niceties could have done very well. After several turbulent years in which she actively shared in the erratic performance of the Clinton administration in the White House, Hillary Rodham Clinton has confessed to be wobbling, stumbling, falling flat on her face: "While accepting the blame for her unfavorable public image, she said she was still bewildered by perceptions of her."

In Washington, in a discussion with a group of women writers, she empha-sized how "surprised" she was "at the way people seem to perceive me." Is it merely a seeming perception of an image? But, when the meeting was over she had to face the question whether the problem was only an optical one of apparent apparitions. Could it be that the critics, the voters, the People, were incensed at real mistakes, and no imagism about them? Weren't there genuine snafus issuing out of doughy half-baked notions? She did look back for a moment with a burst of candor: "I would have done a lot of things differently, but I am confident I would have made different mistakes."

This is admirable self-doubt in the skeptical tradition of Karl Popper (who paid classic tribute to the role of mistakes in the course of human progress). But who will vote for, or have confidence in, a tribune who confidently prom-ises yet another round of dismal errors?

This is Hillary Clinton's problem, not ours. Ours is the vocabulary of poli-tics which may, under some happy circumstances, carry the burden of wit and wisdom. "Naive and dumb" are her own words for her political record. But she still has hopes for some kind of "image makeover." From now on out there will be, "hopefully," no "lack of politically savvy advice." She will be "figuring out the dynamics." Her view that "results speak for themselves" will win out in the end. But what if the "results" are based on her going on inexorably to make those "different mistakes"? Politics are a puzzlement, and the American words don't quite fit into the little vertical and horizontal squares which spell out real meanings and acceptable alternatives.

And who will instruct her in the wiles of *savvy dynamics?* And will the White House train or plane stop somewhere–as in the famous U.S. Air Force One's pause at the L.A. airport, to give time for the *friseur* to do the president's haircut–long enough to enable the First Lady to get cued into the real low-down? The moment is right: "At first you are sort of stunned...." But really, you know, she is kind of ready: "I didn't get this whole image creation thing. I see what it can do but I'm not sure I get it."*

The Washington perception is that, slowly but surely, she will indeed be getting it and, in the fullness of time, sort of "getting there."

In point of cruel fact, the confessional was altogether botched. In the week that followed, the White House was involved yet again in a petty wrangle as to exactly who had "leaked" the secret "off-the-record" chitchat with the Washington press corps (or a half-dozen selected correspondents, all women). The *Washington Post*'s representative insisted that she had asked for approval, and had received it, for publishing the "bits" that appeared in the paper the next day. Hillary denied any such thing.

So, in the end, the First Lady had indeed proved herself capable of making an honest, self-deprecating gesture, a winning move to break a losing streak; but she had, with a pinch of the old pride, made the mistake of trying to keep it confidential. A proverb has it: If you work both sides of the street, don't expect to find both of them sunny.

The current seductiveness of the sight-and-sound of *perception* still suggests a touch of elegance, that it is still pleasant to the ear and impressive on the page. More than that, it must have in its reinforced popularity a certain intellectual flexibility as one of its hidden semantic properties. If, at the one end of the spectrum, our perceptive observer can perceive with incontrovertible 20/20 accuracy, at the other extreme his perception wallows in subjectivity, blurring into illusion, error, and fallacy.

It is almost as if its career as a buzzword in up-to-the-minute journalism had a secret reserve derived from the long Western tradition of disputation over cognition, or over whether what one *thinks* one sees is *really* out there. Plato

---

*   The quotations from Hillary Rodham Clinton are from the *New York Times*, *Newsweek* , and the *IHT* (11 January 1995).

registered only shadowy resemblances; and if there were indeed serious discrepancies between the real and the apparent, then Blake (and, following him, Aldous Huxley) thought "the doors of perception" could be "cleansed." Thus, *perception* has been able to incorporate a standard meaning and also its opposite. The variations we have been documenting evince an uncanny adaptability, and what we can only call a transmogrification of a word has still many meanings to go. We can no longer be surprised when *perception* can turn up perceptible bits of reality as well as imperceptible insightful interpretations–both of which challenge those erratic misperceptions which are astigmatic or myopic–for it can lead the observer to see anything whatsoever and understand nothing at all.

A thoughtful foreign-policy analyst of the *Washington Post* recently made an effort to analyze the "lawyerly mind" of President Clinton. In view of the legal melodrama (impeachment and all that) which was being played out on the American stage, it was increasingly hard to pick and choose among the major players and their adversarial roles. Yet, as Jim Hoagland put it, "In this theater, perception produces its own reality."[1] These means- or "mode"-of-production guarantees that a thousand and more blooming realities will emerge, like Mao's hundred flowers, blighted and short-lived, almost all of them hidden from true recognition. When photographs do not represent accurate pictures and words are not reliable references to fact, how will the media ever mediate between the citizen in society and the historic news-events breaking so fast around him?

Part 4

A Journalist Gets Serious: In P.G. Wodehouse's "Noo Yawk"

*" Here he had touched the
realities. There was something
worth fighting for."*
—P.G. Wodehouse, *"Psmith
Journalist" (1915)*

*"The fact remains that there is not a single
genuine newspaper man,
done in the grand manner, in the whole range
of American fiction...no adequate
portrait of the journalist as a whole, from his
beginnings as a romantic young reporter to his
finish as a Babbitt, correct in every idea and as
hollow as a jug. Here, I believe is genuine
tragedy. Here is the matter that enters
into all fiction of the first class. Here is a
human character in disintegration – the
primary theme of every sound novelist from
Fielding to Zola and from Turgenev
to Joseph Conrad. I know of no American who
starts from a higher level of aspiration than a
journalist. He is in his first phase, genuinely
romantic. He plans to be both an artist and a
moralist – a master of lovely words
and a merchant of sound ideas. He ends,
commonly, as the most depressing
jackass in his community – that is, if his career
goes on to what is called success. He becomes
the repository of all its worst delusions and
superstitions. He becomes the darling of all its
frauds and idiots, and the despair of all its
honest men. He belongs to a good club, and
the initiation fee was his soul."*
—H.L. Mencken *(1926)[1]*

16

The Birth of a Crusader

A literary critic, pondering sadly on the state of the English language and the waywardness of contemporary prose, recently attributed the malaise to (among other sinister causes) the lingering popularity of P.G. Wodehouse. The point was notable. The elegant artificiality of the prose that was meant to transcribe the conversations and the aristocratic complications in the life of Bertie Wooster and his man Jeeves. Echoing an unreal class society of yester-year, it only added to the unnatural stiffness and inauthenticity of our current linguistic usage, especially in the parts of the world where English is a second language and P.G. Wodehouse, in dog-eared copies, is a by-word.

I first took this to be a small joke, a naughty witticism at the expense of a very funny man in his time; but no, it was serious, and I do not object at all. I do not subscribe to the sub-intellectual notion that humor is not good for anything but a laugh.

Nothing appears to be more pernicious among some light-hearted spirits than to try to be serious about a joke. Arthur Koestler once tried it in an ambitious book and got the punchlines regularly wrong. Freud wrote a psychopathology of everyday wit, and was in turn forever subjected to analysis-in-depth himself. Max Eastman explored the enjoyment of laughter, and the most memorable thing about it was the infectious dust jacket featuring the handsome silver-haired author in twinkle-eyed open-mouthed hilarity.

No, if the interpretation of dreams is a nightmare, the discussion of humor is no laughing matter. A recent "structural analysis" of Evelyn Waugh's novel *Put Out More Flags* and a scholarly screed on the comic *Three Men in a Boat* provoked the literary editor of the *Daily Telegraph* into a grim polemic. Critics were excommunicated, the whole genre interdicted: "There must be humourless idiots [David Holloway wrote] who are waiting for an annotated P.G. Wodehouse which will give the source of every quotation that he uses or bends for his own purposes."

Well, there is a lot of source-spotting in Frances Donaldson's biography of P.G. Wodehouse, and she too gets her wrists slapped by yet another proctor:

"[She] tells you all you need to know about Plum [Christopher Warman, writing in *The Times*]. Too much perhaps, for the discussion of his techniques of writing, and the reasons for finding his work funny, for example, almost leave the reader wondering whether it can be funny after all."

And yet I must confess that when the other day, I was chuckling through the Wodehouse Penguin of *Psmith Journalist* (first published in 1915), I was overwhelmed by just this humorless affliction; the longing for an explanation, a bit of esoteric research, for a footnote or two. Those Psmith stories were always something special in the Wodehouse *oeuvre*, and fans often regretted their early abandonment in his writing career. Lady Donaldson notes certain qualities of "intellect...unWodehousian toughness...a kind of ferocity" which are quite unlike anything found in the later books. Psmith in America is especially problematical, for Wodehouse was fascinated by New York, and spent his first Fleet Street pay-cheques on getting to Manhattan. There he tapped a rich vein of social–and verbal–detail which almost made him a documentary or even a "committed" writer, practically disorienting his light-hearted and light-minded strengths as a fiction writer.

Before his entrancing decision to take on a manner "more English" than any other writer, he was perhaps tempted in his room in Manhattan's old Brevoort Hotel on 5th Avenue to try his hand at being "very Noo Yawk." His biographer feels certain that "by now (1915) Wodehouse knew where his real talents lay," and that "Psmith was a bridge...between the youthful period...and the humorous books, with their established castes [casts?] of characters and unchanging format."*

All the more reason, then, to know more about Psmith's American adventures, which revolved around a journalistic crusade against intolerable slum conditions being maintained by crooked property speculators. No sign of Jeeves here.

Make Mine Manhattan

So, without the crack of a smile, I found myself forced to wonder what Wodehouse's New York was really like. How original was his journalistic inspiration, and how pertinent is it–in what his New York paper said, and how it said it–to our problem of "newspaper culture"?

---

*   Frances Donaldson, *P.G. Wodehouse: The Authorized Biography* (1982), p. 91. See also the books on PGW by Benny Green (1981), and David A. Jasen (rev. ed., 1981).

All in all, he understood New York better than, say, Berlin. On the famous "Berlin broadcasts" during World War II (first published in *Encounter*, Oct. and Nov. 1954), see the controversial articles by George Orwell (in *Dickens, Dali & Others*); Malcolm Muggeridge (in *Tread Softly for You Tread on My Jokes*); and in *Encounter* by M (i.e. Richard Mayne) and Ian Sproat (June-July and Sept.-Oct. 1982).

For some it evidently makes no difference, for novels are supposed to capture a truer, or higher, or deeper reality. Who knows, or cares, whether Proust got that evening exactly right at the Duchesse de Guermantes,' or whether Joyce in Zurich had been keeping up with Dublin argot? How could Thomas Mann, writing his *Doktor Faustus* in Californian exile, know how wartime Germans spoke when making their pact with the devil?

Does it matter? Aesthetically, surely not. Literal truth is what we demand only from our historians, not from our novelists. Still, who is there with mind so dulled as not, on occasion, to entertain a certain curiosity about the knowledge of the external world as it interweaves itself through the plots of our storytellers?

An impassioned reader of Balzac like Professor Georg Lukács was absolutely convinced–without ever having looked at any other evidence (documents, statistics, financial records)–that the pageant of a "declining peasantry" and a "rising bourgeoisie" was so accurate as to dovetail scientifically with all the theorems of Marxism-Leninism. No such luck with Wodehouse. And yet on almost every page of the New York adventures of the journalist Psmith in 1915 one is tantalized by the question of how things really were: in the famous German historian's phrase, *wie es eigentlich gewesen ist.* Is the young Wodehouse, "yearn-ing for America" (as he writes in his *Over Seventy*), telling it like it is?

I was stopped on the very first page where the preface explains that very little was "invented," that "most of the incidents in this story are based on actual happenings." Perhaps. But surely what we need for that scholarly annotated edition of Sir Pelham Grenville Wodehouse, full of fine footnotes and ample appendices, are some comparative statistics: "There are several million inhabitants of New York. Not all of them eke out a precarious livelihood by murdering one another." How true. And still one wants to know how many, and how often: for that alarmed sense of mass mayhem which one gets nowadays in New York could not really be–or could it?–an invariable constant.

"The conditions of life in New York are so different from those of London," and indeed they have so remained: more murders are committed in N.Y.C. per annum than in the whole of the U.K. Does nothing change throughout a century? Why do we hear so little about "murderous Manhattan" in Henry James' otherwise marvellously perceptive pages about New York in his *American Scene*?

There are social observers who are persuaded that whatever is actually happening is constantly reflected in the same preconceived emotions of an intellectual class who attend to the register of urban sins (and virtues)...and who see to it that it always adds up to something unprecedented and outrageous. Irving Kristol once scandalized his *New York Times* read-ers by arguing that seventy-five or a hundred years ago America's liberals were protesting as vociferously against racist tensions, traffic jams, urban decay, and street-corner violence as they do today. Are things always the same, the more they change? Does nothing get better, nothing worse?

Wodehouse is here writing of a pre-World War I America:

> In New York one may find every class of paper which the imagination can conceive. Every grade of society is catered for. If an Esquimau came to New York, the first thing he would find on the bookstalls in all probability would be the *Blubber Magazine*, or some similar production written by Esquimaux for Esquimaux. Everybody reads in New York, and reads all the time. The New Yorker peruses his favourite newspaper while he is being jammed into a crowded compartment on the subway or leaping like an antelope into a moving street car.

I suppose the U.S. Publishers Association could provide us with a table of comparative statistics, breaking down American sales, reading habits, and specialist publications. For my own part I found on one of my recent visits to New York an announcement from a Queens' publishing house which caters to "orthodox Jewish homosexual subscribers," that a new magazine would be appearing to appeal to "gay Black converts." Cool, man; cool like an Esquimau.

Of Cops and Subways: Red-Hot Stuff

Taken altogether, Wodehouse's vignettes of New York around 1914-15 are vivid and in-cisive, and the language of the day (I take it, on faith, to be such) rendered with a keen ear and a careful pen. This, and a curious socio-political element (those slummy crime-controlled tenements), quite belies the later Wodehouse formula which, as he put it, was "I believe there are two ways of writing novels. One is mine, making a sort of musical comedy without music and ignoring real life altogether; the other is going right deep down into life and not caring a damn." But the point of *Psmith Journalist* is that the Old Etonian Psmith learned, while still retaining his monocle, to care a damn–that "deep down" there *was* "something worth fighting for."

Psmith was one of those people who are content to accept most of the happenings of life in an airy spirit of tolerance. Life had been more or less of a game with him up till now. In his previous encounters with those with whom fate had brought him in contact there had been little at stake. The prize of victory had been merely a comfortable feeling of having had the best of a battle of wits; the penalty of defeat nothing worse than the discomfort of having failed to score. But this tenement business was different. Here he had touched the realities. There was something worth fighting for. His lot had been cast in pleasant places, and the sight of actual raw misery had come home to him with an added force from that circumstance. He was fully aware of the risks that he must run.

If this sounds not unlike the young affluent Manhattan publisher of the *Village Voice* finding a cause in the radical idealism of the 1960s, it was because P.G. somehow got it all uncannily right. Here is Psmith's credo when he first takes over his New York paper and decides to change its editorial course:

> briefly, my idea is that *Cosy Moments* should become red hot stuff. I could wish its tone to be such that the public will wonder why we do not print it on asbestos. We must chronicle all the live events of the day, murders, fires, and the like, in a manner which will make our readers' spines thrill. Above all, we must be the guardians of the People's rights. We must be a searchlight, showing up the dark spot in the souls of those who would endeavour in any way to do the *People* in the eye. We must detect the wrongdoer, and deliver him such a series of resentful biffs that he will abandon his little games and become a model citizen.

There were at least two daily newspapers in New York which in the past dozen years have remodelled their editorial course along lines which would have pleased Psmith. (The *P* is silent: "Like the tomb. Compare such words as ptarmigan, psalm, and phthisis.")

Had he gone on, Psmith might have become the Joseph Pulitzer of the day, which is only to say that Wodehouse some eighty years ago managed to sense in Manhattan that paradoxical mix of civic alarm and metropolitan pride which is recognizable even today in the "Big Apple" of Mayor Ed Koch and Rudy Giuliani and their successors. Here is Wodehouse's vignette of the Subway (that fearful underground which is currently being "improved" so that graffiti on trains and stations can in future be easily washed off):

> Conversation on the subway is impossible. The ingenious gentlemen who con-structed it started with the object of making it noisy. Not ordinarily noisy, like a ton of coal falling on to a sheet of tin, but really noisy. So they fashioned the pillars of thin steel, and the sleepers of thin wood, and loosened all the nuts, and now a Subway train in motion suggests a prolonged dynamite explosion blended with the voice of some great catastrophe.

Evidently he never lost his affectionate tone (it is there in his late letters), although in his final emigration he hardly ever ventured forth from his ocean-side house on Long Island. Unlike the hard local men of angry protest literature he knew that there were "two New Yorks."

> One is a modern, well-policed city, through which one may walk from end to end without encountering adventure. The other is a city as full of sinister in-trigue, of whisperings and conspiracies, of battle, murder, and sudden death in dark by-ways, as any town of medieval Italy. Given certain conditions, anything may happen to any one in New York.

How "well-policed" New York may have been then, or now, one has to leave to the an-notations of the scholarly sociologists. They will also have to record whether police strategy and tactics have changed much when caught up in the altercations of gangland wars or ethnic riots of more recent years.

The behaviour of the New York policeman in affairs of this kind is based on principles of the soundest practical wisdom. The unthinking man would rush in and attempt to crush the combat in its earliest and fiercest stages. The New York policeman, knowing the importance of his own safety, and the significance of the gangsman's, permits the opposing forces to hammer each other into a certain distaste for battle, and then, when both sides have begun to have enough of it, rushes in himself and clubs everything in sight. It is an admirable process in its results, but is sure rather than swift.

"*Gangsman*"? The Dictionary (Webster; Random House; Partridge) lists *gangster* as common twentieth-century usage, and one finds it of course in the Manhattan pages of O. Henry, Ring Lardner, Damon Runyon, Mark Hellinger.* One wonders whether young Plum always got the word, phrase, inflection, slangy innovation quite right. Here were stranger charac-ters than, dash it, the Jeeves and Bertie Woosters to come.

I suspect that his unusually good ear just missed the off-color *double entendre* in words like *lay* and *hump* (pp. 65, 100). Would a New York landlord refer to the eviction or dispossession of a rent-due tenant by saying, "*Then it's outside for theirs*"(p. 114)? I take his word for it that drunk was "*to get gay*"(pp. 148, 154) and that "*a real skiddoo*" (p. 146) was something different from its more familiar "23-skiddoo" usage. But would a N.Y. boxer praise a newspaper's muckracking articles by saying "*They're to the good*"?

Wodehouse hesitates sometimes, and uncertainly puts quote marks around drawing a good "gate" in a reference to box-office receipts; and he takes refuge in the recondite in explaining what a *sitz-redacteur* was (and I may well have learned it in Manhattan in the same sort of German émigré printing-plant that he did). But he is soon again his confident self with gats, coons, dagoes, jeans (as early as that), simoleons, and the like. He confidently lets Psmith say, "*This act is going to be a scream*"; and, having learned fast, Psmith ventures the remark that crooked politicians were finished because "the right plan would be to put the complete kybosh (if I may use the expression)" on their chances.

---

*   The Burchfield *Supplement* (1972) to the *Oxford English Dictionary* cites first American newspaper usages of 1896 and 1911. Wodehouse is quoted for "gangster" from his *Blandings Castle* of 1935.

"*Gangsman*" the *O.E.D.* records as "a dock porter" (1793) and as "one who has charge of a gang of workmen" (1863). Evidently Wodehouse brought a lot of verbal baggage with him across the Atlantic.

17

Facts, From Homer to Kafka
(Elmore Leonard)

Verisimilitude and Fictions

An additional remark on such expressions, their origins, authenticity, and recognizability. For an issue has been raised which, at a rather more complex intellectual level, has been argued about endlessly by philosophers and aestheticians, and especially by historians of the written word. And I hesitate in this place to go on to consider the controversial one-to-one correspondence theory of names, words, and literary descriptions, of "nominalist" fallacies in the relationship between what we say and the realities we suppose we are designating. More forbidding than that, it involves a problem of language employed by gifted writers (and even by some voluble hacks) and its various elements of realism and/or imagination.

I have already registered some skeptical qualifications about literature's verisimilitude in the criticism of the Wodehouse texts (see above). Writers–as high as novelists and poets, as low as journalists–have a penchant for inventing, for making things up, for imposing their cunning ways with words on duller realities. What we get on a printed page is not necessarily what they heard (and saw) in the public and private places of their lifetime experience. What Homer records in the adventures of Odysseus as "conventional customs" and "common expressions" in ancient Greece and on the high Mediterranean seas are not–contrary to the learned argument of my college teacher in classics, the estimable Sir Moses Finley–automatically to be accepted as having a "realistic" correspondence. One can be certain that, like all great poets, Homer regularly made up that which he ascribed literally to others. He listened sensitively and was not deaf; but he *was* blind, and what he described as Odysseus' Ithaca in the far-away Aegean may well have been the green hills and deep harbors of a neighboring island.* The Homeric passages could be (and probably were) a brilliant and poetic version of a returning sailor's tale, "second-hand" if you will as in the transmission of all oral-traditional composition. For almost three thousand years we have been left with an insoluble puzzle: What is "accurate" and what is "fantasy" in the scientific attempts to describe what appeared to be happenings in the ancient world? Doubtless the pioneering digs of Heinrich Schliemann's celebrated expeditions pushed back the date of a knowable Greek past from the first Olympic games in 776 BC into the second millennium BC; but they had their weaknesses (writes a French biographer), for they "blurred the line between real experience and events described in Homer's epics." Schliemann even believed, as his critics have noted incredulously, that "he had seen the fig tree where Romulus and Remus, the legendary founders of Rome, were abandoned!"[1]

These remarks may appear to be a digression, but they are indeed connected to many of our concerns in the newspaper culture: the growth of "faction" which mixes fact with fiction; the naive journalistic assumptions about "covering a story" and reporting reality, "being there" and "seeing for oneself," corroborating facts from "at least two sources," etc.

As M.I. Finley insisted–in my view, quite unconvincingly–in his well-known book on *The World of Odysseus* (rev. ed., 1978, p. 9), it was "beside the point that the narrative is a collection of fictions from beginning to end." He also defended his "attempt to employ Greek myths and traditions and the Homeric poems in a historical reconstruction" in his *Use and Abuse of History* (1975, chapter 1).**

---

*   I refer here to the long controversy among historians and archaeologists – among them Heinrich Schliemann, Wilhelm Dörpfeld, and Professor M.I. Finley (who in his American years tried to teach me "ancient history" in New York's City College).

The dispute was as to whether Homer was describing, not Ithaca, but the "half-island" of Levkas as the home of Odysseus' royal castle (the "real" remains of which Dörpfeld assumed he found in his famous Leucadian digs). Since when are poets realists who confine their descriptions to the "true facts"? Can their work ever be construed as "documentary"?

**   The scholarly article on the whole subject by Ian Morris (a classicist in Jesus College, Cambridge) is both lively and learned. He is cogent in the detailed critique of his colleague M.I. Finley and the "materialist" school of thought devoted to the almost literal use of available literary sources (here the Homeric poems) as reliable news of the ancient world. He is alert to, and trenchant on, all others who impose anachronistic and self-serving modern theories on thousand-year-old texts.

But he is embarrassingly unconvincing when he turns moralist, and discovers the deceits of ideology. He then offers us an alternative view that the great classical texts illustrate another social reality: namely, how ideology in the *Odyssey* and the *Iliad* justify class dominance, and how propagandistic role-models in the 8th-century B.C. try to persuade the unruly *demos* that Heroes and Gods sanctify the existing order of things. (Sir Moses Finley may have gotten some of the archaeological evidence wrong, but he would never have put up with such "vulgar Marxism.") See Ian Morris' polemical (and flawed) study of "The Use and Abuse of Homer," in *Classical Antiquity*, vol. 5, no. 1 (April 1986), pp. 81-138.)

Most critical historians in the post-Schliemann era contend that the *Odyssey* and the *Iliad* are *not* "history books" and we should not be using them today as documentary sources. Such recent works that do exploit them in this way have been rejected as "counterfeit history," as unreliable or romantic as, say, Schliemann himself, digging at "Troy" and naming his own children Agamemnon and Andromache.

> He believed [writes a French archaeologist] that a two-handled drinking cup he found illustrated a type of jug celebrated in the *Iliad*–the *depas amphikypellon*. But his readiness to see proof of the truth of the Homeric poems in every object he unearthed led Schliemann astray. Today the vessel in question is dated considerably earlier, between 2600 and 1800 BC.

It is said that Schliemann's great achievement was to have inaugurated "investigative" archaeology; but, not unlike "investigative" journalism, its spectacular results were often haphazard. "The relation of ancient tradition to the realities on the ground thus could not be taken automatically for granted."[2]

As for Wilhelm Dörpfeld, his rather more academic follower, in his work on his Leucadian excavations, he found the ruins of an ancient castle from the Homeric era; and before the dig was accidentally flooded, he presented it to the world as the "real" site where Odysseus "actually" sat as king. This is, as we would say today, *kind of/sort of true*, in the way *fiction* on the basis of so-called *"factoids"* becomes *faction* and passes itself off as historical reality.[3]

When I visited (in Florence, in the 1950s) Bernard Berenson, the art critic and historian, his monologue at the well-attended *I Tatti* luncheon table was peppered with cracks about a book about the *Odyssey* "which talked of it as a sociological document only." He interrupted his own conversation to observe bitterly that the book had a "fabulous success," and he registered with biting sarcasm that the American author "was at once offered chairs in Oxford as well as Cambridge...." My old teacher, Moses Finley, in an address to the Classical Association when he was its President defended once again his use of Literature as a reflection of Society. He became, in the end, a Regius Professor at Cambridge and was knighted by the Queen; but the habits of "reductionism" or "holism" came, as I suspect, from Sir Moses' early teaching days in the Marxian atmosphere of City College in the 1930s. Ideology suggested that details in the superstructure could be reduced to, and wholly explained by, the historic forces in the social base. We were all persuaded at the time that everything was connected to everything, that every cultural fact was "relevant" and thus, properly understood, could illuminate great truths about the fundamentals of any society, past and present.[4]

Troubled by "some details of scene and action," a recent American translator of *The Odyssey* (Robert Fitzgerald, 1961) confesses to his perplexities when wandering on location in Ithaca, and he discusses in his Postscript the historical complexities of adjusting Homer's descriptions of the island (had he ever visited it?) with the real geographical facts. He also mentions "Leukas" which some "have believed to be Homer's Ithaca" and tries to account for the poet's "errors" and "confusions." A hundred keen-eyed critics before him have similarly tried to match the sites of Odysseus' coves and harbors, as Homer unforgettably described them, with the maps of real places.

All these efforts are based on the dubious assumption that the ancient Greek poet was recording such details in the documentary spirit of, say, the ancient Greek geographer, Strabo. The camp of reportorial realism stands opposed to the school of poetic truth.

In the end Fitzgerald argues that the original text which has "told us so much" about the eighth century B.C. is itself "a translation"–by which he means the rendering into Homer's metered language of "an action invented and elaborated in the imagination." It is, after all, an exemplary work of art. In his introduction to the Fitzgerald edition, the Nobel-prize-winning poet Seamus Heaney also insists that "the main thing is that his [Homer's] sense of the world was the work of his imagination" and that "everything in *The Odyssey* has been moved from the condition of factuality to the condition of vision."[5]

Writers of what is thought of as great and truthful prose are often newcomers and strangers or, at least, distant and estranged observers, and sometimes even foreigners. Their work, accordingly, is full of hits and misses. John Updike knows little about Brazil and even less about Portuguese speech, and he was harshly judged by critics for these mundane shortcomings when he published his extraordinary novel, *Brazil* (1994). Yet how much did Franz Kafka know about the far-away U.S.A., which he had never visited, when he wrote his profound novel about *Amerika*.* We are properly indifferent–and I have already mentioned Proust, Joyce, Mann–to such erratic considerations when we feel that larger truths are to be had.

Still, a grave misunderstanding arises when we take for literal or documentary accuracy what are only instruments in a greater literary enterprise. None of us are infallible witnesses; but, about most of what is written and published which is even remotely connected to our knowledge and experience, one tends confidently to say: "No, I'm afraid that's not *exactly* what it was like....Real people speak differently, behave differently." There is (as we have seen) artifice in the art of quotation.

---

*   Klaus Mann, in his preface to the American edition of Kafka's *Amerika* (1941), has written: "When he conceived his novel *Amerika* in 1913 [in Prague], he knew no Americans and understood very little English. His only sources of information were the few books he had read – and his own poetic imagination."

Among the "few books" were Benjamin Franklin's autobiography and the poetry of Walt Whitman whom Kafka said he "greatly admired."

So when I am prompted to record my own personal doubts and skepticism about the written and published word–in the "hot copy" of the latest editions of our newspapers as well as in "the conditions of factuality" of the classical allusions in our ancient epics–it is because my own good will and my will to believe are so often sorely tried and caught out by surprise. Yes, I believed in Homeric verisimilitude, and was taken in.

Hollywood Villains and Pulp-Fiction Hoods

When the contemporary press devotes itself to what it calls, with the obligatory dash of collegiate knowingness, "the culture of violence," it must necessarily confront the problem of dealing with its sub-culture, the language of violence. For if it is indeed a culture (and even if it is not), it will have its special vocabulary: loaded words which would convey extreme emotions of hostility and hatred; sinister verbal signals for aggression; clever euphemisms to mask, among other illegalities, the foul deed of murder. In our time popular crime fiction has been usually given the task of supplying the realism that newspaper reportage, for all its grim overground detail, has been sedulously avoiding.

How did the underworld creatures of Murder Incorporated talk in the 1930s? What was the conventional gangster lingo in the Speakeasy decade of the 1920s on Chicago's South Side? The newspaper accounts of the day, and even the regular magazine features of reminiscence, are surely not the place to find out. A novelist with some literary empathy can reconstruct imaginatively the way "Lepke" Buchalter or Al Capone talked–although the law-court transcripts (made when New York and Chicago prosecuting attorneys brought them to trial) would be, for obvious reasons, of only limited help. In court as in film, in front of His Honor the Judge as well as before the Film Censor Will Hays, acts tended to get cleaned up. The "Scarfaces" didn't always talk as Paul Muni or Jimmy Cagney did in the movies. But times do change. "Bugsy" Siegel sounded more like his old self in the Warren Beatty film in the 1980s. Any killer, in the Hollywood cinema of the 1990s, especially in the scripts of Quentin Tarantino (*Pulp Fiction*, etc.), talks "dirty realism"…as art moves heavily forward trying to simulate truth.

On the other hand, there is some evidence that life, in this matter of the vocabulary of violence, is imitating art. Many criminals, in bouts of sensitive self-criticism, have confessed how they liked to copy the "style"–in dress, in speech, in efficiency–which attracted them in the gangster culture glamorously shaped by Warner Brothers, George Raft, Richard Widmark, Mike Hammer, Elmore Leonard, and last but not least by the effing hit-man eloquence of John Travolta. Hollywood villains and pulp-fiction hoods impersonate role models for would-be Mr. Bigs. Not unlike straighter characters among the millions, our crooks also (as a poet once put it) *"live their lives in the cinema/ on an aluminum screen…"*

After such knowledge, there must be a modicum of understanding when in sectors of the serious Western press there is a tendency in the reportage of the criminal underworld to include a daring suggestion or two of the way the gangsters actually talk. Edward G. Robinson wouldn't be the Man Himself without his chewed-up cigar and at least a few undeleted expletives. I offer only one example, and that from the British press; and it also serves to counter the innocent notion that the Ira Gershwin-difference (*"potatoes...tomatoes"*) also divides our profanities and obscenities from the usages on opposite sides of the ocean (as in *"ass/arse")."*

Here is the well-edited *Sunday Times* following up a number of cold-blooded murders which are "upping the ante" in Liverpool's underworld. "The subsequent shootings and torchings have created a new culture of violence, and left the city hankering for the 'good old days' of fisticuffs." Its reporter, a man named Smith, writes at substantial length and gives every impression that his research has been conscientious and his motive was neither to shock nor to titillate but to tell it, professionally, "like it is." The excellent account of a few "flashpoints in a gangland turf war" might have been penned by journalists like Hemingway and Dos Passos when they were doing their youthful stint as newspaper reporters:"The violence is organized, after a fashion. people are apt to call it 'gangland' or 'underworld,' as if it were going on somewhere else, instead of nearby and all around. Men in balaclavas and bandannas, men wearing body armor. Young men, many not yet 30; some men who do not expect to see 30 and a few who won't. This is just how it is. The big picture. The scenic backdrop." Having said that, he can't fail to go on to record how it sounds, to print a few snatches of the sound-track (which, in its original entirety, must have rivaled Henry Miller rewriting Ed McBain).The tiny asterisks are drafted to do heavy duty. Colin Ungi is one of the gunmen facing, presumably, an unsympathetic bespectacled female judge:

> When Colin appeared in court for possession of fire-arms, he was refused bail. Abuse was shouted at the magistrate from the large group of Colin's family and friends at the back of the court. "F***ing twat. Four-eyed c***." Later that day, back in Liverpool 8 there was a small, contained riot outside Black George's pub. Three cars were set on fire by a dozen or so people wearing balaclavas among a crowd of about 100, mainly young white men.

One good expletive deserves another, and the racial balance is preserved. For Johnny Phillips is a black man and the pub-owner of *Black George*, and he felt that the police were "not doing enough to protect him and his family": "The police went to see him and thought he was being abusive and uncooperative. 'F*** off, sausage head,' he is said to have told the detective who was supposed to be investigating the shooting." The score now, as far as f-words were concerned, was even-steven. But in reality, as in pulp fiction, the racial outsider still remained the main target:

He hoped it would be quick, not one of those pain things. You couldn't know when it was going to happen. One minute you could be happy or whatever, going about your business, and next minute, that's it. The end. Goodnight.

This is how it is and continues to be, living in death's shadow.[6]

Mutual Reinforcement

It is a fact that writers who, mostly, lead desk-bound unadventurous lives, are overly susceptible to literature that takes them to places they've never been. Journalism also serves to give us good talk–or charming conversation, or rough dialogue (as in the above)–we never heard from rowdy characters whom in all our born days we won't ever run into. My infatuation, for example, with Elmore Leonard, most of whose thirty-odd short novels I have devoured in paperback, is a case in point; and if his latest newspaper interview is not suspect to the same doubts and pinch-of-salt skepticism I have already raised (does he *really* talk this way? did he *actually* say that?) I learned another lesson in what our linguistic philosophers call epistemology: that is, the very "nature of knowledge" interdicts the naive taking of things at face value.

Elmore Leonard writes crime fiction, and was a cult favorite for decades until Hollywood filmmakers, enjoying their new era of "dirty realism," were able to get away with scenes and soundtracks which could unashamedly re-produce his raciness. He has now become massively successful and internationally famous, even if his reputation is based on the aforementioned misunderstanding: namely, that writers, who are only masters of virtual reality, actually take you to real places you never dreamed of. In Elmore's case, you get to hang around low-down bars and cafés where the riff-raff plot their skullduggery and you can hear every word! He is celebrated indeed as "the poet laureate of wild assholes with revolvers"; and since, alas, I do not know such types (not armed or disarmed, not in New York, or London, or Berlin) I let myself be guided by Elmore and his "inexhaustible flair for the nervous rhythms of contemporary urban speech"; and one sure came away richer by a whole new world.

The newspaper reporter for the *New York Times* who flew out some time ago to Michigan to interview the master of the seedy underworld certainly did not intend to unmask, or debunk, or otherwise expose a reader's illusions. He also wanted to tell-it-like-it-is, to abide by the golden rule of our newspaper culture; and perhaps he did. Only along the way he confessed that "there's a tendency to confuse appearance with reality." I quote this disenchanting passage from the interview, not the least of its virtues being an illustration of how newspaper culture and literary culture can lock horns.

There's a tendency in the United States to confuse appearance with reality. It's like that when you meet Elmore Leonard.

He writes these tough-guy books like *"Get Shorty," "Riding the Rap," "LaBrava"* and *"Stick."* They are loaded with taut dialogue, violence and marvelous characters, inept lowlifes out to score big.

But Leonard himself? A pussy-cat.

An Elmore Leonard character he's not. He doesn't lurk in Miami bars or prowl Detroit's meaner streets. He doesn't consort with confidence men, retired strippers or people who deal in controlled substances.

Well, the writer as a person, his niceness and homely manner, was never the issue; Tolstoy did not need to be bigger than Buonaparte to pen an indictment of Napoleon's war and peace; and Proust did not have to leave his cork-lined apartment in the Boulevard Haussmann for grand parties and elegant salons in order to remember the past with its graces. The reality was in the prose, and the prose was true.

Alas, Elmore's transcriptions of "real speech spoken by common men" was all contrived, and essentially artificial. All the rich expletives which cascaded from the mouths of Elmore Leonard's pimps and gangsters, underworld con- and hit-men, whores on the street and gays in bordellos and bath-houses, were all made up. He–and I with him–never left the writing room: "he sits at a desk all day and wrestles with words."[7] The man lives openly in the overworld, as do all us nice readers who faithfully wallow, vicariously, in the sleaze he cleanly composes, all day, at his desk. He wrestles with words, but his strongest grip is only a half-nelson.

H.L. Mencken, who had (as lexicographers are wont to have) a fuller grip on words, offers us a clue to the twists and turns that involve this kind of vocabulary from P.G. Wodehouse to Elmore Leonard. He observes in his *American Language* that "hard-boiled fiction from America has influenced English speech and writing. The boys' papers have heroes who speak as nearly American as the author can imagine to make them." Thus, English characters imitate American characters who are "*invented*" by American novelists who "*imagine*" their hardboiled speech which, in turn, gets imitated by tough real-life gangsters.

But before the transatlantic Anglo-American drama sets in there is an interplay on the U.S. home scene which is simlarly paradoxical. It is well-known that writers on the subject of espionage have, from E. Phillips Oppenheim to John le Carré, colorfully shaped the style and vocabulary of authentic cloak-and-dagger spies in the field. Historians of the criminal underworld have also noted the "mutual reinforcement" between real-life gangsters and their fictional counterparts (in, say, the stories of Damon Runyon and Raymond Chandler). It is not only in the way they speak–above all, in their slang and circumlocutions for crime, murder, and its swag–but also in their operational deviousness. The books fill many shelves: *Goodfellas* by Nicholas Pileggi, *Honor Thy Father* by Gay Talese, *Donnie Brasco* by Joseph Pistone, Peter Maas' *The Valachi Papers*. Some research has documented, for example, the influence of the genre of gangster movies, heightened by Mario Puzo's novels and *The Godfather* films by Francis Ford Coppola, on the various New York "Mafia families."

As a matter of fact, in one of the most recent trials (1997) this kind of "faction" was featured. The defection of Salvatore (Sammy the Bull) Gravano dealt serious blows to the Mafia rings, for he was the highest-ranking best-informed Mafia hitman ever to turn State's evidence. The courtroom reporters stated openly a certain consternation at the mix of fiction and non-fiction with which they had to deal: "The Gigante trial is a case study in how the Mafia and mass entertainment media have melded together to such an extent that it is difficult to tell where criminal mayhem stops and cutting-edge marketing begins." When Gravano took the witness stand to "sing" or "tell all," he had already published a best-selling book, *Underboss* (1997). According to Blaine Harden, the *Washington Post*'s trial reporter, "Mr. Gravano personified the way in which real mob executions and make-believe mass-market depictions of same have cross-fertilized each other." Peter Maas helped him to write his book. But Gravano's own television confessions–especially his account of "rubbing out some 19 dirty rats"–were so convincing that Hollywood studios offered him multi-million dollar deals to make a real-action movie of the Mafia underworld.But they already have! Had not Francis Coppola won so many prizes for his film series on how the warring mobsters took each other for a bloody ride? And "Sammy the Bull," explaining why "killing came easy to me," recalls how the 1972 film *The Godfather* (the historic first Puzo-Coppola collaboration) was instrumental in molding his self-image: "I left that movie stunned....I mean, I floated out of the theater. That was our life. It was incredible. And not only the mob end, not just the mobsters and the killing and all that [expletive], but that wedding in the beginning, the music and the dancing, it was us." And the language? Was it theirs, their very own? The *Post* saw fit to delete the expletives but the screen scenarios were peppered with the real thing. Or had skillful writers–with an ear for "the everyday" (Orwell) and the "common touch" (Hemingway) and "the very language of men" (Wordsworth)– made it all up? Or maybe only the best bits?

The images and the Hollywood taglines that go with them remain vivifying, in time becoming platitudinous until yet another film based on a new novel comes along with more original conceits. For now Mario Puzo and Francis Ford Coppola appear to be sufficient unto the day. As the Mafia mobster Sammy "the Bull" Gravano testified about a gang-land takeover: "I just bullied my way in. I said I was going to make them an offer they couldn't refuse. I didn't have to explain. I imagine they all saw *The Godfather*" (Peter Maas, *Underboss*, 1997, p. 216).

This kind of literary inspiration reinforces, if in a perverse way, the old Goethean notion of a world literature. As crime spreads and best-selling books get universally translated, the so-called *mimesis* between local texts and distant characters become more and more outlandish. Who would have thought in Stalin's day that within the century a writer like Mario Puzo would be more influential than Tolstoy or Pasternak or Solzhenitsyn? A post-Soviet mafia goes from strength to strength in the new Russian underworld, and one leading Moscow gangster–"Star, a 44-year-old godfather who presides over an eastern Russian region the size of Scotland"–has revealed the formative role-model of his life: "He modelled himself, he said, on Vito Corleone, the central figure of *The Godfather,* the Mario Puzo novel made into a Hollywood blockbuster starring Marlon Brando. He read the book six times while in prison, memorizing Corleone's monologues and copying his manners." He quotes aphorisms made famous by New York godfathers, talks eloquently about the ideal of honor as if he were to the Sicilian manner born; but, curiously enough, he and his "family" all carry the portrait of Lenin as a tattoo on their chests. Why Lenin? "Because in the old days we used to say that a Soviet execution platoon would never shoot at his portrait. Others had Stalin on their backs as well." How did the Puzo godfathers in Manhattan manage without this extra bit of protection? Would a tattoo of Mussolini have helped? or of President Roosevelt? Exemptions run out. The Leninist-Stalinist vests are not so bullet-proof any more.[8]

It has become a very thin line–that traditional frontier between reality and make-believe, between the authenticity of the historian and the imagination of the writer who embellishes–melodramatizes–with a scraggly hand and hardly visible corrections. Espionage was never the same again when the CIA men at their Langley, Virginia, headquarters–as well as the MI-6 officers in London (and, who knows? the KGB in the old Lubyanka in Soviet Moscow)–thrilled to the pages of the contemporary school of spy thrillers from John le Carré to Len Deighton. Agents took on new names and identities ("moles," for example); and the devious conventions of secret, furtive behavior took on new polish. Many a conspiracy in the world of intelligence came to a nasty end because counter-control officers on the other side knew the plot–for they had read the same book. The most glamorous spy chief of the day, Markus "Mischa" Wolf successfully headed the East German DDR espionage corps. He is generally said to be the model for John le Carré's arch-villain of the Cold War, "Karla" of Moscow Control–le Carré (David Cornwall) served in West Germany as a youthful member of Britain's MI-6. And only recently, to complete the circle of "factoid" vanity, Wolf wrote his memoirs and remarked that he had been "a fan" of the novelist he inspired.[9]

Demythologization usually breeds new myths of its own. A "new genre" in crime fiction or a dramatically different shade in black-and-white gangster films appears to displace old stereotypes and freshen up perceptions of life and death in the underworld. Faces change: scrawny or dumpy figures like Jimmy Cagney and Edward G. Robinson give way to syndicate slicksters like Warren Beatty and Al Pacino. Writers who once operated under severe restrictions came to enjoy new opportunities, new freedoms: at once tougher and more taciturn as in Raymond Chandler, and more loquaciously foul-mouthed as in Quentin Tarantino. Time was when crime never paid–and the Little Caesars and the Public Enemies always ended badly. In recent years it all seems to have the golden touch and a happy end. The stars of "gangsta rap" have been earning millions, and if they didn't happen to shoot each other or commit accidental suicide in their hotel rooms while on tour, they are still rapping profitably today. As for the new generation of "Families" (viz. *The Sopranos*) "they live, grow old and die without ever seeing the inside of a jail or getting shot...." Our welfare state extends protection to the oddest people.

One newspaper, in welcoming the popular new American TV series, which chronicles the waves of crime initiated by the Soprano family in the boondocks of New Jersey, credits these films with "transforming the mafia genre, for years drowning in its own mythology...." The change, I submit, is hardly visible to the naked eye (the dozens of Family members are all type-cast from a Little Italy Central Casting and bear names like Gandolfini and Chianese). Nor is it audible to the attentive ear (assaulted and deafened by the f-word at the estimated rate of two-to-the-minute in 60-minute installments)....But it is, somehow, a little bit different and thus capable of establishing itself as "a landmark in American television drama." In the case of *The Sopranos*, the TV-series has attracted national awards for being the best, the finest, the truest, the best-written thing of its kind since the days of Humphrey Bogart's Philip Marlowe and Marlon Brando's Don Corleone.

The author appears to be kind of/sort of proud that he has "obviously done a good job of creating a real universe...." This is, as self-praise, one cosmos too far; what he means is the creation of an unreal, or virtual, universe, full of "self-referential stuff" and Hollywood quotations. One newspaper interviewer expressed his enthusiasm this way: "...*The Sopranos* doesn't just piece together mob lore from the movies; it also makes gags and knowing references to them...." The knowledgeability, or knowingness, is impressive. One of the Sporanos shoots a kid in the foot "for giving him cheek"...just like in the film *Goodfellas*. Another Sporano tries, but (alas) gets rejected, to get an analysis by a new psycho-therapist...who duly explains that even Robert DeNiro was similarly rejected in his latest gangster movie. Finally, the *Soprano* women, or at least one of them, try their hand at impersonating the star Diane Keaton playing a Corleone mob wife.

These achievements in a new kind of literary ingenuity were possible–far, far from Stendhal's classic image of a mirror under a carriage, directly reflecting earthy realities–only with the opportunity of using a cable channel rather than being constricted to the orthodoxies of a U.S. mainstream TV network. A foreign admirer in London explained in the *Times* that this was "crucial to its complexity and intelligence." On the major American television networks (NBC, CBS, ABC) gangster stories are known to be twisted to "moralistic ends." As David Chase, the *Soprano* author, revealed, "We could not have told stories the way we have...." Part of the genre-busting story-telling is, of course, photographic excursions into, at the very least, half-nudity and a dialogue rich in repetitive expletives. But that is only by-the-by (or so runs the official credo). Chase argues, "Being on network television would have meant losing so much more than the bare breasts and the swearing. We would have lost *The Sopranos*." The deepest *motif* which holds the artistic achievement together is clearly its non-ethical ethos....its victory over the usual–the, conventional, boring–"moral resolution," its transcendence over the establishment's theses that crime-does-not-pay and that he-who-lives-by-the-bullet-dies-by-the-same. One newspaper headline suggested the onset of a new "maturity."

A 'FAMILY DRAMA' FOR GROWN-UPS

Kids eveidently are acculturated when young to want the dramatic simplicities of good guys *vs.* bad guys. But their parents now thirst for "complexity and intelligence." *The Times* of London's correspondent puts his finger on the point: "...Chase has created a central character we're on the side of even when we've seen him garrotte someone on screen." Let no one think that garnering sympathy for killers is an easy job. Cursing like troopers and undressing like strip-tease artists are the least of it. In one episode I saw a young Hassidic Jew, long-bearded in a wide-brimmed black-hat, brutally wasted–it was dark in the Jersey tunnel which was the scene-of-the-crime, and it could be he was strangled. Apparently his wheeling-and-dealing got in the way of Tony Soprano. In the next episode Tony made a noble effort–with a dash of fashionable Freudian remorse–to tell it to his psychoanalyst...like, you know, DeNiro tried to do in *Analyze This*...

It would be shortsighted to take all this as a simple case of fiction imitating life imitating fiction. The deception is contrived in a hall of mirrors, and the reflections become more substantial than when the mirror images were first spotted. A report of an FBI wire-tap (in the year 2000, and it happened to be in, of all places, New Jersey) picked up local *mafiosi* talk about the TV series–"wondering how its makers could know so much." The tape overheard one mobster, described as desk-policeman are wont to do, as "a heavyset waste management executive" ("waste" as garbage-disposal? or "to waste" as contract-killer?): "Every week there's another one of us there...."[10]

What is remarkable (and we have noted it before) is that each such breakthrough has nothing to do with greater approximation of American underworld realities, with a more accurate representation of the crime and the criminal, abroad in the land. Truth and social (or: anti-social) realism are irrelevant; for in such cases the imaginative writers who were responsible for memorable character, for twisted plotting and catchy dialogue, were simply making it up–with, to be sure, unprecedented dexterity–out of whole cloth. Just as Elmore Leonard fashioned his distinctive breakthrough from the big-time of Capone-type gangsters to the small-time of "the shysters and the losers" by sitting quietly at his writing table in Detroit and gloriously dreaming it all on to the page…just so did the author of the much-heralded *The Sopranos*–David Chase, an Italian-American whose family changed its name from De Cesare in the 1920s–find his inspiration within himself. He made the Sopranos sing and remained quite oblivious to the grubby or bloody realities of the external world. As he confessed, "This is probably not going to be the answer that anyone likes to hear, but I don't know any real mobsters." So much for social realism and documentary truth. Undaunted the newspaper interviewer went on to question him about the show's sociological kinkiness, from the *capo*'s addiction to psychoanalysis (old-style mobsters would confess only to priests; and sometimes to their mothers in the kitchen) to the fateful unmanly turns in their love life. As brutish, ruthless Tony says: "Psychiatry and cunnilingus have brought us to this." This may be original, perceptive and even true; but David Chase does not offer it, however stimulating the thesis might be, as an authoritative footnote to Kinsey research into male Italo-American sexuality. Everything can be posited in an imagined world, and also its opposite. It is the outlandish world of a writer's whim, and David Chase pays tribute to the whimsy of his forerunners, the innovative Coppola, Scorsese and Mario Puzo, and the gangs they influenced: "…*The Godfather* is everything to these people. It's their Bible, their Koran. Their *Mona Lisa*, their Eiffel Tower. It's their thing." This mish-mash, this spaghetti *al dente* of an ideology, serves "these people" well. They are a gifted writer's fictional people. Chase has now prepared a second series of the successful *Sopranos* for a U.S. cable channel. Home Box Office has given him, yet another reporter happily noted, "a freedom with language and nudity" that wouldn't be possible on the mainstream channels of "network TV." It also puts a rather safe distance from the fixed sensitivities of ethnic correctness. The estimable Quentin Curtis, the film critic and interviewer I have been quoting, even sensed that what yesterday was taken as a slur and a dark stain on the image of a proud people, is giving way to a sense that, after all, Columbus who discovered America was also a kind of "tough guinea."*[11] They were "all wops like me," as Luigi Barzini used to say, in tireless provocation.

---

* "**Guinea, ginny.** *(Derog.)* An Italian, a person of Italian descent….Wide W.W.II use. *Very derog*….1932: 'A tough Ginney bootlegger by the name of Gregorio…' (Damon Runyon)." Wentworth & Flexner, *Dictionary of American Slang* (2nd, suppl. ed. 1975), p. 234.

On its derivation, Mencken is puzzled by its "changed meaning," for it was originally an 18th-19th-century reference to "a Negro from guinea" – but "when it came to signify an Italian I do not know." H.L. Mencken, *The American Language, Supplement One* (1952), p. 606.

One positive strand has persisted, and in this case still touched evidently by the original ethnic pride. According to Green, "*Guinea Negro*" still refers to "a mixed-race group native to Maryland, Virginia and West Virginia…." *Cassell Dictionary of Slang* (ed. Jonathon Green, 1998), p. 543.

A British coin made from West Africa gold – the *guinea* – was first struck in 1613 and until recently was worth 21 shillings (i.e., one shilling more than a pound). To be

A last word about the novelist's modesty. His achievement is a fictional reality imposed by his lively imagination on an underworld which found its agreeable identity only after related characters were verbally sketched on a printed page or pictured in a movie, or both. A literary man's modest disclaimer that he had merely graphically copied "the real thing" is often only a shrewd plea for even more recognition of a fiction-writer's fantasies and, whatever the hard facts, his very own basic creativity. His personal powers are flattered by the paradox that he can imitate life on the basis of no personal first-hand experience at all.

It was so at the very beginning of the contemporary renaissance of the urban outlaw in a black limousine, carrying a sub-machine gun in a sinister violin case, or pointing a sawed-off shot-gun at his Southside rivals. Mario Puzo, whose "*Godfather*" novels were worldwide best-sellers and became Hollywood film hits, created the modern legend of "The Mafia." But, as he was the first to confess, "… 'I'm ashamed to admit that I wrote *The Godfather* [1969] entirely from research. I never met a real honest-to-god gangster….Real gangsters refused to believe that I had never been in the rackets. He added: 'But all of them loved the book.' And later the movie…."[12] The legend became reality, and the question was discarded as to whether the perception was at first hand or second. But beyond the entertainment value of the brutality and the delinquency, one perennial issue remained. Some Italo-Americans continued to object that the crowded panorama of bloody murderers and criminal racketeers was ethnically unflattering. The Italians back home in the *Mezzogiorno*, especially in Sicily, also looked askance at the representation of "Families" of *mafiosi* and devotees of "*Omerta*." As Luigi Barzini used to argue, "Our Italianate vices are different and are our very own; they are home-grown and not made in Hollywood…." In the end, the sociology and anthropology (and, to be sure, the decorative accompanying obscenities) may well have been different… but the mayhem was the same. Lots of shooting; many corpses; dead men tell no tales.[13]

What is nowadays reflected in politics and in the novel passes through a hall of mirrors. Real-life gangsters imitate Hollywood caricatures, but if the correspondence is not all one way it is also not a two-dimensional matter of copy-cat style: lingo, swagger, menacing mien. The fiction comes back to haunt the reality, and vice versa; once the mirrors are in place, the confounding of images is endless. In the O.J. Simpson case (which we have dealt with in another context), Detective Mark Fuhrman's literary ambitions proved to be a

---

billed (and to have to pay) for services in guineas, far from being *derog.*, was part of the lifestyle of the English élite.

Pejoratives often profit from being ambiguous. Words sometimes take the liberty of living double-lives, and getting away with it.

turning point. He had wanted to write a cops-and-robbers story based on his own experience *and* on what he had learned from re-reading his favorite crime books (especially Joseph Wambaugh's)–and the "scenario" was admitted as relevant evidence to the real-life L.A. double-murder of the beautiful ex-Mrs. Simpson and her friend Ron Goldman.

As Linda Deutsch reported in her Associated Press dispatch (16 August 1996), Defense Attorney Johnnie Cochran had told her that "This is perhaps the biggest thing that's happened in any case in this country in this decade." Fuhrman in California sensed the public demand for "gritty realism about life on the streets"; and so he "told some stories and did some play-acting." The would-be author put the stories (in the phrase he uses for the literary art and technique evidently most congenial to him) "through the meat-grinder of my own imagination....They were embellished, exaggerated, even entirely made up." He admitted he said "horrible things" (the n-word, forty-one times in the recorded tapes); but he told the *Los Angeles Times* that Joe Wambaugh in *The Choir Boys* also said it repeatedly (fourteen times). He had a point. A Hollywood producer or director might well have edited it down in the final cut to a decent dirty dozen.

The verdict of the Los Angeles jury, in favor of O. J. Simpson's innocence, was generally ascribed to these so-called "Fuhrman tapes" on which the ill-starred L.A. detective tried to let loose his imaginative (and verbal) powers along the lines of his literary idol, Joe Wambaugh. He thought of Wambaugh's admirable work as "boisterous...free-wheeling...Rabelaisian...bizarre... chilling." The able reporter Lawrence Schiller put together the best-selling prison book for O.J. Simpson, placing the working press well inside the crime story. The reputedly "best detective" on the Los Angeles police force, Fuhrman, tried to rival "America's premier cop novelist"; and Fuhrman's own Hollywoodesque dialogue was indeed so bizarre, so boisterous and Rabelaisian that it induced a criminal-court jury to acquit the accused. Simpson was later found guilty of murder by a jury in a civil court which was charged to assess responsibility for "fatal damages."

There is a strange "Bermuda triangle" here in which all realities fly high in only to disappear. We mourn for old certainties. Law and order were easier to comprehend, and even to maintain, when gangsters didn't read books and learn new tricks in homicide. There was a time when cops didn't entertain literary ambitions and confuse the minds of juries with images from movie stories.[14]

18

Jewish Gangsters and the East Side Story

An Untold Story

As for those anti-Semites and color-bigots of yore, how *did* they really talk? Modern records are a modest, limited source; and the historians of ancient eras find slim pickings among the sparse Græco-Roman inscriptions and fragmentary manuscripts. For the J-word I can recommend a three-volume compilation which translates every scrap of evidence which has come down to us pertaining to the Biblical people whom the serene Marcus Aurelius found "more troublesome" than any other in the Roman Empire of his reign.[1]

But no one evidently has been able to recover a vocabulary of demotic invective. The former Jewish military commander, Flavius Josephus, who defected to the Romans, mounts in his famous polemic *Against Apion* (*circa* 100 A.D.) a spirited defense of his old co-religionists, taking apart the anti-Semitic prejudices of his day argument by argument–but where was "the beef," the low juicy expletives among the bigots that so aroused his ancestral pro-Semitism? What dirty names had Josephus himself been called?

In our own day we have from time to time been surprised by written evidence which we had hitherto assumed to be unavailable to historians who were interested in "the language like she is really spoke." One such contemporary find throws some light onto the period in "little old Noo Yawk" where P.G. Wodehouse had been researching the ways his fictional characters should realistically be made to talk. The standard literature on the subject proved to be, for various ideological reasons, minimal or misleading. We know the names of notorious gangsters who came out of East Side Manhattan or Brooklyn ghettoes–Louis "Lepke" Buchalter, Dutch Schultz, Benjamin "Bugsy" Siegel, Meyer Lansky, among others–but did this handful, as one historian of "the Jewish gangster" has recently insisted, constitute "an enormously complex, richly endowed culture of vice and criminality"? Michael Gold, a *Daily Worker* columnist I read as a boy, touched on the subject in his *Jews Without Money* (1930); but he would, wouldn't he. Gold's Marxian Communism led him to see "capitalist society" as a ruthlessly exploitative environment. Especially so in the crowded East Side where millions of East European Jews found refuge in the high-immigration years of 1870-1925, when despairing young girls took to prostitution and desperate young men took to crime.

There were other less dogmatic-ideological ways of looking at the story. In the case of Irving Howe and his authoritative work, *World of Our Fathers* (1976), "the underworld culture" was dismissed as insignificant or non-existent. Howe wrote: "in the life of the immigrant community as a whole, crime was a marginal phenomenon, a pathology discoloring the process of collective assertion and adjustment." It remained for one historian, Albert Fried, chronicling *The Rise and Fall of the Jewish Gangster in America* (1980/1993), to deny the marginality. He rejected the impression of mere discoloration (as in Howe); ignored an enlightened turn to liberal and radical protest movements (as in Gold); and flew the flag of his own peculiar pride, a Jewish contribution to "an undying American tradition"–running rackets...gangsterdom.[2]

Well, again, how did they talk? What do the written records show? Was it in broken English, fractured Yiddish, a new East-Side pushcart argot? The newspapers of the day were arid, at least on this score; although, in general, Irving Howe found the files of the *Jewish Daily Forward* "an incomparable reservoir of material–repertorial, impressionistic, sociological, polemical." (My grandfather read the competing newspaper, *The Day*, "*der Tog,*"every day of his life in America.)

As for academic historians, they were distracted by the spectacle of "the Melting Pot," that assertive adjustment by which, in a single generation, an Americanized middle-class came into being and a plethora of fine English-prose writers emerged, from Abraham Cahan to Saul Bellow. (One of my aunts used to clip for me as a literary model to follow the English-language column of Dr. S. Margoshes in *The Day* of the 1920s. I can still remember the elegant rhythm of his long, ornate sentences.)

But Professor Fried found a new, authentic source in a breath-taking trick of research as if he had, like Mark Twain's Connecticut Yankee, hauled back the voices of the past that were lost in outer space. Apparently, some years after the turn of the century in New York, when the crime rate in downtown Manhattan (especially in the East Side ghetto) became disturbingly high and disagreeably prominent, a watchdog committee had been set up. The initiating force was a group of influential German-American Jews. The rich élite of the European migration were alarmed that the East Side crooks, lower-Manhattan whores, and the bearded shylocks–all clearly "a rich culture," says Fried–would be bringing all Jewry into disrepute. They hired a man called Abe Shoenfeld, and his team of private investigators, to look into the matter. They gave him a few years to fulfill his "important and highly confidential assignment." He would gather the facts; they would try to re-establish respectability.

The Schoenfeld documents are worth mentioning for the special light they shed on the slang (and its etymological roots) of New York in its day.*

Abe Shoenfeld and his reporters visited the bordellos on East Broadway and Grand Street, and talked with the girls and their *macks* (pimps) who worked Second Avenue. Shoenfeld turned up regularly at all the crowded hangouts: the cafés, casinos, pool halls, and other shady seedbeds of delinquency. His staff made lists of the habitués, the longest of which was under "*guns.*" (A "gun," surely, was not a "gunsel" or a gunman but short for *gonniff,* a small-time petty crook, mostly pickpocketing for his "*fagin*" or money-lending "*shylock.*") Taken together the cast of characters on the streets between Delancey and Rivington resembled nothing so much as the *dramatis personae* of a plot in a story by Ring Lardner or Damon Runyon, O. Henry or Mark Hellinger: "Big Aleck...Lefty Louis...Candy Kid Phil...Chaim the Mummy...Dopey Benny...and Little Natie ('not the one from Broome Street')." There is in this kind of name-tagging, found not only among the Jewish and Italian immi-grants but among all the "greenhorns" in the new world, a resourceful effort to communicate in a strange tongue with a limited vocabulary. It flaunts a lively, original color and even a quasi-biblical allusiveness as if Noah on his Ark were suddenly discovering striking differences and individuality, one by one.

Some East Side locutions persisted. A term like"*wise guy*" (big shot) re-mained in Houston Street circulation and appears exactly in this respectful, unironical way in Brooklyn's Italo-American *Mafia* families across the river almost a century later. A few words and phrases get exhausted and displaced. Abe Shoenfeld's "*gun-mol*" is a crook's woman or associate; but *moll*** has fallen victim to, among other things, a feministic cleansing of *macho* lan-guage. His *guerilla* (later "gorilla") was prescient, a partisan spelling in a time pre-dating the gun-toting cult of Che Guevara.

Still and all, there is the wholeness of a sound track that is still missing. It was, I surmise, replete with rude phrases that would have been worthy of an establishment's blue pencil, studded with words that deserved to be disguised by asterisks. I am tempted to note as "typical" that in Irving Howe's monumen-tal volume on the world of the fathers his "Glossary of Yiddish Terms" does not even include the godfatherly *gonniff* (crook) or any old bits of profanity, viz.

---

*   I have not as yet been able to consult the original Shoenfeld papers which were collected in Manhattan by Judah P. Magnes, a well-known teacher and philosopher who later became a founding professor of the Hebrew University in Jerusalem. Rabbi Magnes' "archive on the Jewish underworld" (Fried) was included in his personal file when he left Manhattan's Temple Emanuel-El for Palestine in 1922.

**   *Moll* dates back to 17th-century usage for "prostitute." The attribution of *gunsel* is, usually, to the Yiddish and German: *gentsel, Gänzlein* (gosling). *Oxford Dictionary of Modern Slang*, pp. 93, 139. Jonathon Green claims (*Slang Down the Ages*, p. 227) that *gonnsel* – "a young homosexual companion," most famously personified in Elmer, the young inadequate hoodlum of Dashiell Hammett's *Maltese Falcon* (1930, filmed in 1941) – "is often mistranslated as gunman."

"mommser" (bastard, s.o.b.). Evidently these were Jews not only without money but lacking a coarse language in which to engage in the rough trade. More than that, none of the authorities I consulted on the subject of gangsters in the East Side story pay the least attention to whether the gunsels and the macks with their molls were ever armed–or if so, where they got their weapons…or how they carried them, and what make and calibre they happened to be. A gangster culture comes out of the barrel of a gun. A so-called "rich underworld culture" hangs in there barely, if it appears to be without special vocabulary or appropriate weapons, speechless as well as defenseless. No wonder this kind of gangsterism "rose and fell" so quickly.

This is a world I never knew. If I am permitted another passing personal remark, I was born and grew up in the "suburban" Bronx ghetto, in a second-generation neighborhood where one not even suspected the depravity in the Lower Manhattan's East Side neighborhoods of our fathers. Living not in the past or even the present but for the "American future," a brilliant ghetto graduate like Morris Raphael Cohen became our philosophy teacher at City College and another East Side son, Dan Bell (now a professor at Harvard), became my co-editor at the *New Leader*, the social-democrat weekly newspaper at the Rand School on 15th Street. The wild, sinful life on Houston Street or Hester Street was a piece of missing or lost history, too shameful to share. In my boyhood I never recall hearing talk of sin, ruin, vice, and corruption. Looking at the stars, proud of those who "made it" and achieved success, my mother hummed the pretty songs of Molly Picon and my father made arrangements to attend the new theater play featuring Maurice Schwartz; my sister and I listened to Eddie Cantor's comedy show on the radio; and my grandfather leafed through a conservative morning journal or read the books on his own shelves. The world we knew, and now remember, was one of diligent schoolboys (on the way to "making good"), of mainstream singers and actors of East Side stages who told us sad and sentimental tales (but only with a happy end). No, we were oblivious to the "underworld culture"–its historian has now, in the Afterword to his revised edition (1993), downgraded it to an "underworld subculture." However long its transitional phase of depravity ran, in our youth there appeared to be room only for hearsay of the social idealism of an Abraham Cahan and a Morris Hilliquit and a David Dubinsky in the garment center; also the prowess of a young ethnic athlete named Hank Greenberg who was swatting home-runs on a sand-lot in Crotona Park. The dark epic saga of Abe Schoenfeld's East Side manuscripts was, possibly, suppressed; was, probably, repressed. It has a story which still has, surely, fully to be told.[3]

The Grunt and the Growl

There is a special pathos to this kind of drama that appeals to journalists and historians; but, then, all things are fated to decline and fall and little remains other than a few remembered names (and some anecdotes that go with them). The modern daily press, then and now, has always had a cultural penchant for the "monickers"; and in the constant repetition–John Nolan will always be "Legs Diamond," Benjamin Siegel "Bugsy," Arthur Flegenheimer (most improbably) "Dutch Schultz," Louis Buchalter "Lepke," Irving Wechsler "Waxey Gordon"–it at once trivialized and made immortal.

Human detail makes killers a size smaller, more human, and therefore rather less terrifying. During the trial in 1996 of one of the last of the powerful Mafia bosses, John Gotti of the "Gambino family" was given a daily artist-illustrated sartorial report as he sat nattily in the courtroom. We were reliably informed about the cut of the cloth of his Armani suit...the wide knot in his silk tie, the shade of blue in his new shirt (the *Newsday* reporters didn't miss a thing). This could be reckoned among the least of the press' misdemeanors in covering the "big, bad, and beautiful" in the murderous underworld. The gangsters appeared to be larger than life (or death). The ugly violence was unfailingly deplored, but there was no lack of breathless admiration for–or, at least, recognition of–Al Capone's bravura, Lucky Luciano's cunning, Meyer Lansky's administrative ingenuity, Frank Costello's political instincts, and so forth. As Gotti once said in defense of his public flamboyance, "You got to go in there with your suits, your jewelry. Put it in their face. When people go to the circus, they don't want to see clowns. They want to see fucking lions and tigers, and that's what we are" (Peter Maas and Salvatore Gravano, *Underboss* [1997], p. 411).

Peter Maas is of two minds about this. The Mafia at a certain stage in its notoriety needed a favorable public image, and he thinks Gotti rose to the occasion–and dressed for it. "He looked the way Americans wanted a gangster to look. It was as if he had studied every gangster movie ever made and absorbed the lessons in his own persona." And yet Maas sympathized with Gotti's "underboss," his deputy who in the final act "betrayed" him, turned against him, gave full incriminating testimony to the prosecuting attorneys. He senses that Sammy Gravano was right when he made his basic complaint about Mafia bosses in the limelight. What did they think they were up to?–mixing and mingling with TV stars, sitting for a portrait by Andy Warhol, and similar gags? "That wasn't me, to go somewhere just to be seen. We're not actors, we're not actresses. We're gangsters and racketeers. We're not supposed to be known to the public. We're a secret society. What kind of secret is this?" Both boss and underboss had a point, and it made for one of the large fatal contradictions which destroyed what they both called and revered as "the life." The underworld could not live in the overworld. When racketeering became profitably organized Big Business, the whole chaotic, small-time structure of the phantasm that they were chasing–it could be called "gangster capitalism"–fell apart.

The reporter Peter Maas whom I have been quoting–a latter-day Psmith to whom we are indebted for a wealth of rich, invaluable book-length detail

about New York crime–makes an acute observation about how moral values
get suspended for long periods of time during the intensive coverage of gangland murder stories. Still, a bias shows; an attitude is expressed between the
lines; hardened reporters (and their cynical tabloid editors) are seen to be
"rooting for" one side or another. Maas himself, in his two books on *Cosa
Nostra* killers, can't help turning out to be something of a fan or rooter for one
or another of his protagonists, both of whom had turned state's evidence against
their own Mafia families. *The Valachi Papers* (1969) first shed light on the
Cosa Nostra, "our thing." In his more recent narrative which recounts "the
story of Sammy the Bull Gravano" (1997), he waxes indignant at the prejudices of our newspaper culture against the man who was sufficiently brave
enough–and (well, yes) heroic and moral enough–to break his oath and "spill
the beans." From the newspapers a reader would, alas, come away with the
impression that Gravano who finally saw the light–"I'm finally doing the right
thing," he confessed–was really the dark villain: "I've been reading all this
stuff about me, like I'm the devil. I'm a rat. I'm a canary. I'm a stool pigeon. I'm
a piece of shit. I'm a traitor....Which side are these reporters on?" More than
that, he was a squealer...a traitor...a snitch. The obloquy which was poured on
the gangster's head at this moment of truth and remorse, if not redemption,
moves Maas to a sympathetic defense of the ethics of a turncoat. He resents the
attitudes of *Newsday* and the *New York Times* which "shared a nearly universal
perception that Sammy's sole motivation was to spare himself life in prison."
After the plea-bargaining deal with the F.B.I. Gravano was given a light sentence, was paroled, and has now been living in freedom (if in daily danger of
revenge).

As the historian A.J.P. Taylor once contended in a discussion program with
me (and he was, as always, pretty persuasive), no good biography can be
written of a man's life without some element of sympathy or approval for even
the most disagreeable character. (I allowed Bismarck and Napoleon, but pleaded
an exception for Hitler, for Stalin.) Accordingly, we have now a "balanced"
view of a Mafioso:

> Whenever we got a Soviet defector [said a senior FBI officer, recalling the days of the
> Cold War] he was treated like a hero, a guy who had seen the light, and now was
> helping our side, doing the right thing. Yet *Cosa Nostra* has done far more to damage
> the well-being of the United States than the Soviet Union ever did. And here was Gotti
> portrayed as some sort of folk hero and Sammy as a Judas. It didn't make any sense.
> Where were our values?[4]

This was Sammy the Bull's last charge. In his one and only memorable
phrase (the rest are only variations which we covered in our previous chapters
on the f-word), he had announced to the astonished F.B.I. director, "I want to
switch governments." For some he had been a "prince" in an underworld
empire–for others, a style-setter in a "gangster culture." He was seen as a

culture hero in a racketeering life-style; or as a soldier on active duty in an underworld army. But no one had ever surmised that the mob thought of itself somehow as *a government*. It wasn't. Perhaps the phrase was a snippet of an ambitious influence from the counter-cultural pretensions of the 1960s: alternative power-centers, sort of. But these squalid gangs represented neither a social system nor a state-within-a-state with self-legitimating rules of governance. It aspired to be a "gangster capitalism" but it became increasingly marginalized in American society and was reduced to an urban excrescence.

Some sensitive reporters have caught an old, familiar note of dissent and disenchantment, as another quasi-ideology produced a God, or Godfather, that failed. It had a few ideas but they were thin, and its so-called ideals were even more anemic. They would die for honor and a loyalty oath, but they lived for greed. They wanted a good old-fashioned life and traditional values for "the family" but they wound up living isolated in fortified villas, with underpaid servants (and one henchman was "whacked out," i.e., killed, for wearing, on the same day, the same hand-painted necktie as the boss). They made no famous last stand, with their smoking guns causing a big bang; and they had no language for even the most elementary of memorial inscriptions: They couldn't even spell: "Here fell heroes and their freinds." They whined and whimpered. One of them picked up a hackneyed middlebrow phrase to the effect that they were being victimized in "a victim culture."

"What did I do," so Johnny Dio asked, "that J.P. Morgan didn't do?...It's all a racket. Isn't Wall Street a racket?"

Will any of their names be remembered? All of them, Jews and Gentiles alike, traveled a short while toward the sun and (to adapt Spender's poetic phrase) left the vivid air signed with their dishonor. Their world rose and fell. The reference to executives of organized crime as "Mafiosi" has just phraseological significance. A few survived, and passed on the very American lesson for permanent success–Don't rob the banks. Own them.

But those names! And nicknames! Surely they will last a little longer, for they were reminders of their existential reality, of a strange and savage Europe, the primitive old world of their immigrant fathers, forever separating them from the Smiths and the Joneses, living uptown or on the West Side or in the suburbs or further out in the country. Their monickers–or, in older slang, handles–were signatures in an elemental melodrama of outlaws and rebels, of strangers in a new land. One night in 1936, when the young and energetic District Attorney, Thomas E. ("Tom") Dewey, was going after the vice rings in the Manhattan of Lucky Luciano (and the campaign finally brought this particular Godfather a sentence of life imprisonment–and eventual deportation), the New York police arrested a host of prostitutes, madams, pimps, and other whore-house personnel. Among them the following *"madams"* were later persuaded to testify: "Nigger Ruth, Sadie the Chink, Jenny the Factory, Polack Frances, Silver-tongued Elsie, Gashouse Lil, Frisco Jean, and Cokey Flo."[5]

Luciano protested that he had nothing to do with the ladies in question, "not with none of those broads." But luck ran out for him: the jury disbelieved. Luciano ended with a whimper in his *Last Testament*-memoir, earning himself a humiliating tag of "cry-baby" by whining about "Dewey's crap," about "that little shit with the mustache," and how "Dewey was such a goddamned racketeer himself, in a legal way, that he crawled up my back with a frame and stabbed me…." There was no excuse for a Godfather and the head of a Family to be crying, out loud, and in mixed metaphors yet.

In all of this we are, as I have suggested, close to that abstract school of nominalist thought which argues that names are substantial, are emblems of reality, and can entertain a half-life of their own. Accordingly, I close this discussion of personal nomenclature by referring to one historian who, similarly, has been "taking liberties" by associating visual images with the sound of words. Our scholar of New York gangsterdom (Albert Fried) has read all the contemporary accounts and insists that "the sound of their names did chill the bones, did paralyze the will, did lend themselves to metaphors of assault, enslavement, destruction." The gunsels were, in point of fact, "as ferocious and as cunning and indefatigable as their reputations made them out to be." Newspaper stories made their nicknames household words.

But who today remembers–and why, and how–Louis "Lepke" Buchalter and Jacob "Gurrah" Shapiro? Do the newspaper headlines still live? "The invocation of [Lepke's] name–and Gurrah's by way of contrast–came to exert its own effect, as though one tempted fate simply by uttering them. The sound of 'Lepke' can easily call up images of a wolf–*lupus, lupo*–creeping up on an unsuspecting prey for the kill; 'Gurrah' suggests, perhaps, a huge growling beast.."[6] One Godfather boasted that his family consisted of all lions and tigers. But the circus has moved on. All that's left are memories of the grunts and the growls.

And so back to P.G. Wodehouse. We left him with Psmith in New York, wrestling with words, trying to get a fuller grip on "realities." Wasn't he also a stranger in a world he never really knew? Or, like so many other newcomers to these shores, had he quickly discovered "something worth fighting for"? Do these things happen "only in America"?

19

Was This How Things Really Were?

"Why America? I have often wondered about that." So Wodehouse wrote in his memoir *Over Seventy* (1957), and offered the touching explanation, for whatever it's worth: "This yearning I had to visit America...was due principally, I think, to the fact that I was an enthusiastic boxer in those days and had a boyish reverence for America's pugilists—James J. Corbett, James J. Jeffries, Tom Sharkey, Kid McCoy and the rest of them." At any rate "Kid Brady" became an heroic figure in Psmith's crusade against "raw actual misery" and, con-sequently, we often find ourselves at the ringside of adolescent longing.

The contest was short but energetic. At intervals the combatants would cling affectionately to one another, and on these occasions the red-jerseyed man, still chewing gum and still wearing the same air of being lost in abstract thought, would split up the mass by the simple method of ploughing his way between the pair. Towards the end of the first round Thomas, eluding a left swing, put Patrick neatly to the floor, where the latter remained for the necessary ten seconds.

This Wodehouse could have seen, and could have written in prim and proper gentlemanly prose, in London. But if he longed for something more and different, for "the realities," he found some of them in the bars and gyms of the New York sporting underworld. Here is Pugsy Maloney explaining the cat in his arms ("It's a kitty what I got in de street") to Billy Windsor (who, combining "the toughest of muscle with the softest of hearts," was "always ready at any moment to become the champion of the oppressed on the slightest provocation"):

> "I wasn't hoitin' her....Dere was two fellers in de street sickin' a dawg on to her. An' I come up an' says, G'wan! What do youse t'ink you're doin,' fussin' de poor dumb animal!?' An' one of de guys, he says, 'G'wan! Who do youse t'ink youse is?' An' I says, 'I'm de guy what's going' to swat youse on de coco if youse don't quit fussin' de poor dumb animal.' So wit dat he makes a break at swattin' me one, an' I brings her in here, cos I t'inks, maybe you'll look after her."

Was this the way the Pugsy Maloneys spoke in New York in 1915? I don't know, and I can't imagine who does.

Mark Twain's *Connecticut Yankee* apparatus might catch the voices on a bygone wave-length, and today we have archives of "oral history," with a tape for every conceivable accent, inflection, and ethnic lilt. But the history of the language "as spoken by common men" depends necessarily on works of contrived fiction, artfully recorded. and confidently defended on the theory that the truth is in the poetry. Yet there is, also, and historians have unfailingly insisted on it, a poetry in the truth. It may well be that the ephemeral "spirit of the age," or zeitgeist, is impossible to recapture...*temps perdu.* But at least we ought to be able to sense or imagine the difference. Wodehouse commentators often miss the point. J.B. Priestley once wrote: "In the matter of wildly metaphorical slang he has beaten the Americans at their own game. Meet a New York crook of Mr Wodehouse's invention and you find he talks not as such crooks actually do talk, but as they would like to talk."

This drives us into a roundabout, indeed a vicious circle, for how could Jolly Jack Priestley himself have had the faintest notion of how New York crooks "would like to talk"? How could he know which part of their rich vernacular was native to their own speech and what they had picked up in a cinema showing a movie following the plot of a book? Or is it the wild fate of all social reality, its words and deeds, to find an ultimate existence, a final form, in the related fantasies of fiction? The actual Père Goriots are all dead, but Balzac remains our living source.

For a book or two young P.G. Wodehouse became a poet of "million-footed Manhattan." The Pugsy Maloneys are gone, but Plum's "little old Noo Yawk" lives. It encapsulates a lesson for us in an older newspaper culture: what the papers used to say, and how a novelist of the day imagined they said it.

Part 5

In the Crossfire of the Media Wars

*"The majority of our educated classes is
suffering from a curious epidemic.
They are not stage-struck, indeed; that would
have been a minor infatuation....
No, from the beginning of the present
excitements – the barbarian war,
the Armenian disaster, the succession of
victories – you cannot find a man
but is writing history; nay, every one you meet
is a Thucydides, a Herodotus, a Xenophon. The
old saying must be true, and war be
the father of all things, seeing what a litter of
historians it has now teemed forth at birth."*
—Lucian *(120-200 A.D.)*

*"The first thing to notice is the continued, and
equal, vigor both of 'the introspective,' and
'the aesthesis' meanings. Preserved by the
insulating power of the context, they flourish
happily side by side without the slightest mutual
contamination. Here are two lines from Pope*

*'What thin partitions sense
from thought divide
While pure Description held
the place of sense....'*

*Description fills up the void by lack of
profundity, of pertinent comment on life, of
intellectual meat."*
—C.S. Lewis, *"Studies in Words" (1960)[1]*

20

Spin Doctors and Other Quacks

Whether this analogy was worth pursuing is dubious, and questionable also is the offhand verbal snappiness of coy and careless reference to the "obscene" qualities in American political life. Why should this be? When "the culture of obscenity" (in films, books, advertising, soft porn, etc.) becomes identified with the inalienable right to have fun, freedom, and the pursuit of self-fulfilment, how can you belatedly set limits and at the last moment call for abiding by the rules and regulations of ethical standards? This is how. "You haven't had a good laugh until you hear the 'MF'-word, and others unsuitable for family newspapers, get a workout the likes of which they haven't had since the fuzzy-cheeked revolutionaries took over Columbia University in the 1960s." This is showy knowledgeability, quite irrelevant to the argumentative thrust of such analysis the pundit intended to offer his readers; in fact, it obscures it. (I was delayed by taking a moment to figure out what the "MF"-word was; and others, even less familiar with fuzzy-cheeked argot, may take a bit longer.)

The columnist in question, Mr. Edwin Yoder, Jr., went on for a few more paragraphs on the "savagery and irresponsibility" in that particular electoral campaign (mostly on the part of the Republicans who, in the revised "f-word" of the day, "starting futzing around"); and all this without even the vaguest suggestion about where the serious reader could look to find the causes of such democratic degradation. But that kind of Lippmannesque inquiry might lose the coast-to-coast syndicate some readers, hooked nowadays on the "new journalism" of *biff-boom-bang*. So many of our late-twentieth-century pundits flaunt this kind of fin-de-siècle insouciance, mixed with a measure of fancy writing and school-boy pretense...and, in this case, the climax of the following highfalutin' conclusion: "Meanwhile, hearing the White House and Republicans match wits over the meaning of the election, we are in for the greatest exercise in spin since Penelope held the suitors of Ithaca at bay pending the return of Ulysses from the Trojan War."[2] Homer would also have had his difficulties with "spin" (as well as "monte" and "*MF*"), although the Greeks would surely have a word for it all.

I remain with the question: Can one always grasp the meaning of what the newspaper reports? Its dispatch is intended to be simple, readily meaningful. But how much slips away because of "in-language" to which the average reader is "out"?...because of some story's relatively recondite vocabulary which can't be further reduced to a common enough denominator.

Finance is the most obvious example. The scientific achievement of a Nobel-Prize winner is another. Sports pages are the most regular winners in the contest for losing readers who do not happen to be *au courant* with the-rules-and-regulations (and jargon) of the game in question. An important meeting of the American Basketball Association—playfully, as always, headlined as NBA TIGHTENS THE RULES TO LOOSEN UP THE GAME—came to the following decision that mystified me (a basketball fan of sorts): "There will be stricter guidelines regarding illegal defenses, with the defenders in the lane no longer allowed 2.9 seconds before they must double-team the ball."[3]

Entymologists have had—when one examines all the "derivations unknown" and "presumed origins," both lost in the mists of time—a rather hit-and-miss record in the analysis of old words. How should they fare better with the new coinages? These turn up every day, bright and clever and (mostly) short-lived. Sometimes they can be ascribed to a wit, a songster, an ad man, a TV comic, even an unlikely academic (McLuhan and his global village and the-media-is-the-message; Charles Reich and his greening of America). But more often than not there are rival claimants for introducing "*Right on!*," "*Cool, man!*" or "*You slay me*" or "*the decision-making process.*" On occasion a new coinage is a phrase in search of a meaning, and if doesn't get it, it can survive only as a kind of rare Lewis Carroll nonsense-syllable. Recently, on British television, that worthy wit and dramatist, Alan Bennett, introduced some equally worthy contemporary with the words: "And there's not a lot of what I call splother about her." The next day it was quoted by the TV critic in the *Independent* (14 November 1994) with the words: "I haven't got a clue what this means either, but it seemed somehow appropriate." Being somehow appropriate can vaguely cover a vast number of vivid verbalizations.

And indeed a paragraph later the TV man in the *Independent* was complaining about some lack of "modernization" in a BBC dramatization of classic stories. He illustrated his point (and inserted her parenthetical explanations) with this: "Indeed, subtitles might be necessary for today's youth to understand phrases like 'rotten swizz' ('well uncool') or 'horrid, hateful little boy' ('wus')." I doubt whether Eric Partridge or H.L. Mencken could help us out in this sticky thicket. Slang is overrated as the shortest line between a word and a meaning. It can be *in* when most readers are out–new-fangled when they are old-fashioned–fast, vivid, and shiny where we're slow and dull...and, well, uncool. (Maybe I'm beginning to get it....)

In the admirable coverage of economic and financial events which Wall Street correspondents contribute from New York to the *International Herald Tribune*, there is much weighty atten-tion given to "basic trends" and "large movements." But the "hard facts," which newspapers are supposed to live by, are not easy to gather in evidence. Careful readers can readily spot the holes in the argument for boom or bust, inflation or deflation, higher wages or lower profits, and the like.

Recently a new and useful phrase has come into journalistic practice which passes muster for evidence–*"anecdotal evidence."* In a story about "good news about jobs"—but then why is Wall Street (with its eye on inflation) so glum?–the reporter makes a significant qualification: "Anecdotal evidence hints at." What this means, in older formulations, is that *some say* that the very opposite may well be the case. The new phrase–borrowed, I suspect, from professional academic historians who are systematic enough to classify a half-dozen different forms of evidence–serves to cover up a newspaper's uncer-tainty by giving it a highfalutin' credibility.

What exactly is *"anecdotal evidence"?* An "anecdote" by itself is of dubi-ous value; it re-ferred, originally, to something unpublished, usually items of gossip (cf. *The Shorter O.E.D.*, vol. I, p. 69). Nowadays, if it is not something concocted by press agent hacks, it is an untrustworthy mélange of rumour, tittle-tattle, and hearsay: at best a tale twice-told and thrice-embellished. And so: Beware of "Anecdotal Evidence," a "buzz-word" of our currently "In-language." If wittily told the anecdote can induce a smile; it can never prove a point.

Occasionally a verbal sophistication slips through in a newspaper story and counters a measure of our despair at fable being taken for fact, uncertain-ties offered as faits accomplis. Harsh economic realities help, for often punish-ing difficulties are the best taskmasters for wayward prose. Thus, a startling realism overtook the new leadership of the Sony Corporation in Los Angeles after some years of inept management. A half-dozen top executives were dis-missed until hopes ran high again with the appointment (in October 1996) of a man named John Calley. The most striking thing about the selection of the new Sony president and chief operating officer was that *"he has great contact with reality"*–a connection which, as the Los Angeles correspondent of the *New York Times* observed, "is relatively rare in the business." With what had all the others been in great contact? Shadowy unreal configurations in the dark rooms of their Hollywood studios? The President of the Japanese parent com-pany, Nobuyuki Idei, had been increasingly alarmed at the overspending and the poor box-office results of what Columbia and TriStar had been turning out as "Sony entertainment." Calley was the man who could save the day, and one remark about his approach to "reality" was impressive and indeed rare: "It would seem arrogant to talk about this," he said. "I'm utterly unfamiliar with the problems there. I have all the anecdotal stuff like everyone else." Does this imply that anecdotal evidence is too thin to determine hard cases? To know all the stories is far from being in the big picture–familiarity with serious problems takes sterner stuff. Anecdotes, in other words, are suddenly not good enough, and certainly do not constitute reliable evidence to move around a million dollars or a billion yen. Being in contact with reality and the familiarity with colorful little stories that people like to talk about may be two different things. This distinction may go far.[4]

In the face of the confusion and obscurity, in which so many journalistic efforts at bright clever writing result, one sometimes longs for the old-time hacks and their dull prose without a college education. Sometimes the fault is the attempt to convey some relatively "in-side" information in a snap-crackle-pop way. The business pages of our major dailies virtually vibrate with this kind of thing–the news being the Virtual World Entertainment Corporation of Chicago has contracted for "systems to run its Battle Tech games," and the deal is that "it will provide the technological fuel to enable the computer game junkies to go into Virtual World's game centers, don headsets equipped with twin television screens and take up their data guns." (*IHT*, 14 November 1994). One cannot but be vaguely unsure what all this means, and what exactly is going to be going on except, as the playful headline writer put it: REAL SALES BUT VIRTUAL PROFIT—suggesting, I suppose, that one can either get rich or go bankrupt that way.

But this kind of verbal disarray becomes rather more deleterious when the subject becomes increasingly academic or philosophical, as they sometimes do on the literary pages of our newspapers where often a regular book-reviewer tries to wrestle several times a week with substantial intellectual problems, most of which are too top heavy to be carried in a lightweight 850-word column. Here is the knowing regular book reviewer of the *Washington Post*, Mr. Jonathan Yardley, agreeing with some author who is "steeped in the great inescapable truth about the human condition," namely that decay, loss, and oblivion are the way of the world. He affirms (on a grey Monday morning in November) that "eventually we'll be part of the same, lukewarm, uniformly distributed soup." What, then, matters success or failure, or indeed religious faith? "[T]his is certain: We all lose in the end."[5] It may be certain to the village atheists in the *Washington Post*, but the last time I heard there was a vast community out there of Christian believers (and one can here reckon additional millions of Jews and Muslims to that multitude) who are equally certain that with earthly loss an eternity is won, that, for them, in the end the divine ultimate purpose triumphs. I do not happen to be among them, but the casual peremptory tone in speaking of the highest matters is surely dismaying so early in the morning.

A "little learning" leads one into intellectual temptations, and it is as dangerous in theology as the sophomoric simplicities in sociology and anthropology that I have been citing. On another page in the paper William Safire was just confessing that he and his band of word-sleuths had been stumped by the Pope's usage (in his best-selling book *"Crossing the Threshold of Hope"*) of the concept of "soteriology." They looked the hard word up, and found that–following a parable in the Gospel of Luke: "The seed is the word of God"–it meant the doctrine of salvation. Some prefer it to soup, but this may no longer be news.

I am hard put to find in all the journalism which was spent on celebrating, or commemorating, the grand anniversary (the twenty-fifth) of that explosive pseudo-revolutionary phenomenon known as '68, wherein gifted extroverted students became, for a brief season, heroic figures in the media for the transformation of a rotten society governed by grown-ups. In Paris Danny Cohn-Bendit was taking power on behalf of the imagination; in London Tariq Ali was climbing the com-manding heights of Grosvenor Square; in Berlin Rudi Dutschke was refunctioning alienation into a liberation ideology; and in the USA Mario Savio and Mark Rudd and Bernardine Dohrn (where are they all now?) were fed up on all the b— s—— and ready to give it to all the m— f—— in the Establishment, but for real.

For my own part, I liked the idea of the eighty-five-year-old former Tory minister and old-time Fleet Street journalist (he was, he once told me, in Africa with Evelyn Waugh when *Scoop* was dreamed up) coming up with the most pertinent reminiscence, a snippet of a song lifted by a Scottish lass named Mary Hopkin, and he quoted it as evidence that even then one could be "plugged in." Here is Lord (William) Deedes humming the sentiments that a whole generation twenty-five years later tried to repress:

> *Those were the days, my friends.*
> *We thought they'd never end....*
> *We'd live the life we chose.*
> *We'd fight and never lose...*
> *We were young and sure to have our way.*

On the same day the *Daily Telegraph* also came up with a paragraph of new prose from a young English student wrestling with the problem of her own generation's point of view, if such there be. She devoted herself to answering a questionnaire which was to evaluate a thousand reports about Youth Today. Hedonism is, it seems, high on the agenda for every one of "Thatcher's children"–disco-dancing, clubbing, imbibing alcohol and drugs, in short pure pleasure-seeking, unite the generation....

And then Miss Imogen Edwards Jones commented memorably (and how far are we from the '68ers and their concerns for power and liberation!): "So my generation is optimistic, hedonistic, anti-establishment, and more feminist than the one which went before [presumably the generation of the '80s]. But the most worrying thing about the report is that, there I was thinking how cool and original I was...only to learn that I am just a cliché." (*Daily Telegraph*, 29 September 1994). Rare it is for a newspaper on any odd Thursday to flash such wit and wisdom. A half-century ago, as I recall, a New York intellectual named Harold Rosenberg achieved im-mortal quotability with his phrase about his own self-centred egoistic generation of deep and original thinkers–he indicted the "the Herd of Independent Minds."

21

Images of Violence, Words of War

Hoping for a Moral Resonance

Suggestive snippets in the quality Western press–and where else could we find such a plethora of cues to be getting on with?–do raise larger and more fundamental questions of psychology and even philosophy. I do not have the space nor indeed the competence to go into them here. But the matters that have been broached in the above–especially the nature of "reality" and "unreality"–are put by reporters as well as by pundits in the newspapers in a serious context (when they are writing at their very best); and they should be touched upon critically here. Although I know from argumentative international round-table discussions (where I have on occasion offered a summary of my views presented here) that the conventional self-confidence of the professionals tends to get ruffled, I trust my self-critical remarks can be accepted by my readers as fair and truthful. For, as the poet hopefully said, the truth wounds only to cure–but, as I have always conceded, some criticism can be negative, hurtful, sinister, and even deadly. This is the danger: when our fault-finding degenerates into a kind of total or totalitarian critique of the press and other media that we have, into a root-and-branch rejection of our System of Communication in the name of some utopian Alternative Culture. We remember the style of Dr. Herbert Marcuse and Prof. Noam Chomsky. *We* were all being fed nothing but "lies...repressive distortions...or imperialist ideology"–whereas *they* knew the truth, the real details of what is happening in the world–and this dazzling enlightenment came from sources, secret and unimpeachable, which they never took the trouble to reveal. No, the gurus with a special pipeline to truth and reality cannot help us.

For, as in the famous one-liner of the American wit, Will Rogers, we all know only what we read in the papers. If the papers vary enough, we can pick and choose, evaluate dispatches and editorials, compare the stories coming out in New York, or London, or Paris, or Tokyo, contrast the impact of the written word against the filmed chronicles of TV documentary (featuring foreign correspondents who happened to be there) and even get some assistance from weekly and monthly journals, and (last, but not least) from hard-backs...a long and thoughtful book-length analysis never harmed anybody. So it is that the press enables us to criticize the press, gives us the material to reflect seriously about the state of the world–in our case (in this section) about war and violence, prejudice and propaganda, and the peculiar malaise which appears to be overcoming our perceptions of what is going on. Are the new realities– which include carnage of the millions (including women and children)–too overwhelming for us to take? Are the complications–age-old tribal and racial prejudices, with invidious narrowness on all sides–too difficult for us to comprehend and thus to do anything sensible about?

Another poet has given us a striking and subtle guideline. In a line of verse that has been much quoted, T.S. Eliot remarked that "human kind cannot bear very much reality..." he meant either, or perhaps both (as is the way of memorable poets), of two things. A certain level of reality-perception is reached, and then there is a blockage. Or, if the disagreeable realities confronting us mount up to monstrously unmanageable proportions, then there is a blackout. One is quantitative, the other qualitative; and the ominous change from quantity-to-quality hovers darkly.

Consider the Balkan realities involving the civil war carnage of the 1990s. A correspondent writing from the Croatian capital, Zagreb, ponders this puzzling problem of blockage and blackout (for which there is, as always, a formidable German word, *Apperzeptions-verweigerung*, or perception-denial): "Appalling images have been captured by television cameras. The response from the West has been paltry." This is not simply a newspaper shot fired across the bow of television crews; for it is the obvious case that the press of the West has *also* recorded, in graphic prose, appalling scenes and have gone on, with similarly paltry effect, to express outrage and call for major correc-tive action. Still, one tends to expect that pictures are, or can be, more effective than words. The massacred bodies of children lying on a street in Sarajevo can make for a shocking declarative sentence–but it represents an infinitely more outrageous scene on your screen at home. Or does it? Our Zagreb correspondent suggests: "Perhaps the inertia has stemmed from the plethora of images of violence flashing across television screens. The images are increasingly indistinguishable and so seem to carry no moral resonance" (*New York Times/IHT*, 14 March 1995). What has gone wrong? For the practitioners of documentary film they can only hope to set things right with ever more—film. And the journalists are equally persistent and just as tireless in the reporting of stories that overwhelm us with yet another example of "man's inhumanity to man" (which, as the poet Robert Burns thought, "makes countless thousands mourn").

But just as the vivid prose of conventional war reporting becomes banal, platitudinous, and even soporific with its year-in, year-out descriptions of war's atrocities—how can today's story still move one, short of getting a piece by a Tolstoy and a black-and-white sketch by a Goya?—so do pictures, even by hand-held cameras with crackling sound of nearby gunfire, become lifeless clichés.

The committed French intellectual, Bernard-Henri Lévy, wants to mourn for the good cause of Bosnia; in his Zolaesque way he castigated the moral collapse of the West. His film *Bosna!* was called "the most vitriolic condemnation of the Western world's military inaction." And he explained, "I made this movie because I handle a camera better than I handle a gun." The trouble with this option is that "the handling of a gun" will produce those bleeding bodies in a Yugoslav village, the handling of the camera produces a thousand additional pic-tures which have apparently lost their power to induce real emotions, excite public opinion, change actual politics. A crusader's moral offensive against "ethnic cleansing" is somehow, somewhere, jammed up between his very lively camera and our very flat screen.

Too bad that we have now almost lost once-popular buzz-words with the tensile strength of "moral equivalence." It became a kind of cliché in its day (coined, I believe, by Jeane Kirkpatrick in a famous *Commentary* article in the early 1980s). But it never moved far away from its original meaningful content which was clear but not simple. That is to say, "moral" actually meant *immoral*–for the argument was about "equivalent vices" of two antagonistic societies, in the catchword of the day, "Kolyma *vs.* Coca-Cola," that is, the Soviet's Gulag evil as opposed to America's insipid national drink. As for "equivalent," it really signified "unequivalent" since it was rarely posited that both Cold War enemies were "as bad as" each other. It only suggested that in a revised world-view the main enemy was actually the war-mongering USA. Other Western powers, allied with eternally aggressive Germany and still-imperialist England, were all seduced by their own anti-Communist propaganda. Whereas the peace-loving elements remained neutral and even handed. They could, in trust and indeed in friendship, forge a united front with such pacific anti-nuclear initiatives coming from the much-maligned camp of the Soviet Union...and other Communist powers that had suffered so long in the isolation of a *cordon sanitaire.*

Built-in apparent paradoxes give a phrase an especially useful dimension; and we have seen innumerable examples when *cool* meant *hot, peace* meant *war, democracy* dictatorship–a circular image of *revolution* came to signify *linear* progress–and to be *bested* really meant to be *worsted.* A small idea, or a fragmentary enthusiasm, or an attractive conceit, hangs fast to such usages despite historical inflation and platitudinous repetition.

Even the so-called "Doctrine" of Moral Equivalence–now that the Cold War is over and a half-century of ideological argument has all but ceased–has not completely disappeared from shorthand usage in our newspaper culture. Debates over the past recur every now and then, and editorial writers and columnists look backward and take up old semantic cudgels. A writer in the

New York Post (in February 1999), discussing the 16-part television documentary series on *"The Cold War"* with Ted Turner's CNN being the prime target as well as British TV-producer, Sir Jeremy Isaacs, argued: "Leftists of the 1960s often preached the 'moral equivalence' of America and Soviet Russia. Some leftists still do. It always seemed like an incomprehensible belief. But perhaps as we *can* explain it–as an unconscious admission of kinship between Soviet ideas and the mainstream American intelligentsia's..."The phrase also emerged briefly in the transatlantic controversy over the Hollywood "Oscar" to Elia Kazan. The London press had a special concern for the story since many of Kazan's old Party-line friends (Carl Foreman, Donald Ogden Stewart, et al.) took refuge in England during the McCarthyite "witch-hunt" of the 1950s, with which Kazan is said to have famously cooperated. As in the old days the stormy polemics which broke out were loaded with metaphors and catch-phrases, glued onto the preserved clippings of that repository of newspaper culture, "the Morgue." Was it really a *witch-hunt*–and the notion was memorably dramatized in Arthur Miller's play *The Crucible* about the so-called Salem Witches of seventeenth-century Massachusetts? But anti-Communists, then and now, rushed to point out the "unsoundness of the metaphor"–for witches, by and large, didn't exist, whereas communists did ("and recently-opened KGB files tend to support the 'hysterical' estimate of their numbers, rather than, say, Arthur Miller's")....Again, did the blacklisting of Party liners and fellow-travellers of the day really amount to *"persecution"*? An article in the *Spectator* was entitled "Persecution Mania," and it continued to dissent in despair at threadbare myths still circulating in "the Hollywood Left's warped idea of Cold War history, especially its own." Old scraps of political history were reprinted in the *New York Times*: Bernard Weinraub's long and detailed dispatches from Hollywood where all the "Kazan victims," still alive, were quoted. One bitterly suggested that "someone should shoot him [i.e., Elia Kazan]"–as if Stalin's sometime GPU killers could still be imported to put paid to the enemies of the people. In the *New York Post*, a young columnist explained the culture wars of almost ancient history –

> In Russia, the 1950s meant the ongoing Gulag–the massive network of concentration camps where supposed enemies of the people labored, rotted and died. In the United States, Sen. Joseph McCarthy spent a few years harassing left-wingers. Although we now know that McCarthy was basically right that Soviet agents (or former agents) were cleverly concealed around American society, he was also a lout, and the nation soon tired of his bullying and put him out of business....

Thus, a simple lesson of an immoral imputation of equivalence is still pertinent; and the *Spectator*'s American correspondent puts it, if possible, even more forcefully still in the relevant language of yesteryear. Mark Steyn was also trying to explain "why the fact that the Soviet Union went belly up a decade ago seems barely to have impinged on showbiz proponents of the theory of 'moral equivalence'...." How could they make "an equation of a few underemployed screenwriters with Stalin's mountain of corpses"? Alas, it was "merely the more robust examples of the entertainment industry's enduring belief in 'moral equivalence'...."[1]

An Ether of Indecision and Obfuscation

At what point, then, do we cease being able to "stand very much reality?" —afraid in Conrad's "heart of darkness" to contemplate "The horror! The horror!"

Another filmmaker, Marcel Ophuls, concedes that journalism *has* done its job in explaining the war and exposing its cruelties, often at great risk. "The problem with Bosnia, Ophuls discovers, is something deeper: the nature of the Western societies in which the news reports end up. These societies seem increasingly unwilling to see, increasingly unable to feel." And so it is that Ophuls has made, in his *"The Troubles We've Seen"* (1994), a documentary film not about the war but about how it is being reported—obviously with words that fall short, and with pictures that fail to move in the way that mankind used to respond to appalling realities. If the message is not getting through, the messengers must seek faults in themselves; and, perhaps, in the whole system of sights and sounds in our contemporary com-munication networks.

Once again a lone despairing observer turns to vague notions of a culpable society, a.k.a. a corrupted culture, which is alienating human beings from authentic feelings: "Against this backdrop, the words and images from the journalists in Ophuls's documentary become deprived of sense, and their news dispatches float off into an ether of indecision or obfuscation." The culture seems to have grown mouldy. "Culturally," he says, "the signs are even more ominous." (They would be, wouldn't they?) Marcel Ophuls, whose previous work—on French collaborationism, on German concentration camps—managed to evoke memorable chords of anger and pity and distress, is now filled with a Spenglerian sense of gloom and doom. I do not think he is not merely rationalizing the lack of commercial box-office success of his lat-est efforts; he may well be entitled to put his sweeping argument: "No violence, real or fictional, is taken seriously any longer. It's all just imagery–video clips."

Artists in the past often persuaded themselves that their imagism, reflected in poetic words and imaginative pictures, was the true reality and "all that ye need to know." The language of literature and art gave us the deeper knowledge of the external world with which we had to cope; and it endowed us with the means by which we were actually "able to see...able to feel." There is, I sense, a new *Weltschmerz* in the phrase dismissing "just imagery." When images fail, virtual unreality has come again.

The dogs of war keep on barking, but our apathy to the news about its tragic savagery sets in on three levels–in reverse time order, on the level of the far-away readership which represses its natural interest and sympathy in the surfeit of distressing details; on the level of the foreign-desk editors who weary easily of "on-and-on-going stories" and instruct their reporters to hunt after other headlines; and, finally and most dismaying, on the killing fields themselves when benumbed survivors and decimated fratricidal armies give up on their original attempts to "tell the world" (which was also a way of obtaining foreign aid and support).

No correspondent stays for very long in the endangered war zones, and when a fresh face arrives to catch up on the latest butcheries, our newspaper culture shows itself unusually receptive (for a day or so). The new man is sure to make yet another attempt to recapture the pathos of war and, perhaps, make the anthologies of fine wartime writing. Chechnya flares up, and there is another grisly dispatch from Grozny. At the moment there is peace in Bosnia-Herzegovina, but the readers can only take just so much of the stench of bodies being exhumed after the massacres of ethnic cleansing. And here is a new *New York Times* correspondent, James C. McKinley, Jr., flying into a still-smoldering danger zone somewhere and trying his hand at finding words and sentences to convey the horror of a mini-holocaust–

> The dead were laid out on the ground in front of the still-smoldering tea factory. Someone had covered a few of the bodies with old shawls and rags. People who had come to find their relatives tiptoed down the line of the dead, gingerly picking up the rags with shaking hands.
> One woman lifted the corner of a bloody cloth, caught her breath and began to cry. There was a baby underneath. The baby's head had been hollowed out by a bullet fired from close range. The skull was empty, fragile, a broken gourd. The eyes were missing. The child was not her kin, but that did not matter.

Nor, I suspect, did it matter to the reader himself who, by this time, is caught up in the concern for good prose rather more than for another heart-breaking scene in a three-year-old civil war. In October 1993 Tutsi officers assassinated the first Hutu president in a failed coup, and the massacres claimed some 150,000 lives, mostly women and children.

The vignette was vivid (but the "tiptoeing" and the "gingerly," not to mention the "broken gourd," were a little self-conscious). The interview with a survivor was conventional ("When they came and started shooting, I ran and hid in the bushes."). The latest body count was dispiriting: sixty-two corpses on last Friday, mostly Tutsi women and children....Even if we could feel, and grasp, and *see* the scene, could we do anything about it? To help? To ease the panic "of people caught in their morning routines trying to flee, of children being shot down in the back as they ran, of women being hacked down with their children, of houses being set afire with dead and dying people inside."[2] If we could be outraged enough, we might have been moved to prod the UN, the West, or even Julius K. Nyerere himself (the former Tanzanian president) who was negotiating the Western-backed plan to deploy troops from neighboring African nations to stop the violence. But then how much confidence in the UN's Boutros Ghali, in the Western powers, and indeed in the momentarily stable neighboring nations has our media reportage left us with? Our newspaper culture goes to all the wars, but is entrapped by apathy and pinned down by helplessness.

22

How Not to Report a War (Lebanon 1982)

The *Oxford English Dictionary*'s definition of *hypocrisy* is, alas, all too pertinent: "The assuming of a false appearance of virtue or goodness, with dissimulation of real character or inclinations...."

The *Times* of London's account of how, during the Falklands War, the Spanish language press "failed the test of truth" set out eloquently the vices of unprofessionalism (and worse) in the reporting of military hostilities to a democratic public which had "a right to know." Readers were fed "biased" accounts. They should have been able to "learn more objectively about what was going on in the world around them." Official one-sided versions of what was happening were "handled uncritically." There was a lamentable lack of "respect for the facts." Editors and correspondents were "erratic in their judgments." Newspapers "over-identified" with one cause in the conflict.

Then one war followed another in the awful news of the day: tension over the Falklands in the spring, and alarm over Lebanon in the summer. Here, too, in the train of the Israeli invasion of 6 June 1982, there was a right to know–to receive unbiased news stories; to learn objectively what was happening in the Middle East explosion; to obtain from intelligent experienced foreign correspondents each day critically evaluated accounts of official communiqués; to offer, where appropriate, some shrewdly informed judgements on fast-breaking events; and, above all, to prevent partisan, emotional over-identification with one side or the other which would blur, distort, and even poison the atmosphere of public opinion.

In this perspective one can only report, with distress and some sense of betrayal, the failure of its own "test of truth" on the part of The *Times* and indeed of a substantial part of the British press. (Not to mention the Americans whose grievous shortcomings have often been detailed.)[1] It was an abysmal performance. Each day a concerned reader in London had to struggle his way through loaded dispatches, misleading headlines, deceptive photographs, supererogatory asides, irrelevant patches of purple prose, as well as whole blank areas of non-information unprovided by reporters who were too incompetent or too prejudiced to get around to them, or undemanded by editors who had no sense of the "big picture" or of the vital details that go to make it up.

The technical deficiencies were the least of it. On 9 August the *Times* reported the softening of the Begin cabinet on whether all the PLO should leave at once or in stages. Although the story told of the "compromise on offer" (namely, a requirement that only a "majority of the PLO" had first to leave) the headline insisted on reporting that it was a "HARD LINE." When the first guerrillas were about to embark from Beirut harbor, the *Times* headline (21 August) read: WHAT NOW FOR THE PLO IN EXILE AND BITTERNESS?–as if the Lebanon had in ten years become their homeland and not also a bitter place of "exile" (from, last time around, King Hussein's Jordan). One doubts that the trade-unions would allow it, but the *Times* might well make a new start by firing all of its headline writers. Not even the editor seems to be able to control their idiosyncrasies. On 13 August he wrote a not unreasonable leading article on why some of Israel's policies "make it difficult just now to be her friend." However, the catchpenny caption read:

THE PATHOLOGY OF PERSECUTION MANIA

In the text there was no indication of what pathology, what persecution mania. But then the *Times* is still relatively new to the modern practice of having the headline match the story. Understatement used to be its strength, misstatement is now its weakness.

On the pictorial side it is in a relatively unassailable position since it publishes so few photographs. An evaluation of the pictures shown on television would take us too far afield, and too deep into the morass of deception. In the *Standard* (London, 18 August) I note one revealing example: the TV pictures shown on ITN of Belsen-like children in a mental hospital in Beirut. A check was made with a leading nutritionist in West Beirut. He indicated that although the pictures were new, the cases were old. "The Lebanon was well known for its endemic illnesses; and what was shown were not the symptoms of nine weeks of war...."

The case of "Reagan's Little Girl" was even more grievous since (as Hugh Davies reported in the *Daily Telegraph*, 24 August) –

> President Reagan keeps a photograph of a 'maimed' child victim of the war in Lebanon on his desk at the Oval Office. The photograph was used by the President to berate Mr. Shamir (Israeli) Foreign Minister, during a chilly 20-minute interview in Washington.
>
> The news agency photograph, distributed worldwide earlier this month, showed a nurse feeding a 7-month-old baby who was said to have lost both arms after being burned in a bombing.

The caption in the *Washington Post* (and, presumably, throughout the world press) reported that the child had been wounded when an Israeli jet hit an East Beirut suburb during a raid on Palestinian positions.

An Israeli investigation launched by the chief of staff, General Eitan, concluded that their Air Force was not in fact involved: "The tragic incident was proved to be the direct result of indiscriminate shelling by the PLO."

The Israeli Health Minister, Eliezer Shostock, dispatched a special team to find the baby. The picture had been taken in a Beirut hospital where the child was treated with his mother. The mother and baby boy (not girl, as the newspapers reported) had been released from hospital, and they were traced to a Lebanese village. Professor Baruch Modan (the Health Ministry's director-general) visited the baby and his mother. He was found to be far from seriously injured and "in good health." He had suffered some burns, but neither arm had been amputated, although one was still strapped to his side because of a fracture. According to the *Daily Mail* which reproduced the picture on 25 August: "The original picture does appear to show a nurse placing her hand around the stump of an arm." But it was evidently clear from the original that the apparent "stump" was in fact the top of the milk bottle which the nurse had been feeding the child.* I take these details from the two dispatches in the *Mail* and the *Telegraph*, neither of which take the trouble to mention the name of the world-wide news agency involved or indicate any follow-up curiosity as to how this kind of discreditable photo service was possible. The *Telegraph* headline ran: BEGIN DISCREDITS PHOTO....The *Mail* kept a strange distance from its own story by running the headline: 'TRUTH' ABOUT WAR BABY picture.

Had the *Times* published the picture of Yasser Arafat grinning (why so happy when conceding such a grievous point?) as Congressman McCloskey dramatically announced the PLO's recognition of Israel, the readers might have been able to take a properly skeptical attitude to the canard. But it didn't; so its correspondent in a front page story headline "ARAFAT SIGNS PLEDGE TO RECOGNIZE ISRAEL" could, in his studied naivety, report nothing less than "an historic breakthrough." The facsimile of the signed document in question, reproduced one day later (27 July), revealed clearly that Arafat had mentioned no specific resolutions, no diplomatic details, indeed had only made a very "general" gesture–facts which led most serious European newspapers and their correspondents to take the whole devious affair as a questionable show of public relations. Small wonder that the editor of the *Times*, evidently reading only his own paper, could come to the extraordinary conclusion (27 July) that, in the ultimate peace, "the PLO's participation offers by far the best chance that an eventual settlement would win the consent of the mass of the Palestinian people..." As if the Palestinian electorate would ever be asked to say yes, or no, or maybe, to anything proposed by this sterling band of plebiscitarian democrats!

---

*   The excellent West German *FAZ* reporter recorded on 26 August that it was the United Press International that distributed the picture and its false details. A week later the UPI confirmed the error, without apologies.

No, we were all grateful for the lack of pictures in the *Times*. They did not publish photographs of Yasser Arafat kissing babies, or embracing Lebanese widows to console them (see the *Observer*, 15 August, p. 8))–arranged and calculated publicity shots that any self-respecting newspaper editor, otherwise so alert to "news-management," would toss into the waste-paper basket.

What also should have gone into the trash of the day were the attempts of the young, dashing correspondents of the *Times*, short on space and long on literary ambition, to make a name for themselves as fine writers under fire. Especially grotesque–and even painful on the eyes, so early in the morning– were the juvenile efforts of Messrs. Robert Fisk and Christopher Walker, representing the *Times* in Beirut and Jerusalem, respectively. Walker was no talker, and Fisk would take every risk–but, ah, what a way they had with words! In the beginning, when the Israelis captured Beaufort Castle in the Lebanon, the Times' man heard the echoes of the clanking armor of the Crusades. (Oxford evidently still teaches its undergraduates medieval history.) By 6 August, Robert Fisk was reporting on "Dante's Inferno." On the same day he was inspired enough to move a few centuries forward in the potted cultural history which he brought along with him in his baton's bag. Now he was deep into the age of Leonardo and Michelangelo, and covering his beat he discovered: "Salma is a beautiful woman with dark eyes and the sort of smile that Renaissance artists used to give to Madonnas...." Later on he reported that "I saw a guerilla a few yards away kissing a small baby, its mother with her head in her hands, an older woman raising her arms toward the man's face, an El Greco of beseeching eyes and hands" (*Times*, 23 August 1982). And soon he is well into the nineteenth century as the Beirut battle resumes: "a rain of golden flares dropped down from the night sky between the clouds like the closing moments of some Wagnerian epic, all movement and garish color." But he hastened to assure us it was not yet "the twilight of the gods."

Nor do the flights of literary pseudery get any better even if we are spared the putative source (say, Jules Verne): "The explosions were muffled, like doors slamming somewhere deep beneath the earth" (*Times*, 7 August 1982). All was grist to his mill, geology, literature, music, the arts. But in the midst of it all he couldn't leave off letting you know he was also something of a cinema buff: "It was meant to be something of an epic departure....On Saturday, driving down to the port amid the lorry-loads of guerrillas, the whole affair had more in common with Fellini, a passage through a place of ruins, of gunfire so loud it made your head sing...." (*Times*, 23 August 1982).

How was it that there was room for these kinds of schoolboy exercises in purple prose and not for a whole host of prosaic military and political details, without which no reader could form an opinion for himself? It remains a mystery of an afflicted Fleet Street journalism ("singing heads" indeed!). Why did we have to know on 28 July, wasting four valuable lines of expensive cold type, that Robert Fisk that day had seen among the detritus of a bomb attack "a complete set of Collins' blue-covered Illustrated Encyclopedia, riven into shreds beside the ruined houses..."? What journalistic urgency required us to know that it all somehow reminded him of "a lunatic cameo of old photographs of the London blitz"? Why had he time to put to paper all this fancy stuff for his file-of-clippings book–and no time to tell us whether he had been able to put any challenging question to Arafat at the Congressman McCloskey conference. Why had he no space to interview a single Arab Ambassador as to why they were making such difficulties about taking the Palestinian guerrillas into their own countries? Or a moment's quiet to report what possible impact the revelations of murder and terror which had obtained in the PLO state-within-a-state in Lebanon might have on the reigning European political notion that Arafat's "moderates" were a force to be welcomed in the West Bank and Gaza? More than that, why wasn't there time to report on why the PLO had consented so quickly to "abandon ship"–especially when no *Times* report ever indicated that the PLO guerrillas (only "civilians") had even been hit, or that even one of their headquarters (only "refugee camps") had been bombed.

Thus, we had our fill of Dante, and Leonardo, and Wagner, of El Greco and Fellini–but precious little Clausewitz. The impressionistic mannerism left us, alas, with an impression not of war and its consequences but only of a penchant for gaudy phrases. Robert Fisk had time and space for everything but the telling of some all-important military detail. As Hemingway once told Dos Passos in Spain, beware of sentimentalists on the front line! The American *Herald Tribune*, true to its Paris traditions, reported soberly on "heavy fighting" and "intense opposition." With Messrs. Walker and Fisk, everything was always "savage" and "horrifying." At one point, feeling so badly about it all (War being Hell, as is well known), Fisk breaks down and tells us (7 August) that in the Beirut devastation: "we turned our backs in something akin to shame and fled."

His flight took him back, presumably, to the Hotel Commodore (which had just been bombed).

At some point the plight of Fisk of the *Times* began to break our hearts. He had to witness the humiliating "exodus" of the brave and valiant fighters he had been reporting so vividly for years, nobler chaps than he had ever known, sacrificing all in a finer cause than he had ever covered: "When I found Mustafa yesterday morning, leading his two small sons to the lorries that would take them to the Beirut port, he smiled in an embarrassed way. He was sad, he said. He did not know what would happen in the future. Of course the PLO would survive. But when we shook hands, he was glad to be asked no more questions." Rigorously loyal to his duty as a professional journalist (which, some would have thought, was always to go on asking questions), he began to ponder–Wordsworth, one suspects, sneaking in here–thoughts too deep for tears: "And when I turned back I found my friend weeping uncontrollably. He was not lamenting an individual's fate. There was something far deeper than that at stake yesterday morning…." We held our breath while he plumbed the depths of the problems; it was all so "sad and monstrous." But in the end we were left only with this wondrous thought: "and amid this madness one wondered how many would have stayed to die, how many understood what was happening, how many had done terrible things in the Lebanon these past seven years since the civil war gave the Palestinians power"[2] (*Times*, 23 August).

But, back at the bombed Hotel Commodore, had the bombing been intentional? To be sure the Israelis had admitted how much they hated the kind of reporting that the Western correspondents had been dispatching from West Beirut (thus getting around the efforts of the Jerusalem censors to do their version of a "Falkland blackout" of all horrific military oeprations). But, then, were the Israelis doing that kind of pinpoint bombing? On 5 August we were told by Robert Fisk in Beirut that "To describe the shelling as indiscriminate would be something of an understatement." Christopher Walker, cabling from Jerusalem, was only slightly more tentative in referring to the "apparent random nature" of the bombing. Between the two of them we came away with the firm notion that the Beirut bombing was "haphazard" and "inaccurate." But suddenly, when it suited these certified ordnance experts assembled, it became "precision bombing." The French ambassador's residence had been struck, and for a change the infamously random bombsters had "the target in their sight" and had made a "deliberate" hit.

The editors of the *New York Times* eliminated the word "indiscriminate" from their front-page report by Thomas Friedman in Beirut (5 August). Friedman was outraged by the omission. He wrote, in an internal memo (quoted in the *New Statesman*, 27 August), "I am filled with profound sadness…I feel thoroughly humiliated." He explained: "My God, your own reporter's hotel was hit 30 feet from his room and there are no Palestinian positions in the Commodore…."

Now, Fleet Street fun-and-games apart, it is of some international public interest to know just what the Israeli bombing strategy was, and whether (whatever it was) it turned out to be wild and inefficient, destroying homes, schools and hospitals in hit-or-miss fashion (and we saw the film in living color on TV)–or perhaps "uncannily precise" (and the SAM-8s were in fact eliminated in the Syrian-held Bekaa Valley). Was General Sharon, in other words, a "Bomber" Harris, willing to raze a civilian city in order to achieve a military advantage (and who was there to photograph the hospitals in Hamburg and Dresden?)–or was the point of it all the brilliant PLO checkmate maneuver, against superior Israeli forces, of using the homes, schools and hospitals as a shield against all-out attack?

Only when it was all over did the little self-censored truths emerge. Now John Bulloch could write (as he probably couldn't in his weekly column in *Al Nahar*, the Arabic Beirut newspaper) of the Palestinian guerrillas: "They set themselves above the law, they terrorized, extorted, and inflicted their own summary punishments..." (*Daily Telegraph*, 20 August). The patient newspaper reader had been carefully protected for so long from any "unevenhanded" reporting which might make him think too badly of a force which, however extreme and violent, was after all, "fighting for an idea"–now, at long last, he was offered a hitherto hidden dimension of reality.

Now it could all be told. Fisk's dispatch on 21 August went so far as to hint darkly at "corruption" in the PLO's leadership, at the dishonor of PLO officers who had gone off (with wives) to Damascus "and had not returned to fight." The man's colorful vivacity now gave way to a sour bitterness as the defeat of the PLO and "their betrayal" drove him to some version of a familiar "stab-in-the-back" theory: "the guerrillas of the PLO will be at the mercy of Arab regimes which have no love for revolutionary instability and which were thus content to leave the PLO to its doom...." The revolution, obviously, was being devoured by reaction: "Having received no real military assistance from Jordan, Iraq, Egypt, South Yemen, Algeria or Tunisia, Arafat is now consigning his men to those comatose nations, handing them over, in fact, to the security services of a whole series of largely repressive regimes." There were new tones, new touches. Was he trying to tell us that, in the end, honor was only due to "the thoughtful" Khalil Wazzir ("Abu Jihad," an Arafat commander throughout the siege) who had been "privately wishing the PLO had adopted a more bellicose spirit in the last days"?

I suspect it is a vain hope to expect to have serious questions answered by even the most serious of our daily newspapers. Correspondents were too preoccupied telling us how they felt and what they thought about the hellishness of war to be able to inform us as to what was actually going on. Editors–the *Times'* were once satisfied to cover the Korean war in the 1950s via their correspondent in India–were too gentlemanly to instruct their young men in the field to stop sermonizing, at the least they should cease and desist from cheap and easy journalistic tricks. The sophisticated *New Yorker* editors used to classify them under the cynical Quotes-Which-We-Doubt-Ever-Got-Said and Department-of-Raised-Eyebrows; and to make some professionally worthy attempt to do justice to the dimensions of the tragedy by going in for hard, crisp, straight reporting.

But perhaps this is, as I say, asking too much in a world of depreciating, if not collapsing, journalistic standards. What can one really expect from editors who, failing "the test of truth" in their aberrant headlines, their wayward reportage and unbalanced editorializing, seek to add to the zero-sum of the paper's insights and illuminations by publishing (6 August) a piece by a playwright set out to Beirut by the Bertrand Russell Peace Foundation for three days? Under a headline which would have disgraced flashy popular papers like the *Sun* or the *Daily Mirror*–TEA AND 7-UP AS THE BOMBS FALL–a playwright called Howard Brenton reported on his instructive visit to PLO headquarters and his nice impressions of taking drinks with the PLO fighters ("the wine bottles and vine leaves printed on the table's oil-cloth are indelibly stamped on my mind"): "I thought I would meet a bunch of thugs in West Beirut; instead I met the Palestinians, an attractive, witty, endlessly resourceful lot, with a love of story-telling and argument; in short, so like Jewish friends I have in England…." As for me, don't get me wrong–some of my own best friends are moderate guerrilla fighters in Chairman Arafat's underground headquarters, wherever they may happen to be at the moment–or in Osama Bin Laden's Afghanistan redoubt.

23

Interchangeable Tragedy

One Catastrophe at a Time

Our problem persists: the saturation point of journalistic prose, and the information overload of television pictures.

Short of the extraordinary, imaginative quality which suffused the writing about war by Leo Tolstoy, Theodor Fontane, Henri Barbusse, Erich Maria Remarque, and other literary masters, conventional newspaper writing about battlefields, with their ruins and casualties, soon reaches the point of no return on the investment–of emotion, morality, human sympathy–put in by the worthy correspon-dent on the front.

Human sensibilities were outraged by singular events in previous centuries. One recalls the headless bodies of the victims of Jacobin terror in the later stages of the French Revolution–the despair of the few survivors of the massacre of Chios (pictured in Delacroix' famous oil painting of 1824–diverse war crimes in the Crimea and in the Balkans. These events, and many others, provoked, aroused, and sustained angry popular feelings commensurate with the outrage. Nowadays when messages arrive from innumerable global villages about homicide, or fratricide, or genocide in countless wars and revolutions, it is helpless apathy that is registered. Battles begin to bore; slaughter satiates.

A clear awareness of this overload coefficient marked the career of one of the most famous European TV-news personalities. Hanns Joachim Friedrichs, who dominated the German commentary programs during the 1980s, modeled himself on the American "anchormen" (especially Walter Cronkite); and one guideline was his much-quoted maxim: "You can't broadcast more than one catastrophe per evening."[1] Newspapermen, with a slight snicker, contrasted this iron rationing of the bad news with their own truthful abandon in covering all disasters simultaneously: an earthquake on the front page, a fire and a flood on the second, a serial-murder's gore on the third, and a long feature on one or the other ongoing ethnic wars detailing civilian casualties (women raped, children bayoneted) to round off the day's news.

But whatever the media, electronic or print, there remains the new and transforming factor of satiety, or saturation, or the paralyzing condition known as "compassion fatigue."

Often we find the correspondent, covering wars and other catastrophes, trying to put some cool space between him and his story. At times this calls for a measure of intellectual distance; at other times it turns out to be, literally, mileage. (One famous London newspaper tried covering the Korean War in the early 1950s from its bureau in India. No significant improvements in memorable objectivity or perspective resulted.) At best the "long shots" do avoid some distracting minor detail and can sum up conveniently all the important aspects of the main news. Usually the compacted message is a nondescript effort as in the following paragraphs which I quote from the *Washington Post*'s story on another of the murderous raids in Algeria, actually filed by the *Post*'s man in the far-away French capital: "*Paris.*—As many as 200 Algerians died early Tuesday in a suburb of Algiers at the hands of attacks presumed to be Muslim militants dedicated to the overthrow of the government." He then goes on to record:

> ...the massacre in the village of Baraki, a few kilometers east of the capital, bore all the trademarks of the near-nightly butchery of men, women, and children that has plagued Algeria for the past several weeks. Armed groups of several dozen men enter villages, slit throats, disembowel pregnant women, behead children, shoot the survivors and burn their bodies, plunder and incinerate dwellings, and carry off young women.[2]

There may be, I sense, an abstraction too many in this catalogue of terrorist horror. Can it be that straight news telling and ethical (or emotional) impact are mutually exclusive?

In the following quotation from a dispatch to the *New York Times*, one would be hard put precisely to identify the tragic scene which its war correspondent, Steven Erlanger, tries so hard to record truthfully. Was it the carnage in Kosovo or in Bosnia? The brutalities in Burundi and Rwanda? The desolation in Mozambique or Angola? A historic reminiscence of the killing fields of Cambodia after the massacres of Pol Pot? The last days of the violence in Vietnam? Or a more recent ethnic or clannish cleansing in Somalia?

> Disoriented people wander aimlessly along dusty, cratered streets through the rubbish of civilization: broken furniture, a child's sweater, twisted girders, a women's wig, charred dolls, dangling pipes, felled street lamps, severed electrical and telephone wires jangling, moving like some weird mutant spider in the wind....

No, it is a scene in Grozny, in a lull between the Russian-Chechen offensives (March 1995). One may re-member the "mutant spider" for a few moments but then we will be overcome by more lurid sketches of human tragedies spiralling into endless death and darkness:

Doctors expect epidemics of cholera, diphtheria, dysentery and other diseases, with unknown numbers of bodies, civilian and military, buried quickly just be-neath the crumbling soil of blasted courtyards and ragged parks....The tread of a tank, twisted and brown with rust and caked dirt, lies like the fossilized back-bone of a long-dead monster.[3]

This is still the *Times'* Erlanger in Grozny; and, once again, we may remember the "mon-strous fossil." But after the next day's reports about the renewed combat in Afghanistan and among the Serbs and Croats it is understandable that we may think we are in devastated Kabul or Bihac. We turn away wearily from the morning papers' vivid accounts of the death and destruction which, alas, have become interchangeable.

If each man is supposed to die alone, and each ruined city perishes in its own way, then the worldwide overload of print and pictures, of universal and ubiquitous badness, is introducing a monotone sameness: We are witnessing a flattening of the rounded globe, a blurring of the natural contours, a benumbed indifference to the mournful message of *"the horror! the horror!"* No victim is a tragedy unto himself; but he is becoming faceless and nameless in the crowded, unending rush hour of the evening headlines and video clips.

The pioneering TV programs of the new mode of perception and receptiveness are those film anthologies of *biff-boom-bang* disaster snippets that cut from burning buildings and collapsing bridges to oil rig explosions and pile-up highway crashes, not to mention air-borne suicides jumping in free fall from rooftops. The couch-potato impassivity is a mix of lethargy, stolidity, and torpor, in the wake of orgies of vicarious over-excitement. It has become grisly popular entertainment all over, and is a model training session for the new mass insensibility.

Pulling Off a Genocide

The cry of murder used to be shouted from the mountaintops; now the echo in the valley is almost stilled. What has been called moral resonance is fast becoming a memory of the past, of older habits of ethical response.

In the beginning the horror of genocide or of a holocaust was in a class all by itself. Systematic mass murder of a race or a tribe or a whole people was spoken of in hushed dramatic terms; and no journalist or historian dared to compare the unutterable crimes of the present-day world with even the most heinous affairs of yesteryear. German anti-Nazis insisted on the "singularity" of Hitler's elimination of East European Jewry, and no "comparison" was allowed, even with Stalin's liquidation of millions in the old U.S.S.R. A distinguished American historian (Professor Bernard Lewis) was reprimanded by a French court during the 1990s for daring to suggest that the Turkish murder of Armenians in the horrific campaign of 1915 was not systematic or extensive enough to be classified in the genocidal terms of a holocaust. By the time of the emergence of the phrase "ethnic cleansing" for the internecine warfare in disintegrating Yugoslavia, much casuistry had been expended in the arguments about comparative mayhem. Concepts had become clichés, and the reporting of violence, of man's inhumanity to man, had become almost casual. A foreign correspondent in war-torn Zaire quoted an international aid worker in Kisangani: "You've got a bit of everything here. Hutu who have participated in genocide. Serbs who are most probably war criminals and, on the other side, Tutsi-controlled forces that are trying to pull off a genocide on their own."[4] In its easy-going slangy matter-of-factness, as if one were talking about a petty thief pulling off a heist on your local neighborhood bank, the very phrase–"to pull off a genocide of one's own"–suggests the process of barbarization which has overtaken our language and our world order in the present time.

Piecing It Together

I do not mean for these remarks to write off the whole genre of journalistic reportage of war and violence. Undeniably there are passages that stick in the mind: a paragraph that sears, an item that dissolves any apathy. I offer only two exceptional details, both from the newspaper accounts of the Palestine carnage in March 1996 when several Hamas terrorist bombs murdered dozens of Israeli citizens, a great many of them women shoppers and schoolchildren who happened to be passengers riding on the targeted buses. One journalist reported an odd piece of street theater: "Last month in Qalqila, a Palestinian town in the West Bank that Israel recently returned to Palestinian control, Hamas supporters staged a mock bombing of an Israeli bus, while residents looked on or cheered." He added a remark–after, with hindsight, one knew that the street-corner mock-up was not a ritual but a bloody rehearsal–to the effect that this was "outrageous" in the diplomatic context of Middle-East peacemaking.

After the bloody reality of a third bomb (two in Jerusalem, one in Tel Aviv), one mother described the anxiety in the house about the children who had not yet come home from school:

> On television we watch bearded men with white plastic gloves gather body parts. The angry desperation inside me grows. We're making peace! Why are we still scraping children's fingers from the sidewalk.
>
> Little work gets done, as we await the dreaded roll call. The process is too familiar. First, the bodies are pieced together. Then they are moved to a morgue. Families identify the missing.
>
> Anyone who thinks his or her child might have been a victim in bombing is advised to bring dental X-rays. A picture of a jaw is particularly useful.
>
> The file cabinet where I keep the children's vaccination records does not contain a single dental X-ray....I imagine myself dialing the dentist and explaining what pictures I need.

The mother's imagination is infectious; a reader, for a chilling change, can for once sense and identify with the horror and the outrage. Yet for how long?

I also see the television pictures on the evening TV news. For a moment those "bearded men with plastic gloves"–orthodox Jews who deeply feel the religious call "to piece together," to restore the creatures that had been made in the image of God–are no longer inexplicable Biblical figures scurrying around on the scene of the devastation. But they are indeed becoming all "too familiar." The dramatic pictures are repeated again in the late night news and on all other channels. How long before the familiarity breeds the old insensibility? It is not that we have become heartless and unfeeling; the increasingly imperturbable response among the readers and viewers of the world's violent news is less cynical than inert, at best appearing to be disinterested or dispassionate.

Horror can no longer shock. For the tragic sense of death is limited and episodic; none of us can live continuously at a level of loss and outrage. Even the most empathetic of witnesses succumb to a form of compassion fatigue. Survivors take refuge behind a protective shield of emotional distance; remoter spectators soon view scenes of man's inhumanity to man with a wilful and spiritless indifference. Apathy has come again.[5]

I should note the occasional, electrifying exceptions. Historians of mass culture are excessive when they imply an absolutization of the increasing emotional aridity. If an inauthentic indifference mounts demonstrably in all modern societies, there are also the moving hypnotic effects of the mass media–at first in the star-studded world of the cinema, as in the famous Rudolph Valentino funeral at which three female fans among the hundreds of thousands of mourners (in 1926) committed grief-stricken suicide...to the excitable notoriety of the pop pin-up favorites in the tabloids and the deep involvement of fans in TV soap opera's fictional characters. Indeed, there were many unique or unprecedented aspects to the aftermath of the death of Diana, the Princess of Wales (in the shocking Paris car crash of August 1997). Still, what I have called the "interchangeable" elements were striking in the emotional pageant of grief and mourning. One sage commentator (Alistair Cooke) found it sufficient to recycle the Valentino affair and H.L. Mencken's interview with the young matinée idol just before his death and spectacular funeral in New York City. And in the unusual atmosphere of the services for Princess Diana in Westminster Abbey came Elton John's recycling of his sad sentiments at the death of Marilyn Monroe (1962); he sang a revised version of his pop hit song "Candle in the Wind" as his contribution to Diana's last rites. Other candles, other winds–new words, old chords. It made little difference to the tears that were wept in the flower-strewn palace gardens that the grievous sense of loss was, mostly, second-hand.

At its most manipulative moments the mass media and its associated popular culture can succeed in giving life and death full cover; and the coverage includes a sense of personal intimacy. And hence, when in a brutal stroke of fate a loved one is struck down, it can also include convulsive outbursts of heartfelt bereavement. Virtually.[6]

When the Public Cries

It could be that the categories with which we have been recording "the media wars" on this subject of *apathy* and *compassion fatigue,* and the like, are themselves part of the problem, that is, they are fashionable terms which are shaped and distorted in the heat of current controversies. Polemicists charge, as we have seen, pictorial journalism with increasing deceit for its pretenses of virtual reality. Culture-critics maintain that the written word, especially at its everyday journalistic level, is no longer capable of touching moral emotions; that in the face of recent catastrophes it has been another case of "the bland leading the bland."

There is yet another school of thought–and it appears to prevail in the establishments of the world–which dismisses the whole idea that painful images on television and indeed screaming headlines in the press can, or indeed should, goad governments into action. Some Americans dismiss it as "the CNN factor." Moralists among the European intellectual classes periodically raise the cry that "something must be done" to alleviate, or even settle, an intolerable outbreak of injustice and violence. Apparently events did so move in the cases of Iraq's invasion of little Kuwait (leading to the Gulf War); the UN's intervention in strife-torn Bosnia and later the U.S.-led bombing campaign in Kosovo; the brief and disagreeable occupation by various NATO units in Somalia, and in the humanitarian-aid aftermath of various natural catastrophes (hunger and disease, floods and earthquakes) in the Afro-Asian world. Were ethics a moving factor, or was *Realpolitik* decisive?

In a 1997 study for the "Carnegie Commission on Preventing Deadly Conflict" the argument is put forth that "National Interests" are far more powerful than Media Images in determining what action a country takes towards violence and suffering outside its borders: "The national interest increasingly decrees non-intervention; long, hesitating consultation with allies; or, occasionally, a quick entrance and exit. Television pictures play little part in these decisions."[7] Two questions are herewith raised. Is it true that public opinion (no matter how one defines it and measures it) plays "little part"? And is it right that the Jeffersonian watchdogs of a civilized, democratic society should abdicate from, or fail at, their enlightened functions?

The two answers are obviously intertwined, and cannot be taken as separate strands. If the media coverage fails, for whatever reason (from numbing pictorial excess to flaccid prose), then it is all the more a factor in decision-making, for it has left a vacuum in the corridors of power–an inert public opinion alongside which ambitious opportunists can decide as they please. For another, calculating "national interests" can well include, again in the Jeffersonian perspective, "a decent respect for the opinions of mankind"–and images of a nation's self-esteem can also be deemed essential and defended as a proper and serious factor in foreign policy. As one press commentator on the Carnegie/

Gowing report wrote, "The finding is a cheerful one if you are fed up with people in power claiming that the press and television, not they, shape events. But the conclusion is pretty gloomy if, like the report's author, you wish that media coverage, television particularly, could somehow prevent conflict and misery." To be sure, there is gloom in the cheer if one believes, as a severe media critic like Brenda Maddox of the *Times* in London does, that "the top brass" do not take their cues from the media "because the reporting is almost invariably wrong–even if for the most respectable of reasons. The brave reporter standing in the midst of genocide or famine simply cannot get the facts." Ms. Maddox even has her doubts about the phrase itself, the *"true story,"* which she calls "the conventional misnomer for a news report."

Now, nobody is more skeptical than I have been about the pretensions of our newspaper culture to represent all the upright virtues (accuracy, truth, clarity, etc.); but it can only be a trendy canard when one assumes that the reporters get "the true story" *invariably* wrong. That the *real* happening happens "before the cameras and microphones fly in and after they have gone." At which points "the plot often changes direction" in ways that would be *far too complicated* for news desks to explain to their readers and viewers.... In most of the dramatic crises since World War II, with such unfortunate exceptions as have been lamented in these pages, the mainstream of Western journalism have gotten the stories right–badly written at times, often superficial, necessarily incomplete and replete with small errors, but basically true for all that.

Journalism is not exactly historiography. Yet the disparity is habitually used by the "top brass" of the establishments as an excuse to defy a disagreeable public response when their own political agenda requires special rationalization for their waywardness or deviousness. Even the anti-Nazi mid-War reports of the Holocaust were held to be "exaggerated...one-sided...hysterical..."–since if what was being reported about the Nazi death camps was, roughly, "a true story," then Auschwitz-Birkenau would have had to be bombed; and that, for one reason or another, did not suit the Anglo-American high command, was simply "not on."[8]

The final editorial advice offered by Brenda Maddox of the *Times* is, I hasten to say, wise and constructive:

> Not only do 'stories' hold their news value for a very brief time, but globalization of news has been accompanied by increasing parochialism.
> The task for television news editors is clear. Having flown in their reporters to a hot spot and allowing them only a few brief sentences before intoning their byline, they must insist that those in the field explain that the pictures behind them do not tell the whole story.

Too true; but when even parts of the news story capture the immediacy of a human tragedy, there should be no excuse for not expecting a human response. Failing that we must needs return to our original inquiry about the contemporary disjunction between communication and ethics. What's going wrong with words and pictures? Why doesn't the good news delight and the bad news dismay? Apathy be damned, aren't we here to be moved? Hearts and minds together?

This malaise in our newspaper culture touches the essential spirit of our civilization. The ancient Greek spirit, as is well known, ran the whole course from compassion to apathy and denial, and was not (as in the classicist legend) consistently loyal to the principles of tragic literature and its sublime *catharsis*. As Herodotus tells us in his history, the victorious Athenians "showed themselves beyond measure afflicted at the fall of Miletus, in many ways expressing their sympathy." Indeed when a poet made a drama of the fall of the city "the whole theatre burst into tears."

But then the poet was sentenced to pay a fine "for recalling to them their own misfortunes." Thereafter they made a law prohibiting the performance of the play, thus turning their backs on the reminder of the tragedy and its humane emotions.[9]

The Cruel Dilemma

Is there any way out of this dilemma? Tell the story, and apathy and attention-fatigue grows. Play the story down (over the years it is *so* repetitious) or omit it altogether (grisly prose does pall), and a cynical indifference overtakes us. Perhaps one can side step the difficulties by mixing the reportage with choice items of good news? The American ABC television network has instituted a news segment called *"Solutions"* which adds, after all the reports of natural and man-made disasters, a cheerful story of a problem solved: a boy rescued…a conflagration extinguished…a daring social experiment that worked.

But will Somalia make it? In the years of its civil war in the 1990s, and the UN effort to end it included American and European troops who were then hastily withdrawn, the sorely tried East African land steadily supplied grave headlines and odious pictures of death and destruction. Now, only a few years later, little is heard from Mogadishu and all the points inland where the soil had been bloodied. The ruling war lord, at the moment General Abshia, argues that his unreported news nowadays is only good. Somalia is effectively dealing with its problems, coming up with proper (and peaceful) solutions. He can proudly point to new roads, a well-fed population, constructive negotiations among the old hostile tribes, etc. The general even took the initiative in calling a conference, an international roundtable of Western media experts to advise on how to deal with the odd and neglected story of the dog that didn't bite the man. Sir Bob Geldof, of Band-Aid fame, was blunt: "You've got to get this into your heads: television audiences are bored with hearing people whingeing about their problems. They switch right off. They want the problems to go away." Waves of Western sympathy–prompting a readiness to feed the world (and send warm blankets as well)–is in an ebb tide. John Simpson, the much-travelled "World Affairs Editor" of the BBC, confirmed that when all becomes quiet on the fighting fronts, all the war correspondents flee from peace as from a plague:

> Yet here we were, in a prosperous and thriving town whose streets were policed by men in smart new uniforms and the sound of gunfire had gone....
>
> We were sitting in the middle of a solution of sorts, a town which was sorting out its problems with no help from the outside world. And the outside world didn't even care. [10]

Slowly, in the tropical heat (110º F.), the General's Western advisors came to a conclusion. As Simpson reported from clean and prosperous Bosasso –

> What was needed was a less emotional, more rational kind of reporting. Journalists shouldn't always try to wring heart-strings or disgust with images of violence. Aid agencies should accept that the days of mass international appeal were dead. We should scale down our ideas and concentrate on what is really happening.

In the old scales of our newspaper culture this new ethos would be found seriously wanting. What is "really" happening is only half-communicated when the heart-breaking tragedy and the odious images of mass murder are not included in our committed concentration. Are not violence and starvation real happenings? What is being "scaled down" are not our "ideas" but those chunky segments of the true story with which warring politicians cannot cope –and the media no longer have ways of making dire events interesting enough to capture and hold the attention of readers and viewers.

The cruel dilemma remains. The bad news is too barbarous to take; the good news is too dull, too tedious to bear.

Who Can Remain Unmoved (and Why)?

The so-called crisis in the compassion of Western citizenries–reacting (or failing to respond as expected) to the moral challenges of war and violence reported to them by the journalistic communicators of the day–has, of course, multiple causation. The fault lies, in part, in ourselves.

In the current state of modern culture, rich in its variety of diversionary entertainments, sympathy for afflicted peoples–be they our neighbors or far-away folk about which we know nearly nothing–has slipped down the table of humane priorities. Some say we have become increasingly "*de-sensitized*"; others protest against the "*anaesthetic*" impact of a Western overload of all sorts of lurid violence. But still, nations and peoples do–on historic occasion– continue to respond. The public opinion polls in all of the NATO nation-states (nineteen in all) showed substantial majorities of support in the Yugoslav crisis of 1998 (Bosnia) and of 1999 (Kosovo). It gave massive popular backing to the military campaigns launched in the almost futile attempt to halt the "ethnic cleansing" of Muslims, Albanian Kosovars and other victimized populations, dispossessed by Milosevic's Serbian régime intent on mass eviction. The huge humanitarian aid programs were no less determined and impressive.

Yet how was it that in these cases, on these occasions, ordinarily compassion-fatigued folks were aroused to feel enough outrage, sympathy, and anger to make emotion-driven sacrifices? Was there a media miracle? Were the newspaper dispatches and their accompanying front-page photos suddenly more graphic, more effective? Were the cameramen's pictures for the "breaking news" programs of the television stations–I watched the British *BBC World*, the American *CNN* and its German outlet *N-TV* which, taken together, achieved a significant quota of "NATO viewers"–all at once more moving, more intimately piteous?

In point of act, as we have seen, the increasing compassion fatigue was not any kind of ethical exhaustion on the part of viewers and certainly not of readers. The general public was simply bored into apathy. TV pictures were scatter-brained: badly cut, carelessly commentated, concise to the point of bittiness. In addition, a vast distrust was induced, for example, by CNN's Baghdad realism in the Gulf War of the early 1990s–the strips of permitted film were often misleading to the point of deception. (A later clear-cut case of journalistic distortion drove the notorious Peter Arnett, the CNN star war correspondent, into retirement.) Mainstream journalism had other shortcomings, and we have amply documented the deficiencies of existing newspaper prose-styles to tell it, as they once used to, "like it is." The fault, then, was also in the stars, and even the most famous and able of foreign correspondents failed to distinguish themselves significantly.

It seems that nothing is harder to change than a newspaper stylebook. I have already had my share of fun with the mainstream convention of writing garish water-color leads, simulating fascinating old-time short-story-tellers to catch, if not to maintain for long, the reader's attention for a genuine "human interest story" (and not some old-style, tedious dispatch with hard, unchewable news). Now it could be applied to the Balkan tragedy. Even war stories could be soporific if they were being confined, day by day in every briefing, to straightforward half-truths, small prevarications designed not to give anything away to the enemy. What I think of as the fairy-tale touch–journalism's *once-upon-a-time* genre–came plainly into vogue again. Here, for example, is the *Washington Post*'s Peter Finn reporting from somewhere in the Balkans, trying to grab my attention...and failing utterly (before, that is, the onset of my sense of duty to persist and report on the reporters): "KRUMA, Albania.—Life's spiral turned slowly in the Kosovo village of Goden, a collection of 20 whitewashed stone houses with red tile roofs that rested on gentle hills within sight of the Albanian border." On the same day Steven Erlanger of the *New York Times* was reporting from Belgrade, far from gentle hills but with "life's spiral" still turning, if a little faster. Here, *in toto*, is his first, gripping paragraph: "BELGRADE.—Vladimir, like an unknown number of young Serbs, is on the run." More is to be found on the jump page, the continuing story of Vladimir, twenty-four, and what makes him run (he had just deserted from the Yugoslav Army).[11]

Only the day before–rounding out a fortnight's bombing of aerial targets in Yugoslavia–the *New York Times* focused the attention of its readers from the gentle hills to the echoing valleys when its correspondent, Ms. Carlotta Gall, just over the border from Kosovo, reported in a lyrical variation of the one-paragraph lead: "BLACE, Macedonia.–The valley hummed with thousands of voices, the hillside and fields below shifted constantly with the crowds of people. Along the train tracks a steady line of stumbling figures moved forward to join the human mass."[12] If peace ever comes to this benighted area and tourism flourished, these literary talents of Mr. Finn and Ms. Gall could easily rewrite such graphic materials for guidebooks on the natural and attractive assets of the area. Can this be acceptable wartime reporting?

In some quarters of mainstream journalism, as I detect, a few lessons of the recent past have indeed been learned. In the first place, there is a renewed determination to treat official military briefings with skepticism. The old maxim is being dusted off to the effect that truth is the first casualty in a war....On the first days of the NATO bombing campaign our media were guilty of disseminating any graphic or hair-raising story they could stumble upon, dressed up in any sort of inappropriate phraseology which could give it significance. Especially popular were sinister overtones from the Nazi past (*Genocide!*), or from the Stalin era (*the Great Terror!*). Thus, several of the Kosovo representatives at Rambouillet, where Milosevic had refused to sign a negotiated agreement, had been reportedly murdered–later that week they were interviewed, alive, including Ibrahim Rugova. 100,000 Kosavars had been rounded up for a "concentration camp" in the Pristina sports stadium–an Agence France Presse reporter rushed over and found the place empty. One paper was literary enough to report that the Yugoslav Army had an Orwellian strategy of "identity obliteration"–which only meant that refugees on the Macedonian and Albanian borders were being deprived of their passports, and this caused refugee difficulties but did not exactly amount to a social lobotomy.

One London newspaper learned its lesson very quickly, and published on its fifth page of an enterprising 8-page supplement a warning against exaggeration which, from then on, it would heed (*but not yet*: the story was headlined, "Slaughter of the Innocents," the supplement "A Pitiless War"): "...With so many men missing and so little known of their whereabouts, concentration camps, and the use of hostages as human shields, remain possible. In the absence of confirmation, United Nations officials bridled at references to 'genocide' in Washington, saying that there was simply no evidence to support the use of the term."[13] But the chastened team of eleven foreign reporters that the paper had assembled to sum up the Balkan War up to date did succeed in signalling the transition to a soberer style of verisimilitude which could be read to be believed.

No tricks and turns. No phraseological twists to grab your attention, to stop you in your tracks, to ease you into the next and slightly longer paragraph. Perhaps the old-fashioned impact was due, mainly, to the smaller scale of the tragic events transpiring, when the pain and suffering of single individuals or young families with small children had to be grasped...and not, in mind-defeating contrast, the millions of corpses of Auschwitz or of the great killing fields of Cambodia and Rwanda. Here is one leanly written incident (it could be that the fancy-prose flights were probably trimmed away by wary editors). It is presumably totally true; it reads as if it were honest and accurate and, in general, destined to help revive (hopefully) the Western compassion which characterizes the empathy of "good Samaritans" for the less fortunate.

> The injuries of the Guci family from Demjan, near the city of Djakovica, showed what could have happened to anybody who defied the order to go. The faces of Besa Guci, 26, and her husband, Dull, a 64-year-old farm worker, were encrusted with black scabs yesterday. Their eldest boy, Ullka, 6, was cut on the left cheek. The youngest surviving child, four-year-old Ull, was so traumatised that he could not speak. The couple's baby was dead.
>
> On Tuesday they were at home when the Serbs gave them an hour to get out. They could not explain why they stayed; they seemed to have been paralysed by fear. When their hour was up, the Serbs started firing on the village from tanks. The first barrage hit their home.
>
> "The wall exploded and I was without sense," said Besa Guci. "I was holding my baby girl. When I looked at her the explosion had taken away half of her head. She was 18 months old. Her name was Drincesh."
>
> Despite the shelling, the Gucis buried their baby in the garden and then began walking. They passed several bodies by the side of the road before meeting a nephew on his tractor. He was towing a cart full of refugees and gave them a lift. Four other villages around Demjan were emptied and burnt by the Serbs, they said. It was three days before they arrived at the Morina border point....

Even the mistranslations serve the modest cause of honest reporting. Most newspaper renderings of foreign interviews make the Russian man-in-the-street sound like a Cheapside cockney; Swiss eye-witness' quotes sound like Ernie Pyle's staccato; and a Balkan peasant emerges like a character out of Marquez or a Vargas Llosa novel set in an Andes mountain village. Besa Guci probably did say in his original Serbo-Croat that the explosions had *knocked her senseless*; "I was without sense" is a quick, faulty transcription, but says it better. More than that, it restores our battered confidence, so mis-used by the journalistic counterfeit which passes for real out of a deep need for reader identification. We respond best to the fate of the familiar–what is strange can be alienating–to identify with the downtrodden the victims must at least sound "like us."

Of such tiny seeds do small, sympathetic truths grow.[14]

The more woeful tales emerged, especially on the refugee-crowded Kosovo borders with Albania and Macedonia, the less reserves were left for correspondents to tell their readers or listeners swiftly and directly what they were observing in the tragic turmoil. Language, like everything else, was increasingly in short supply as thousands of displaced persons tried to *"hunker down"* somewhere, their temporary camps without *"infra-structure"* and any kind of *"logistics."* The former (*"infra-structure"*) was an overemployed buzz-word by which was meant mainly water, and food and toilets, and shelter...would naming them strain the qualities of mercy? The latter (*"logistics"*) was another heavy-hooded word; it was obsessively repeated to disguise, in part, the early incompetence of the aid agencies, and served to suggest knowingly the culpable absence of delivery and distribution. Small wonder that the *New York Times* correspondent, with some of the most conscientious young writers in the business, went on trying to tease readers into a sharper sense of the horrendous realities. Attention-catching leads hammered down at us with the bomb-like persistence of raids in the first weeks of aerial strikes. From the Yugoslav capital the *Times* reporter sent this: *"Belgrade.*–Aca Singer, who lost 65 members of his family in the Holocaust, says he did not survive Auschwitz to die from an American bomb." If, at first, the relevance of this piquant bit of melancholy association is not entirely obvious, it becomes evident as you get past the first paragraph that the small Jewish community in Serbia may also, like almost everybody else, get hit by U.S. Cruise missiles...and then heartfelt troubled questions will begin to be thrown at American Jewish politicians. Among them: Defense Secretary William Cohen; National Security Advisor Samuel "Sandy" Berger; White House spokesman James Rubin. The latter serves as spokesman to Secretary of State Madeleine Albright who, we are truly reminded, "is not Jewish although she has Jewish relatives."

Last but not least, the old-style Slav anti-Semitism lurking in Milosevic's ruins will presumably be targeting NATO's supreme commander in the Yugoslav campaign, four-star U.S. General Wesley K. Clark...who discovered his "roots" rather late in life, only in his post-West Point twenties–as one "investigative" story revealed, under a five-column headline: *Discovery Gave Clark a Personal Reason to Fight 'Cleansing'*. He had been adopted and raised as a Protestant (in Little Rock, Arkansas), but–wait for it!–was the grandson of a Russian Jewish immigrant named Jacob Nemerovsky...who had emigrated to the USA...under a false passport.[15] At this point, the ethnic byways of a good newspaper-story seem to be getting a tortuous detour or two away from the main line.

It was another *Washington Post* correspondent who captured the award for the shortest one-paragraph lead of the week: it not only compelled curiosity but fulfilled its promise of a plaintive tale of woe, without sentimental excesses. *Post* reporter David Finkel wrote: *"Brazde, Macedonia.*–This time it's a man crying."

Presumably all of his previous stories from the refugee front were accounts of the wailing of women and children; this time it was different. It took ten other paragraphs before we learned the cause of his lament–the distressing separation of the man from his wife and children. There was the additional anguish that they were suffering the loss and lostness even more cruelly:

> ...Which means that they could be here. Right now. Wondering where he is.
>   Not knowing that he is at the fence, under a half-dead tree, with six singing birds in its branches once again looking at the pictures in his wallet, once again crying.

I will spare the reader the additional telegrammic flashes of fancy writing which just managed to escape the fate that all young journalists are warned against–sinking into the bathos of sob stories, or mawkish tearjerkers. Here is a bit more of the effort of an impressionable literary fellow (favorite author: Stephen Crane) trying to capture the red badge of despair. And one should note the fine reportorial instinct which turned Mr. David Finkel's head to count the singing birds in the half-dead tree...for the story is moving sadly to its conclusion where the tears will mingle with hope: "...Down the dirt road not too far, just far enough to breathe some different air. Walks away in bare feet, soon passing a half-dead tree with six birds no longer singing in it and no weeping man sitting beneath it, either...." Mr. Finkel should be thanking his lucky stars that he is a print-reporter for an open-minded Washington newspaper. If he were a TV correspondent he would have been instructed by the home-office's hard-headed anchorman to *stop repeat stop* interviewing refugees and get his cameraman to get a good, angled shot of any, or all, of those songless birds in the half-dead tree.[16]

Truth and Poetry

The idea of "compassion fatigue" is a simplistic one, reducing a multitude of complexities to a plain tag. It assumes that the normal response to a truthful representation by reporters or cameramen of the realities of war and its accompanying horrors would (and should) always be a humane one. Public concern leads to ethical involvement–mixing sympathies and revulsion into a highly moral response, either of political outrage or pacifistic protest, or both at once, in a demonstration of humanist integrity. If such be not the end-result, then the prose was faulty or the picture blurred. A mediocre writer fails to be evocative enough, too weak to etch the words cuttingly into the conscience of mankind. A harassed photographer misses his best angle-shots, or if he does manage to shoot them graphically then they, more often than not, will never reach his eager and deserving audience because of military censorship, or home-office editing, or some other regrettable obstacles to "telling it like it is."

The exceptions to this enlightened conception of modern man's normal reaction to killing and cruelty are so numerous as to suggest paradoxical opposites. The sight of corpses can revolt and also fascinate–violence may frighten…and also inspire to do likewise. More than that, the putatively truthful recording of realities may be partisan, and its detectable prejudices will soon appear threadbare. An accurate snapshot can distort a larger scene or context–a ringing sentence, an eloquent repetition (*"War is hell!"*), begins to pall.

One of the most senior and experienced of Western war correspondents has put together a picture and televised what he calls "True Terror." It records mostly the appalling carnage of recent anti-American bombings and makes yet another professional effort "to push the parameters outward." But even he is often plagued with doubts about the journalistic credo that the truth will make us all free…all the while moving us to tears, illuminating our minds with deeper understanding, stirring us to proper and proportionate civic reaction. Will his documentary film be "upsetting" anyone in prime time? Should he warn the viewers of what is to come, knowing that "…a big helping of photogenic horror is often akin to pornography. Images of faces convulsed in horror, bodies contorted beyond recognition are, for many, compulsive viewing…."[17]

No, there is no short or convenient media formula for the journalistic effort to get the facts, to tell the truth, to come up with a big story, to serve (and even save) mankind. The best reporters, always in a small minority, are often candid enough to admit fallibility: "I must condense a day's events into a few minutes. I choose only those words and images that will give my report the greatest impact. I have to accept that I am telling half a story, skimming over it, much unsaid and unshown. That is the nature of TV news and, given the limitations of airtime (and, we are told, viewers' attention spans), it will always be so." After such knowledge, what hope for a minute more, even an additional half-hour of "hard truths," of photogenic horror? There is encouragement in the recently updated (June 1998) code of the Broadcasting Standards Commission to the effect: "Broadcasters have a duty to show real life in a violent world….To seek to prevent broadcasters from telling and retelling hard truths would be a substantial disservice both to democracy and to our understanding of the human condition." True, and civic enough. But most viewers in Britain as well as in the U.S.A. are convinced that there is already too much violence on their screens—bloody violence of any or all sorts, factual and fictional…"too many casualties." And this leads directly to Para. 49 of the code: "There are significant concerns about the portrayal of violence which broadcasters need to take into concern." Between the Scylla of "real life" and the Charybdis of "significant concerns," there is no easy solution to the dilemma of such extreme situations: the truth appalls. Michael Nicholson, an admirable veteran of many wars (and whom I have been citing here), was one of those British reporters trying to cover the Falklands War when Prime Minister Margaret Thatcher issued her complete "press blackout." In the absence of any words or pictures, small wonder that the depiction of the South Atlantic conflict took on almost comic-strip proportions (*Aargh! Pow! Boom!*). Not once, as Nicholson recalls, was "the reality" shown on the screen. "The gallant wounded, yes. The dead and dying, no!"

Thus, on most strenuous occasions, there has been no "fatigue" setting in—the truth had not even a chance to raise a sweat. And so the old-fashioned and even unsophisticated belief persists in the newspaper culture that because of "...editorial censorship so much of the world's atrocities are well-kept secrets...our editors sanitise suffering and glamourise and falsify war to such an extent that they almost succeed in making it an acceptable means of settling international and tribal vendettas." Peace *is* beautiful, and because we have heard it before is no reason to close our ears to one more "strangled cry" (in John Strachey's memorable phrase): "...as we prepare to hang up our boots, we leave the world very much as we found it. All we have done is advertise its ills; we have done nothing to cure them. It is as savage and treacherous as ever." If hand-held camcorders were a curative, then the images of war and violence on our screens could restore the savage world to wholeness and harmony. Rather more convincing, alas, is the poet's surmise that humankind cannot stand too much reality.

Speaking of poets it could be, in the last analysis (and by-and-large), that prose is quite helpless in the face of ultimate things. It only touches on tragedy, hurriedly; it snatches at reality, forgettably. If this is so we can appreciate the modest suggestion of one newspaper that only poetry, at its best, can take on the challenge of "telling it like it is" or was. The editor offered his readers these convincing lines from a fine Welsh poet named Dannie Abse:

> What is the name of your country?
> Its frontiers keep changing.
> What is the Capital of your country?
> The town where blood issued
> through the cold and hot water taps.
> What is your National Anthem?
> The ancient fugue of screams.
> Who are your compatriots?
> The crippled, the groping blinded,
> the war dead not yet in their dungeons
> Who is your leader?
> Death's trumpet-tongued fool.

These verses were first published in 1989 and reprinted in the *Times* a decade later, a decade in which a cold war was ended and several others began, in which frontiers (at least in Balkan Europe) kept changing and names of countries newly given, a decade of "blood...screams...war dead," and leading the compatriots was recognizably "Death's trumpet-tongued fool."[18]

I am also tempted to borrow here the words that once served the sixteenth-century poet (Thomas Wyatt) when in a flight of metaphor he railed against a wild mode that was "*stalking*" him, and in "*that strange fashion of forsaking*" was always "*busily seeking/with a continual change*" something which he called (in a new coinage) "*newfangledness.*" The latter word seems today too light and casual for the grave implication that what was being forsaken were great and meaningful things; but once they sounded sinister. Words which gravely warn are always in short supply.

A century later Thomas Hobbes was issuing in his *Leviathan* (1651) the gravest warnings against "metaphors" and "senseless and ambiguous words"– for "reasoning upon them is wandering amongst innumerable absurdities...." The end, for Hobbes, of all such "foolish fires of metaphorics" was "contention, and sedition, and contempt."

"*Buzz words*" were then referred to as "*bug-words*"–from an old Welsh association of *bugs* with specters and objects of terror, as in *bogey* and *bugbear* in Shakespeare's *Timon*: "Thou shalt not fright me with thye bugbeare words." Shakespeare's *Twelfth Night* (3:1) marks the old and still "newfangled" point for me: "*They that dally nicely with words may quickly make them wanton.*"[19]

24

Of Realities and *Realpolitik*

All Compassion Spent

This is a book about "newspaper culture," not about foreign policy. But since the cultural fatigue which has paralyzed the international community has mostly been about the conflict in ex-Yugoslavia with its disorienting effects on governmental policy-makers as well as intellectual élites, a few words to disengage the two themes may be in order.

There were moments in the past, and I have touched upon some of them, when moral awareness and emotional consequences in the face of some intolerable wrong-doing put public opinion in motion which, in turn, put pressure on governmental leaders, if they weren't already so strongly motivated. And in the face of possible apathy or stolidity, powers could be pushed into taking action. Little of this traditional democratic process–Bagehot thought of it as "the physics" of an open constitutional society–had been discernable in the mid-1990s.

This may have been a throwback to the *Realpolitik* of olden days; and public indifference could have been ascribed to the low-level intensity of diplomatic ditherings. Television and other communication disorders were, at first, only be playing a minor role in the tragic Balkan impasse. There is a hopelessly civilized cynicism in the face of the tribal flare-up of age-old popular vendettas. There are lingering Western sympathies for the Serbians, even if they happen to be the aggressors; as a French diplomat said, "We have our principles on one side, and our friends on the other." In post-Hitler Germany we witnessed a national conversion to pacifist behavior when confronting military situations anywhere, even dangerously close to home; and with the Italians the Germans evince a post-Axis indisposition to indulge in belligerent altercations where a citizen-in-uniform can get hurt (and even killed). In the end, and the surmise lies near, it may all be part of a natural emergence of a new balance-of-power system of rivalries in a neo-nationalistic *Machtpolitik* wherein a few make war, many die, all negotiate, each proffer secret or ambivalent compromise deals, and nothing seems to get resolved.

For I did not mean to imply, as do most of the cultural responses I have been glossing, that there is (necessarily, at least in complex power-politics) a simple relation between moral emotion and sound policy. Outrage can be selective, seeing excesses in a one-eyed perspective. Anger can mislead, and striking a robust blow for peace, or justice, or diffuse humanitarianism may deepen tragedies. Still, there are also ethical consequences to what comes out as international apathy or torpor. One important European commentary entitled "Bosnia & Morality," came to the conclusion that the "poisonous brew" of a realistic awareness of evil and a cowardly (or, perhaps, prudent) policy of inaction has led to an unprecedented "European Self-Contempt." The zigzag course of U.S. foreign policy, leading suddenly to NATO's seventy-eight days of bombing to induce a break in the Sarajevo blockade, did not help the sorely tried spirits. Thus, bewildering basic questions of hard politics and dithering alliance strategy have, presumably, played as large a role in determining inertia as the superstructure's "atmospheric" problem of *realities unperceived* and *all compassion spent.*[1]

Yet, even in this analysis, there loomed the new factor of television which relays, despite all its blurs, "the suffering of unfortunate peoples into one's own living room." The 1969 remark is from the German anthropologist Arnold Gehlen; but the thought was already familiar to millions of Americans since the escalation of the bloodshed in the Vietnam war of the mid-1960s. The *FAZ* wrote:

> To be aware of what is going on and to do nothing is the contradiction which is afflicting our moral integrity. We are attentive viewers, even outraged spectators, but ethical failures. European public opinion everywhere seems to share the same burden of self-contempt....We are supposed to be building a "new Europe" with virtues of dignity and respect among old once-fratricidal peoples. But we have inaugurated it with a moral catastrophe. (Jan Ross, *FAZ*, 20 July 1995)

Still and all, the malaise is multi-national, multi-cultural, multi-causal.

Challenging the Pictorial Dogma

Reflective newspaper editors, when they are not casting aspersions on the ability of the television medium to come to grips with world realities, occasionally puzzle over their own incapacities in a vaguely self-critical way. I turn again to a German source. In a recent issue of one of the most earnest of European dailies, the *Frankfurter Allgemeine Zeitung*,[2] one of its writers counted some 121 violent conflicts in the world during 1994, among them were reckoned ten very bloody civil wars. He was, as a well-informed observer, quite confident that "we know very much and will get to know more." But there was an element of doubt in his tone, and it came not from the intellectual scepticism of his academic traditions but from the more pragmatic professional experiences in a sorely tried newspaper culture: "Are the horrors that dominate the foreground of our information the whole of the reality? Does that which we are reading and seeing constitute truly what has been happening?" Well, it may be a little late in the day to be asking such epistemological questions if the an-swers are in the negative. (Someone, or something, may have accomplished the most gigantic disinformation program ever.) Another writer in the same paper quickly descended from soaring metaphysics and targeted the enemy next door in the television studio. Here—as we heard so often in the internecine war of the media—were the sources of error and distortion, manipulation and misrepresentation, all adding up (again as among our cynical Italian colleagues) to *virtual unreality.*

The story that prompted this particular recrimination was a television account of how the Turkish army was using, in its offensive against the Kurds across the Iraqi border, weapons "made-in-Germany"; hence the *Bundesrepublik* should cease and desist from military collaboration with its NATO ally. Pictures were shown of a *Panzer* movement in South-East Turkey; and a former Colonel in the defunct East-German DDR-Army identified the vehicles so deployed to the last mechanical detail. The Bonn government subsequently denied the charge. It insisted that it had *not* included old East-German army stocks in its military deliveries to the Turks, and showed another set of pictures of the tank in question in *Russian* territory, suggesting that the Turks might have, and probably had, purchased the controversial vehicles from Russian ar-mored supplies.

Thus, this particular build-up of a Turkish-German diplomatic crisis was based on false premises. Was it an error? Doubtless. Could it have been a malicious misrepresentation? Possibly. But something larger and deeper was (as it always is) involved.

The *FAZ* writer (1 April 1995) sees in the case of the readily identifiable "BTR-60 Panzer" not only the sinister hand of television irresponsibility but also, more deviously, the black magic of computer manipulation.

> In the era of "virtual reality" everything possible can be done with pictures, apart from proving indisputably that such-and-such is really the case. To present what is not, or to touch it up, and even to roll back what has actually taken place, is nowadays very easy—thanks to *"blue screen"* and *"paint box".*...
>
> To detect this will become increasingly difficult. Politicians who have never met each other can be assembled in a group photo. Peaceful demonstrations can be converted into riots, and bloody battles re-pictured as harmless military opera-tions. A document can be reconstructed as if it were the genuine article itself.... And if the pictorial manipulators so wish, even the dead can be made to come to life again.
>
> So it is that in television nothing is impossible between fiction and truth....

One small hope is still present, and the valiant defender of newspaper culture does not stoop to the advice of so many defeatists: namely, pressing the off (or *aus*) button on your of-fending TV set. He proposes a grand solution, even utopian in its proportions—the de-mythologization of the pictorial dogma, namely, the assumption that you can believe what you see. One must broadcast the universal critical message: "Perfect manipulation is now technically feasible." Once this is recognized, then there should be little further trouble with naiveté and gullibility, as in this case with Panzers that have "readily identifiable" features. Features can be faked, identities fabricated.

The truth, presumably, will out. You'd better *not* believe.

The Shadows of a "Virtual Unreality"

I do not want to be misunderstood. The detection of ulterior motives in the opinionated reportage involving the press's critique of television does not, by and for itself, invalidate the journalist's case against the misdemeanors of the milky screen. In point of fact the quality of television broadcasting, aggravated by the cutthroat competition between the public and the private stations (at least in Western Europe), has been visibly deteriorating. And I have in various places in these pages indicated the "spiritual crises" which have gripped the other-wise sturdy souls of the BBC in London and the ARD in Cologne and Hamburg, not to mention hard-pressed colleagues in the USA and elsewhere, where public TV has achieved certain standards. They are all struggling to survive, to keep in the running with their populistic profit-making competitors, by going down-market with some semblance of dignity.

Their difficulties are not merely due to the pressure of audience ratings which tend to reflect the lowest common denominator of attention and entertainment. There are also twinges of professional conscience–for well-meaning news-editors and foreign correspondents have admitted to over-simplification and even gross deception as on-the-spot reporters, in a few sentences and with the most colorful film footage available, try to present the news of wars and alarums. A newly appointed director of the formidable German public TV network has gone so far as to accuse television, including his own stations, of the heinous sin of "disinformation." The intendant, Fritz Pleitgen, has served as a working journalist in most of the leading capitals of East and West; and on his appointment he even played with the notion of abandoning the news-gathering function altogether:

> The television camera is everywhere, but it can't get anywhere near a representation of reality....What's worse is that in each country the viewer gets to feel that he is at the center of the world's events. Most of the world he never gets to see, only when it is disastrously involved in a drought, or a massacre, or a plague. Whole continents happen to disappear, like Atlantis....
>
> The authorities manipulate us, and we manipulate our audience....It's no longer a matter of slight distortions, half-truths, or erratic interpretations. The differences between the world on TV and reality [*zwischen Fernsehwelt und Wirklichkeit*] could not be greater. We are on the path to the incurable habits of disinformation. I am afraid that

the more our television communication develops, the more distant it becomes from reality.[3]

The outlandish collapse of almost all institutions in Italy in the mid-1990s has underlined the dangers of things to come. Thus, the world press in its graphic reporting of the "Berlesconi scandal"–the *tangentopoli* which has continued to afflict Italian society with a prime minister running the country to the hollow plaudits of the TV stations that he owns–has elaborated eagerly on the large, civilizational lesson that could be learned, even if it is to its own media advantage.

The meteoric career of one star figure, Paolo Liguori, began as a youthful ultra-leftist with the terrorists of *Lotta Continua,* went through intermediate stages with the anti-Communist *Il Giornale* and the Christian *Il Sabato,* and wound up as a media commentator of great popularity. His shady style has given a neologism to the print journalists: *liguorizzare.* One Italian journalist explains: "It means to invent an item, dress it up with supporting facts, and present it as if it were all true." The nightly program called *Striscia la Notizia* was watched by upwards of 7 million, and the *Guardian*'s correspondent described it as: "a quick-fire televised comic-strip, an aggressive cocktail of news and variety. A huge red puppet–now a national institution–is a special reporter. There are dancing girls and incessant, hysterical canned laughter." Even the producer of the program no longer needs to rationalize what is being presented by mouthing his excuses in the old antiquated terms of public-spirited communications media. "What you see on television," one TV producer confesses, "is what we want you to see and is necessarily a falsification." The commentaries are "phoney," the interviews staged; the quiz shows are rigged, and the winning lottery numbers fixed. "For this kind of TV," the *Guardian* writes, "the whole world is a game show"—and, evidently, just as fraudulent: "Others have unmasked fake magicians, phoney draws, and actors in the place of supposedly real-life protagonists....Accusations fly that some fakes have been faked themselves."[4]

The cynicism of the Italians and the alarmism of the Germans may prove to be saving graces in the complex developments ahead. Nothing in the end will be taken seriously in Italy, not its reality, not its mirror images; and the Germans are already attempting to see whether they can control, and indeed censor, what is coming up to overwhelm them.

The American impulse to optimism (as so often in the past) is in sharp contrast to a European world-weariness; it resists even doubts and uncertainties–although disenchantment will come in time, gushing forth spasmodically in "culture criticism" and self-critical "media studies." In the first flush of technological discovery the utopian sense of hope is still naive and untroubled. The founding director of the Media Lab at the Massachusetts Institute of Technology and the high priest of the so-called "Digital Revolution" was asked–in (as we were expressly assured by *Newsweek*) "real time"–whether some conceivable developments might "frighten" him. No, he found everything "exhilarating," for he was a "self-proclaimed optimist about the digital age." He found "cyberspace as a notion" to be "benevolent...where people help each other to be free." If so, he might be encouraged to campaign for an alternative united-nations organization in harmony with this prospect of "electronic bliss." The Digital Master's words do not exactly sound like a call for a new Charter of Four Freedoms or Universal Human Rights; but since these have been overshadowed by the sheer unbenevolence of nations in our time we might try to make do as well as we can with MIT prose:

> The Internet has already altered our conception of time. Will it do the same to our conception of reality?
> For the time being, our process of converting bits into atoms is not very mature. But as it becomes more sophisticated, when we can display holographic images that we can enter, when we develop a tactile interface that we can explore with our other senses, the Internet will provide us [with] something that will be almost indistinguishable from the real world.[5]

As so often in the history of language, a word of some semantic charm with an association to a stronger factor somewhere in the society (or culture, if you will) buzzes to popularity. It creates the impression that its diffusion is irresistible; and its parallelism, in other lands or even languages, appears to be uncanny. The vocabulary of English political leaders (also, every now and then, of men-of-letters) is replete with traditional literary values, going back to such formidable phrasemakers as Isaac D'Israeli's son, the Prime Minister Benjamin, and indeed to Cromwell's wordsmith, John Milton. And so it is not unexpected that knowledgeable etymological spirits in the press should pick quarrelsome quibbles. Nit-picking is not confined to the Clinton White House, and its "frantic semantics." Prime Minister Tony Blair, in one of the innumerable British debates over "Europe" and its spreading single currency, the so-called *euro*, was once characteristically involved in a familiar terminological dispute. It was almost medieval in its scholasticism, were it not for the difference that dogmatic certainties were not involved but only muddled ambiguities. A parliamentary reporter in Westminster (Matthew Parris) reported: "...To sound contemplative Mr. Blair reaches for his V-words: 'vision' and 'values'. These are beginning to excite derision." Worse was to come, when he noted another keynote in this prime minister's approach to persuasion: "...The word 'real' kept cropping up. We must get real. The euro is happening–like it or not. There is no opposing reality, 'no going back' (in his words) 'from the road to the future'. The euro simply is." Different perceptions of reality are allowable, for this depends on entitlements (i.e., some see more sharply than others). But factional equivocation about the word *is*–in President Clinton's Washington as in Blair's London–makes hostile etymologists of everyone in the chamber within hearing distance.

The two-letter word's relationship to past and future–to what "*was*" and to what "*will be*"–has seriously weakened. "Get into what is the real world today!" shouted the prime minister. And the reporter observed that "this was met with hoots." The reality to be "gotten into" is not *is* but "*could* be" or "*might* be." "*Is*" makes the past more relevant, the future immanent, if not present.

Careless, easygoing verbiage has relaxed the sense of tense. We expect "the vision thing" while we wait, in a busy democracy, to be handed a ghostwritten text evocatively studded with new "keynotes" and catchphrases. They herald the contemplative sound. They should prove that the leaders (and their staff) are "getting *with it*" or, if populistic enough, are already there. A V-word or two, a refurbishing of several C- or L-words, may suggest to conservative as well as liberal supporters that the leader is…right on.[6]

Weasel Words and the Look of Things

Few readers can be unaware of the political implications in contemporary affairs of personal dress and appearance: from top to toe. On all sides we are confronted by the electoral miracles of make-over: *e.g.* the effective change in Mrs. Margaret Thatcher's coiffure and couture (which presumably helped to keep her in Downing Street for so long)…across to the near-futile attempts to straighten out President Richard Nixon's "duck-walk" (and at the same time keep him clean-shaven of his five o'clock shadow)–from Joschka Fischer's quick change from the street-fighter's uniform of the German Left (roll-collar shirt, jeans, sneakers) into the double-breasted garb of an Armani-suited foreign minister and popular European statesman…across to Hillary Clinton's late presidential trousered *chic* which groomed her for senatorial politics in New York.

Little is needed to keep in the running except an attractive and well-placed snap-shot or two. To be sure, true photographs can be manipulated, and the simplest measure of the distortion now known as "spin" is to glamorize the positive and under-light the negative. But, generally speaking, the elementary contrast between even "*Before*" and "*After*" pictures manages to tell the story. The two newspaper portraits which illustrated the makeover of British Cabinet Minister Clare Short spoke louder than a thousand words of a fashion-editor's florid prose. More complex pictorial problems in political contexts of rather more gravity–say, the television coverage of the Kosovo war (seventy-eight days in the spring of 1999)–call for differentiated analysis of a different order.

I shall overlook the crude charges of cynical propagandistic manipulation. Milosevic supporters in Belgrade were at a loss to explain convincingly the movement of hundreds of thousands of Kosovarans, fleeing (mostly under duress) across the neighboring foreign borders into hastily improvised refugee camps in Albania and Macedonia. They blamed it first–without international echo (but credulously believed at home)–on the NATO bombing raid; but the innumerable heart-breaking refugee tales told another story. Second, they charged Hollywood-style manipulation and montage. Goran Matic in Belgrade, the Yugoslav propaganda chief and Milosevic's "minister-without-portfolio," made the following charge (11 May 1999): "...NATO hired thousands of ethnic Albanians to act the part of refugees, traipsing in circles 'so as to seem like vast numbers of people on the run.'"[7] If Goran Matic's moviegoers would believe that, they would believe anything (and apparently they did).

The theory behind this misconception was a familiar one of simple-minded skepticism. What film footage leaves behind is an Illusion: a hand-held representation of a Reality caught at a contrived angle. It is not a black-and-white statement of facts, a documentary recording of events, as they were (or are...or ever could be credited as being).

So far, so good–if, that is, one wants to go in for philosophizing in this manner about the metaphysics of any kind of reliable knowledge of the external world. But the cast of thousands of hired extras (men, women, and children suitably attired for the occasion) is a fish of another water, a *canard* of another flight. No one ever saw–even caught a glimpse of, let alone interviewed–any one of such actors who, replicated and quickly inter-cut, could make for a convincing mass scene in D.W. Griffith's *Birth of a Nation*, or posed as Napoleon's "traipsters" in the battles of Bondarchuk's eight-hour *War and Peace*, or the innumerable Alec Guinness-led British POWs, whistling their way across the Bridge of the River Kwai....Among the vast international press corps, camped for months as the refugees in their tens of thousands flooded through the check-points along the Kosovaran frontier with Albania and Macedonia, there were indeed some thousand enterprising traipsters, all looking for a story. They were altogether unlikely to overlook a hoax of such proportions, a piece of counterfeit of such conspicuous fraudulence, historic and world-scandalizing.

The hunger for such a "scoop" I found especially ravenous on the part of the media of such NATO allies (Italy; Greece) which have for one ethnic or ethical reason or another taken some measure of official, critical distance from the "humanitarian" war aims of NATO's anti-Serbian alliance. The Italians fear being "swamped" by unwanted illegal immigrants. The Greek press, suddenly unanimous in its solidarity with Orthodox believers, was almost monolithic in its accounts of the strategic failings, tactical shortcomings, cynical errors, and other unforgivable misconceptions of the American high command. Some anti-war Greek militants went so far as to demolish the statue in Athens of President Harry S. Truman–whose "Truman Doctrine" had been credited with having saved civil war-torn post-war Greece from falling into the hands of the communists and becoming, in quick time, a Soviet satellite. Truman was "decapitated," and his sculptured head lay on the mid-town sidewalk. When the then U.S. Defense Secretary, William Cohen, arrived in Athens months later to patch up the Alliance, his motorcade passed the "toppled Truman" (only a pair of bronze shoes remained on the pedestal).[8]

But even more than the dissident opinions of unwilling, recalcitrant allies in Greece and in Italy, the spectacle of a reunited German Republic going off to war for the first time since Hitler's day offered provocative points of departure for analysts of newspaper and media culture.

This had nothing to do with the daily reports of wayward loyalties or vacillating commitments. Quite the contrary. The German spokesmen stood out in the European ensemble; two eloquent ministers who were in charge of the Kosovo campaign, Scharping at Defense and Fischer at Foreign Affairs. If anything they were (as old soldiers put it) "over the top." Scharping's commitment to the destruction of the Yugoslav régime took him so far as to identify Milosevic with Hitler (evidently nothing less than opposing an evil *Führer* would justify "a just war"); and Fischer also led a chorus of former pacifists who denounced "the Holocaust in Kosovo." Both men were strong in their support of NATO alliance policy–the first German military commitment in half-a-century. But they were loud and excessive in their oratorical appeals to a population (and to their own inner circle) who had been saturated with peace-loving sentiment and the piquant prospect of never having ever to go to war again...except in strict self-defense and in the "singular" event of another "Hitler" and another "Auschwitz," both of which they were pledged to oppose even by force of arms.

The politics of the threatening Kosovo campaign–or rather its German ideology–was further distorted by the fact that the moderate Left as well as the Far Left, peace-loving as they were, would rather die than identify themselves as "anti-Communist." Their hostility to the totalitarianism of the Soviet Union–and, especially, to its *DDR* satellite régime in Eastern Germany–was for decades notoriously low-key. Even the proper officials of the Bonn Establishment were very reluctant (and hence, at best, very tepid) cold warriors. And so it behooved Minister Joschka Fischer to identify the Belgrade enemy as..."Fascism!" [*Stormy applause*] That Milosevic was a life-long Marxist-Leninist Communist (if of Tito's heretical persuasion), that he was re-introducing the old *Internationale* anthem to be sung to the unfurling of the old red flag, was sedulously kept out of prevailing rhetoric. Fischer's half-a-dozen outbursts in the German *Bundestag*–impassioned, magniloquent–were marred only by the suspicion (could it have only been on my own part?) that he was commanding the Abraham Lincoln Brigade in the Spanish Civil War in the 1930s. He talked himself into the pose of a Loyalist in the struggle against an evil General-Franco-fascist. Hadn't Picasso showed us in his *Guernica* the truth about the atrocities? Joschka felt more comfortable, even a shade more sincere, crying *No Pasaran*!

Nor was this all. It was a peculiarity of the newspaper culture that its language of journalism often faces unconscious or unwitting dilemmas. A Hamburg columnist or a Cologne TV interviewer of *Bundeswehr* officers in a camp near Macedonia, were hesitant to press on too critically–for they would seem

to be letting down a great humanitarian-national cause led not by the reactionary Right but legitimated as a Just War by the liberal Left. And if they publicly
collaborated in the official violence, taking "collateral damage" in their stride–
rationalized as having "less than 1% error," including embassies, schools,
hospitals, etc.–they felt in their heart of hearts that they might be betraying the
most sterling pacifist tradition in the German past with its sacred oath: *Nie
wieder Krieg!* (*Never again war!*)

I was not alone in sensing that there was a perceptible nostalgia for the
good old golden days of resounding political protest. Once upon a time a
single photograph, shot on a Vietnam street (the Saigon police chief with his
pistol to the head of a cringing youthful civilian), went around the world.
Ideologies need such "defining moments." A naked little girl, aflame and
running to escape a napalm inferno…an American flag, burning to purposeful
glee. Those were the years when there were symbols galore.

The Kosovo crises were singularly bereft of such symbolic ideological
connectedness. For a few evenings the picture of Milosevic's supporters–rush-
ing to assemble on a Danube bridge, carrying the Target-Symbol circled on
their placards or dyed on their T-shirts–seemed to emerge as a "permanent
icon." But it faded quickly before the popular shot of Slobodan playing some
piece of classic jazz before going to bed during the nightly air raid on Belgrade.
Keen-eared reporters also gave us a byte of Heavy Metal which was evidently
played during the bombing raids by American airmen, just doing their duty.
But in a week or so nothing was ever heard again of Milosevic's saxophone;
and when NATO's bombing actually destroyed a few Danube bridges (and
much else), the Target-T-shirt became, as one Belgrade reporter had it, "uncool."
Pop rock had almost made it. But they bombed in Belgrade.

Are these reportorial details of mere passing significance in an account of
newspaper culture? Hardly. The pop-cult temperament craves for what it fancies to be iconic; the '68 mind, still addicted to its fixes of yesteryear, longs for
what it declared to be defining moments. One conversation on the highest
level of eyewitness history–and it is no scrap of ephemera, inflated to historic
symbolism–is pertinent, and perhaps even conclusive. A *Washington Post*
correspondent informed us that the day after the Chinese Embassy bombing,
President Clinton complained to Prime Minister Tony Blair of Britain that the
news coverage was not fully presenting the moral dimensions of the war. Referring to one of the Serbian atrocities which had been the cause of the Kosovo
war, the president said to the prime minister: "…If we had one TV picture of the
15 men being roped together and burned alive, people would be wondering
why we haven't leveled the place." One wonders what the professional hoaxters
in their dark rooms were up to when there was such a crying need–just one TV
picture!–for their counterfeiting services.

Even with this hidden, internal tension, the German engagement in the
Allied cause never faltered. But there were wobbles. Would the unreconstructed

wing of the Green Party manage to depose "the warmonger" Joschka Fischer? Would the various television news programs with their incessant *Specials* bore the German citizenry into indifference? Or, possibly, frighten them into hesitation, caution, paralysis? Could they ever be persuaded to take the "militaristic" step of supplying "ground troops (*Bodentruppen*)" for possible combat and probable casualties? If so, would it give their pacifistic wing of Fischer's Green party the opportunity to dismiss him and thus put paid to the existing Red-Green governing coalition? Small faction-fights can cause great defeats. *Der Spiegel* ventured their wartime prediction that Germany as well as Italy and Greece would defect from the Kosovo alliance, and thus disintegrate the role of the U.S.-led NATO in post-Communist Europe. It was a close-run thing.

And the same tensions with the same ambivalent sound effects were played out in the subsequent crisis wherein the German government pledged "unconditional support" for the USA in its "Bush war against terror" and had to step warily, even with open trucks laden with food-aid, before crossing the border into the Afghanistan war zone.

Reporting the Sartorial Details

If serious verse is increasingly turned to by journalists with a desperate old-fashioned faith that "*the truth is in the poetry*," our new-fangled sociology or "cultural criticism" as popularly practiced in the print media appears more threadbare than ever. And if European journalism has shown itself to be more self-critical than the American, it is largely because the '68 generation in the U.S.A.–the bulk of which was never close to the theoretical inspiration of, say, the school of Dr. Herbert Marcuse–hardly ever thought (although down the line they responded to the pop version) in abstract or intellectual terms.

Thus, one European newspaper commentator, on the occasion of the seventy-nine-day NATO aerial war against the Yugoslav Serbs over Kosovo, lamented the intellectual disarray in young and old alike. He registered a huge, empty silence where "Pop Thinkers" had once filled the scene with slogans, analyses, theories, all products of the *Weltanschauung* which accompanied the Students Revolt and its radical devotion to an alternative life-style. Had ideology, as it periodically does, failed again? What happened to the militant *Peace Now* demonstrations which as late as the 1980s had effectively marshalled all the anti-war forces of a "Vietnik" anti-Americanism? The very sight of a NATO weapon, "made in U.S.A.," could trigger a mass protest at an Allied air base or a U.S. Army headquarters. And only recently the *Friedenskämpfer* in Germany had won their long struggle through all the German courts to allow them (under the flag of free speech) lawfully to denounce all the world's standing armies, especially their own, with the classic quote, "All Soldiers Are Murderers [Alle Soldaten sind Mörder]."

Could it be that this militant school of Pop-Thought had exhausted itself, or perhaps developed a flaw, a methodological failing? From the original intellectual inspiration of the Frankfurt School of "subtle [i.e., not vulgar] Marxism," developed by Messrs. Max Horkheimer and T.W. Adorno (and Dr. Herbert Marcuse belonged to the main circle), young social rebels had learned and cultivated one trick: an ingenious short-cut from a small reported fact to a large, comprehensive world-revolutionary posture. The images and icons of '68, "the way we were then," reinforced over the years the politics of a youth culture, flaunting idiosyncrasies of speech and informalities of dress. Shock was the means–an alternative vision of growing up...and hanging around together–was the end.

The Establishment was not merely there to be defied but to be dismayed. Signals on the surface pointed unfailingly to the systematic evil thereof. One European journalist (Christoph Amend, writing in the Berlin *Tagesspiegel*) registered the passing of a movement and its ideology, which embraced a whole Western school of Pop interpretation. The wearing of a tie (or a bra) could signify a dastardly betrayal of the movement to the straight Establishment. But with political power in a "Red [the S.P.D.]-Green" coalition government in Germany came a dramatic bourgeoisification. Since the popular electoral turn to the Left in 1998 several ministers in the new German government–Foreign Secretary Joschka Fischer and the prime minister himself, Gerhard Schroeder, both in their day vociferous Peace Demonstrators and indeed "street-fighters" in the mélées of '68–were photographed in Parliament and in all international conferences wearing starched white collars, Italian-cut single- and double-breasted suits, with matching bits of fancy haberdashery. No wonder they approved the bombing of Yugoslavia! No surprise that they even sent German *Bundeswehr* troops to the Balkans to help NATO make war. They had all pleaded for "*the liquidation of NATO*" only a few years ago as youthful rebels, marching through the streets waving banners, wearing open-laced sneakers and shabby blue jeans. Foreign Minister Joschka Fischer still sometimes turned out in remnants of his old ideological uniform when he had to defend his pro-war military strategy in Kosovo to his Green Party; half of them are still anti-war pacifists to whom bombs–and indeed the helmets, boots, and combat-jackets of the soldiers who deliver them–are anathema. The matter of dress, at least in contemporary German liberal-left politics, is anything but trivial; and newspapers have newly extended their conventional Paris-driven fashion consciousness to report such details. It was once considered *infra dig*, except in cases of "what the bride wore." More and more what the wives are wearing in their husbands' political campaigns for high office appears to reflect itself in public opinion polls, notably in the USA. Especially in trial-crime reporting it turns out to be, in the light of the impressionistic vulnerabilities of juries (and their focus groups), revealing and often decisive. The color of a dress, the length of a skirt, the fit of a sweater or blouse, even the heel-size of a pair of shoes: all have been known to play a role in events and hence have become relevant newsworthy items.

If I may be permitted a personal digression, I remember meeting Chancellor Willy Brandt in a hotel room in London on a landmark visit to Britain. In the 1970s he was the first post-war German to be invited to Coventry to speak on an occasion to commemorate the English city's aerial devastation by Hitler's *Luftwaffe*. He was accompanied by his powerful party boss, Herbert Wehner, the ex-Communist ideologist and *Bundestag* leader of the Social Democrats. Brandt was busy changing his clothes for an official diplomatic dinner that night in Westminster. Wehner would not come along, for he had not packed his dark suit and he would never ever put on a dinner jacket (called in German "*ein Smoking*"), not to speak of a tuxedo. He was, after all, not a "bourgeois" politician. Not wearing fancy togs was to remain loyal to one's class.

On that occasion, in the Hotel Claridge suite, I made a few unfortunate remarks to the effect that it was a primitive and absurd taboo to assign such significance to clothes and their political import. And, at the moment, what was *Genosse* Wehner himself wearing? A brownish sports jacket, wrinkled and worn out in spots, with corduroy patches at the elbows–the perfect sartorial symbol of old English country gentlemen. The moral of the story? It is grotesque to confound the cut of one's textile apparel with political correctness and ethical values....The shabbiness of one underclass turns out to be the *chic* of another overclass.

Willy Brandt, slipping into his *Smoking* and skilfully tying the bow in his "black tie," merely laughed. Herbert Wehner would not be moved and did not take kindly to the ironic critique of his socialist integrity. Would Karl Marx ever have donned "evening wear" to attend a ceremonial dinner in St. James' Palace? Would Vladimir Ilyich have changed his leather barricade-cap for a shiny, brushed bowler hat? Wehner pulled a long face, and in fact (although we had known each other for twenty years) he never greeted me again. As for his relations with Brandt, in whose chancellorship he was an all-powerful make-or-break Party boss, there were strains and tensions even then when they were still travelling together. And when, years later, Wehner withdrew the rank-and-file support of the bureaucratic Social-Democratic party machine and Chancellor Willy Brandt was forced to resign, the final falling-out between the two ex-Marxists had also a "sartorial" element.

The historic break, as I was reliably informed, occurred on a visit to Moscow where Wehner had once been in wartime communist exile. He had been a "guest" in the sinister Hotel Lux where all the faithful comrades had denounced each other in the 1930s and tried desperately to show their exclusive loyalty to Comrade Stalin. Wehner's preoccupation during the Moscow Show-Trials (1936-1938) was to make up lists of underground or exiled comrades (including many of his next-door Hotel Lux neighbors) who might not just have been unwaveringly loyal Bolsheviks by Stalinist standards....

A picture on the front page of the day-old Western newspaper Wehner had been reading in Moscow showed a smiling *Bundeskanzler*, enjoying himself at a gala affair in Washington. Willy Brandt was *dancing* on the grand ball-room floor. And he was wearing, yet again, a glossy dinner jacket and well-knotted black tie. In Moscow (in the early 1970s), on his return to revisit his old Marxist-Leninist haunts, out of some still unrevealed, unexplained political behavior, Wehner made a slight, casual disparaging remark about *Kanzler* Brandt to the foreign press (mostly West German) hanging around the hotel lobby; and when it reached Bonn a "final crisis" set in. Brandt fell, Wehner survived.[9]

The visible surface of events–and, as we like to believe, its deeper meaning–is hard to record and even more difficult to grasp. But then again newspapers are not destined to offer us complete knowledge. They often come up with erratic detail and get, under pressure of deadlines, important little facts wrong. Can men of letters in their novels–and/or historians in their scholarly tomes–come to the rescue and get it right for posterity? I would think that most serious journalists in our day would find it difficult to disagree with Saul Bellow, writing about the Bellow ("Chick")-Ravelstein ("Allan Bloom") argument, as summed up in his latest novel:

> Ravelstein had come to agree that it was important to note how people looked. Their ideas are not enough–their theoretical convictions and political views. If you don't take into account their haircuts, the hang of their pants, their taste in skirts and blouses, their style of driving a car or eating a dinner, your knowledge is incomplete....

The unanswered question is whether the credo of completeness is binding on journalists–who don't have time (or, most of the days, the space) to cover the news and still make an inventory of "how people looked." Or on novel-ists–who delight in making things up with their fictions aspiring to a higher truthfulness. And/or on historians: whose minds are inevitably influenced nowadays by the works of fiction they have read and are often victimized or, more frequently, misled by their primary sources, among which are the main-stream newspapers considered to be reliable. It amounts to a vicious circle turning from facts to fiction and then, at the next curve, to faction. (Professor Fritz Stern, for example, citing Theodor Fontane and paying him homage as a graphic source for comprehension of the period he wrote about in his Bleichroeder biography.)

"Attention must be paid," Arthur Miller said in a celebrated instruction. "Take everything into account," says Saul Bellow, especially how people looked, dressed, ate, behaved themselves behind a wheel. To the extent that the newspaper's written words compete with the prose of literature and the footnoted narrative of historians, journalism feels compelled to take up a hand at transcendental trivia. As we have seen, many wind up wallowing in superficiality (and monotonous vulgarity). Many more devise a portrait of recogniz-able realism, and then add to the picture "warts and all" as their prejudices dictate. A few come up with rare illuminations of that "hard, gemlike flame" which Walter Pater considered to be "success in life."[10]

I have only to make the point that on the Left, especially among old Bolsheviks and other dedicated *revoluzzer*, the personal politics of protocol is never trivial or unimportant, indeed it is rarely very far from passionate convictions of one stripe or another. What does one wear when mounting the barricades? It seems outlandish that in the midst of the Kosovo war, with its million forlorn refugees, the media still focused their camera on the cut of Chancellor Schroeder's daily change of Italian single-breasted two-piece suits (Armani? Versace? Brioni?) as the matching silk ties flashed in the klieg lights. The sartorial melodrama was even heightened in the Afghanistan crisis and the attempt to capture Osama bin Laden, who was appealing to world public opinion in long white flowing robes, accentuating his full-fledged black beard. The desperate U.S. president, winning support in Shanghai for his "international coalition against Terror," donned a shiny blue mandarin jacket to gleam alongside the iridescent Chinese leadership which offered him "solidarity." As for the two Green Party ministers in the Schroeder Berlin cabinet–Fischer, and yet another street-marching militant, Jürgen Trittin, whose modest dark ties now discreetly harmonized with his dark polo shirts, thus softening the shock of the "betrayal" (i.e., capitulation to the bourgeoisie)–each looked on television screens and front-page newspaper photos every inch the formidable German Establishment figure. They never seemed to be "comfortable with" the new attire. The image appeared to be all.

Clothes Maketh the Man, Unmaketh the Woman

On the American scene there is an altogether more impervious element in the sartorial routines of the Establishment. There may be fanciful or aggressively casual deviations over the week-end (or on vacation)–it all began perhaps with the innovative "Truman shirt" in the 1940s–but the standard attire, except for students on campus or pop stars and their fans, is fashionably unexceptionable. Rare is the figure who turns up on Wall Street or on Capitol Hill without a suit jacket, buttoned-up shirt, and knotted tie. Still, there are moments when the U.S. press touches a nerve, and there seems to be an alarmed, pained reaction from the great American public as if some important national code had been violated.

One of the more outlandish days of recent scandal was, in my view, the small incident when President Clinton, having ordered a special Hollywood hairdresser to attend to him, held up California air-traffic while his coiffure was being done in Air Force One, expensively parked on a runway of the L.A. airport. It caused a storm of derision. We *do* want our heroes–or leading men who, for a time or a term or two, play the role–to look ever so good. They should appear (unlike, say, Nixon) squeaky clean and closely shaven. Even looking *chic* is permissible. But there is a conventional line which should not be crossed, and it marks a primping self-indulgence too far. Narcissism throws a dark shadow, and conspicuous vanity loses votes.

In the United States, the old world's ideology of apparel only apparently plays less of a role. Textiles always had a special place in the traditional European dreams of a utopia and the revolutionary characters who would bring it about. In Sir Thomas More's utopian island, blue uniforms (among other items of attire) had distinctive significance. The French Jacobins, with their red bonnets and fluttering trousers, broke with all styles that had ever graced the seats of power. Newborn Americans, fashioning their new world, dressed out of primitive necessities rather than intellectual design. President Andrew Jackson, making his backwoodsman's radical thrust, might well put on a singular appearance in his Daniel Boone's fur hat; but his White House presence was rather prim and proper. Abraham Lincoln's aspect struck a dark, saturnine note which befitted an era when millions of Civil War casualties were being mourned...and Theodore Roosevelt's flair was flamboyant enough to match his bully pulpit. The stricter military forms of men's wear had always for ex-colonials a hated touch of British redcoat hostility; and even in a well-disciplined American expeditionary force in World War Two, the doughboys wore a floppy little brimless cap at a rakish angle, in which a Napoleonic or a Hessian grenadier wouldn't be caught dead.

On the more recent American scene there is–at least in the highest political circles–a pendulum swing in contemporary style which is roughly equivalent to the Washington electoral alternation between liberal-left Democrats and the right-of-center conservative Republicans. Some observers, much too impressed with the shenanigans of the '68 generation, were misled by the dramatic triumph in the White House of Jimmy Carter's cohorts in blue jeans. Brash Yankee laxity had at last appeared in the most official of stylish places. Loose and improvised was the manner of all the president's men. Those energetic spirits whom Napoleon (or Madame de Staël to whom he was talking) called the *idéologues* had long awaited a new cosmic turning. A culture that had pushed frontiers over far-away horizons and "won the West" should produce a wild informality, sporting open-collar shirts. That no ties were to be worn was taken to be a small sign of a larger liberation that broke all knots and restrictions, all twists and folds that uselessly encumbered the free human spirit. If it was a great change, it was a revolution of the casual. *"Come as you are"* was the strict order of the day.

There is little point in overloading these pages with the Thermidorean reversal of radical change in the long years of Ronald Reagan's administration. The president himself slipped on occasion into his Wrangler jackets and his Levi-Strauss trousers, and even topped it all off with a Stetson hat, mounting a well-saddled horse. But this was not for real. All the pieces, if not the animal, were movie wardrobe leftovers. What mattered was that nothing was obligatory, *de rigueur*. If you were happy wearing a three-piece suit, so be it. Ideological correctness was out. You could be as you were, or are, or wanted to be. Especially if the attire was clean and, if possible, sharply pressed.

In the Clinton years nobody really ever attempted to reverse the reversal. The forty-second president of the United States was too busy trying to be himself, or to try and find out who he was (or might be), to be consistently playing a role-model for Americans who were still yearning for the old and yet enjoying the new.

In the first days of the George W. Bush administration (as I write), the pendulum has swung again. The *New York Times* reported, with its usual awkwardness in choosing words and concepts, that Bush was providing another "corporate model for the White House." This was beside the mark. In one European newspaper this phrase was expatiated into a thesis that a new corporativism had arrived, that the United States was becoming something of a "corporative" or "corporate" state. No way. It was more like the return of the collar button into the buttonhole. One Washington correspondent gave us this vivid snapshot:

> The days when Clinton used to stroll around the White House in a baseball cap and tracksuit, munching on a banana smothered in peanut butter, while aides lolled in antique armchairs with their feet on their desks, have given way to a starched regime that prizes punctuality and efficiency. All make staff are now expected to wear jackets and ties in the Oval Office....[11]

Still, in an international context, conventional middle-class norms can send different signals in various directions. There are Kremlinologists who have won fame by predicting shifting policies according to the changing Bolshevik fashions in which, say, Stalin wore or discarded his military Marshal's uniform, often in dazzling white gabardine. They reflected on the headwear to be seen in Red Square on high Soviet occasions: Malenkov, just before his fall, showed himself bare-headed; Beria covered a balding head with a bushy fur-hat; others took to wearing fedoras and adding a medal or two to the five or six strands of colorful Party decorations pinned on to their suit-jackets.[12]

The sartorial question, notoriously embarrassing as it has been in the political polemics of German politics, has not gone completely unnoticed in foreign diplomatic circles. Perhaps only a woman's eye could have caught it, especially Mme. Madeleine Albright's: she, whose short skirts and tight-fitting blouses have themselves been the subject of some controversy and consternation. Why do public personalities persist in sending sartorial signals of questionable meaning? Mme. Albright may not have seen herself plain as she sat among prim Arab diplomats in the Middle East–but she appears to have a perceptive eye for what her well-dressed counterpart in Berlin has been wearing. She knows that the German foreign minister, Joschka Fischer, was once a Marxist-Leninist street fighter in the old '68 days (headband, open collar, torn jeans; all obligatory) and she appreciates the change that has come over the man. In one recent interview Mrs. Albright quoted Fischer as saying to her, on the occasion of the fiftieth anniversary of the NATO military alliance, "I could never have believed that I would have ever attended a NATO meeting, and dressed in a three-piece suit!..." I venture to suggest that vests and single-breasted jackets will be coming into their place in the history of Western ideology.[13]

In capitalist societies the significant movements on the Left or on the Right have to be read another way. The French nationalist, Le Pen, never turned up in a solid single-colored shirt which might hint at the nature of his black- or brown-shirted bid for power. German revolutionary radicals who for many long militant years slept in their sweat-shirts and jeans–when the demos and picket-lines called for day-and-night endurance–now signal their readiness to compromise for top jobs in a Left coalition government by...polishing their shoes and combing out their long unruly curls.

Are such details to be taken seriously? When a dullard on my morning newspaper fails to give me these kinds of facts I am forced to peer with eagle eyes at the televised news wherein apparel necessarily fills the screen, and close-ups can catch tell-tale five-o'clock-shadows. In this fashion one can register the varieties of top- and rain-coats; the disappearance of berets (long since transferred from the arty Parisian Left Bank to élite paratrooper barracks); the photo-op challenge to European Ministers of their two- and three button suit-jackets (when there is no time to button them all up...and to check one's trouser zipper as one steps out of the limousine); the victory of white starched shirt-collars (at least in the highest circles who figure in the newsreels regularly) over loose open-necked casualness.

Women's apparel as signals on the political scene is harder to read–especially when complicated by personal style in jewellery (ear-rings, strings of pearls, brooches, etc.). Berlin observers note that the German Foreign Minister Joschka Fischer was well on his way to general acceptability (after his '68-radical past) when he added a white pocket kerchief to his designer suit-jacket. Washington critics reported that U.S. foreign policy might have been slightly more successful if Mrs. Albright had abandoned her tight above-the-knees skirts and wore longer, looser-fitting garments. They made a good pair–the radical whose parents came from Hungary and made it to the top of the German cabinet and the Czech refugee who often didn't quite convince Washington of her accent and apparel.

In the first stage of alternative dressing to "defy and dismay" the Establishment, female attire simply copied casual male informalities. When the sartorial gestures become rather more complex there is little lee-way for cross-over dressing–for, that is, the woman party leader in the European Parliament who once chained herself to Strasbourg iron gates and for the pacifistic militant who used to do the Easter march in the rain to Aldermaston with her fellow-protesters. Old dress codes remain rather mean and paltry when they don't go further than the tailored two-piece suit (what the Germans call "*die Power-Uniform*") and any old blouse-and-skirt combination. Expressive and extrovert movements are being deprived of yet another demonstrative symbol. Eccentric emblematic signals seem to be going out of fashion this year. Everybody is beginning to look like everybody else.

For most European editors and reporters it is still "a gender story," observed along the traditional perception of clothes making the man. In Germany nowadays most of the positions in the power-sharing Green Party are "manned' by women who enjoy the quota advantages of a fifty-fifty division of the spoils. And most of these women in the public limelight have until now resisted the blandishments of *embourgeoisement*. They have never–or not yet–changed their casual ready-to-wear; and most of them refrain (even in front of the camera) from any close-up-friendly cosmetic retouching. They may always look fairly dishevelled on the 6 o'clock news, a few of them indeed like something out of John Knox's "monstrous regiment of women" of, say, 1558. But what still holds them together–certainly far more than coalition politics–is that the male leadership in the Schroeder cabinet, with its newly-clad sartorial elegance and makeover hair-do's, appears unattractive, even distasteful to them. When you come right down to it, i.e., to their basic sense of core character, the off-putting camouflage by which one dresses up fashionably to seduce the electorate is for "the wimmin" embarrassing, corrupting, and altogether alienating. (I have met a few more reasonable women, in German politics and journalism, who insist that to look so impeccably unkempt takes some doing, taking almost as long in fact as a hair-do session with the nearest *coiffeuse*.)

The alert English mainstream press does report such differences among the Green counterparts on the London Left. Here is the *Daily Telegraph* venting its Tory joy at the "make-over" of Clare Short, a Far Left agit-prop figure of old, and now domesticated in the Tony Blair New Labour cabinet:

CLARE SHORT TIRED OF FEMINISM WITH A TOUCH OF LIP GLOSS.
It was the lipstick you noticed first. A flattering pink, glistening with the faintest sheen of lip gloss. Then the eyes, shaped eyebrows, and gamine haircut....

It was (according to the story written by the paper's Fashion editor, Hilary Alexander) enough to make every follower of the blunt-speaking radical gasp in dismay. The image-makers, she concludes, have finally gotten their hands on the Cabinet's scruffy rebel. Only yesterday she had been seen on TV borrowing a pair of ill-fitting brown boots to march around the refugee camps outside Kosovo. Today she was discussing world issues, "poised and pretty...both word and picture perfect. Her make-up was a triumph."

For her counterpart, in turn, the stylish French socialist Edith Cresson, it all proved to be a total disaster. Mitterand's short-lived choice for prime minister of France had her brilliant career ended by a forced resignation from one of the highest posts in the High European Commission in Brussels. Her poised and attractive eloquence could not rally enough of her old comrades on the EU Left from the indictment on the general charges of "bureaucratic sleaze." A German radical commentator said, "She doesn't even look innocent...."

But innocent or guilty of what? Regular visits to the tony hair-dresser and to the *chic* dress-maker can undermine a sense of solidarity on the militant feminist Left. In a Europe which has socialists heading governments in France, Germany, and Britain there is a danger of gender-model confusion and disarray. A small sector of comradely support can disastrously crumble away; for, in point of fact, a few males prefer frumpery in politics, and a good many females prefer the way the battle-axes of yesteryear used to look. Whether figures of fun or objects of nostalgia, every vote lost is a step closer to an old career of cooking in the kitchen for the children. Or who would be wanting to mount the barricades with the made-over Clare Short? The Fashion Editor's enthusiasm can be dispiriting and counter-revolutionary –

> ...Eyes were emphasized with the merest hint of eyeliner and a soft browny-grey shadow. Brows were newly-shaped too. And those lips, from which the truth–a concept alien to many politicians–emerged in the past with regular abandon, were gleaming, moistened and perfectly on message.
> The blunt-cut bob that sat on her jawline had gone too. Miss Short sported instead a new style achieved by what hairdressers call feathering–cutting into the hair to give a soft ragged edge rather than a sharp unflattering line.
> The navy silk trouser suit was an excellent choice. It looked as if it could have been Jaeger. The neckline was rounded, rather than severe, and the white buttons matched the white silk shell top underneath. Perhaps the middle buttons were a little too strained for comfort, but that could have been because she was sitting down.
> Let's hope the new 'Clare flair' was not a one-off..[14]

IF clothes maketh the man, the fads of fashion unmake the politician who primps away his or her street-cred. If it's not a pants length too high or a tight skirt too short with a hemline too far, then it's the whole cut of an outfit which is suspiciously obsessive or just a wrinkle too casual. The ageing veterans of the '68 generation no longer appear to be readily identifiable as rebels and radicals. The Western world embraced, torn blue jeans and all, the easy-going ready-to-wear; and whole societies followed the new uniformities by coming-and-going as they were.

To be sure, nobody came casually to the U.S. Senate–nor to the House of Commons–where certain old and traditional formalities prevailed. But the Mario Savios and the Bernadine Dohrns of '68 notoriety have not yet been elected to high or important public offices which would present sartorial dilemmas.

Daniel Cohn-Bendit, perhaps the most memorable name in the European Student Movement of the 1960s, is still in the news and on the TV screens. He has neatly fudged his personal problem as to what he should be wearing when he goes about his quasi-philanthropic business of doing little bits of good here and there–from improving Franco-German kindergartens to recanting (rather convincingly) almost all of his ideological errors which made him such a terror in *les événements* of the Sorbonne riots. His torn sweaters and his shock of red hair are no longer around the boulevards to make a good paragraph in a quick and colorful newspaper story. He dresses now with calculated diffidence; and nobody notices any more the markings of his sneakers or the color of his polo shirts. A year or so ago (it was in late June 2000) we happened, unexpectedly, to be sitting at the same podium. Not only were we, in the ensuing discussion, in shocking general agreement; we were wearing the same sort of shabby sports jacket (with reinforced elbow patches). It was kind of embarrassing.

On the German scene the break with the dishevelment of the militant past was, on occasion, as breathtaking as Ms. Clare Short's makeover and Foreign Minister Joschka Fischer's three-piece Brioni suits, if not altogether as duplicitous. The current and very loquacious spokeswoman of the Green Left in the Berlin *Bundestag*, Claudia Roth, appears almost nightly on the TV newscasts with a fashionably cut-and-dyed pageboy *coiffure*; and she makes a point of wearing–indeed flamboyantly, for she is a youngish and rather comely creature–a dashing scarf around her bare neck-line and broad shoulders. The scarves are chosen, as she once demonstrated to a TV cameraman, from a personal collection which was designed to fit every political occasion. She wore, suitably enough, a long black shawl on that awful 11th of September when her once-pacifist and anti-NATO party, now in the government coalition, had to commit itself "unconditionally" to Chancellor Schroeder's solidarity for President Bush's "War against Terrorism."

One stylistic hold-out from the old street-demonstration days is Hans-Christian Ströbele, and he may be "the exception that proves the rule."[15] Most of Hans-Christian Ströbele's German comrades, the banner-wavers and the slogan-chanters and even the street fighters, pose properly nowadays for the cameras which record every idiosyncrasy of attire. Ströbele is a battle-tested *idéologue* and, not unlike Robespierre and his devotion to Jacobin virtue, he remains ruthless with class enemies and all they represent. He hates the Establishment with whatever camouflage the contemporary capitalist system succeeded in disguising itself to hide its oppressive techniques of manipulation and global exploitation. He has cultivated a cool and quiet contempt that has burned vividly for decades. Ströbele was one of the lawyers–along with Otto Schily, a Green defector who became one of the most powerful Ministers in the Schroeder cabinet–who defended the so-called "Baader-Meinhof gang"; and he was expelled from the Bar Association (in 1975) for ethical transgressions (i.e., violating the ethical code for defense counsel when he smuggled messages in and out of jail). He was originally a member of the Social Democratic

Party, gracing its indestructible left wing; but he was expelled for ideological transgressions by referring to *RAF*-terrorist clients as "comrades." He approved, or seemed to be apologizing for, Iraq's bombardment of Israel during the "Desert Storm" war of 1991. This provoked important defections in the ranks of the Left (usually, figures like Henryk M. Broder, who were anti-anti-Semitic and pro-Zionist). He went on to be, with unflagging consistency, a prime agitator against the Western policies in Yugoslavia, opposing the *NATO* "out-of-area" presence in Bosnia as well as Kosovo, not to mention Montenegro. Almost singlehandedly, he brought the *Bundestag* muckraking investigation into the Christian Democrat corruption scandals to the entrapment and fall of the great figures of the Reunification Revolution of 1989, Chancellor Helmut Kohl and CDU Party leader Wolfgang Schäuble.

Did Robespierre always wear his *tricot* (or, perhaps, his *culottes*) in the Reign of Terror? Ströbele (b. 1939), the ubiquitous inquisitor in German political life these days, regularly appears wearing his fearsome uniform...unfailingly it consists of a pair of faded blue jean trousers; a short, shabby denim *blouson*; an open, unbuttoned shirt (with no tie and no knot to uncurl the crumpled collar). And–the sartorial touch of genius–the gleaming whiter-than-white seam of his peek-a-boo undershirt.

At a talk show many years ago we, Ströbele and I, argued amiably during a truce in the Cold War (after Nixon and Khrushchev and before Reagan and Gorbachov). To the alarm of the moderator at the microphone I ventured to congratulate Ströbele on his impeccable attire (I think I said: *gear*), so politically correct and *so* well laundered. Squeezing in another thought in the silence of a five-second byte, I muttered some additional admiration for his ready supply of presentable T-shirts. But what would he do when, some morning, a *V*-shirt happened to turn up in his *trousseau*? And suddenly there would be, for the agit-prop of the day, no tell-tale chest patch, no emblematic all-cotton eminently washable medallion on his neckline....

As a lifelong devotee of V-shirts (made by the Fruit of the Loom people), I knew that my question was not disinterested, and could be ignored; which it was. For years on years Ströbele has continued to exhibit that bit of T-shirt whiteness just at the point where neck meets breast-plate. It was, I thought, uncannily reminiscent of the Jacobin insignia which Jacques Louis David, a happy survivor of the guillotine, painted into his memorable portraits of *les amis de la grande révolution* (mostly victims like Marat, or Napoleonic generals).

Ströbele, like his companions on the Left who have survived the "*big chill*" (Daniel Cohn-Bendit, Jürgen Trittin, Joschka Fischer, et al.), has "made it" to the mainstream. He has gathered strength from every crusading skirmish, from every corruption scandal he exposes, from every wrongdoer he catches red-handed. For a stylish *revoluzzer*, with a good ear for the tunes of the day, there was indeed life after '68. In more recent years Ströbele has been zealously at the forefront of almost any parliamentary altercation which involved human rights, animal rights, civil rights, and other good causes.

If the garment discreetly covered up for a macho hairy chest, it also reassuringly suggested a touch of that cleanliness which is close to godliness. Come to think of it, this ideologized under-thing could become one of the most famous pieces of men's wear–at least since Marlon Brando ran around in Stanley Kowalski's sleeveless sweaty undershirt in the days when Tennessee Williams' *Streetcar* was offering manly images to remember.

In the U.S. mainstream press there has been for a long time now a reasonable amount of immunization against what is archly called hype. It keeps out of the paper the usual run of publicity tricks and other public-relations ploys involving clients who pose for "newsy" pictures and/or allow themselves to be quoted as saying something quotable or doing something reportable. Many newcomers to the Washington political scene are eager to do their new jobs without welcoming–or even conspicuously deploring–what seems to strike a serious newspaper editor as personal details which carry enough "human interest" to publicize in his paper.

Thus, I have read a dozen or so richly detailed profiles–in the U.S. as well as European press–of Ms. Condoleezza Rice who was President-elect George W. Bush's surprising (she was a woman, she was black, she was intelligent) choice as his National Security adviser…a post that had been previously held by such towering intellectual personalities as McGeorge Bundy, Henry Kissinger, Zbigniew Brzezinski. Every scrap of information about Ms. Rice would help a newspaper reader make some sense of American foreign policy and cast some light on a new president's first faltering efforts on the international scene. I was delighted by some investigative reporter's thoughtful quotations from her previous academic work on security problems. I was charmed by the glossy magazine treatments, lavishly illustrated, featuring her femininity. The striking portrait in *Vogue*–by Annie Leibovitz (in the tradition of Man Ray and Richard Avedon, if not Helmut Newton)–was singular and, in certain circles, provocative.

It seems that Ms. Rice, the first woman to hold such a senior position in the White House, had been trained as a classical pianist; and she had to make a choice between a career in academe or in music. The Leibovitz photograph, as one paper reported (and it reprinted it, and why not?), "presents a striking contrast to Miss Rice's normal image." The normal image (always with its implicit abnormalities)–which is always a factor in the editorial process of judging what is or is not fit to print–is one of an "intense intellectual." As a would-be concert pianist she is photographed sitting in front of her baby grand in an elegant strapless ballroom-gown. (Not unlike, one might say, her musical sisters: Jessye Norman, Kathleen Battle, et al.)

Did this photograph "belie her public reputation"? Evidently it suggested a flamboyance which didn't suit well with advising on grave issues of war and peace. One mainstream newspaper–in London, during the tense beginnings of the Anglo-American military engagement against the Taliban régime in Afghanistan–published the *Vogue* photograph, and in a fit of concern of the place and impact of clothes and especially female dress in world politics, tried to ward off the demons that usually plague crossover gender politics. We are insistently instructed in the other side of the picture: "Miss Rice is not known for a flamboyant dress sense...." (What if she were, conscripting a dress sense to counter her counterpart's flowing Arab robes?...) We are pointedly reminded that even during the balls celebrating the inauguration of President Bush earlier that year she preferred "a plain wool-knit dress rather than a ballgown." There is, as I have been suggesting, a hidden ideological message in the clothes we choose to wear., their cut, color and conventionality.

It appears, once again, that to go to war–or even to attend to its declaration–one has to dress properly, appropriately. The press' political correspondents have to cover the story with the expertise on *couture* of the paper's fashion reporters. Washington was at the time on a war footing, and the *Daily Telegraph*'s U.S. correspondent needed to reassure his British readers who were all taken to be stalwart defenders of yet another Anglo-American special relationship: "For day-to-day wear, Miss Rice is most likely to be found in a grey trouser suit and low-heeled shoes. Her skirts are nearly always cut below the knee and she rarely wears bright colors...." It is good to remind oneself that it was the American Ralph Waldo Emerson who supported in Boston the first edition of Thomas Carlyle's *Sartor Resartus* (1836, "The tailor repatched"). The speculations of an imaginary Professor Teufelsdröckh led to the conclusion that "all symbols, forms, and human institutions are properly clothes, and as such temporary...."[16]

Making It Up

There is a school of thought which contends that only journalism can be permitted, in the very haste of things, to be approximate. Newspapers are destined to get only the general gist but not the literal and certainly not the deeper truth. Still, scholarly historians, who are supposed to be the repositories of exact transcription and documentation, use these very journalistic texts to which their own work is supposed to stand in sharp contrast.

More than that, history can only be silent when a corroborating letter or a relevant diary entry–or some other identifiably reliable source–is simply *not* there. In the above case of Wehner/Breloer the most dramatic and revealing incident occurred in the filming of a long, excruciating silence which we know to have happened. In most biographical portraits words can be quoted or devised. Here no dialogue or soliloquy needs to be listened to....And a true portrait of the man emerges, out of a hushed nothingness.

There is just no simple way of making a record of what-it-was-like or a lifelike representation with warts and all. Even profound and revered historians sometimes speculate, and mere journalists often get it exactly right. A histo-

rian like Thucydides–whose fabricated speeches were put into the mouths of
all the essential heroes and villains of ancient Greek history–has been recognized for millennia as the great Western founder of "scientific history." A
contemporary playwright like Michael Frayn wrestles with this classical heritage when trying to illuminate aspects of contemporary history which journalists have left unresolved (*viz.* the sinister Nazi atom-bomb which Werner
Heisenberg might have built for Hitler in World War II). Thucydides insisted
that he had avoided all "story-telling"; but when he found it impossible to
remember "exact wording," then he made each orator speak, "as in my opinion
he would have done in the circumstances but keeping as close as I could to the
train of thought that guided the actual speech...."

Frayn in his striking play entitled *Copenhagen* (1998) the Heisenberg drama
has its wartime climax in the house of his scientific mentor, the Danish half-
Jewish physicist Niels Bohr. It follows this historic line–taking "journalistic
license," or (some would say) taking more liberties with hard facts than most
editors of history would allow. He surmised what the trains of thought were. He
departs from the known historical record. His protagonists make unprecedented
observations and suggest paths-not-taken of adventurous consequence. He
"reaches the parts" where recorded and recordable history cannot reach.

Is he not guilty of "license" in the sense of "excess, abuse of freedom"? Isn't
he, after all, just making it all up? How can a playwright's "make-believe
world," arranged on a footlighted stage on which actors impute motives and
suspect temptations, serve to illuminate a real world which calls for a remorse-
less discipline on behalf of factuality and truthfulness?

Many serious playgoers were convinced by Frayn's drama. I saw *Copenhagen*
in a London performance in 1999 and after some intellectual difficulties about
accommodating fiction to non-fiction I found his credo acceptable:

> ...The great challenge facing the storyteller and the historian alike is to get inside
> people's heads, to stand where they stood and see the world as they saw it, to make
> some informed estimate of their motives and intentions–and this is precisely where
> recorded and recordable history cannot reach. Even when all the external evidence has
> been mastered, the only way into the protagonists' heads is through the imagination.

I am still troubled that in accepting this the last consequence may be the
subversion of the ideal purposes of both Journalism and History. The journalistic effort may record diligently all the facts and conjectures; the historical
enterprise should be assessing coherently and reasonably all causes and possibilities. Yet only art has the license to surmise–to approach the past, invasively–
to dare to reveal the ultimate truth, if such there be.[17]

Nobel Advice

Some sectors of the intelligentsia have already given up, thrown in the
towel; technology is inflicting virtual–some predict actual–Hiroshima on the

fragile, shaky structures of old-fashioned cultural life. At a recent conference in Milan (December 1995), ten Nobel-Prize-winners assembled to discuss the onset of an "Information Society" and its highways and byways. The American physicist present, Murray Gell-Mann, thought that the "information boom" which is accompanying the current craze for computers and their loaded Internet potential was a global universal inundation of "Disinformation" or, at best, of badly-organized information. The Latin-American poet, the late Octavio Paz, offered the even more dismal proposition that what is wrong and disastrous about "virtual reality" is *not* that it is a hindrance to perception, a screened barrier to living awareness, an unjust impediment to true minds, etc., etc. The virtual approximation of reality is *really like* real reality; endlessly various, thoroughly random and chaotic. The virtual approximate reality will only be compounding life's troubles, in an intimate imitation of all our personal vices and confusions. The prevalent chaos—and the poet, among other artists, comes to give a semblance of visible order and audible meaning—will merely be replicated. If chaos is to come again (and again) in an "age unbred," then the only hope for the artist is to salvage a "cultural niche" for himself in which a few can remain creative, original, authentic. The world's free market-places may continue to flourish, but the market's efficient mechanism leaves little room for such traditional, old-time qualities such as "culture...justice...compassion."

The African poet and playwright, Wole Soyinka (Nobel prize-winner, 1986), was sunk in even greater despair (possibly also because they were now hanging writers in his native Nigeria). He mourned the future of private images, of the keepers of the word—"this amulet of a secular priesthood, prophets of earthly expectations." Was there, then, among them some promising "medicine-man" who would come to cure what was ailing us all?

Which leaves us, for the moment, where we started out from in the history of the concept of culture—somewhere between E.B. Tylor's "primitives" and James G. Frazer's "magicians"—in dark, tribal homelands, driven by incomprehensible and uncontrollable forces, longing for the golden bough. The consequence of opening up new dimensions is that we have become lost in time won, and we can be comforted only by the cosmic fact that some say *even then* we would have a *culture.*[18]

Hegel, and Holding Fast

If the newspapers tend to get the last word in the argument between press and television, and especially in the precarious field of film hoaxes and the pseudo-documentary simulation of virtual reality, they both share "the camera-eye," whose pictures in print or on the screen have been increasingly manipulated for ignoble purposes. The *paparazzi*, as they have been called since Fellini's *Dolce Vita* movie of 1960, have now become an endangered species. Laws are being prepared in various Western lands to control them and

reduce their ingenious invasions of privacy which result in sensationally intimate long-lens snapshots that tabloids everywhere flaunt. Rather more clumsy
and heavier TV equipment handicaps the video competition–an agile and
resourceful photographer manages to pry indefatigably.

With the result that men and women in the news-headlines suffer regular
"ambushes by the camera." And when the cameramen are prevented from zoom-
ing in on real scenes, will they not be desperate enough to use new technology
to fake the forbidden scenes which "tell all"? One lamentable professional
still-photographer, conceding the regrettable "invasion of privacy," went on
to confess to yet another deplorable practice of current media photography:
"More and more, final printed images are being modified by electronic manipulation that gives them less and less faithfulness to whatever was in front of
the camera in the first place" (A.L. Cotcher, commenting in the *Times*, 24
August 1996, p. 19, on the *Times* article by Libby Purves, "Ambushed by the
Camera," 20 August 1996).

I want to back-pedal a bit in order to intrude a word of caution. It is not
merely a matter of local gossip and its home-grown purveyors. We have also to
do here with what English or American papers are saying about far-away countries about which the editors seem to know everything. They do not. Inaccuracy through over-simplification is a standard vice even among the best of
journalists–and there are a number of other discountable elements which can
reduce the force and validity of the dark message.

There is the factor, frequently mentioned in the previous pages, of the
industrial bias of the newspaper industry against the television conglomerates
and the heirs of the old studio moguls in Hollywood. There is also, mixing
with prejudice and exaggeration, the excessive impressionism of professional
doomsayers. The clocks are always ticking to midnight. Our press has developed what can be called a primordial predilection for gloom-and-doom, for
the item of bad news writ large. On occasions when culture or civilization
appears to be involved the story can take on apocalyptic tones. The world as
we have known it is going down the tubes–total evil is on the verge of a
disastrous triumph–our society has lost its grip on realities–the end is nigh.

Having said that, we still remain with the basic, if somewhat qualified, truth
that the tragedy of our televised communication system is that (Marshal
McLuhan, to the contrary notwithstanding) the medium is, and has, no message. Its mind is as blank as the screen on your Sony set in the off-position: a
small light may be blinking but there is no illumination. Certainly this is no
new fear on the part of observers of Western civilization and its discontents. I
recall that dark suspicion of even that most optimistic spirit in the eighteenth-
century French Enlightenment, Diderot, who warned in the *Encyclopédie:* "if
it happens that there should be in society men interested in forming, as it were,
centers of shadow, even the people will find itself plunged into a profound

darkness." Such shadowy forces are not only in the formative stage in Italy (according to our British reporters) but they have (according to Americans) been long at work at their interests in the USA. As for those Teutonically entrenched cultural institutions, the high-minded and heavily subsidized major networks of the reunited Germany, observant insiders have also detected signs of an onsetting darkness. (In the profound words of Pogo in the cartoon, some of them are saying: We have met the enemy, and they is us....) I quote only one *jeremiad* on the subject—which is, of course, subject to the qualifications I have made above.

A *Washington Post* columnist named Bob Herbert was venting his outrage at the mental level of U.S. schoolchildren who could not pass an examination in history and public affairs of the most elementary kind. Polls and tests had revealed that enormous percentages did not know "who ordered the nuclear attack on Japan" or even that "it was on Japan that President Truman ordered the dropping of the A-bomb"; and these, and similar, scholastic shortcomings were ascribed to "our being, to a large extent, a nation of nitwits." The cause? Films that are being "made for morons"; TV entertainment which, when Mr. Herbert got around to looking at it, was "so much worse–so much more stupid–than anything I had imagined." He concluded:

> None of this would be important if we were talking only about fads, goofy things that make a momentary appearance, spark a chuckle and pass harmlessly from sight. But that is not what is going on. Americans are surrounded by a deep and abiding stupidity. Radio talk-show hosts, contemptuous of facts and disdainful toward truth, spew venom—and mindless listeners all across the country cheer....Alarms should be clanging from coast to coast. An ignorant populace is a populace in danger....People who willingly swim in a sea of ig-norance can blame themselves when the quality of their lives deteriorates....
>
> (*Washington Post/IHT*, 2 March 1995)

This, too, can only be accepted with some grains of salt. Yet the despairing cry of a popular culture in deep agonized trouble is, again, a sign of the temper of the times. More than that, it can be taken as a revealing indicator (more or less roughly) of the shape of things to come. Things can always get worse; but can the primal scream of protest in our press be pitched any louder?

For the consolation of philosophy while contemplating this degraded drama of cultures traduced, is a heartfelt sense of gratitude for the printed word, at least in its cultured context of civilized journalism. What would we do without our reliable morning newspaper! It may yet prove to be the one instrument to preserve our sanity on going into a new, unreal century which is likely to take on forms *alla italiana*: "Everyday reality has been replaced by televised reality, which is itself being dismantled, and no one has any idea what is real and what is not."

I am desperately reminded of the way in which the German thinker, Hegel, retained his hold on the less than ideal outside world of his own day. Before he proceeded to get to work on his philosophical manuscripts at his writing table he first made sure to check out his mail box and see whether his newspapers had come. He held them fast in his hand: it was good to know in the light of the morning that the outside world, with its very real realities, was still there....May our own grip be so sure.

25

Spielberg, Or the Hollywood Scapegoat

The gravest accusations of historic guilt are always extravagant, are indeed barely credible (except in the rarest cases of tragic mass murder) and even when encountered in the most professional historiography need to be examined with critical care. How much more so in the context of newspaper cultures when the charges are formulated journalistically–and supported only by a reporter's quick recollection of evidence from adventitiously available sources.

We have been documenting the contemporary suspicion that our civilization–or, at least, its moral sense and capacity for human sympathy and decent ethical response–has been subject to a certain anesthetization. As we have seen, it has been a major theme of newspaper editorializing, wherein all the media, old as well as new, have come in for their share of the accountability. Criticism has been pointing a finger at every aspect of communication to find the sinister fault. Television has been everywhere isolated as the major factor. But the press campaign on behalf of the written and printed word–as against the photograph and the motion picture–has itself faltered when it, in turn, has been charged with apathy, verbal exhaustion, and an incapacity to make tragic news real and involving to its readership. Meanwhile, back in the studio, the TV editors look askance at their big brothers, the Hollywood filmmakers who have taken charge in their block-busting kind of way of the fantasy life of vast populations of moviegoers.

Who, or what, is to blame? Where is the conspiracy? Something is wrong, and we would like to have news, good or bad, that the villainy has been spotted and that the alarm has been sounded. In our times novelists have been blamed for wars and poets for peace (or, at least, pacifism). Marcel Proust's novel was famously charged with being responsible for the Fall of France in 1940, and the pacifist mid-Weimar tunes of Brecht-Weill for diverse German failings which led to ruin and damnation. The pattern is irresistible and irresponsible. The latest to take place in our newspaper culture's mission to report on the decline of the West, its quest to find the key to nothing less than the crisis of contemporary civilization, is a youngish American of much talent, vast wealth, and infinite jest–Steven Spielberg.

I take one newspaper article from the many which–even since the world-wide cinema success of *Jaws* (1975), *Close Encounters of the Third Kind* (1977), *Indiana Jones* (1989), *Jurassic Park* (1993), *The Lost World* (1997)– formulates the extravagant charge of historic guilt I have referred to above. It's almost a scoop to find and interview the man who symbolized the malaise. Hollywood–as in so many other ideologies of accusation–is the scene of the crime. Once it was merely content to fabricate dreams we would live by; now it has moved to usurp and make superfluous the whole human imagination. There was once time and space in our lives for magical childhood images; now there is room only for special effects. Once upon a time there used to be fairy tales and a Peter Pan wondrousness but, alas, no longer: "No, we would yawn; not unless they're digital, computerised, animatronic fairies zapping around the skies, preferably pursued by a velociraptor." No, according to the indict-ment, the man is supposed to be the boy wonder with the boundless imagina-tion, but, "his boundless imagination has shrunk everybody else's....His images have planted themselves in America's–and the world's–collective conscious-ness: the shark fin moving ominously across the surface of the water, the bicycling boy silhouetted against the moon, the tyrannosaurus's foot sud-denly stamping down in front of the jeep."

After such charges it will be increasingly difficult for Steven Spielberg to bask easily in the popularity of America's (and the world's) children. It is one thing for an artist to establish himself as baby-friendly, quite another to be mercilessly ribbed for infantilism. The increasing orientation of the Holly-wood film production to ever younger audiences has led to the critical suspi-cion, especially since the spate of new movies trying to revive a taste for fairy tales (and even more: a whimsical fancy for fairies), that "we should be al-lowed to remain children for ever." One newspaper columnist of the *Sunday Times* joins in the ranks of the critics who are pillorying Spielberg: "The one great message the LA producers agree it is safe to deliver to the masses is that growing up is bad. From *ET* to *Hook*, Steven Spielberg has done his best to keep us in short pants, if not nappies."[1] There is supposed to be a law of diminishing returns at work here. Not, of course, in the cash receipts them-selves. *Jurassic Park* is already the biggest grossing film of all time; and *The Lost World* grossed $200 million in its first six weeks. The charge is "the remorseless desensitizing of the audience." Much is made of laughter among youngsters who were seeing Spielberg's film about the Nazi/Jewish holocaust, *Schindler's List*. A woman is shot in the head at close range, and this was greeted by the remark, "Oh, man, was that *cool!*"

The critic's logic is relentless:

after two decades of joky terror, from *Jaws* to *Jurassic Park*–after films that cannot move us because every human element has been eradicated–why should we be surprised that audiences find it increasingly hard to feel *real* terror?...The most telling moment in *Schindler's List* is a small one, in a black-and-white film, one little girl's coat suddenly turns red....Reality–even the reality of the Holocaust–wasn't enough for Spielberg. He had to trump it–to show, as he always does, how much better the movies are than reality.

One would have thought that the sterling integrity of a film like *Schindler's List* would have been taken as the exception to Hollywood make-believe, that it would have provided at least some extenuating circumstances for the rest of the indictment. The little red coat is a scene that lasts all of nine seconds; and approve the surrealistic touch or not, it surely betrays a moment of personal emotion. But for the newspaper critic who wants to round out a large, resonating argument, explaining in several thousand words on a Sunday morning some ultimate truths, nothing will stop him from completing his case against "the little Jewish boy who wanted desperately to blend in has succeeded to the point where any kind of individual expression seems beyond him...all the human shadings Spielberg has never been able to master."

We have come a long dialectical way in the argument about reality and apathy, compassion fatigue and diplomatic indifference, civility and hardness of heart. Even a resounding editorial cry against "desensitization" may have its own insensitive notes (here a slight touch of anti-Semitism). Especially when one takes into consideration that ever since the earliest days of the movies being made on the Californian west coast, there has always been a "Spielberg" at the dark center of what is taken to be the Evil of Hollywood. The despised names are interchangeable–D.W. Griffith (for the critics of a racist America); Will Hays (for liberal defenders of enlightened censor-free culture); Louis B. Mayer (for the Nazi propagandists against a Judæo-Bolshevik decadence); and any and all American studio heads for Stalin's Marxist critics who despised capitalism's "escapism" and its "bourgeois dream world". There have been, and will be, others.

What it amounts to is that when political and cultural debate becomes desperate and violent it turns out also to be about a struggle to size up the dimensions of life and art, to take the measure of reality. Mine is bigger than yours; yours is smaller than mine. As the man who hated Spielberg concluded his bill of charges –

Everything has to be 'larger than life'–even the Holocaust, which was surely quite large enough. That one dismal directorial touch in *Schindler's List* reminds you of how decadent films have become. Steven Spielberg's films are bigger than ever, but they're so much smaller than life.

I offer this as a representative example of an effort to work towards a philosophy for our newspaper culture, a characteristic piece of intellectual journalism, and I would not have taken you, dear reader, through it at such length if I did not think it contained bits of the best and the worst of what the papers say.[2]

26

Journalism and Jewry

A Coincidence of Background

It is a remarkable coincidence–although others tend to read something deeper into it–that two of the greatest mainstream newspapers were bought and brought to publishing success by German-Jewish immigrant families. Their success stories are well known–how Adolph Ochs transformed a little Manhattan publication to the formidable *New York Times* (so identified with his descendants, the Sulzbergers) and how Eugene Meyer (with the help of his daughter Katharine Graham and her energetic husband, the volatile Philip Graham) guided the struggling *Washington Post* to journalistic pre-eminence. It is equally remarkable that ownership and control of these formidable institutions have remained within their own families. None of the great WASP families in journalism–from Hearst to Scripps to Bennett–have been able to manage such a "dynasty."

But the simple reference to the "racial" or "religious" background of the two families who have played such an influential role in American life raises so many complex issues that many historians of the U.S. press have taken quick and easy ways out–that the factor of "Jewishness" explains everything or, alternatively, nothing at all. For being "German Jews," if that is what the founding fathers were, covers a multitude of Old World roots and a very tangled underbrush of adaptation and integration in the New World.

Eugene was American-born of (as we are officially told) "a distinguished family from Alsace-Lorraine, France." Still, his father's birthplace was for much of the last century-and-a-half German; Goethe had studied in German-speaking Strasbourg (and when I happened to turn up for its liberation from the Nazis in 1945 I read the local newspaper which proclaimed on its front-page headline: ELSASS IST FREI!). Eugene Meyer, at thirteen, had declined to take his bar mitzvah and went on to marry Agnes Ernst, an impressive descendant of a long Hannoverian line of Lutheran ministers; she accepted the hand of her "rich Jewish beau" and was confident that he would come to be "considered as not Jewish rather than she was Jewish...." But, as her daughter Katharine writes, "She was deeply hurt, however,...by suddenly being touched by social discrimination in New York."[1]

Chicago was even worse. In the aftermath of the dramatic sale of the Washington newspaper to Eugene Meyer, the powerful right-wing publisher Colonel McCormick of the *Chicago Tribune* had left some loose strings. A few copyrights to valuable features were overlooked. Meyer, a brilliant financier, didn't really know what comic strips actually were and indeed how important "the funnies" were to a paper's daily circulation. (He could have asked me, then aged twelve, and an avid reader of the four comic-strips at issue–*Andy Gump*, *Gasoline Alley*, *Dick Tracy*, and *Winnie Winkle*...Iwouldn't for the world have missed an installment, then syndicated in New York in the *Daily News*.) The rights turned out to have been "swiped" by Col. McCormick's cousin (Eleanor Medill "Cissy" Patterson); and for years "Cissy"–also the sister of the *News'* publisher, Joe Patterson–fought a legal battle to defend her four popular features. The case went up to the U.S. Supreme Court (1935). Meyer and the *Post* won.

Whereupon Cissy sent the winner a present "so as not to disappoint you." It was packaged in a florist's box in which some orchids decorated a smaller box which, in turn, contained a lump of raw, red, fleshy meat. Meyer's daughter recorded the incident drily as an "unpleasantly loaded reference to Shylock" This must be recorded as one of the understatements of the century. Not even in Hitler's Third Reich when they often highlighted the anti-Semitic twists of Shakespeare's *Merchant of Venice* did they ever think of translating the metaphor of "a pound of flesh" into an ominous literalness of a dripping reality. A younger American generation–these were the 1930s–may not have appreciated the full force of the unpleasantness. As Katharine Meyer (as she was then) remembers, "Sensitive subjects were rarely mentioned at our house, but three were particularly taboo–money, my father's being Jewish, and sex....I was totally–incredibly–unaware of anti-Semitism." It must have been a factor in the *Post*'s "newspaper culture," invisible or audible, subtle or tangible, during the whole of the half-century from that day in the 1930s when Eugene Meyer made his innocent Washington purchase of a small, unreadable, bankrupt newspaper to the secret tapes of President Richard Nixon venting his profane fury at the fearless Jewish journals that had been exposing his Watergate misdemeanors.[2]

Jewish Stories, Yiddish Words

Such deep-seated complexes about "roots" and "identity" and ancestral origins made for embarrassing uncertainties and conspicuous instabilities in many editorial attitudes of the great pre-eminent "Jewish-owned" newspaper over many decades. It would, to be sure, be remiss to be tempted to do any cheap and easy psychoanalysis of the *New York Times* and its journalistic style

and political commitments. Complexes are notoriously complex. Some curious and peculiar decisions–say, about the private education of the next generation of the family heirs (with grandchildren often confined to total ignorance
of their ancestral origins), or about the denominational profile of the paper's
leading editors and executives (a Gentile dynasty of WASPs with names like
Turner Catledge and Amory Bradford)–are surely directly connected. One has
to take into account, and estimate the obvious influences of, the special psy-
chic problems of European ethnic groups in the great transatlantic process of
Americanization. Who assimilated faster? Who failed to integrate fully and
were to be marked (and marred) by a lingering alienation?

Certain other attitudes have, over the years, been psychologized about by
critics (ascribing bouts of inexplicable stubbornness or off-putting arrogance
to "anal-erotic" determinants shaping a traditionally harassed minority, etc.).
Such behavior patterns may well have something to do with the nervousness
of a leadership/ownership which infects a whole organization with its own
reluctance to live and work in a reasonable peace with itself.

One small, if revealing, item. For an unconscionably long time, as we have
noted earlier, the *New York Times* refused to publish letters of correction or
otherwise admit a factual error, even an astigmatic editorial bias, and set it
right. This species of invincible editorial vanity exhausted itself one fine day,
and now with a certain discreet prominence "Corrections" are regularly published at the bottom of page 2. The column of diverse items has an arch note of
stiffness and stuffiness, and obviously it will never exude the fun of acknowl-
edging egg-on-their-faces which other mainstream papers enjoy when they
get around to putting the record straight. I am thinking of the more informal
Washington Post under the Grahams (and their appointed Ombudsmen), and
the old unbending *Manchester Guardian* when it moved to London (and
became sprightly and even brazen)....The reader is also reminded of the difficulties (I have already recounted them in another place) that afflicted "the
language of journalism" as-she-is-spoke in Times Square when it came to the
incursion of Yiddishisms into the slang, argot and pop jargon quoted by *Times*
reporters as they diligently covered Broadway, or the Bronx, or any other rich
"Big Apple" story, for the edification of endlessly inquisitive New York readers. As they would put it *today*–when the good ethnically correct news-story
had become its regular *shtick* (but never *then*, not on your nelly!)–they just
could not muster up the *chutzpah* to make a breakthrough; they behaved like
a *kvetch*. At long last the demotic of *shmooze* could be quoted, could be
bandied about, as if it were indeed the natural speech of the common language.

Under the circumstances–an editorial movement from haughty if furtive
self-censorship to excessive overcompensation–it necessarily became too much
of a muchness; and less would have been more. I remember Isaac Bashevis
Singer in Manhattan, reading a copy of the morning newspaper at a corner

table of his favorite Upper West Side cafeteria, wincing at the proliferation of the *mamaloshen*. He had been awarded a Nobel Prize in literature for novels which had been originally written in Yiddish. Now he was mourning for his mother tongue in exile when it was obviously being reduced to comic turns, fun-and-games.*

To be sure, words of import to Jews and to Jewry in general are not confined to the playful and lighthearted excursions into Yiddish etymology. Anti-Semitic excesses are rarely characterized by the role which Yiddishisms can play in the context of hatred, contempt, and obloquy. Only very occasionally is one startled by a press report in which an old Hebrew or Israeli allusion can trigger an emotional reaction in the mind (or, perhaps, the unconscious) of a newspaper reader: a loaded word which by sheer accident (or, perhaps, coincidence) can steer into the murkier regions of racialism.

The other day I spotted an item in the New York press–not in the *Times*, but in the *Daily News*–which reported the case of a murder in nearby New Jersey. A man had arranged for two "hit-men" to kill his wife. He happened to be a rabbi, in charge of a flourishing synagogue in Cherry Hill's Jewish community. He was, at this point, arrested and charged, found guilty, and his first and only plea for understanding and/or innocence was in these unfortunate terms: "Everything was *kosher*...." What did this mean? That the murder was somehow "clean" and "approved"? Or that the conspiracy to murder (which could bring for "the philandering rabbi" a death sentence) was somehow okay, right on, according to tribal rules?

To rationalize his bloody deed with a most unpopular ritualistic act (at least for non-Jews) was not exactly a skillful Talmudist tactic. The *Daily News* quoted the *"kosher"* phrase several times in the text. What may have been left in the communications residue was the reinforced association with blood, murder, and estranging Jewish practices. This may be considered to be only a small and even trivial contribution in the larger tragic context of things. But there are those that are convinced that every such bit helps the Holocaust: the next one, that is.

---

*   He once told me the story of his older brother's deep linguistic dilemma. I.J. (for Israel Joseph) was also a successful Yiddish-writing novelist; but in the late 1920s, at the height of his career and the lowpoint of his linguistic self-confidence, he announced to the Warsaw (and New York) press that he no longer considered himself "a Yiddish writer." For an alternative, he began studying French, and then German. His vocabulary was paltry, his sentences ungainly...it was all too difficult. He returned to his original language, and was pleased to get good European and American translations for his *Yoshe Kalb* (1933) and *The Brothers Ashkenazy* (1936). Still, he retained (as his brother tells it) twinges of "humiliation."

Small unrecognized languages secrete their own sense of shame; but sometimes the full story ranges from a humiliating sense of inferiority to boisterous joy in reviving the remnants. See: Isaac Bashevis Singer's preface to I.J. Singer's *Yoshe Kalb* (formerly *The Sinner*; tr. Maurice Samuel, 1965), pp. v-x.

For the *Times* and for mainstream journalism everywhere in the Western world, such "bits" are not passing items in the kaleidoscope of breaking stories–now a black man picked up on charges of rape, or an Italianate character suspected of a gangland Mafia-type killing, or yet another Jewish financier involved in large-scale fraud in Wall Street wheeler-dealing…and other similar reinforcements of tribal stereotypes in the popular tabloidized mind. The *Times* has tried to do its best over a half-century of troubled self-consciousness. Its credo, as I myself heard it from a senior *Times* editor was: Tell the truthful story. Omit that which might be inflammatory and, hopefully, irrelevant. Ration the facts that might fuel the fires of murderous misunderstanding, and cool the controversy which might lose its temper….I have previously recorded some of the hits and misses, and suggested that there can be no hard and fast rules in this inevitably painful pragmatism of trial and error. Sometimes the biographical date which has been "cleaned up" distorts the public understanding of an important issue. Sometimes the graphic quote which has been accurately ascribed to a passing hooligan or to an insidious ringleader goes on to cause a riot of hate and fury. For sure, the *Times* has won some, and lost some.

The dilemma, and its horns, remain. The other day (in February 2003), one of the *Times'* sports writers tried to assemble the data of increasing "racism" in the athletic games of the day. The very collation of the details in America, in Europe, and elsewhere, could be considered provocative…since the situation can be taken to be relatively controllable if the abuse and sometimes the ensuing violence is merely "local" and growing out of local issues. Despair mounts when one becomes aware of its near universal extent; and, perversely, the hooligan takes heart when he suddenly is aware that he is part of a million-footed mob: *Je suis partout!*…The journalistic analysis is not very incisive, but the tone is serious, even grave: "…Almost every country in Europe has racist signs, chants and even violence at soccer stadiums, particularly from rightist groups that single out blacks, Jews, Muslims or other ethnic groups. Some demonstrators say they do it only to unsettle the opposing team, but the evidence is that the hatreds go much deeper." George Vecsey goes on, as his wont, to register the telling detail; for one thing, the consequence of an unexpected influx of skillful African players into the games of newly opened-up Eastern Europe–the so-called "*monkey chant.*" What this precisely is (if one has never heard it in a vociferous stadium) is hard to describe without a sort of musical notation. It may have something to do with the whooping cries of Tarzan and/ or the enraged grunting of King Kong; but it is related to the jungle's primitivism if not to an echo of Charles Darwin's scheme of things. In any case, sports reporters find it more convenient to write about the "*monkey chant's*" being whooped up against one or another unpopular African player rather than refer to "insulting expletives" or, every now and them, the N-word itself. Moreover, the chants out of the forest primeval have a kind of naïve improvisational quality about them and, when transcribed, seem apparently quite harmless.

When England played Slovakia recently hostile fans chanted "*oooh-oooh-oooh*" at two black players on the field. Somewhat hurt feelings are surely the result but the wounds cannot, in the very nature of the guttural non-verbal defiance, go very deep. In addition to which the "*monkey noises*" have rather different intonations in various phonic cultures, and what is menacing in the hubbub of Barcelona is only an indifferent din in the hullabaloo of Bratislava. Still, it is dispiriting to think of a mean little corps of racist hooligans trying to perfect the ugliness of their "*ooohs*"–practicing noisome noise in front of the mirror, like Brecht's Hitler in *Arturo Ui*–in time for the next World Cup.

The presence in our sports stadia of the spirit of the real Hitler is another thing; although Nazi echoes are often relatively harmless in the repetition of slogans long made into empty clichés by thousands of hours of World War II made-for-TV Grade-B-movies. The *Times* reports from Austria: "When Maccabi Haifa met Sturm Graz in a European tournament the Israeli team was heckled with swastikas and chants of '*Sieg Heil*'...." Rather more insidious is the phonetic ingenuity of the London hooligans who have been targeting not the players on the field (there are almost no Jewish soccer stars) but the fans in the stadium, for the Tottenham team had a large Jewish following. (Again, I quote the *Times*' detail.) Evidently the tumult and the shouting have come up with "...a hissing sound, simulating gas chambers." This is combined with a massed chorus crying out, in a somewhat original turn of phrase, "*Yiddos! Yiddos!*" This bears enough resemblance to the well-known targets of the Nazi genocide (*Jews*, *Juden*, *juifs*, *Yids*, *zhids*) so as to refresh the enthusiasm of little monsters who might have been relaxing with all the talk about the banality of evil. There are enemies out there, to be settled with....*kiddoes*, *bozoes*, and *yiddoes*. I am not sure that, in this particular case, the reporter for the *Times* was right to consider this nasty bit as news fit to print. Was it "doublechecked" (i.e., with Buchenwald as well as Auschwitz)? Did the gas actually hiss? Some concentration camp literature refers to a whirring or a rattling noise, some to an inaudible sound or to a deathly silence. The onomatopeia is devious. The *Times*' news report may well have something to do with the compulsive drive to demonstrate the great newspaper-of-record's anxiety about its being cool, disinterested, and objective on a very delicate issue. It is an honorable concern; but, under the circumstances, the whole troubled atmosphere is not a very reliable context for coming to sound and consistent editorial judgment.[3]

The contradictions are built in; the ambivalences are endemic. When is the *Times* reporting in the highest moral spirit of private discretion? And when is it "telling it like it is," coming clean, going all the way (or almost), outbursting with daring detail? It mostly depends on whether (and when) you believe the old dictum–André Gide's, I think–about the truth really wounding only to heal. A romantic ideal result, devoutly to be wished...but in "interesting times" there are always Chinese complications.

Desirable Sorts

Anti-Semitism has many strands, and there are differences between the established prejudice which aims its barbs against a class of rich publishers who happen to be of Jewish descent as against the poisoned arrows targeted on the poor workaday journalists whom they employ in a generally Gentile world. The narrow-minded bias which "discriminated against" the Ochs/Sulzbergers and the Meyers was mostly ad hominem. The families had both old money and polished manners, and their national acculturation was impeccable; but WASP America had an unpleasantly loaded name for them–"*Jews…*"–and the various emotions involved ranged from suspicion to contempt. What of the writers, the reporters whom they hired, the editors whom they regularly appointed and evidently favored? Did they have a prose style or a journalistic attitude which could by any stretch of the imagination be judged to be "Jewish"?

Great and respectable figures in American journalism, such as the admirable (in most respects) H.L. Mencken, took it for granted that "Jews were different." I suspect that I may have been peripherally involved in this absurd bit of bigotry. In my ambitious youthful years I had offered outlines of one or two books to the distinguished New York publishing house of Alfred A. Knopf. I had editorial difficulties, and I attributed them to the grapevine rumor that Mencken, who was on Knopf's board, was "anti-Semitic." Later on I found this item in Mencken's published diary, which commented on a Knopf plan to "get out of New York" (i.e., into the WASP suburbs): "…He [Knopf] realized himself that there are now too many Jews in his office. Once he gets to Westchester county he should be able to find supplies of labor of a more desirable sort" (Baltimore, 19 September 1946). Even some sort of desirable authors. But certain types, so populous in New York, had to be discouraged before they proliferated. Mencken was always interested in students and young would-be American intellectuals. I recall the drama when Merle Curti, that fine historian at Columbia University, was to transfer to the faculty of Johns Hopkins University in Mencken's beloved Baltimore. He welcomed it, and this decision was also praised by Samuel Eliot Morison, a distinguished friend: "…I asked him [Morison] what sort of students he was encountering. He said that they were mainly Jews, and few of them showed any capacity…."(Baltimore, February 10, 1942). It so happened that Merle Curti was my *Doktorvater* when I was a Ph.D. candidate at Columbia in just that year. In our conversations after weekly seminars Curti occasionally alluded to Mencken's prejudices and recommended that I "give him a miss" when I moved south to Washington, D.C. to report for military service in the Pentagon (with billets in nearby Alexandria). If I didn't want to wind up in the Quartermaster Corps handling pots-and-pans for the Infantry's kitchens (which I did) I would need every friend I could muster on behalf of my "desirable capacity." The recommendations of Merle Curti together with the other Columbia stalwarts, Professors Henry Steele

Commager and Allan Nevins, earned me an appointment as a "combat historian."* Mencken's sentiments might have put me on a blacklist.

One other personal note on this period when the anti-Semitic phobia was
evidently rife and rampant...and most Jewish families, eagerly making their
way in the *goldene medina*, were remarkably oblivious to established nativist
antipathies. My colleague on the City College newspaper, the *Campus*, was a
sports columnist named Philip Minoff. In his last piece for the paper he wrote–
bright, brazen, boyish–an unashamed plea for a job now that he was a college
graduate and available for assignment in the great, wide world. He joyously
accepted an offer from the editor of the *Philadelphia Inquirer*. When we had a
reunion after a year and he was no longer a "try-out" but a fully-fledged
newsman on the paper's staff–*not* "a journalist" who, he quipped, was only a
reporter-out-of-a-job. I found my old classmate full of bitter insights into his
new life "in the sticks" where every morning, as he narrated it, he walked into
the long City Room towards the cubby-hole in the end-corner where a free and
empty desk had been assigned to him. And with every step he felt all eyes
staring out upon him and with the silent identification, "There goes the New
York Jew...." None of us, ambitious sons of Brooklyn and the Bronx, who came
to maturity on Manhattan's Convent Avenue (our grassless college campus),
had ever sensed–perhaps it was a flaw in our ghetto sensibilities–that we could
be so labelled, that we were all wearing, somewhere, a five-pointed star, the
badge of sufferance. Philip Minoff returned to Manhattan and, commensurate
with his talents (still bright, brazen, boyish), lived out a successful journalistic
career as a well-known film and television critic for the magazine *Cue*. His by-
line never again fell "under a quota" (or so he was convinced).

Back across the Atlantic it was rather different. In the long years I spent in
London it became obvious that the problem I would set for myself in this
chapter was not easy to cope with, given a youthful American background.
neither Mencken nor Stanley Walker, to whom I have looked for journalistic
guidance, could provide benchmarks. Nor indeed could, on the other side of
the pale, the experiences of the Sulzbergers and the Meyers; for there were in
England no Jewish-owned newspapers, and the journalistic ambitions of striv-

---

*   I was issued a *Leica* camera and a *Smith-Corona* portable typewriter (on which I am
     still typing this); and we were instructed to prepare for the final offensive against
     Hitler which would liberate Strasbourg and therewith the whole of France. The
     subsequent crossing of the Rhine was to initiate the last offensive against the Nazis'
     so-called *Third Reich* and begin the victorious occupation of post-Hitler Germany.
        Before I "shipped out" of Richmond I visited Ellen Glasgow, the grand old lady
     of Virginia letters; and I gave the curmudgeonly H.L. Mencken in nearby Baltimore
     a wide berth, the recommended "miss." Ellen Glasgow gave me a copy of her latest
     novel, *Vein of Iron*, and invited me to come back "after the war"; but she had died,
     aged 72, in 1945.

ing British Jews took other, and more disquieting turns. The case of Frederic Raphael I found to be surprising and instructive.

He is an excellent writer and critic, and has enjoyed much success for his novels, and other contributions to the world of cinema, London theater, television, and magazines. His journalism has been consistently on the highest level. But now, looking back on his long and (for most of his colleagues) enviable career, he confesses to its pains and humiliations; and what emerges from his autobiographical chronicle (*A Spoilt Boy*, 2003) is that a young man's turn to writing was, in his English case, not an Americanesque tale of assimilation and integration–like young Phil Minoff...like Irving Kristol, and Daniel Bell...and, come to think of it, like me. Writing became the instrument of maintaining and protecting his separateness. His very success underlined his cultural nonacceptance and his persistent alienation...unlike his Jewish counterparts in the U.S.A.: Bellow, Roth, Ben Hecht, Walter Lippmann, et al.

For Raphael had an American mother and an English father...which in an English private school (Charterhouse in Sussex) very much complicated his estrangement among the upper-class schoolboys who taunted and bullied "the New York Jew" in the well-known sadistic behavior patterns. He was lonely, ostracized, near suicidal. As he says, "I cursed my father with the curse he laid on me by first fathering a Jew and then sending me to school among the Philistines." Young Raphael could not understand what he had done to deserve so much enmity. In a schoolboy letter he wrote:

> ...Here I do not exist. For days no one has spoken to me. I am the Yid. I never thought I would write like this. It was never my intention....[But] I have never really suffered till now. All my friends, or those I thought my friends, have turned against me....They mimic Jews all day, and mimic me too. I sit here and shiver. I am powerless. I do not know what I have done or why God has treated me like this. I do not know why there are Jews or why I must be here. I would sooner be dead. Perhaps I soon shall be....I am not a person. I am a thing: the Yid. It's true, isn't it? I am the Yid..

Now an old and reputable writer, he looks back on his youthful letter and admits that it was artful, callow, self-pitying and accusing. He now thinks that he was acquiescing in his own helplessness "by the relish of its description." By describing his unfortunate predicament, by putting words down on paper, he was "almost literally" coming to terms with it: "Once a thing is said it is no longer the thing it was. I was being forced into being a writer....The writer has the sad consolation of hoping, in the end, to have the last word...." It was a bleak ambition and a desperate intention, but it served to end his woeful state of apartness. A vocation "settled in" on him like a calling. "...Isolation had been thrust upon me. Now I embraced it and rejected the common world: writing needed only pen and paper...."

Still and all, he had to live and work in the common world, and in most of his talented texts he showed himself to be cool and distant, critical and a shade vindictive. One of his anti-Semitic schoolboy enemies became, with a slight change of name, the Jewish hero of *The Glittering Prizes* (1976), one of Raphael's best-known scenarios. But the man's life and work amounted, in my judgement, to very much more than a career of point-scoring; and, indeed, even substantially more than the enlightened outrage of a Sunday supplement feature which presented the distressing story of an "outcast." The *Sunday Times* headline read: "As a New York Jew transposed to an English public school, Frederic Raphael ran into anti-Semitism in its most naked form."

Naked forms are sometimes less revealing than well-dressed phenomena which mix and mingle in the best circles to insidious effect. What interests us more in the context of this chapter are the peculiar, if not idiosyncratic, careers of writers with special powers who–in journalism, literature and elsewhere– derive from an old tradition which valued literacy (based on a single good book) and were driven by an almost inexplicable sense of chosenness: of making choices and choosing words.[4]

And yet, and yet....In those early days, the ubiquitous Anglo-Saxon–WASP had not yet come into usage–context of all American institutions was unimaginably constricting. In my turn I also tried to make my own mark in mainstream East Coast journalism. But the prospects even in New York ap- peared to be strangely forbidding. The personnel policies of the *New York Times*, of "Jewish-owned" repute, seemed so inscrutable for young Ameri- cans who wanted to (and did) participate fully in twentieth-century Ameri- can life; and they considered "one generation" enough time and space for acceptable integration and assimilation. Any kind of rebarbative ethnicities would, I am afraid, be taking a little longer. I read the "star by-lines" of the *Times* with not a little envy and a sense of unachievable prominence. Men named Turner Catledge and James Reston and John Kieran made the run- ning, their names coming trippingly off the tongue. But whose sentences shone memorably out of the elegant anonymity of the editorial-page col- umn, "*Topics of the Times*"? I heard the whisper: Simeon Strunsky, Meyer Berger.

And what of all those fine writers across the street in the *Herald-Trib*– Dorothy Thompson and Percy Hammond and Virgil Thomson and Richard Watts and F.P.A. (Franklin P. Adams)? Later on one learned the neurotic iden- tity-crisis secrets of a Walter Lippmann, slyly maintaining his high authority by camouflaging his low roots.

I somehow finagled a brief interview with Stanley Walker, the famed city editor of the *New York Herald-Tribune* (as it then was). He was the very model of a brilliant Manhattan newspaperman, the legendary "Man with the Green Eyeshade." He still had his Texas accent (which gave me a bit of trouble), and he talked of ambitious things that could only find their place in a utopian agenda. He raised great and stimulating questions, as I recall.

Whether there was any sense in the idea that a respectable high-class so-phisticated newspaper of tabloid size could ever find a place in New York? (Ralph Ingersoll was already trying this with his ill-fated *PM*; which Mencken excommunicated from "American journalism" and acidly referred to as "sim-ply a Yiddish paper printed in English.")

How to explain that the best political cartoonists were either subversive radicals or foreigners? (Who could approach Thomas Nast or Honoré Daumier?)

Why was "culture" such a difficult nettle for American journalists to handle? It was no longer a disgrace to read a book. But only a few years ago, said Walker in the early 1940s, a graduate of a university's school of journalism tried to impress himself upon editors for a job by boasting that he had not read a book in some four years!

How come newspapermen are so incurious even about…newspapers? Walker was dismayed that many New York newspapermen haven't read a British paper (or an out-of-town American paper) in years; he found the sub-intellectual level of life appalling.…

These appear to be timeless questions, very much relevant as my readers will readily observe to my concerns in this book, where the struggle with the "Semitic problem" has been discussed. Still, even in Stanley Walker's day, when the struggle with the "Semitic problem" was not a public issue (Stanley Walker died in Lampasas, Texas, in 1962, still editing, still ques-tioning), the subject often came up. Some of his writings have been col-lected, and I choose a passage to quote as a fitting document on this whole problem of ethnicity which I was presumably too shy–another word for self-censoring–to toss into the discussion so long ago. As Stanley Walker wrote (in 1934):

> Racial inheritance probably has little to do with journalistic expertness, and yet most men who have got ahead in American journalism have been of Irish, English or Scottish blood. There have been a few Germans, and fewer from the Scandinavian countries. French blood? Sometimes, but not often. And a good Italian newspaper man is so rare that he belongs in the Smithsonian Institution. Of all reporters, the Irish, if they have a poetic streak in them and can stay reasonably sober, probably make the best.

What of the Jews? Do they have enough "cultural" reserves? And how strong is the pull of so-called "roots"? (Walker could return to Texas and put out a small-town newspaper. Could I ever have made my way back to Lodz?): "Jewish reporters are impossible to classify; some are cloddish, some brilliant, some level-headed, some itching with messianic afflictions, some profligate, and some close-fisted and scheming. One thing surely may be said about them: most Jews know enough not to drink too much."

There are still thorny problems here somewhere; but I am afraid that alco-holism is not even the half of it.[5]

Smoking Typewriters

American eyes (and ears), more finely attuned to obvious unsubtleties, readily spot the strategy of indirect ascription in ethnic identification. Who gets to wear the j- or -n-word labels, and how are they tagged? Many States-side readers of more recent newspaper stories about English and other European Jews "in the headlines" even take the neutral or anodyne references to be a kind of defamation by defense. Which is to suggest that even the good will of *anti*-Anti-Semitism is, in the context of journalistic controversy (and not only there), likely to have undesirable side effects ("some of my best friends are Jews" has long been taken to be a phrase of craven hypocrisy, a comic cliché). Irony would have it that defending the Jews proves to be as offensive as the original anti-Semitism.

1. In the British legal wrangle (1998) over the extradition of Chile's General Pinochet, the retired dictator was arrested while taking medical treatment in a London hospital and was, in the first judicial instance, facing deportation to Spain. A Spanish judge had been pressing charges for torture and murder of its nationals in the Pinochet time of terror. The deciding vote in the British House of Lords which provides the judges for the U.K.'s supreme court–they decided three to two in favor of extradition–was cast by a Lord Hoffman. The tabloid press then revealed that Leonard Hoffman *Q.C.*, as he once was, served (as did his wife Lady Hoffman) in prominent organizational functions of Amnesty International. It was Amnesty which had been officially pressing the case for extradition in the name of "human rights." Lord Hoffman, therefore, was grievously remiss in not having disqualified himself on account of possible prejudice or "conflict of interest." If his "liberal politics" were, strictly speaking, relevant to the ethos of non-partisanship, were then *all* aspects of his race, creed, or religious ancestry equally pertinent? Fleet Street editors have always been sensitive to names in their headlines, and "Hoffman" was surely foreign, possibly Jewish and thus not without a traditional Hebrew or Teutonic piquancy. Not that the man at the center of the "mis-trial" which led to new hearings and a second trial did not have a few other vulnerable, seductive qualities which would add to the dark suggestion of alienation: "…With simian features, wiry frame, lascivious grin and long judicial wig, Lord 'Lennie' Hoffman puts one in mind of [a] great music hall comedian….We need to know more than we used to know about the man beneath the powdered wigs and in the case of Hoffman…we have a judge-about-town with a fondness for night-clubs and a gimlet eye for a well-turned ankle."[6] But this was not all. Yet to come, beyond the monkey business, was the sly touch of Semitism. As the *Sunday Times* reported of "the Man who is regarded by many as the cleverest of the law lords": "…Where other Jewish boys got bicycles for their bar mitzvahs, Hoffman asked for a typewriter." And everybody knows what can happen to clever and devious young men who use typewriters to cover a secret agenda….

2. Paying similar backhanded homage to a tribal cleverness, the novelist and critic A.N. Wilson mounted a singular protest at the dastardly allusiveness which had outraged him in the reportage of the allegations of "disloyalty" against Dominic Lawson, the editor of the *Sunday Telegraph* and, formerly, of the *Spectator* in London. (He was also the son of Lord [Nigel] Lawson, chancellor of the Exchequer in Mrs. Thatcher's cabinet.) His familiar by-line made the headlines when a disgruntled MI-6 employee charged Lawson with being a "secret agent." In this context where one would have thought the matter of ethnic or religious origins was irrelevant, there crept into the press discussion an outlandish note of Captain Dreyfus and of the implication of sinister foreign espionage. A.N. Wilson was angered by it, and wrote in his *Standard* column:

> …What struck me about the anti-Dominic diatribes was their arguably anti-Semitic tone. He is described as too clever, devious, working behind the scenes to some agenda hidden from the rest of us. 'Immensely unlovable if immensely talented' was one comment. Why not say 'Bloody Jew'? That, at least, is how it must have come across to some readers.[7]

This would have been the first that many readers (like this one) had in fact heard of it; the element of racism or rancor in the news was not so obvious at first sight. I had not spotted it. Harmless prejudice may creep into a story when it is fast breaking; but it takes at least a day or two for serious hate to insinuate itself and then raise its ungodly head.

Such ethnically incorrect prejudice doesn't travel well across the Atlantic. One day later the *New York Times* published a long dispatch from its London correspondent, Sarah Lyall, under the headline: "BRITISH PRESS UNCOVERS SPY SCANDAL OF ITS OWN." It did not mention the "Semitic" complications. "Objectively speaking," the so-called "Jewish element" in the story was evidently far-fetched and hence not "fit to print." But since what the British press was uncovering revealed a little Dreyfusard sore at the center of it, the omission was glaring and culpable.

But then again, how could the correct spirits in Times Square bring themselves to report that a distinguished editorial colleague had been called "*a bl—dy J***" or some other eminently deletable expletive?[8]

Starting to Think

The anti-racialist detection of verbal slurs depends itself on a semantic sensitivity amounting almost to a zealous 24/7 alertness to any kind of unkind suggestion. It is a given that you have to know all the words intimately before you can be outraged by the worst of them. Accordingly, in personal conversation one tends to play very safe by using circumlocutions which, in turn, are not always reliable. (Thus: when is "*a native*" not a term of colonialist contempt? When he, or she, is "a red Indian" and now oddly to be known as a *Native American*..)Words can be two-faced.

In the media most of the publicity is given to the half-dozen or so populistic derogations whose every usage, calculated or casual, can be seized upon to make the ethnically correct point. It follows that one is very much surprised when some unusual "racialist" incident turns up whose ambiguity or complexity catches us unprepared. I would have surmised that hyphenated Americans from Japan or China do still have their difficulties when serving in the U.S. Army. The American G.I. on one of the many Afro-Asian fighting fronts since World War II has never been famous for delicate language. (Bill Mauldin's well-known and justly celebrated cartoons of the 1940s had their vocabulary cleaned up before publication.)

But most of the epithets that were once so necessary to maintain a steady level of combative hostility and, above all, a sense of manly superiority, tend to lose half of their bite over time, viz. "frog...kraut...wop...jerry...limey...dago." What about "gook"?

One post-*nisei* G.I., or Japanese-American soldier, serving with the U.S. Army in Vietnam, recalled recently the moment when he looked at a *gook* casualty in Saigon and was struck–evidently for the very first, surprising time– by the fact that "the enemy had an Asian face." But he rushes to add that "I was never called a *gook* during my tour of Vietnam." A strong civic dose of Americanization can give one the accent, the gestures, and general demeanor (if not quite the skin-color) of a new identity; it extends to the elemental *Weltanschauung* which makes for a group solidarity laced with mutual tolerance (albeit amongst themselves, with a narrow-minded hostility for "*the others*"). One G.I. veteran states, as a historian has recorded (and it was recently quoted in the *Washington Post*): "After I had been in Vietnam a while I started to think, 'If the Vietnamese are the enemy, I don't have to treat them like human beings'. Vietnam was a very undeveloped country. I started to think that any culture that was underdeveloped was not equal to our own....As much as I despise the word gook, it seemed very appropriate over there." He "*started to think*"....That–and especially "thinking" about what one fancies to be one's own *culture* and how it differs from foreign *cultures*–is (as we shall see) one of the most dangerous irrational exercises of our contemporary experience. Malignity is not usually motiveless, and hateful antipathies are rarely altogether mindless. They are often the beginning of a thought-process, with persons "starting to think" and going badly wrong. Taking thought is not necessarily a guarantee to wind up with a rational or logical conclusion. When the best newspapers follow up a continuing story of such prejudice and hostility (in Herzegovina as well as Harlem), they can pin-point with deadly accuracy the onset of an invidious ethnic correctness.[9]

There is, to be sure, always a follow-up to the continuing story. The language of journalism flourishes on colorful detail; and the colors of racism–and its semantic suggestiveness–almost always find a place in even the most innocent of reportage. Conscientious reporters, rounding out a dispatch, often feel obliged to offer all the background facts and thus, on occasion, perpetuate the memory of old-time narrow-mindedness. It was an ordinary day of a fairly important golf tournament, the "Johnny Walker Classic" in Perth, and the correspondent for the *Independent* in London was simply describing some of the difficulties of the South African champion, Retief Goosen, to maintain his lead in the European competition. All the usual sports-writing clichés were trotted out, and they made for a quiet and harmless read–the South African was "*just trying to hang in there,*" he was telling himself "*to stay calm and focused,*" etc. Then came a phrase which was memorable and inevitably opened old wounds...on one decisive hole Goosen sliced the ball into the bush. It was only routine that the reporter would explain that Goosen had "...sliced it into a bush whose locally known name has been changed from 'black boy' to 'grass tree' for obvious reasons." For a South African, saddled with the memories of the burdensome vocabulary of *apartheid*, "black" and "boy" were among the standard cuss-words–*nomen* was *omen*. The man took a penalty drop on that fateful first hole, but caught the branches of the "grass tree" with his next shot, moving the golf ball only about ten yards....The spirit of *black boy* was obviously taking its revenge. Or, at least, we who follow such stories were vividly reminded of the racist relapses of only yesterday. No such interesting words are ever allowed to slip away into oblivion. Once they are judged fit to print, they live on, keeping old wounds open and festering.[10]

Prejudice by Ricochet

It is the fate of some national or ethnic stereotypes, when they are weakened and especially vulnerable–indeed when they are mortally wounded by telling exceptions and convincing evidence to the contrary–simply and strangely to survive, to persist, to linger (or, as we would say nowadays, to linger on). The Jews are an especially good example since they have been around a long time now, perhaps longer in the surviving records of history than any other single ethnic or tribal group, and tragically subject to periodical acts of genocide. It could be that Jewry could qualify for the questionable honor of a first prize not for strictly *tribal* reasons but for its peculiar faith, its non-proselytizing (hence estranging) religion with its so-called theological provocations.

George Steiner once defended his thesis of Jewish sufferance as a historic result of its "dizzying concept of monotheism." He was convinced that the new belief in Jehovah, a few millennia back in time, unsettled irreparably primordial man's devotion to gods, demons, and other articles of traditional faith. Being the "chosen people" of a single Lord Almighty was a Jewish singularity too far, and it was all simply too much to take, too heavy a burden on the part of the eternal *goy* in the rest of the world and its unchosen peoples.

Even if one doesn't accept the Steiner thesis–tentatively posed in his T.S. Eliot lectures in 1971–it could be that a number of other popular and recurrent hatreds stretch back farther in history, far back into thus far unrecorded aeons.

"Skin-color differences" which still divide since time immemorial the light-
and dark brown peoples in the Indian sub-continent (tan Brahmins in the
north, black Untouchables in the south). Or *"hair differences"* which set north
and south islanders apart in the Japanese peninsula. Or *"height differences"*
which still cause bitter animosities in Hutu and Tutsi Africa among the long
and the short and the tall....[11]

The Jews are not alone in the atrocious mass graves of history (and pre-
history). But the writers in the remnant, from the Pentateuch to the diary of
Anne Frank, were always literary and eloquent enough to leave memorable
traces of the sorry story, of the casualties on "the eternal road." These are the
penalties for being unremittingly literate. And some readers of the pogrom
narrative of misdeeds from Haman to Hitler wee provoked to go on to do
likewise.

I have already mentioned the ancient debates in the Roman Empire–between Flavius Josephus, the Hebrew general who defected to Rome (but remained a patriotic defender of his defeated people) and an anti-Semitic
pamphleteer in imperial Rome named Apion. Apion's charges appear frighten-
ingly familiar; and Josephus' polemical replies have become over centuries
and millennia conventionally routine. Some historical research has deepened
the whole controversy to include the "racial" epithets and ethnic "smears"
which troubled the Jewish community of Pharaonic Egypt. Those were the
years after Ikhnaton when enough-became-enough, and Moses–not unlike
innumerable rabbinical prophets to Zionists like Theodor Herzl and Chaim
Weizmann in other centuries–rallied his people to leave en masse. And they
did leave for other shores, for another land, promised or otherwise.[12]

If such invidious charges against a people appear to be unchanging over
long periods of historical time, it could signify either of two things–that, in the
first place, the perceived vices of the unpopular people in question actually
provoked the same nasty responses or, in a familiar bit of genocidal repartee,
that the Jews in their peculiar and characteristic life-styles brought anti-Semitism
upon themselves. Thus, the victims are responsible for their victimization. (As
the Germans say, *der Opfer ist schuld*; or: the corpses are culpable.) The perpe-
trators are permanently locked into their hardness of heart and mind. Is the
meanness inexpungeable? Well, if Jews are held never to change, so their
critics and enemies remain implacable and unchanging. In the second place
(and alternatively), the familiar patterns of wilful prejudice–of arbitrary discrimination and a diffused hate-they-neighbor syndrome–are so invincibly
embedded in human behavior in history that the pro's-and-con's of communal
strife deviate only ever so slightly in the various and repetitious tragedies of
expulsion and purge, of pogrom and massacre...and Holocaust.

There is another factor in the apparently eternal road to victimization. The
resonances across millennia are clear enough, but they become reinforced by
a singular kind of echo within an echo, so that we know now that recent

massacres were perpetrated in Nigeria by the Hausa tribes because they felt (or were told to feel) that their hateful enemies, the Ibos, were *"the Jews of Nigeria"* (i.e., greedy, exploitative, conspiratorial, and…well, *different*). A thousand miles away, on the other side of Africa, the "hapless Hebrews" were receiving another set of blows by ricochet when–in the tribal quarrels of twentieth-century Kenya–the same guilt-by-association was fastened on to minorities by the majorities who operate according to the primitive old saw, "Give a dog a bad name and hang him…."

I met several times with Tom Mboya, one of the stalwart young men around Jomo Kenyatta who were pioneering the Kenyan anti-colonial independence movements in the 1950s and 1960s during the first years of enthused African national liberation. (Mboya was murdered in downtown Nairobi in the year 1969.) I remember, with some embarrassment, his forlorn efforts on several occasions to try and explain to me the probable futility of his agitating for constitutional minority-rights guarantees to be written into the fundamentals of the new state of Kenya. I talked of Thomas Jefferson and Oliver Wendell Holmes and a great American judicial tradition; and he wearily recognized the importance of legal guarantees of a bill of rights. To be sure, he wanted them all to be relevant in the new Kenya–but he remained skeptical. Local tribal animosities were too deep-seated, with roots stretching back (perhaps) into times unrecorded. Did he sense his own transience on the scene? It takes a rich political culture, nurtured on Voltaire and John Stuart Mill (among other seminal forces–Gandhi, perhaps…Buddha and Jesus, maybe) to protect the civil liberties of strange and different neighbors–all those Others!–struggling to survive among aggressive majorities. Minority men (and as we saw from Kabul, Minority Women) always live in times of trouble.

"You see, I am a member of the Luo, a small tribe, alert, industrious, ambitious. But the predominant clan is the Kikuyu. And they think of us as '*the Jews of East Africa.*' And you know what happened to the Jews…."

I have reason to believe that in our century this kind of loaded "trial by Jewry" plays a variable factor in the episodes of ethnic cleansing which have been recorded in the Balkans…in certain Shi'ite (and Sunni) provinces of the Moslem world…and even, as I surmise, among the various Eskimo peoples bickering for pole position in the Arctic race for exclusive Inuit identity.

There is, thus, an incremental anti-Semitism by calculated mistaken identification–whereby some local enemies somewhere on the five continents get classified as "Jews" and are, thereupon, victimized, attacked, assaulted with second-hand passions and emotions illicitly borrowed from other dark genocidal episodes that happen to insinuate themselves into the violent controversy.

Nor is this all. History knows various kinds of spin: and some twists and turns come up with grotesque variations. Let me mention one example from contemporary Japan.

Japan's Identity and Its Jewish Fantasies

In a visit there in the 1950s, during the early years of their post-war reconstruction and their dynamic incursion on to the world's industrial markets, I was introduced to a number of remarkable intellectuals who happened to revere, as I did, the same German philosopher–Karl Jaspers. Indeed they set up flowering "*Jasper-Klubs*" to spread his version of the "Existentialism" which was so popular in the day. What I learned subsequently I can only reconstruct by surmises.

Jaspers–whose house I was privileged to frequent: in Heidelberg in the 1940s, later in Basel (where he was given a university chair, following on from Nietzsche and Jakob Burckhardt)–was a sterling humanist and anti-Nazi, and he had been removed from his university post by the Hitlerites as early as 1937. His wife, in danger throughout the Third Reich, was a Jewess. (Her brother, Gustav Mayer, was in Oxford exile and was the author of a sympathetic two-volume biography of Friedrich Engels.) When the U.S. occupation of Western Germany relaxed, I met many guests in the little house in Heidelberg's Plöckstrass; and they ranged from Hannah Arendt and Golo Mann, both "Jewish" students of Jaspers in the old Weimar days...to strange Japanese emissaries who spoke no German but revered the tall, silver-haired charismatic philosopher...and went home to establish those small study-groups in various Japanese cities. They were especially inspired and respectful when they learned of Mrs. Gertrude Jaspers' ancestral Old Testament faith.

I move from the tragic and the bizarre to the apparently trivial. But in the dark ambiguities of thinking in stereotypes and hating in convenient analogies which history in its clutter and litter just leaves lying around, nothing should be blithely overlooked.

I am sure that there were genuine moral sentiments–as well as purely academic motivations–involved in the special interest the Japanese exhibited so extensively in certain aspects of German life in the post-war ruins and occupation. It paralleled so very much of their own Douglas MacArthur years. I heard the Heidelberg philosopher himself express admiration for the conscientious work of the Japanese translators and bibliographers of the "Karl Jasper Clubs." But I could not then (or now) suppress the suspicion that a great deal of the devotion of the devotees was fed by the mistaken, if useful and serving, notion that the Germans who were the protagonists of their little intellectual drama all happened to be "Jews." As one academic study of Japanese attitudes put it: "...In the post-war period, as the facts of the Holocaust became known, many Japanese relieved their sense of war guilt by identifying with the Jews, the quintessential victims of war...." This was a form of psycho-cultural prevarication that Arthur Koestler would have characterized as a political neurosis. I was constantly astonished by its symptomology.

Anne Frank's *Diary* sold in the millions of copies; and, in honor of the noble Jewish teenage victim, a Japanese company called Anne Co. Ltd. went so far as to market a popular brand of sanitary napkins ("Anne's Day," which was also reliably reported to be a euphemism for menstruation in Japan). In the Japanese theater the Broadway hit of *shtetl* life based on Sholom Aleichem's Yiddish tales, *Fiddler on the Roof*, soon became the longest running musical in Japanese history. A best-selling book of 1986 (by Masami Uno) argued on the thesis of its very title, *If You Understand the Jews, You Will Understand Japan*. The melodramatic plot thickened when, also in the 1980s, an Israeli writer named Joseph Eidelberg argued that his close study of the Old Testament and of many curious traits of ancient Hebrew life and laws led him to the conclusion: the Japanese were descended from the Jews. Eidelberg's Japanese edition (tr. 1984) dramatized this in its subtitle "*The Road from Exodus to Japan*": the islands of the setting sun were the last stop and happy fate of the so-called "ten lost tribes."[13]

This was, to be sure, all based on a massive misunderstanding, profound (or, at the very least, regaling) in its cross-eyed cultural complications and almost incomprehensible in its mélange of enthusiasm, guile, and self-delusion. Even in the early post-war days of my own visits to Japan there were, as I have hinted in my "Japanese anecdotes," indications that nothing was as it appeared to be.[14] Some of the leading American Japanologists then resident in Japan–I mention only two who were my friends, Herbert Passin and Theodore Cohen–were Jews who were treated with the greatest respect in the robust Tokyo intellectual life during and after the U.S. occupation. (Cohen did a monumental two-volume biography of General Douglas MacArthur; and Passin was an influential Columbia University anthropologist whose mastery of things Japanese was unrivalled.)[15]

Even then there were suspicions of dark secrets, although every Japanese problem in those days appeared to be something of a mystery wrapped in an enigma. There was, as I was told, in almost every major bookstore in the land something that was called "a Jewish corner"; but only few adventurous souls ventured to find out what appeared to be pro-Semitic was, in point of fact, in a characteristic Japanese paradox, anti-Semitic. After all, somebody had taken the trouble to consult no less than 104 standard dictionaries and discovered that they all contained derogatory definitions of the word "Jew." Some of our local friends attributed this, with painful politeness, to "the Bard"...i.e., to the baleful influence of Shakespeare's *Merchant of Venice*, of course...and evidently the Shylock character was the most popular among Japanese actors doing Western theater...with fifty-six stagings in recent years (ten times more than *Hamlet*).

My intention is not to make a psychodrama of all this, and I hurry through a rich and fascinating cross-cultural relationship which the *New York Times* broke with a breathtaking story on 12 March 1987 to the effect that flagrantly anti-Semitic books had become sensational bestsellers in Japan, selling millions of copies. In that year no less than 82 books were available on the shelves with the J-word in the title. And those titles promised the secrets of *The Jewish Plot to Control the World*, offered a guide to *The Expert Way of Reading the Protocols* (i.e., of Zion), and (complete in one volume) revealed *The Secret of Jewish Power That Moves the World*.*

Historians treat the *Times* story as something of a historic scoop, exposing little known racialist currents. But neither Tokyo nor New York quite managed to understand each other–either before or after Sato Masaki, a Japanese press officer, met with the editors of the *Times* in New York (in that year, 1987) and proceeded to ask how many Jewish journalists were employed at the *Times* and why the paper carried so many "Jewish" stories. One history of the subject records: "...Sato's questions were tactless and displayed astounding naiveté....{But}the intense reaction he received bewildered Japanese observers who failed to understand what he had done wrong."

What the *Times* editors might be forgiven not to have understood is that the Japanese consider their anti-Semitism really to be a form of *pro*-Semitism; and even their repetitions from *The Protocols* and *Mein Kampf* and other vicious classics of anti-Semitic literature were (or so they think) intended to praise the Jews, not to bury them. The quasi-occult literature stocked in the "Jewish corner" of Tokyo and Kyoto bookstores were now spilling out of the bookish ghetto and on to the main shelves, front tables, and window exhibits. The problematical books on the "success stories" of cunning Jewish activists on the world scene were now "coming out" as per popular demand. A vast readership was evidently longing to go out and do likewise. "Judeo-Bolshevism" (founded by Karl Marx from a rabbinical family), which had been a contending role model for world domination, was proving to be an ignominious failure. Surely "Judeo-Capitalism" (with all its little Shylocks doing their best) had a better chance of making it, no?[16]

What had happened to that old, proud national genealogy which had ascribed Japanese genes to a lost tribal exodus from ancient Israel? What remained of the touching pop-cult identification of "Japs and Jews," two small peoples of a common heritage, fated to suffer and survive for they had been chosen to achieve greater things? Where had they all gone, the dancing fiddlers and the luminous Anne Franks who had sung and bled for us?

Well, they were still there–for "Jews in the Japanese Mind" did not operate in accord with rational rules of logic and geometry, and no distance between two points would ever be effected by a short straight line. The Jews and the Japanese were both hated and hateful peoples, and the latter would learn from the former the occult knowledge of successful conspiracy...of the secret way of accumulating wealth and world power...of finally fulfilling their appointed

---

*   Thereafter regular journalistic attention was paid to the strange role of "Jews in the Japanese Mind." See: "Japanese Book Praises Hitler for Politics," *New York Times*, 8 June 1994; and "Hitler Book Is Withdrawn by Japanese," *New York Times*, 15 June 1994.

destiny. Both peoples had nearly faced extinction; and both were on the slow, difficult, erratic paths to make historic comebacks. The Japanese too had been in the fires of a Holocaust; sad to contemplate, a few more Hiroshima- or Nagasaki-bombs would have finished them off forever.

Here, in some kind of confounded sense of history and ultimate destiny, was another fanciful story of a people who could ascribe their near destruction to the perception–(in the Japanese case) their very own arbitrariness–that "they were just like the Jews." The Japanese were anti-Semitic without really having any Jews to harm. They were pro-Semitic for they would be, as a successor people, the chosen fulfillment of what had to be. Ideologies in the Orient are different, and this one was never fated to be dominant in culture or in politics. It was only a case of the mythological pursuing the uncredible.

But the reader will not have come with me all this way without a suspicion that, in my analysis, myths can be fictions spun out of whole cloth and yet be irrefragably real; and what appears to be incredible is often lent simple-minded credence. More than that, there seems to be no individual intellect or communal belief system so strong or fine-webbed as to resist all of such mental aberrations all of the time. In the case of the Japanese and their deeply troubled relationship to the Jews and to anti-Semitism, an especially lively imagination compensated for having evolved in history along the Pacific rim, so far from the scene of the action. Sometimes the linkage is easy and straightforward: "…Christ's appearance out of the ranks of the Jews was merely a rehearsal for the appearance of the real messiah from Japan." Rather more difficult (but ultimately more rewarding) is establishing a kind of cosmic or cosmological anthropology in which marvellous foreign histories become part of one's own fable, and what is fabulous turns out to be one's manifest destiny. (Is this, again, a case of splendid imitation?)

I am told that the Takenouchi Document is "apocryphal" and said to be in possession of the self-proclaimed descendents of Takenouchi Sukune, a semi-historical figure from the third or fourth century A.D. It is supposed to have been written in the mystical script of "the Age of the Gods" (which presumably existed in Japan prior to the linguistic adoption of Chinese characters). In that golden age language was a universal bond, mixing all human communication (including Hebrew, Greek, Egyptian hieroglyphics, Sumerian, the Roman alphabet, Sanskrit, and Chinese). All in all, the *Document* documents the saga of Japan as the source of (no less) all human civilization, "unifying within itself all the world's cultures in peace and harmony…." How did it come to pass that Japan relinquished–obviously–its global hegemony? Certain primeval natural disasters, lost in time. But there was time enough for a renaissance–and in the seventh century A.D., or thereabouts, all the world's greatest religious leaders (including Moses, the Buddha, Lao-tzu, Confucius, Christ, and Muhammed) came to Japan to study…before returning to their respective lands to preach the true Way.[17]

Having established that, it follows as the rising sun follows the setting sun that there is a complementarity of Japanese and Jewish history. Both the Japanese and the Jews are descended from the gods; but since the former are, not unsurprisingly, more precious to Jehovah than the latter, it is in the final "unshrouding of history" preordained that the savior of the world should come from...Japan.

Other prophets pick up from there, when day and night become one, and in its unearthly light villains become heroes, victims turn out to be innocent, anti-Semites emerge as friends of Zion. As one Tokyo author wrote fairly recently, defending her edition of *The Protocols of the Elders*: "...I will reveal the leaders of the Jews, who, though they are disguised as evildoers, once unmasked will be seen to be the truly righteous, the avatars of true holiness, the embodiment of the mission chosen by God."

I append a short final note here on the causes and sources of extraordinary misperception that distorted a foreigner's view of Japanese attitudes towards race and identity, towards pro-Judaism (which did not involve support for the real-existing state of Israel) and an anti-Semitism (which did not necessarily preclude admiration for the Hebrew heritage). Nothing was what it seemed to be. One could read sedulously the impeccable English editions of the great daily newspapers–*Asahi*, *Mainichi*, and *Yomiuri*–and be intensively well informed but, in the end, none the wiser.

1. In the first place, an attractive but delusional comparison between the two great "Axis Powers" of World War II, Germany and Japan, was conventional wisdom for almost half-a-century. Bi-national references were readily made, and obvious similarities were emphasized. But, in the final analysis, it amounted to a too simple coupling of Prime Ministers Yoshida and Adenauer who presided over the post-war reconstruction of their respective ruined societies.

Germany was "different" too. No neo-Nazi movements made serious or permanent incursions in the new German democracy; the line of demarcation to the shameful past was drawn so tightly that even the copyright to Hitler's *Mein Kampf* was monopolized by the new anti-Nazi establishment...to the extent that permission to reprint (even for scholars, even for university libraries) was systematically denied. The five terms of Shigeru Yoshida seemed to be similarly clean and forward-looking. In his conservative decencies he appeared to be so like his counterpart Dr. Konrad Adenauer in Bonn that it was inconceivable that post-war Japanese society should be harboring a secret cache of "black" literature about the Jews–which was strictly impossible and also intellectually inconceivable in post-Hitler Germany. The early misperception, as I say, contributed to a seriously erratic interpretation. Other later observers (among them, Ian Buruma) came to adjust the blurred focus. Japan *was* different...or appeared to be different, if only we knew what to compare it with...apart, that is, from our own self-centered idiosyncratic selves. All was sui generis.[18]

2. In the second place, newspapermen cannot reasonably be expected to have a working familiarity with all the languages being spoken in the countries of their foreign assignments. They can, after a fashion, make do with translations, although these are for the most part dull, erratic, and frequently misleading. So long as the correspondent is aware of, and makes allowances for, the missing dimension of accuracy, indeed of subtlety or special insight, then some competent work can be done. Educated readers have learned to be wary of the writer abroad who cannot even hold a brief conversation with his proverbial taxi driver but who presumes to pontificate about the largest matters of indigenous politics and personality. I confess to my own small sins in Japan.

My misdemeanors were complicated by the fact I tried to pass judgement on what I saw rather than what I heard or read with the prospect of the aforementioned pitfalls. My first impressions were garnered in the years long before Japan astonished the world by becoming an economic superpower, that is, before, for example, the Japanese industrial miracle came to be producing "one out of every four automobiles in the world...." In my day I thought the Japanese were making, in the quip of the times, "very nice old cars": the contraptions were ungainly, precarious vehicles, and unstylish to boot. The breakthrough to state-of-the-art technology and design was soon to come. Some of the change was already present when U.S. magazine photographers enthused over their new Nikon cameras (e.g., as I recall, David Duncan, of *Life* magazine and *Magnum*). In a casual newspaper interview in Tokyo I happened to make some unguarded, outlandish remark, to be sure eminently quotable, about the future of all the motor cars, and photographic equipment and silicon chips and whatnot, that was beginning to come off the high-tech Japanese assembly lines for worldwide export. Unwittingly perhaps I gave them, on the eve of their greatest triumph ever on the world stage, a slogan that comforted their deepest complex by assuaging their troubled sense of inferiority in a copycat culture. I was quoted as saying, "First-class imitation is better than second-class originality." I never heard the last of it.

It became for several years–a happy period when the Japanese recovered some of their national self-assurance–a buzz-word incantation which seemed to bless that Japanese emergence as an industrial (and financial) power of its own. I had long since returned to the West...but still, little gifts and other signs of appreciation caught up with me. For Christmas I was given several bottles of the best *Saké* from the editors of *Yomiuri shimbun*. On birthdays there arrived from *Asahi Shimbun* potted plants with special flower arrangements. The publishers of *Mainichi Shimbun* shipped, on several occasions, a case of "homemade" Yokohama beer famously copied from Bavarian brewers half-a-century before. And from all three formidable daily newspapers there was for a long time to come the prompt delivery of their English-language editions.

I spent much time reading in them assiduously. But only slowly did it dawn on me that here too did that old Italian saw obtain: *traduttore, traditore* ("the translator is a traitor"). Truths, large and small, inevitably disappear in such cross-cultural enterprises. Deliberate and purposeful editorial influence (viz., omitting certain embarrassing stories, playing down others) compete in the patterns of distortion and disinformation with subtler, less obvious factors. I refer to the quality of translation and the limitations of so-called exact renderings between two tongues which are, in many ways, culturally incompatible. The simplest words in an everyday vocabulary can prove treacherous. The difference...between the *Mainichi* which discussed seriously the *Protocols* which "the Elders of Zion" bequeathed to the world (a devious tsarist- Russian forgery) and the civilized literacy of their version of the newspaper I read...was deep. The gulf between the liberal ideology of the *Asahi* journalism in the enlightened post-MacArthur years and the Imperial newspaper which faithfully (and sympathetically) reported on the doings of its Axis ally (e.g., Hitler's "Nuremberg Racial Laws" of 1935) was striking and sinister. To follow the injunction to "say it in plain English" was no guarantee at all of accuracy and true meaning. Between the lapses in technical competence and the historic loyalties of an old society...falls a shadow.

As in many other places in these volumes it would take us far afield to consider the implications of what began as an exercise in journalistic curiosity in Tokyo long ago in the last century. I still follow the English-language press wherever it rears its forlorn head. I receive (and look at) the weekend copy of the *Kuwait Times* which, every ten years or so–I write during the second Gulf War of the second President Bush–becomes a journalistic source of burning significance. More importantly perhaps, there are those unfortunate English-language supplements of the *Corriere della Sera* (Milan) and *Kateremini* (Athens) which present themselves unreadably as supplements to the *International Herald-Tribune* (Paris). They are the very models of a good journalistic idea badly done.

Of Japs and Germans

I leave to last the question: Can it, in the very nature of things, be well done? I am of two minds. That excellent (and, deservedly, distinguished) daily German newspaper, the *Frankfurter Allgemeine Zeitung* has tried, with its high standards and lofty ambitions, to do an English-language version of the paper, also to be inserted in the European copies of the *Herald-Trib*. It lasted about two years (2000-2002), and was an undeniable *succès d'estime*. It was readable, sophisticated, and altogether indispensable for a substantial readership which has to follow European affairs without a working knowledge of the German language. In many respects, in my view, it represented a major cultural achievement in the evolution of the new Europe. For mostly financial or budgetary reasons it was short lived (and its weekly successor is a different product altogether).

Yet in its story of "great success and small failure" there was, I suggest, a Tokyo element of cultural disaster which I have described above in its Japanese context.

The duplicitous factor in its makeup was far from being any kind of political ruse or editorial subterfuge. The new Frankfurt paper reflected consistently the broad liberal-conservative values which brought the post-Hitler Germany back into a European civic culture. The fault line can be detected in the very nature of "the language of journalism." What went wrong came from the irreducible difference between two major languages and cultures; they have much in common, but it would be stolid to overlook their distinct and perhaps unbridgeable differences. In a word, we were confronted each day with an interpretation of reality–what happened yesterday? And what did it mean?–which was perceived in one language and then formulated in another. First-class translators did their best, catching double meanings, ingeniously retrieving a bit of slang to give equivalent flavor, paying sensitive attention to nuances of opinion and rhythms of argument. But, aye, there's the rub....

The English language as it has flourished in our time is practiced at any place and moment of time by a veritable higgledy-piggledy ragamuffin band of "native speakers." The coterie of valiant translators and interpreters consist, of course, of bilingual Englishmen and Americans, but also of New Zealanders and Australians, not to speak of well-educated South Africans, Hong Kong Chinese, Indians, and Pakistanis. Each adds, inevitably, a note of his own to a translated text. Inconsistent spellings and punctuation are the very least of it. Various euphemisms for such profanity and obscenity as may turn up in a breaking news story are, at the other extreme, not decisive. What *is* deceptive and duplicitous is the smell, sound and color of the general statement that is being made every day in the name of a nation, language, and culture. This was consistently misleading.

The Germans, as they emerge from the original *F.A.Z.*, are indubitably "Teutonic." They are, in their political behavior, a bit stodgy and in their cultural energy a shade ponderous. Their prose, especially in the famous *Feuilleton* pages of the *F.A.Z.*, tends to be at once elaborate and elegant, convoluted and long-winded. They still don't believe in indentations, and some column-long dispatches or commentaries consist of one dense, relentless paragraph. Their slang is often borrowed (and mispronounced as well as misused) from the innovative English demotic, and when it returns in translation becomes usually an absurd or misleading expletive. (The f-word and the s-word have had, as I have already documented in these pages, wild and silly careers as they commute between German jargon and Anglo-American patois.)

All in all, a serious and intelligent broadsheet newspaper is Janus-faced when it aspires to bestride two cultures. The protagonist is recognizable, to be sure; but he behaves like a *Doppelgänger*. For all my admiration of what the *Frankfurter* attempted–and it was singular in the history of journalism–I felt curiously uneasy and discomfited, and increasingly so as Germany within Europe moved into a grave crisis in the first years of the new century. A thousand foreign observers of the unprecedented troubles in the European Union and in the NATO military alliance felt that they had not quite expected a new and drastic turn of German policy. Was it a new Germany discovering a "*Sonderweg*"? Who were these "different Germans"?

We had become familiar over long post-war decades–from Konrad Adenauer to Gerhard Schröder, from Heinrich Böll to Günter Grass–with original figures as they lived and breathed. But who were these new protagonists on the German scene? They were kind of breezy guys...fast on the uptake...and just okay (or right-on) in tough situations. We seemed to be suddenly dealing with a whole new cast of characters. Their statements were full of brief sentences and short paragraphs. If it hadn't occurred to foreign observers before, they were...come to think of it...*just like us!*

And just at the high and relaxed point of so-called Western solidarity the grievous splits developed in Europe and in Euro-American relations; and they undermined the old picture of the Germans as pliant and pleasing *yea*-sayers and left us upset with a bunch of noisy unpredictable *nay*-sayers.

To be sure, no single factor or cause was responsible. Not merely "the language of journalism" had been somehow transvalued. We had to look at all the possible flaws in perception.

27

White House Storm, Or "Hurricane Monica"

The Scabrous Scoop

The salacious "body language" which the Monica Lewinsky affair–involving President Clinton in the White House's august Oval Room (or neighboring trysting places)–ushered in a time for serious American media which tried men's souls. Words were used in broadcasts, tapes, latest bulletins on "the scandal," which referred to well-known bodily functions but normally only in an obscene context. There was much shock and alienation in the land, not a little disgust. The professional press critics were put into their "condemnatory mode," and in turn, as the *New York Times* observed, "the whiff of condemnation" puts many reporters and editors into "*mea culpa* overdrive." As one of its own columnists expostulated–

> Suddenly it's all right to junk all rules of journalism by amplifying rumors floated by faceless well-poisoners identified only as sources.
> Suddenly it's all right to speculate in clinical language about sexual activities once considered so unorthodox that even the raciest newspapers refused to acknowledge their existence. Rumors are reported–only rumors that a "semen-stained" garment is lurking in the wings. (*Russell Baker*)

Well, this was overstated and rather inaccurate, for it wasn't suddenly all right. The *Chicago Tribune* avoided using the phrase "oral sex" (and hence refrained from reporting the joke going the rounds in Washington about the "Oral Room").* Editors found themselves debating whether to use words like

---

*   This follows a previous Presidential usage – "the nooky room" – so designated by Lyndon B. Johnson, then leader of the Senate, for his private place in the Capitol where he would entertain his illicit liaisons. It was quoted by David Maraniss in the *Washington Post* as a precedent for public officials who suffer from the difficulties of controlling their sexual drive. *"Nookie"* is given in the *Oxford Dictionary of Modern Slang* as "sexual intercourse...(perh. from *nook*, secluded corner)," p. 152. Greene's *Slang Down the Ages* suggests a French derivative *(nug)* and refers to a 17th-century "nugging house." See also David Maraniss, "Patterns of Denial Joined to the Appetites of Power," *Washington Post/IHT*, 26 January 1998, pp. 1, 6.

"semen" on the nightly news; and even to repeat more than once or twice "scandal" on a single front page. The *Christian Science Monitor* referred to semen as "residue." Several newspapers refused to run the widely syndicated "*Doonsbury*" comic strip in which the famed satirist, Gary Trudeau, referred to the sex allegations gripping the nation in language which a few American editors found "offensive and inappropriate." Some moved the panels from the comics to the editorial page; others dropped them altogether.

No, it was not suddenly all right. One widely read Washington columnist confessed that she had recoiled "in the seventh week of the squalid White House sex scandal" from a social life in the capital–presumably she meant cocktail-party gossip and dinner conversation–which had "changed beyond recognition." She had long championed the liberal cause of a free access to all the facts in the name of a citizen's inalienable right to know. But enough was enough for Mary McGrory: "when *Newsweek* described in lurid detail where Bill Clinton had guided the hand of a lady caller as they dallied in a nook off the Oval Office, I thought my right to know had been carried too far."[1]

The whole story of whether the President had seduced (or she him) a comely young intern-secretary in the West Wing of his official residence, and its implications for all collateral consequences from adultery to perjury, was widely held to be "the most difficult story" that the newspaper editors, for a fast-breaking long weekend, had to deal with in contemporary journalism. Humorists had a field day. Art Buchwald seized upon subjects for his column that had been "no-no topics for years and years," such as "telephone sex " (which he described as "a popular method of becoming intimate with a person without turning the encounter into a contact sport"). He was elated that what he called "phone love" had finally put paid to the old and primitive era of heavy breathers. Stand-up comics on late-nite television stood up and recycled old raunchy jokes to the irritated embarrassment of a President who, paradoxically enough, maintained his political popularity in the U.S. public opinion polls. The great American public bought more newspapers to follow the latest saucy tid-bit–and tuned into more broadcasts to catch the latest news–at the same time deepening its moral distaste for media that had no compunctions about stooping so low.[2] Pollsters for ABC television reported that 75 percent of the public felt that there was too much media coverage of the tawdry allegations but, nonetheless, it consumed that coverage voraciously (switch-on audiences were up, advertisers rushed to book additional time).

There was one special response that is worth noting, and it is, in its way, at once historic and trivial; for in a culture whose business is business there is always a corner of the marketplace in which great events will always be taken to be convenient plugs for one or another patented product. The publisher of *Playboy* magazine–which had pioneered the outing of soft-porn pornography in word and picture since the "sexual revolution" of the 1960s—was exultant. President Jimmy Carter, in a celebrated confession, had once told Hugh Hefner that he had, on occasion, "lusted in my heart" (i.e., after one or another desirable female). Now the lust had been made flesh, and in the Oval Office yet. "We have a playboy in the White House," Hefner rejoiced, as if his *Playboy* enterprises had just been awarded the Presidential seal or an Executive medal of honor. If anything, profanity and adultery, among other so-called vices, had received the Good Housekeeping seal-of-approval or, even, an eternal sell-by date.* He felt that a lifetime of single-minded devotion to erotic ideals, officially ostracized as lewd and lascivious, had been finally justified. He was especially titillated that the President and one of his closest advisors had admitted that, when they were together and having some fun, the p-word had been one of their favorite subjects of conversation. This prompted the publisher of *Playboy* to wax lyrical, if not philosophical: "It ['Pussy'] is the one great mystery, the one genuine grace note, the one true power. It is guaranteed to bring out a sense of play in a grown man, and it holds us in its sway from adolescence until death."

He was happy about the whole affair (and the more the merrier), for it was all "a triumph in the history of the sexual revolution." He had to remember to pay tribute to the memory of Lenny Bruce and Robert Mapplethorpe in their time struggling against the "bluenoses" and "moral charlatans." He pronounced it "the final battle in this century-long culture war."

> Whatever the truth of the allegations against Clinton....we have had a national teach-in on the sex lives of former presidents, on oral sex and seduction, on the value of tiny gifts and late-night phone calls, on discretion and reckless abandon. The sexually charged atmosphere of the White House has lit a thousand points of lust–around water-coolers, on the Internet, in bedrooms, on telephones–and a thousand points of tolerance. We are human. We are sexual....

If Hugh Hefner had his way the history of the Republic could be written in a short, direct line from the *Federalist* papers and Monroe's Doctrine to the precepts of *Playboy* porn.[3]

---

*   The stratagem – "innocence by association" – of connecting *Playboy*, its nude centerfolds and bimbo-bunny night-clubs, with real-existing sexual scandal is not original or unprecedented. Less playful, more outlandish was the unfortunate sponsorship of a post-War prime-time TV-documentary film about the Auschwitz concentration camp by a U.S. gas company. Again, an adman's celebration of the Teutonic national virtue of *"German efficiency"* was once featured in an advertising campaign for *Lufthansa.* (I pointed this out at the time to one of the bosses of the airline in Cologne; I received no reply; but my letter did, according to a report in *Time* magazine about "counter-productive" publicity, lead to the campaign's abrogation. Not all is fair in love and war.)

Return to the Brickbat Days

Even some more proper voices in the establishment found no contradictions in the popular response to scandal, i.e., between the high of moral outrage and the low of pleasurable puritanical titillation. It was a welcome sign, so a *Washington Post* writer argued, of sophistication when Americans in their tens of millions have finally learned to distinguish between private affairs and public ones...and, possibly, daring to conclude that not every illicit sexual relationship between consenting adults is a sign of the decadence of the Republic and a portent of national collapse. The editors of the *New York Times* shared this pious optimism to suggest that out of the debris of what they called "Hurricane Monica": "the Clinton crisis may produce a new, more worldly way of judging the private lives of candidates and office-holders." But such a "new, more worldly way" will have its price; and if mainstream American journalism is prepared to pay it, it may find itself regularly targeted as the tainted messenger that brings the dirty news.

To be sure, the self-criticism voiced in the press by a few angry voices was not confined to the new semi-candor with which the lascivious detail of a sex scandal was reported. Marvin Kalb, a former newspaper and TV reporter (now a "Press, Politics & Public Policy" Institute director at Harvard), despaired of the newspaper culture ever recovering its dignity. The loss of "reputation and legitimacy" in the frenzied coverage of the Lewinsky story would handicap the media for a long time in its civic function of "defense of democracy and freedom." How could, Kalb asked bitterly, our press sink to such unprofessional levels? Facts were assumed, innuendoes proliferated. The cry in every newspaper office was: Scoop now, double-check later.

In the *Washington Post* Richard Harwood went on in the same vein, diplomatically naming no names, but crediting the *Post*-owned *Newsweek* with assembling "the basic facts," criticizing all the others who rushed to embellish and embroider. As for the *New York Times*, it appeared to be taking refuge in the consolations of history, and published a surprising article which seemed to pooh-pooh the self-critical argument that "the American press is once again at risk–grave risk!–of abandoning its proud tradition of sobriety, fairness and impartiality." Evidently the tradition was a myth. It never *was*...never was *genuine*. Alexis de Tocqueville might have been persuaded (in a famous impression of 1831-2) that the praiseworthy press he encountered was not only guaranteeing democracy in America but "maintaining civilization." Not so. A *Times* writer, in a rare debunking mode, insisted that the free press of that Jacksonian day regularly devoted itself to politicians' sex lives (real or fictitious)–deepening a real, earlier, earthier tradition of "a press that called Washington an incompetent, Adams a tyrant, and Jefferson a fornicator." Was the newspaper culture ever a model for decorum and dignity? As the *Times* article concluded, with uncharacteristic resignation, "for better or worse, we now seem to be returning to the brickbat days of journalism." We would also be going forward to an age when the old self-censoring bracketeers would not necessarily be deleting all expletives. Foul or fair, speech would be enjoying more freedom than ever.

In Watergate the operational obscenities were mainly connected to political misdemeanors; in the Clinton White House scandal they were returned more literally to some of their original sexological contexts. Nixonite expletives emerged in the heat of partisan hostility. Clinton's no-no's emerged from transgression and escapade, and the lewd chatter thereof. Serious mainstream reporters feel rather more comfortable with high issues of an historic conflict rather than the low antics of a sex scandal. Expletive-strewn soundtracks sound sometimes the same–for there are only a limited number of obscenities, repetitive and interchangeable, which are involved in privately taped conversations. Accordingly, the Nixon and the Clinton affairs, for all the superficial references to déjà vu, had quite a different impact on the press corps and its daily "feeding frenzies" for hitherto unknown facts. One news weekly which for a season specialized in turning up something new and fresh in every number nevertheless admitted that the Lewinsky scoops "don't have the ominous constitutional grandeur of Nixon's break-in or Ronald Reagan's secret Nicaraguan war." Still, there was an "apocalyptic" atmosphere of sorts. "The city is teeming with paranoid prosecutors...studiofulls of talking heads. Everyone, it seems, has a subpoena, a new lawyer, or a defense fund–or all three–and is investigating someone else."[4]

A *New York Times* writer, under the headline "AN ARMAGEDDON OF DIRTY LINEN," viewed with alarm what she called "an apocalypse of scandal"; she shuddered to think what the talk would be like "when the National Conversation on Indecency begins."[6]

A columnist in the *Washington Post* sensed that dangerous times lay ahead. In a dramatic broadcast Mrs. Clinton had expressed the desire for a "rigid zone of privacy" around the personal conduct of the president. Even liberal commentators surmised that she would find for the coming age of liberal enlightenment precious few publicists who would go along with this, for not many journalists and editors can respect this as a reasonable public policy. In "extraordinary circumstances," as even the *New York Times* has wrestled itself into conceding, reporters have a duty to delve into sexual conduct and other "deeply private matters." The hope for a new American worldliness was linked to another saving prospect, namely: "a resurgence of the old conviction that character counts, and that rigorous inquiry into the character of presidential candidates is not an intrusion but a civic obligation." Experience, if nothing else, has taught the *Times* that, at least at the presidential level, "many aspects of character and behavior are relevant to making an informed judgement about a person's ability to lead in a time of crisis."

One crisis was already on, another was about to break. Still, as *Newsweek* reported, the president "seemed to be successfully changing the subject from sex to Saddam." Meanwhile, down at the State Department, two Middle East statesmen, threatening war in a crumbling "peace process," were kept cooling their heels in the capitol when the President was busy answering questions about Ms. Monica Lewinsky. The former White House intern had long since been exiled to the Pentagon building across the Potomac, but then it was discovered that she had been "personally cleared" to re-visit the White House some "37 times.") We live in an inquisitive society, and the media will always insist on its right to snoop...out of, to be sure, the highest of possible motives. They are obliged to intrude.[6]

Some call it snoop, others scoop. Here is the *Washington Post* again, leading a strictly factual story (they got it straight from the First Lady) about the presidential couple in their bedroom –

> *Washington.*—In the early morning darkness of Jan. 21, up in the second-floor bedroom of their residence, the husband awakened his wife and said there was something he had to tell her.
>
> "You're not going to believe this, but...," he began.
>
> "What is this?" she asked quietly.
>
> "but I want to tell you what's in the newspapers," he continued.
>
> That is how Hillary Rodham Clinton learned from her husband that he was in trouble again....[7]

The dialogue sounded gentle and innocuous, but it was the couple's first discussion of reports of new sex allegations involving his adultery and associated lovemaking. As another *Post* journalist, spluttering in outrage, put it: one account of the scandal–published in *Time*–"essentially quoted street language in its reportage that I thought I would never see in a mainstream American publication."[8]

By "essential quotation" was meant our old friends in the Bowdlerization process, dashes and asterisks, doing overtime to make good the expletives (or other obscenities) that were half-deleted. In the newspapers, by and large, there was not much change, i.e., incremental but not fundamental, in this respect from the hoary old days of the Richard Nixon tapes: only that the experienced reader was credited with enough acuity to spot that "the deletion thing" was on again.

The new editorial boldness was, as I have said, over-estimated. Expletives were still being deleted, but not thoroughly so; and the prim editorial explanation in brackets was more concise. Editors were so bold as not to have to specify in so many words that something had been excised. Here is the discreet *New York Times'* edited version of the somewhat more explicit *Newsweek* version of the absolutely explicit tapes of the "girl's talk" conversation between Monica Lewinsky and her friend and confidante Mrs. Linda Tripp. They stopped gossiping when they sensed the trap they were in; then they first fell out, disagreed about denying "the Clinton affair," and serious perjury charges threatened the cover-up, the President and "ob-struction of justice" –

> *Tripp:* Look, Monica, we already know that you're going to lie under oath....If I have to testify it's going to be the opposite of what you say....If I say no, that is [expletive] perjury. That's the bottom line. I will do everything not to be in that position....I think you really believe that this is very easy, and I should say [expletive] it. They can't prove it....Look, I can't lie under oath, so I have to think of a way that I don't have to....I only wish you'd tell me the big one [that I know]. Then I'd know he knew.
> *Lewinsky:* I can't. If I do that I'm just going to [expletive] kill myself....

On the same page of the *International Herald Tribune* which re-published the *Newsweek* excerpts as pedantically adjusted by the *Times*, there was a quotation from Mrs. Clinton which, once again, returned the discourse to the mainstream conventions of yesteryear when simple euphemisms obviated the need for insinuation or camouflage: "I'm sitting here because I love him and I respect him and I honor what we've been through together, and you know, if that's not enough for people, then, heck, don't vote for him." This must be the most lilting use of *heck* since another Southern voice sang it as a rhyme in the ditty, "*I'm a rambling wreck/ from Georgia Tech,/ and a heck of an engineer...*" The rambler was also a heck of a fund-raiser and a heck of a vote-getter.

Bracketeering

Can our newspaper culture go home again, to those old, helluva days of euphemism and periphrasis? On reconsideration the two-word bracket incor-porating "the deletion thing" seemed in Times Square to be a more decent way of getting around foul language. When, in her *New York Times* column, Ms. Maureen Dowd rose to the defense of the president's personal secretary–the estimable Betty Currie who was sorely distressed by the melée over the Oval Room which she had been attending for so many loyal years–she was called "the most poignant casualty of Bill Clinton's carelessness and concupiscence." Ms. Dowd's reference to Monica Lewinsky as "ditsy" was not intended to be sexual (although I have seen one foreign dispatch that translated it as "bo-somy"); but she went on to have to quote one appalled Clintonite. He was disgusted with the President's silence, thus making a victim of Mrs. Currie who was forced to give secret testimony under oath. As a result, "'she gets the living [expletive deleted] kicked out of her'."[9] Obviously the *Times'* editors feel more comfy with the old ways of the house-style. No turning points al-lowed around here.

What remains to be noted in this extraordinary episode in American jour-nalistic practice–if not yet in the political (or personal) history of the Clintons–is the pioneering spirit in which the editors and reporters of *Newsweek* not only broke ground in investigative reporting (a scoop was denied them only at the last minute), but in the artistry with which they distributed the hieroglyphics, in order to maintain scrupulous loyalty to the evidence which they were unabashedly citing and "essentially" quoting.

They had to deal with a coast-to-coast onset of "dirty realism." The talk, and its journalistic transcription, signalled a descent into the demotic which might, in the end, be putting on to the level of national conversation the various strands of profanity and obscenity with which we have been busying ourselves in these chapters–the f-words of traditional low usage; the p- and c-words of the half-illiterate underworld; the scatologically rich s- and b-s-words of the half-educated young radical protesters; the salacity of the pornographers and the earthiness of the military, not to mention the blushing "night words" of conventional mating. These were all popular vocabularies under taboo, all trying to break into print, to get published, to liberate themselves, to find belated recognition in the records of history and literature, politics and diplomacy...and at long last to make the front page in the newspapers we read for a true account of what is happening in the world.

Notable too is that the use and abuse of brackets is beginning to take on a life of its own. Brackets now function far beyond the punctilious intentions of the original academic punctuation style as copy-editors initiate an extra square space to relieve the overcrowded roundness of parentheses. It has its conservative users (*viz.,* the *Times*), loyal to old and set formulas of self-censorship, as well as its carefree abusers who insert brackets as a suggestive catch-all, a grab-bag of unmentionables...as in the *Herald Tribune*'s report about Whoopi Goldberg, the celebrated comedienne, who had "to hold her tongue." The news was that she couldn't use her page or two of "good material" on President Bill Clinton's latest troubles because "'They gave me a whole lot of stuff that I couldn't mess with'....She was reduced to joking about how she wasn't allowed to joke. The closest she got to the edge was a remark about using foul language on television. 'I don't need to say [those words] any more'." Evidently the point was all the New York newscasters and coast-to-coast anchormen were saying them now. What exactly she heard them saying–[those words]–the newspaper report blissfully refrained from telling us; the expletives, however foul, were swallowed up in the maw of those hermetically sealed brackets.[10]

Bracketeering is, I venture to suggest, well on its way to becoming a minor art of journalistic circumlocution. In its latest refinement it avoids the original sin of "participatory obscenity" (whereby you are drafted to guess or spell out the expletive which has been discreetly abbreviated or deleted)–at the same time hinting at the rich palette of dirty realism. A new book about U.S. gangsterdom is described by a writer in the *Los Angeles Times* as replete with "unfiltered language" which, in turn, is defined as language "filled with obscenity, with [the foulest, most vulgar epithets imaginable]!" (Paul Breines, reviewing a book by Rich Cohen entitled *Tough Jews: Fathers, Sons, and Gangster Dreams in Jewish America* (1998), in the *Books* section of the *Los*

Angeles Times, 29 March 1998, p. 4). What is bracketed is still left to the steamy imagination, but the pressure to fill in blank spaces (and to finish sentences hanging in fetid mid-air) has been agreeably turned off.

The New Hedonism

All dirty words are obscene, but some are more dirty than others. The f-word as a casual, if emphatic, adjective or adverbial intensifier, is one thing; the phonic-explosive verb (used, as the grammarian wags say, copulatively) is another. In the two styles of taboo talk, Monica was speaking rough Australian rather than seductive Lawrentian. Her obscenities had more to do with disorderly rudeness than with inspired erotica.

Other related distinctions were borderline cases. Is "having an affair" something more substantial–or less–than having "a sexual relationship"? In the first flush of Presidential rationalization oral sex was said to be different from adultery; for on this line of erotic reasoning (as Monica Lewinsky's testimony suggested) "penetration" was lacking. Lusty newspaper stories reported this data on sex and biology with a straight face, nary a tone of irony. There was little skepticism, few raised eyebrows. New-age love-making has to be given its day in court, telling its story in its own words.

Was the most powerful political figure in the world dallying indiscreetly, after hours, with a buxom young employee? Well, so be it. Is he stuttering when denying it, or looking straight into the television camera? Why does she call him *"Schmucko"* and *"the big creep"*? And will she really "f——g kill" herself, as she says, if things go badly wrong? Her girl friend believed her (but did she literally say it was all "flipping amazing"?).

Newsweek's orthography did the language in question as much justice as the expletives deserve in the half-century since Norman Mailer and James Jones, among others, popularized near-misses with an "effing" wink and a "friggin" nod. Square brackets fill the reader in when ambiguous obscenities become metaphors. An extra alphabetical letter can be easily added, at the front or at the back, if the dullish reader doesn't get it at first glance.

Lewinsky: Look, maybe we should just tell the creep. Maybe we should just say "Don't ever talk to me again, I f—ed you over [by telling others about the relationship]. Now you have the information, do whatever you want with it."

Tripp: I think if he f—ing knew he would settle....This is so amazingly huge to me. I know it's huge to you...I'm being a sh—y friend to you and that's the last thing I want to be....

Following the ineluctable and innumerable f- and s-words, obligatory in the talk of literate female singles (at least since the cultured emphasis in the feminist liberation movement of Dr. Germaine Greer), there is in the *Newsweek* account, echoed a few days later in *Time*'s special report ("Monica and Bill:

the Sordid Tale that Imperils the U.S. President, 2 February 1998, pp. 18-49), a curious, unpracticed usage of a p-word, outed by Hugh Hefner, as it cropped up in the conversations of the President and one of his closest friends and advisors, his enthusiastic ally, Vernon Jordan.

An influential black lawyer, Jordan was called upon (presumably at the instigation of the White House) to be a source of legal counsel and caution to the troubled Ms. Lewinsky. He was also a powerful middleman in getting the girl a new job in far-away New York. His handsome photograph, relaxing in the golf-cart carrying his famous golf partner around the links in their weekly round on the Washington course, was printed everywhere. But he remained silent or otherwise very discreet. Only once had he given an interesting quotable reply to an interviewer's question, asking him what he and his golf partner had been talking about while driving in the buggy across the greenery from hole to hole. According to the *Newsweek* profile which prepared us for the punchline by noting that their "mutual fondness for the ladies is a frequent, if crude, topic of conversation": "Jordan slyly replied: 'We talk pu—y.'" *Time* on the same subject, coming a little late, rounds out the theme by quoting some Washington insider who frequently plays the same greens: "all they talk about is p———." It's the same catty crack, but this time the pounce is a little more gentle. *Time* even finds space to give Jordan a chance to purr his gentlemanly little defense, "There's nothing wrong with a little locker-room talk."

Nor with a little quotation from it in the family newspaper of one's own choice, especially when we can privately pucker our lips and–according to our law of participatory obscenity–silently spell it all out properly. We're in on the act or–at least, in the know–about what's up or what's what. Even in the presence of the children? (Warning: there were at least a hundred newspaper articles during that January week, asking if the young could be allowed to watch, even hear, the evening news.) Well, so far as "p———" is concerned or *"pu—y,"* there is hardly a child in America who hasn't seen once, or maybe twice, that old James Bond movie which features a bewitching blonde who commands a platoon of nubile beauties, all serving the villain of the piece and on occasion tempting 007's weakness for the ladies. She went by the name of Pussy Galore.[11]

Only yesterday the standard euphemism for legendary womanizing had been phrases like "large men of large appetites." But locker-room talk is now gender-free. Nothing any longer is "For Men Only," a puritanical restriction which is in many places currently against the law. It takes two to transgress. Bill Clinton is inspired on the subject of "oral sex" to do research in the Bible– and his conclusion was that it is not therein considered adulterous; he is quoted as arguing: "It was only oral. It was passive. So that does not count." Presumably–a daring presumption on the part of the rumor-mongering press– he convinced Ms. Lewinsky that it was only "penetration" that made a relationship or an affair sinful or improper. For the moment nobody was going *the full Monty....*

I often found it unclear in the newspaper and magazine coverage when the bizarre recital of the *risqué* ended and the ribald schoolboy humor began. One reporter, expanding on the theme of "When Sex is not really having sex," remarked that what was involved wasn't *s-x* at all "but merely an advanced massage technique."

Were the jokes a last desperate resort into which battered old middle-class values huddled for refuge, or were the laugh-in aspects of the whole spectacle something of its comic essence? One school of thought about the national outburst attributed it to the weakening and near-disappearance of the old, lingering Puritanism in the American character: like a dying candle, a final flicker. That is why prim and proper stalwarts could still reprove and remonstrate.

Another school focused on the New Hedonism which would allow nothing to interfere with its pleasures. I was amused to find European correspondents tending to accuse each other of "arrogantly misunderstanding" the real nature of contemporary American society. That led to the consternation in all circles at the public opinion polls which indicated a rising popularity curve for the President the more the scandal took its toll in media embarrassment. But, then, was not *"having a bit of fun"* every man's prerogative? Millions seemed to enjoy the revelations about a man who seemed to be caught out at nothing worse than *"having a good time."* The thesis–facile and suggestive, as is the way of such journalism–is that "fun" has become a way of life, even (as one German newspaper put it) a *Weltanschauung*. With a Walkman in his ear the American strides briskly towards Nirvana: "What's happening in America [wrote the *Frankfurter Allgemeine Zeitung*] is anything else but puritanism. It is the democratization of fun and games, and the trivialization of any impediment, moral or otherwise to having a good time.."[12] One European commentator, his own puritanism tempered by Machiavelli and Metternich, was mystified by the Washington open reaction of sympathy, or nonchalance, over the adulterous affair...but public anger at the lying about it. He thought the courtly covering-up at once gentlemanly and understandable; but making the great historic Oval Room in the White House into a cheap by-the-hour room in a bordello...well, that was the unforgiveable part. (And this just after the scandal of the Lincoln Room in the White House that had been "rented out" overnight to rich Party stalwarts and fund-raisers, and the embarrassment of a "sacred" burial-space in Arlington's Military Cemetery having been given to patriotic but ineligible and undeserving political favorites....)

Commentators watched every wriggle in the latest national opinion polls as if they were *voyeurs* looking through the keyhole at the American psyche disrobing itself, or at least sneaking a glance at the secret "id" of the femme fatale in question. Monica Lewinsky's hometown newspaper, the *Los Angeles Times*, had at one point twenty-six reporters assigned to the story about her (some scurried to interview sometime baby-sitters and ageing kindergarten classmates).[13]

How high was the popular percentage that wanted to ignore the "scandal" and cheer on the President in his earnest attempts to vivify the economy and offer world diplomatic leadership? ("Stupifyingly high," wrote one puzzled liberal columnist.) Could the opinion survey results be interpreted as a popular approval of adultery? or of libertinage in high places? One opinion survey in late February 1998, conducted for the *New York Times* and CBS-TV News, seemed to have startling implications for the conventional interpretation of American political culture and its sexual ethos:

> Many Americans expressed disappointment in Mr. Clinton's personal behavior as president, calling it worse than they expected. But an overwhelming majority, 84 percent agreed with the proposition that 'someone can still be a good president even if they do things in their personal life that you disapprove of'....64 percent called the accusations against Mr. Clinton a private matter having to do with his private life rather than a public matter involving his job as president.

In some ways the response was predictable for it followed well-known popular practices rather than formal lip-service precepts.

IT'S UNDERSTANDABLE TO LIE ABOUT SEX, U.S. PUBLIC SAYS
   New York.—...in the statistical equivalent of a collective shrug, most [Americans] call it understandable for the president to lie about his sexual conduct....[14]

Was this an enlightened ambivalence or, perhaps, a disastrous hypocrisy? On the one hand, the story provided another argument on behalf of the "sophistication" thesis advanced by those who believe in a slow but welcome maturity of Yankee attitudes, boding the coming-of-age of the great American public. On the other, this constituted more evidence of the sad decline of probity as an unimpeachable ideal in American public life. How can private lies ever be reconciled to public morality? Is truth for courtrooms, and not for bedrooms? How will traditional American values fare with the onset of prideful (and in many cases, still shamefaced) double standards? At this rate casuistry will soon be the new required U.S. school-subject added on to the National Curriculum.

Between Oblivion and Immortality

Years have gone by; and according to the script cues, to the *dramatis personae*, ephemeral journalism should have left the stage and historians finally come on to play their roles, re-evaluate circumstances, speak their judgments, close open questions and otherwise give deeper meaning to the hectic drama. Times should offer new views and long perspectives; the stormy events have subsided. But no one has gone back or come forth to resolve the issues of grave public concern which were so blithely neglected when the ongoing and breaking story caught us all up in little scenes and even smaller stage business.

Nowadays the American press, and it is not alone here, rarely mentions the case of Monica Lewinsky which brought the Republic to a practical standstill. She has become a fit subject for only a few kinds of news items. *"Where Are They Now?"* a reporter asks, and nudges his readers' memories with a few facts that fill an empty corner of the features page with half-nostalgic human interest details. (Where does the girl now live? does she have a new boyfriend? has she lost the twenty extra pounds which she was carrying around the last time we asked what happened to....) Oh, Monica also turned up once in London for some private reason or another and she was recognizable enough for small crowds to ask for her autograph. But in her heyday every move was news; and even the grave and earnest *Guardian* was interested in what, during the Great Impeachment of the President, she had for breakfast ("two pancakes and orange juice, and she was dressed in a dark trouser suit"). And also, in those days of celebrity and notoriety she tried a little harder to rise above the pedestrian flatness of her California speech and personality. In a moment of distress and despair, when she was cross-examined about "oral sex" in the White House, her spirits sank and she said she felt *"like Hitler's whore."* This was more like it, trying to give the day a historic ring. But, alas, she erred here, since Hitler had no whores (only a nice Bavarian girl like Eva Braun).

Larger political or ideological notes were attempted on occasion; the Zolaesque phrase, or something like it to hint vaguely at some "Dreysfusard" injustice, lasted a moment and disappeared. When Monica's loyal mother Marcia Lewis heard that she might be facing criminal charges (for perjury, obstructing justice, etc.) she cried out at the unfairness of it all. What was wickedly called at the time "the Starr Chamber proceedings" were compared to...Stalin. Marcia Lewis said these were old and familiar techniques: they were used against her family in the old country, "used very effectively by Josef Stalin, which is why they left Russia...." Once again it was a humanist tone that rang out; but Stalin's travesty of political trials was in the 1930s, and the oppressed Lewinsky family left their tsarist oppressors a half-century before.

Stalin's shadow also passed fleetingly over Bill Clinton's trial testimony as he, far more than the Lewinsky ladies, tried to find a tone and a posture...that would be appropriate for a President and commensurate with the hurly-burly that was raging around him. At one point he said, "...I feel like a character in a novel. I feel like somebody who is surrounded by an oppressive force that is creating a lie about me and I can't get the truth out. I feel like the character in the novel [by Arthur Koestler] *Darkness at Noon*." Well-read Oxonian that he was, he might have spent more quality time feeling like other characters in other novels, say, in Flaubert's *Madame Bovary* or Kafka's *The Trial*. Koestler's

Stalinist context served only for a moment; old Bolshevik dialectics could not convince a soul nowadays. Clinton was at his characteristic best when he was nitpicking about juridical-grammatical meanings leading up to that memorable intervention–straight out of the Magdalene/Balliol debates of his Oxford days (did he ever listen to A.J. Ayer, W.V.O. Quine, Gilbert Ryle?)–"It all depends what you mean by '*is*'.."[15]

Were, then, those turbulent events of the 1990s which we all deemed to be historic utterly lost in insignificance, buried in a garbage-fill under a mountain of sleaze and trivia? I sense that no historian will ever be persuaded that what happens to men and nations, no matter how shoddy and undignified, can be simply relegated to oblivion. Will the Clinton-Lewinsky affair, accordingly, take on a new measure of importance? Beyond, that is, the special place we have assigned to it here in "the language of journalism." One reads and rereads the superfluous volumes of Washington testimony, the wretched detail of the notorious Starr Report, the fading cuttings of the salacious scoops which agitated each new edition of *Time* and *Newsweek*. What remains?–Apart, as I say, from the spectacle of a language and a journalistic tradition writhing in paroxysms of scandal mongering?

One seeks links to the great names of the past who shaped our sensibilities in love and politics. I thought of our two protagonists in a Shakespearean context, from tragic figures, sitting perhaps on the ground and telling sad stories of the death of kings....But no. Our august and upstanding forty-second president and his obliging lover never sat on the carpeted floor of the Oval Room, and the only exchanges of substance which I have been able to find was this egregious paragraph, where puerility speaks to vacuity and pap tickles drivel pink "...Then they started swapping dirty jokes–a Lewinsky specialty–mainly on a Jewish theme. One of Monica's ran, 'Why do Jewish men like to watch porno films backwards? So that they can see the hooker give back the money.' The President responded in kind: 'What do you get when you cross a Jewish-American Princess with an Apple? A computer that won't go down on you.'" They also laughed about the latest batch of raunchy email jokes she had sent him. And as they said goodbye she said, "I love you." Then, as she confessed to her biographer (to whom she presumably told all) she realized that this was too serious a comment in a lighthearted conversation. She added quickly, "*Butthead!*"[16]

All journalism aspires to banner headlines; and yet if its story withstands the tests of time it hopes, in a higher aspiration, to find a worthy page, substantially (more or less) as it was originally reported, in the historian's authentic chronicle of the age. Thus, all events and the event-makers find themselves melodramatically connected to, or associated with, great social and political forces and formidable outsize personalities that have shaped causes and consequences. In the case of the Clinton-Lewinsky episode, we have seen the fitful attempts at "largeness," i.e. at giving the whole affair its due place in the ongoing history of the American Presidency…and perhaps of its increasingly important elements of sex, vice, and corruption in a media-driven democracy which evidently thrives on scandal and sensation. Impeachment is so rare in America's constitutional history that there is an ironclad guarantee that such an unusual indictment will never be forgotten. But once that the grand trial for the impeachment of the President failed, a strange absentmindedness set in. The whole subject matter, blatantly more sexological than juridical, was fated to fritter out in a shamefaced avoidance of any aspect (with the exception, perhaps, of a stained blue dress) of the midnight misdemeanors which were held, quite unbelievably, to have threatened the very foundations of the Republic.

The historians, as I say, have not yet come forward to offer a "revised version" of the Washington drama. It will, when it comes, have to deal with two out-of-area challenges. I document them briefly and hastily since there is neither time nor space to speculate about the future of a story that once "shook the world."

1. There is a form of "social scientism" which pretends to be either sound sociology or stimulating cultural criticism; or both. It plagiarizes the *Kulturkritik* of the German schools (from Max Weber to Horkheimer/Adorno) and takes "theoretical" cues from a whole host of heretics (from Gramsci to Jean Baudrillard). It adds some topical ideological targets-of-opportunity and so continues the good fight on behalf of good causes (Chomsky, Kojève, Foucault, Edward Said). When the mix comes to be shaken well, bubbling over with jiggers of conspiracy, alienation, ecology, globalization, not to mention anti-Americanism and the felonies of Dr. Kissinger, the brew turns out finally to look like this…understandable, I am afraid, only when (and possibly not even then) one knows that the globalized conspiracy has it that President Clinton had been put upon by an Israeli Mossad agent, namely "*Monica Dreyfus,*" and that World Jewry had something to do with it (as it always does) the scandal, the plot, the impeachment, etc.

> Absent concrete evidence to the contrary, sexual conspiracism is a diversion into political anti-rationalism. A preoccupation with social absences and narrative lucunae, critical to Said's theory of contrapunctal analysis, emerges as another form of conspiracy theory. The evidentiary search for marginalized voices rendered invisible becomes conspiracism's search for an invisible and controlling marginality. And an absence of an identifiable central intelligence becomes irrefutable evidence of its presence.

And again:

> Conspiracy obsessions are the end-time of the politics of reason, a nebulous world where explanations are the abject servants of faith. Conspircism begins in the realm of empirical reasoning and then moves on to credit the unsubstantiated ends in a dark zone of exponentially-expanded interconnections and fantasized possibiltiies….

That faith, in turn, encapsulates and expresses a visceral alienation, a reaction to the foreign-ness that Monica the Dark Lady embodies. Conspiracism is the unending pursuit of satanic animation to the world.

Finally –

Everyday reality is filled with imperialist traps, ambushes and torture-machines to make us into docile bodies. Such a vision not only characterizes extreme right thinking, but is also representative of Focuault, Chomsky, Zygmunt Bauman, and Said's 'art of suspicions' and sociologies of invisible knowledge.

There may well be more of this in the years to come. But there are critics who will feel strongly that Bill and Monica have done nothing to deserve it. Better oblivion than such immortality.[17]

2. The alternative, at the other extreme, is history as feuilleton. The prose is easy, the research quick. What scrappy evidence there is commands gleeful acceptance, and is sewn together without a stitch being put wrong. The argument is never raucous, and the theses on behalf of one viewpoint or another are clear and unmistakable. Telling quotations are loosely transcribed from scribbled notes, and what is said to have been said in great confrontations is not necessarily exact and faithful. The "quickie" is rushed into print while the historian moves slowly through his bibliography of primary and secondary sources. It is partisan and insistent where it should only be fair and balanced. It is flippant where measure is needed. The feuilletonist is committed to defend the heroine of his history (heroes are rarer) where the requirements of truth demand only that he be, on occasion, a little less gallant. Let one text speak for itself–here is Andrew Morton rounding off his portrait of Monica Lewinsky (which followed on from his bestseller of "the true story" of the late Princess Diana):

...For just as the O.J. Simpson trial exposed the racial fault line running through American society, so the Monica Lewinsky saga has spotlighted the underlying misogyny that still permeates American life, and particularly the media. Clinton the adulterer and liar is a forgiven man; Monica Lewinsky the temptress is a scorned woman, derided by feminists and conservatives alike. Her loyalty, her honesty and her silence are qualities deemed to be without merit. As far as modern moral America is concerned, for her to be female, young, confident, well groomed, at ease with her sexuality–and loved–constitutes some sort of crime. What is far worse, however, she has committed the greatest sin of all: she is overweight....[18]

Happy End

I have previously mentioned that certain kinds of casuistical arguments were contagious, and in the charged atmosphere grotesque facts mixed with outlandish fictions. The "greatest fun president in history" (Monica Lewinsky, b. 1973) became a figure of fun, and it was a dismal entertainment. Everyone could have a theory–or a creditable source, good for a dishy quote–so long as it was at once smart and smutty. One reporter reported that he knew someone who had heard the Lewinsky-Tripp tapes *in extenso* and the quotable snippet (in *Time*) was that Monica Lewinsky had "facetiously referred to herself as the future 'special assistant to the President for b—j—-'."[19] This brought up, knowingly, all matter of sexological side-lines which had, in the not so distant past, been whipped through the culture by Professor Alfred Kinsey and Dr. Alex Comfort and rather more ornately before them by the *Kama Sutra* and its *pittoresque* pages on "fellatio." Since everybody's erotic education these days is multi-cultural, a few knowledgeable commentators went on to speculate or to suggest or syncopate the related italicized practice of cunnilingus, much celebrated in the Indian classic of love and, surely, the much-needed equalizer in the one-sided macho discussion of the subject.

I must not exaggerate: I have only one reference, and that single mention is not even spelled out. No dashes, no asterisks, no hyphens, no blanks. The *Time* correspondent in question was discussing President Clinton's much-praised skills at evasion and ambiguity–"the logic seems as tortured as a position from the *Kama Sutra*"–and was noting that as in this little local difficulty "time after time he has eluded foes and critics by means of clever verbal games." Alerting with a timely signal ("warning: pun ahead"), he argued that this president had a passion for "cunning linguistics."

So this is what it has all come down to, our earnest century in newspaper history devoted to the theory and practice of publishing, in the interests of a New World Order and a global concept of Jeffersonian liberty, all the news that's fit to print. Walter Lippmann called it "the public philosophy." The lofty metaphysics of it all has suddenly become mired in the mud. The truth which is supposed to help make us free has been packaged in fun-packed little puns and double-entendres which will do the trick and also amuse us (so long as we beware of spelling them out). Playfulness is all. Even the noble Enlightenment has become a clever little verbal game. Toys are us.

Part 6

Intimations of a Post-Profane Era

"It's our worst word, at least of one syllable, and maybe our strongest. Shakespeare, Dickens, Mark Twain never used it, at least in print. Norman Mailer in The Naked and the Dead *(1948) had to render it as fug. Now the F-word is heard in the best regulated living rooms. In American gangsta rap and British working-class novels it appears with more regularity, probably, than the....*
"Do you think English-speakers in general will ever get over getting a charge, positive or negative or both, out of the F-word? I don't....And the next thing you know, fuck will start popping up in Republican Congressmen's novels, and then in Presidential debates, and people will start referring to the third Sunday in June as Mofo's Day....
"No! There are limits!...You know what might actually happen?...A watershed. The trend henceforth may be euphemism. Effing will come back, and other eff-words."
—Roy Blount, Jr., *in* The F Word *(ed. Sheidlower, 1995)[1]*

"...And this brings us to the sex-taboo, from the violation of which abusive swearing draws its chief strength; mention even of the privy parts of the body is protected by the convention which has lost little of its rigidity since mid-Victorian times....It is difficult to determine how far this taboo is governed by the sense of reverence, and how far the feeling is of one of disgust and Puritanic self-hate. But in any case the double function of the taboo'd organs, the progenitive and excretory principles, has confused the grammatic mind of civilization....
"It is only a minor taboo that prevents reference to human excrement, but major swearing is strengthened by lavatory metaphors implying worthlessness or noisesome disgust....
"Now, the odd combinations that a witty and persistent mind could contrive from the breach of several of these taboos at once are far more numerous than appears at first sight...[variations] on the alliterative emphasis and rhythm of swearing, on the maximum nervous reaction that can be got from a normal subject by combinations and permutations of the oath, the results to be recorded on a highly sensitive kymograph....Swearing without a practical element, with only a musical relation between the images it employs. Swearing of universal application and eternal beauty."
—Robert Graves, Lars Porsena *(1927)[2]*

28

A Curse on Boyle's Law

Like the bourgeois old order which, in traditional Marxist theory of revolution, can exhaust itself or be overthrown, the f-word regimen for contemporary language, ubiquitous in books and magazines and cinema, teasingly present in even the most serious daily press, can similarly (a) go into decline and collapse by the sheer combat fatigue of overused profanity; or (b) be drastically displaced by energetic editorial efforts which hold pubertarian expletives in contempt and whose literary spirits prefer to write (and to read) in the richness of "the best of the rich English language."

The trouble with the second prospect–and there is little sign of it anywhere–is that the "frantic semantics" of the f-word world come to taint even its most stalwart critics. They tend to lose themselves in the *melée*–fighting fire with fire, giving the witch-doctors a dose of their own medicine, aggravating the obscenity scene with what the Viennese call a *Retour-kutsche*, "answering back" in kind, uttering an equally childish come-back along the lines of "You're another!" I confess I have so lapsed, if with tongue-in-cheek, on several of these pages.

So we find an accomplished prose writer like Alexander Walker, a critic of fastidious standards and an author of many meritorious books, losing his cool; and in a film review of *American Buffalo* (1996) he insists on giving back to the scabrous screen-writers some of their own salacity. In this case, in a critique entitled "What a Criminal Way with Words," the object of the rude counter-attack is no less prestigious a writer than David Mamet. Mamet's play provided the original story and dialogue. As Walker exploded (and the daily f-word count in his own newspaper doubled correspondingly) –

> Take every second line of a David Mamet play out of the screen version and you might usefully cut the running time in half. 'Who is he?'–'Some guy we spotted.'–'Who?'– 'Some guy.'–'Yeah?'–'Yeah...some guy.' Repetition, f***ing repetition, is what Mamet's technique is built on. The expletives are part and f***ing parcel of it. Delete them, too, and it might finish up a third of its length. So much the better.

This kind of counter-attack amounts to a movement forward by burning the bridges behind. It is a war cry too far, a whoop too loud. Can there, if our well-meaning Walkers go ahead with such retorts in rude revenge, be any way back to a style of clean concision? Where language takes a high road to truth or drama or reality? One knows from all of history that mild-spoken reformers rarely make a dent in a newly established order of things. How would an Orwell, a Mencken, a Karl Kraus have devised a viable strategy for the language, now splashing about in the sewage? Alex Walker, for the moment in anger and dismay, takes it out on everybody in sight, writers and actors alike, including in this matter hapless Dustin Hoffman who symbolizes the transition from his older film *Midnight Cowboy* (1969) to his current *American Buffalo* in which he plays a "four-letter fiend." As Walker writes, meaning to indict "a criminal way with words":

> But anyone remembering *Midnight Cowboy* (which is most of us, I hope) won't be impressed....[There's] no advance on Ratso Ritzo, the small-time hustler he played 27 years ago. Don't remember his needing to explain himself in four-letter words then. But that was before f***ing David Mamet came f***ing into view.[3]

The motives of the retaliation are virtuous; but in the struggle to hold on to older virtues in language and vocabulary this may represent a point of no return, a desperate tactic which hopelessly recognizes that if one can't beat 'em you've got to join 'em.

Roughly the same "Walker's Law" could be applied to *Pulp Fiction* (1994), Quentin Tarantino's popular film which, had the f- (and the M-f-) words been omitted, would also have been shorter by half-an-hour or so. But any kind of tampering or even self-censorship of Tarantino's profanity-ridden scenario would have violated the primitive street-corner aesthetic of "dirty realism." A filmmaker who practices this art believes that the more often he uses the f-word (in any and all of its conversational variants), the sharper the character is etched on the silver screen. Young Tarantino's record-breaking tabulation guaranteed him a gallery of unprecedently vivid gangster types–for, as one movie reviewer estimated, it was repeated several hundred times in the two-hour soundtrack. Each of the small-time mobsters (and mobstresses) achieved starring fame for their impersonating Hollywood actors. They disdained, except in several outbursts in the story into far-fetched Christian theology, to make a straight remark. No beating around the bush for them–they beat the bush to bloody death and buried it in hardening cement....

Inasmuch as Tarantino's films have had a huge success–and for some cult-fans they are prose poems of f-word communication–I have been wondering what an effing asterisk actually means to newspaper readers who are regularly inundated, in their visits to the cinema, by such soggy verbiage. They are no longer mere participants in the obscenity; they have to live with it and in it.

And what of, ultimately, the TV viewer? The sale of the television rights for a prime-time slot would entail a substantial bowdlerization...one suspects that even after a modest clean-up, the historic dialogue (which Tarantino himself wrote, or expostulated) might come out into all our the living rooms as one long blip, with great stretches of soundless dialogue.

Some say that, originally, "pulp fiction" as such was actually crafted for the silent cinema before the coming of "the talkies"; but how many amongst us are practiced lip-readers?

In artistic contexts, as well as in political, there are moments when the revolutionary journalistic breakthrough to a new linguistic realism has a serious and acceptable purposefulness. Most of the usages of what we have classified as "dirty realism" are superfluous; they may have a secret agenda (say, reader titillation in tawdry circulation wars); but the profanity, or a hint or two thereof, is gratuitous. Yet, as I say, on special occasions where candor joins with truthfulness, a reporter can get it rudely right. Thus, the celebrated Italian film director Bernardo Bertolucci is musing about his addiction to mannered, painterly camera shots–and how he was, probably, constitutionally unable to make an ugly, or visually brutal, movie. He recalls that he grew up in the beautiful city of Parma and was influenced by its local painter, Parmigiano, the most decorative of the Mannerist artists. And as he confesses to an interviewer for a Sunday newspaper: "I think beauty is in my DNA. If I were to film a boy rolling around in a pile of shit it would look like gold."[4] The image may be faulted for its "unconscious" Freudian undertones (money has always been excremental in Bertolucci's Marxism), but not for its s-word overtones which are, here, both graphic and revealing.

I am, as the reader may have surmised, of two minds about the shape of things to come. Either the f-word vocabulary will be absorbed and acculturated into our straight speech culture (and a whole school of thought devoutly so wishes), or such taboo words of primal semantics will survive their time of troubles and live to see another day as controversially deletable expletives.

One liberal-left journalist, Francis Wheen, has exhibited his credentials as an "f-word fancier" and bade all optimists to hope. It may be a dread monosyllable for some, but the *Oxford English Dictionary* had an early reference to it from a poem of 1503, and Wheen lists the proud company he wants to keep with such f-word-fanciers as "Florio, Rochester, Burns, Rossetti, Joyce and, of course, D.H. Lawrence." In an article he has written he calls my attention to the thrilling fact that if I looked closely enough I would, by combining "the first letter in each of the first four paragraphs" (from...unless...can...knowledge), find another, unexpurgated usage....This is war-to-the-death, even if with a school-boy's dirty tricks, against "the moral invigilators." They execrably failed to keep the word damn out of polite language; and the angry pickets at *Gone with the Wind* (1939), incensed at Clark Gable/Rhett Butler's "Frankly, my dear, I don't give a *damn!,*" also lost a famous battle. As Wheen writes, "At some point in the next century, more likely than not, the f-word will go the same way." Until then he offers a modest Swiftian proposal that may serve as the basis of a provisional compromise:

> For those who believe that there ought to be at least one taboo in the vocabulary, a simple remedy is available. Once a year, Parliament should pick a word–any word– and outlaw it for the next 12 months, with dire penalties for transgressors. Vernacular English includes thousands of suitable candidates–'ninny-hammer,' for instance, or 'jobbernowl' or 'dickey-dido,' or the evocative 'tootie-dumpattick.'

But, in an aside, he warns against the word "nincompoop" which has been creeping into the BBC and the heated debates in Parliament. According to the *Dictionary of the Vulgar Tongue* (published in 1811) it is said to refer to a man who has never seen his wife's pudenda.[5]

While the visionaries of a pornutopia are full of hope and fun, the dystopians are overladen with forebodings. If our culture should ever legitimate the whole of the obscene vulgarities, with the f-word reigning over all of us like some kinky King or cross-over Queen, they reckon that the day the taboos were definitively broken will go down in the annals of humankind as a day of shame (or, for some, shamelessness). I quote again from the famous text of Professor E.J. Mishan, who made the classic case of why the world should *not* be made safe for pornography. I happened to have published his essay (in the 1970s, in *Encounter*) and, as I recall, he offered it as "a perhaps idiosyncratic view, though not an implausible one."

> The existence of sexual proprieties and taboos enables and requires man to hug his sexual fantasies to himself–to have and to hold, for his private anxieties and delectation, a world within himself of the outlandish and licentious. The emergence of the pornographic society would dissolve the illusion of the peculiarity and power of these sub-surface desires. All potent resources of excitation that lurk like furtive monsters in the dark recesses of his imagination would dissipate and melt away in the glare of public pornography.
>
> For the ordinary man, such a loss could be irreplaceable: the last refuge of his inner world, the guarded sanctuary of his lusts, broken open and all its contents dragged into the market place, there to be made the common stuff of mass entertainment. True, the opportunities for overt sexual titillation become multiplied. But with the loss of each man's secret refuge he might feel much like an animal that has been deprived of its own peculiar odour and identity.[6]

At the moment one side seems to be not only having all the fun but making all the running; the other side appears weary and triste, as if it had already lost its odor and identity. One man's semantic tyranny is another man's furtive freedom.

Those whom Robert Boyle* in the seventeenth century called "protest swearers" have often sniffed victory for the cause in recent years as their fan-

---

*   Robert Boyle, *A Free Discourse against Customary Swearing, and A Dissuasive from Cursing* (1695).

cied "low language" climbed the commanding heights of discourse. In the lexicographical study of the f-word published recently in New York by Random House**–also the publishers of James Joyce's groundbreaking *Ulysses*– the standard two predictions were ventured: Either the f-word will become an everyday commonplace in both high and low usage and ubiquitous wherever English is spoken (and written); or euphemisms, new as well as old, will be making a comeback. (I quote this inspired speculation as a motto to this chapter.)

Boyle himself, uncompromising in his indictment of "swearing and cursing," thought the practice could be boycotted into extinction. So did a whole host of historic figures from Dr. Thomas Bowdler to Will Hays (of classic Hollywood's "Hays Office") as well as the censors of the Lord Chamberlain in Great Britain. I have quoted young Francis Wheen, their sworn enemy and a "protest swearer" if there ever was one. He would be pleased to celebrate at long last the triumph of low language–even at the price of making ordinary a whole ingenious vocabulary which served to shock for centuries as a taboo vulgarity.

Long before him, the illustrious Robert Boyle (whose other "laws" have stood science's test of time) speculated on the future of blasphemies, with their rude words and coarse phrases; and he had impressive recourse to the swear-words of the day, to what in the King James translation of the Epistles (James 1:21) was referred to as "filthiness" and a "superfluity of naughtiness." Little is left of such off-color Biblical texts in the new translations. The good book has been cleaned up only to make way for bad language elsewhere. In certain enlightened quarters hosannahs are in order. As for the guardians of the sacred, they argue that profanities are best left in profane literature.

This historic parting of the ways, dividing the spoils of language into two spheres of influence–the high and the low, the sacred and the profane–was, in the long run of centuries of history, an unstable arrangement, a changeable state of affairs. No such frontiers, so opportunistically drawn, remain permanent. And Robert Boyle himself recognized the inner tensions of a sinful language in a real-existing world. It is likely to become infectious; and, when "curious" and "swear words" are massively quarantined, they tend to become even more "fever'd," contagious and pestilent, "kindling each other by their mutual heat...." How to make amends for the mischief? Are there effectual remedies? The quest for a moral or semantic "Antidote" persisted through the modern era; and no one can contend that even Boyle, one of the great intellects of the day, had grasped the problem. The cause of keeping Protest Swearing "asunder" was doomed, for it proved to be an illusion to believe (as Boyle did) that "each single Brand, after a little Smoaking," would ever go out. I

** "A spooky locution," Roy Blount, Jr., remarks. "A publisher known as Disorderly House would sound less reputable but less unsettling." Preface to *The F Word* (ed. Sheidlower, 1995), p. x.

burden this page with another long quote (from Boyle's 1695 pamphlet against *Customary Swearing, and A Dissuasive from Cursing*), for it sets forth a great utopian theory of a language purged clean of sin and shame.

> As far as conveniency will permit, 'twere fit to fly the Conversation, or at least the Familiarity of protest Swearers....For there being very small (if any) Temptation to it in our natures it is principally imitated from others (as when one yawns, most of the Company, though otherwise uninclined to that act, do usually yawn out of sympathy) and to subsist but as 'tis cherished by Example and Custom (its Motive and its Nurse). And therefore, a very effectual Remedy against Swearing, is by conversing where it is discountenanc'd, forcing that shame of singularity that first begot it, to make amends for the mischief it has occasion'd, by employing it to the ruin of its own Productions. As Physicians make Scorpions their own Antidote by preparing out of them an Oyl that is Sovereign against their Stings. Lovers of the same Sin may (methinks) be resembled unto Firebrands, which being laid together, kindle each other by their mutual heat, but being fever'd and kept so asunder, each single Brand, after a little Smoaking, does itself go out.[7]

Three centuries later the utopian hope characterized the dream of Jean-Paul Sartre in which *les mots* would be as pure as *la Révolution*–as well as various other projects of a universal grammar wherein a liberated culture would be brought into sheer harmony with an ideal freedom.

29

Scholem's Nouns and Verbs

Let me digress in an extra word of warning and caution about the frequency curve in the rise of four-letterization. The countdown in such semantic calculations (used "40 times"…"200," etc.) may well be faulty, since the arithmetical weighting of each individual usage is neglected or undisclosed. Is it meaningfully accurate to tally lurid adjectives and livid adverbs together with active verbs or substantive nouns all in the same end-sum? This means putting in the same calculation the f-word repetitiveness of the Australian syndrome together with a singular explosion-into-expletive of some harrassed Jane Austen character who never brought such a cuss-word over her (or his) lips in the whole of the century. (It is the difference between–see my previous documentation–the obsessive-repetitive language of a Patrick White or Sidney Nolan in the noisy and profane centers Sydney or Melbourne as contrasted with the deliberate calculation of Charlie Chaplin, C.A.R. Crosland, Jacqueline duPré, et al., in more soft-spoken Mayfair.)

There are historians of language who call attention to the larger philological issues involved. For example, Gershom Scholem in his famous analysis of "language mysticism" in medieval Europe stresses the significance of the dramatic shift in twelfth-century France and thirteenth-century Germany of certain words from usages as adjectives and adverbs into the final open usage of "the Noun."

I refer the reader to Gershom Scholem's *Origins of the Kabbalah* (1962; tr. 1987) and his earlier *Major Trends in Jewish Mysticism* (1941). I cannot refrain from quoting a characteristically sovereign, if somewhat offhand, remark of his: "…It is, after all, one of the principles of mystical exegesis to interpret all words, if possible, as nouns."

Some readers may be interested in the whole passage, as a sidelight on what may be involved in my–and any other–exploration into "language." In the beginning, as any historian knows, there were the words of others; and they were inevitably an influence. Scholem wrote, summing up the attempts of the first Kabbalists in the French Provence to come to grips knowingly with the notion of "Unknowability," and even more with the idea of "Infinity" after the primordial surmise of "up to there, where there is no end...":

> ...One of the French Kabbalists read the combination of words that actually represents a phrase as a noun, possibly influenced by the aforementioned kind of adverbial composites and perhaps by some [other] expressions. The sentence now referred to is an elevation or orientation of the thought toward a supreme degree of being....It is, after all, one of the principles of mystical exegesis to interpret all words, if possible, as nouns. This emphasis on the noun character, on the name, may be taken as a more primitive attitude in the mystics' conception of language. In their view language is ultimately founded on a sequence of nouns that are nothing other than the names of the deity itself. In other words, language is itself a texture of mystical names.[1]

In a meticulously close reading of hundreds of recondite and forgotten documents, Scholem reveals underlying lingistic patterns, stressing a number of statagems which figure crucially in dramatic periods, whether theological or scatological, of developing language. True, the contexts are profoundly dissimilar. They are as different as Divine sounds from Satanic tones, descending indeed from ineffable heights to lower depths. Still, the verbal stratagems available to human speech and communication are rather limited. In Scholem's case-study, replete with the complications of Christian gnosis and the obscurities of Hebrew Kabbalah, great importance is placed on a number of "mystical-intuitive" factors which may seem at first glance to be more idiosyncratic than rationally intellectual. I remain convinced that such semantic twists-and-turns may well constitute what A.O. Lovejoy, the great historian of ideas, called "philosophical semantics," providing indispensable clues to the larger movements of language and thought.[2]

Among those revealing clues are (1) whether words are "uttered aloud [and] not only thought." (Prayer is related to the divine murmur and is the mark of clerical orthodoxy; and lip-pursing participation is at the other extreme, the current mark of profane-secular conventions. Nevertheless: I am not unaware of, nor indifferent to, the ineasy discomfort felt by those who (like myself) are disposed to explore such parallelisms in the long process of Western secularization between the semantic ingenuities of old-time Judaeo-Christian traditions and the latter-day phenomenon of "four-letterization" in our everyday discourse.)

(2) How many alphabetical letters are omitted from certain names and concepts...just to be on the safe or discreet side?...(Vowels tend to be dropped and consonants have to bear the burden of hidden identity. Yet YHWH and–curses!–the old "Debill" himself, always manage to show their hand, to tip their mitt.)

(3) The canny grammatical placing of sensitive or heretical sentiments in sentences fraught with dangers and disagreeable consequences. (Adjectives qualify, and are slighter–nouns are more substantial, graver.)

(4) Last but not least, Scholem–and Lovejoy before him–highlighted the intellectual responses; some predictable, some surprising (if not original) which obtain in such turbulent periods of psycho-cultural transition. Namely, the small range of give-and-take argumentation between the dogmatists and heretics, oscillating typically from defiant courage to vacillation....And it strikes the contemporary reader as all-too-familiar! To use the phrase from yet another context, the strict interpreters and the broad interpreters will always be with us. The record of old theological debate, not unlike modern ideological disputation, shows comparable movement between an avant garde and a rear guard...between an intuitive irrationalism (bordering on an ineffable obscurity) as opposed to a cool equanimity (masking a conservative reluctance to recognize the new or to discard the old).

In all of this there is an additional factor which, as I have suggested, is indispensable in evaluating low language and its deleted expletives. I can't imagine that it was not also a component element in the high language of old-time Casuists and Talmudists. I mean the peculiar specific gravity of certain weighty words which–spoken high or low, in awe and reverence or in fear and trembling, in cosmic defiance or lewd apostasy–are burdened with special human messages. Scholem, among others, doesn't appear to reckon with this. In the Judaeo-Christian tradition it was difficult to recognize and acknowledge that even the strongest and most dialectical efforts to mask the hidden name of God or indeed the "filthy conversation" (Peter 2:7)–to hide the divine or the dirty secrets, as the case may be–cannot remain inviolate for long.. Time catches up with the efforts of the noblest piety and the most brazen deviltry. The tetragammaton (the sacred four-letter word) became the name of G-d just as His son was known as "Christ" as if He were the annointed King. Deities take on (and, happily, respond to) the names they are given; and circumlocutions over thousands of years, in flat and routine recital, now emerge as interchangeable. As for profanities, they are no longer whispered, and even when edited, nay truncated, in written transmission they are loud and clear (thanks to what I have called the contemporary printed press' "participatory obscenity"). The least we can do as we are being tempted to cross the lines of traditional prohibitions is to purse our lips and murmur under our breaths, as correctly as we can, that which had remained under taboo and unspoken for so long.

As I say, there is little of this in Scholem. But his books are crowded with instructive glimpses of writers and thinkers weighing their words with a mix of care and cunning. And so have they all, over historic centuries in the experience of language and literature, for if words "in the beginning" can create they can, in the end, destroy.

A man of reason and liberal humanism, Scholem was bewitched by the neglected, and indeed unexplored, corners of recondite scholarship, and his medieval mystics and even the self-styled messiahs (especially Sabbatai Sevi in the seventeenth century) enchanted him. For years on end he buried himself in proverbially dusty archives, piecing together tattered manuscripts, re-translating classical Latin and old Hebrew, doubting specimens of handwriting in copyist's ancient copies, thus rejecting unacceptable forgeries, locating and dating hitherto unknown medieval centers of mystical religiosity...and he was wrenched and shattered by the experience. Here is a passage towards the close in one of his most intense books which reveals the troubled and ambivalent spirit:

> ...Symbols are born, in the last resort, of the memory of an inexpressible content. There is something wrenching and shattering about it. The kabbalists of Gerona [in thirteenth-century Spain between Barcelona and the Pyranees) attempted to contain the symbol within contemplation without permitting it to become pure allegory. This developing interest in the symbolic character of religious life led to the first great wave of mystical commentaries...and the prayers necome mystical symbols of deeply hidden divine realities, whose expression is in itself inaccessible and denied to us....

Seen in this way, even the great and enlightened wortk of Moses Maimonides, *The Guide to the Perplexed* (1204, translated from the original Arabic), becomes something of an intellectual disappointment, even a failure, for it could "at best only lead to the treshhold of mysticism but no further...."

Unbeknownst to me Scholem died (at the age of eighty-five in 1982) during the week I was in Israel, and I only read of his funeral in an announcement published in the *Jerusalem Post*. Did he himself, I wonder, ever cross "the threshhold"? Did he ever openly welcome the onset of the irrational and take leave of the splendid rationalism which informed his whole intellectual journey?

One of the most captivating figures in Scholem's *Origins of the Kabbalah* was Nahmanides, a man of "towering authority." He represented a classic case of a sober rationalist who argued against the heretical mystics...but was, secretly, troubled by the shortcomings of his own orthodoxies. Curiously, Scholem is not wrenched, not to speak of being shattered. Here he appears to be untouched, and writes in one of his cold, apodictic footnotes: "...in reality not even a beginner in philosophy would have had any difficulty resolving the problems that so vexed Nahmanides." Perhaps he should have given us such a beginner's text in philosophy; it might even have resolved more problems than the old enigmatic ones of a medieval rabbi.

Gershom Scholem was a towering figure in the history of ideas and words; and, to return to our point of departure (to wit: statistics of breakthrough, the number of "hits") he knew that simply counting taboo-breaking usages is of small value. One resonant phrase in an apocalyptic moment (or in some melodramatic climax taken to be such) may be worth more than the buzz of a whole babble of believers.

I met Gershom Scholem briefly in post-war Berlin (where he was born as "Gerhard Scholem" in 1897); he was one of the first post-Hitler exiles to visit from "Zion" to which he had emigrated as a young man in 1923. He wrote occasionally for *Der Monat* and *Encounter*; but I often wondered whether, even in the face of a lifetime spent deeply researching the meaning of mystical religion, he was an observant (or practicing) believer. Did he believe that "In the beginning there was the word"? (John, 1:1) Did he hold with the notion, in a kind of semantic creationism, that the Word started it all? Probably not. But he would have happily lost himself in the trail that ancient Greek philosophy (logos, and all that) left on the Judeo-Christian mind.

In one of his books he seems to delight in the rewriting efforts made by one of his favorite thirteenth-century Kabbalah mystics, Isaac the Blind, who was the son of the illustrious Rabad (the traditional acronym of Rabbi Abraham Ben David [1100-1179]) Isaac, perhaps because he was sightless, saw more deeply into Genesis 1:26 which postulated merely that God created man in his own image or likeness. Genesis reedited, or retranslated (i.e., intuitively revised and mystically reinterpreted), would emerge with the real beginnings in Nothing. And from "the Naught" came the providential creation of World and Time and Humankind when the *ideas* were conceived and their first proper *Names* so worded.

More than that: Was God alone? Couldn't He have had all-knowing advisors? Nobody creates new worlds within infinite time and endless space without taking *some* counsel. The true story of Genesis now begins in the plural, not with the singular. "Let *us* make man." *Us*, with the divine help of heavenly advisors and their inspired vocabulary....And what sayeth the advisors?..."And He took counsel with the words that shape reality and by means of which everything was realized."

The words that shape reality....This idea will go far.[3]

Commentators emphasize Scholem's reaction to the narrow-minded prejudices of Jewish scholars who were "wedded to Enlightenment rationalism" and he thereupon created a new and tantalizing field of study which took him into strange (and, for many of his liberal contemporaries, alienating) subjects, "no matter how anomalous and repellent." He bypassed the passionate detractors and admirers of mystical movements; and he straddled the great themes of Judaism as they played out in "empirical, publicly visible, historical actuality" as well as in "inner spiritual events to be grasped through recondite symbolical interpretation."

Thus, he lived in two worlds: one demanded the sense for the ineffable, the other called for words and meanings which were at once reasonable and precise, truthful and transparent. His life and achievement made a triumph of the dual tension, the combined challenge.[4]

30

Robert Graves, Or the Vision of a Post-Profane Era

I have often referred to the 1920s, and to the representative names of Joyce and Lawrence as the watershed in the struggle against literary censorship. The period, and its scandalizing novels, full of words that were immemorially under taboo, signalized the re-entry into the English language of old obscenities as lyrical or half-poetic expressions without which imaginative prose writers could not (or so they insisted) capture the bittersweet realities of life. The purposes of such profanity were high-minded, and the prohibition of "dirty books"–most dramatically in the cases of *Ulysses* and *Lady Chatterley's Lover*–was a grievous, if conventional, misunderstanding of the relationship of language and aesthetics in a noble enterprise of serious literature. By the end of the century the main currents of free-flowing naturalistic vocabulary had become torrential.

Modern communication–from the novel to the news-story–was never to be the same again. Everybody came to write and speak as the demotic demiurge dictated. The diversion of old stagnant streams into fresher swirling currents spilled over every shore. The great defenders of the original movement–viz., Robert Graves, poet-novelist-historian–would not have recognized the inundated landscape nowadays. The case they made at the time was at once modest and profound, but it was mediated at every turn with a sense of irony and paradox which befits the engagement with ultimate things.

In his little book of 1927 on "the future of swearing and improper language" Robert Graves offered *Ulysses* as a masterpiece to be studied "as a manual of contemporary obscenity." Joyce's novel was "a deadly serious work" in which "obscenity is anatomized as it has never been anatomized before." It was an original idea, if a mite fanciful, that to reach the good place (like, perhaps, the Wagnerian hero going through the fire), a heavenly city or a republic of letters, the writer would have to pass through a hell of obscenities to bring himself "as far beyond obscenity as Shakespeare got beyond the lust of which he makes frank confession...." Only then could one transcend "the badness and rankness which obscenity exudes."[1] Graves found it, as he wrote, "quite right" that it should be censored since its chief Anglo-American public could at the best of times be "only an obscene one." For these were unfortunate cases where avant-garde creations are misappropriated by a mass mainstream culture, and high literature gets grossly exploited for low purposes. But he argued that "it [*Ulysses*] was not an obscene book"–on the contrary it was (in his extravagant judgement, warming to the defense) "perhaps the least obscene book ever published." Hence, in the avant-garde's critical sense of mainstream dialectic, "that is why it is censored." Graves' explanation of this paradox was obscurely put before it was clearly understood. In the years to come it threw a useful light on what is living and what is deadly in the efflorescence of the f-word and other obscenities in twentieth-century language: "...Joyce is read as obscene instead of successfully past obscenity."[2] In other words, a handful of artists can, in their profane way, break through to a post-profanity context. They would succeed, like the revolutionaries, where all others had failed. Not for them the helpless tidal swell of obscenities–let others dip in it, touch their toes and splash in it....Some would swim it, not a few drown in it.

Lawrence, mistakenly, thought the invigorated language would wash culture clean, remove the layers of sticky rhetoric from the body of love and its natural impulses and loyalties. That, alas, is not the way the f-word worked. An even "uncleaner" culture–by Lawrentian standards, so resolute against the sickly preoccupation of "sex in the head"–seemed to emerge. And the utopian search for a new touch and intimate tone persisted. How to reach *through* and *past* obscenities? I have recorded only a few moments in our culture–ever hopeful that a profane word or phrase or page, or an obscenely challenging work of art, might signal new epiphanous illuminations–where the established taboos were broken...for want of a better compliment...to good purpose. The occasions were various, the accompanying emotions unimportant. A great comedian (Chaplin) had turned bitter; a crusading socialist (Crosland) was frustrated and angry; a black athlete (Cassius Clay/Muhammed Ali) wanted to shock the dude...and a few other momentary but significant outbursts.

They were, I take it, signals in the Joycean sense adumbrated by Robert Graves that a post-obscenity context was possible. An expletive, hurled with grave human hostility of one sort or another, was a serious response which seemed to come from so far inside them that the words appeared to have a special, vibrant life-force of their own.

At one point, this kind of synonymity amounted to what has been called "a secret language" wherein the defilement which was latent in a word could be evaded by drawing copiously on the legitimate vocabulary for secret obscene images to avoid the appearance of obscenity (confronted with so much contemporary salacity or foul talk or dirty words). I am not certain that this was eternally so. Some journalists, parading "a little knowledge," have tried to argue, with more than usual earnestness, that the plague of foul words and lewd images is of fairly recent origin. One TV-columnist, reviewing a program entitled *Pornography: the Secret History of Civilization* (1999), accepted the "fascinating" thesis (if over-neat) that pornography didn't exist until the excavation of Pompeii and its scandalous effect on the nineteenth-century Victorians. The squeamish English excavators were supposedly horror-struck. Accordingly, some works (which had been an acceptable part of everyday Roman life) were defaced and others locked in a Naples secret museum.

"Only then," we are told, did such material attain the status of the forbidden, and therefore "the lure of the excitingly shameful." After all, the word pornography itself first appeared in English dictionaries in the middle of the nineteenth century. If all this was so (and it probably isn't) then what were our anthropologists and ethnologists going on about ancient totems and taboos? Here is one with an account of taboos in Melanesia and Australia:

> ...And not merely the names themselves but any words that sounded like them are scrupulously avoided, and other words used in their place. A custom of this sort, it is plain, may easily be a potent agent of change in language, for, where it prevails to any considerable extent, many words must constantly become obsolete and new ones spring up.

This, of course, illuminates the out-of-dating of modern popular equivalents to the words "whore" and "harlot" (which, in the end, still have a kind of Biblical immunity). As our ethnologist in the South Seas reported, "New words sprang up everywhere like mushrooms in the night..."; and this, we learn, went as well for the Paraguay Indians.

Should Anglo-American linguists in our own time and place be less successful with new coinages for similarly furtive purposes? Or is the contemporary onslaught against any and all taboos so strong and relentless that only what is robustly old can survive? Will such durable obscenities become slowly legitimized or, at least, increasingly used in everyday speech?[3]

To come up with circumlocutions was in past times an earnest effort to avoid the fearsome wrath of the gods. It is still, even in a secular unbelieving age, too serious an affair to be left to newspaper wordsmiths trying to be amusing for the early morning edition. In the long perspective of cultural or civilized progress, the notion of our language moving "beyond Obscenity" heralds a post-profanity epoch. It suggests a miraculous purification of the language after its "deadly serious" confrontation with all the traditional taboos. It is somehow also related to the Utopian hope of an ideal synthesis emerging out of the utterly antithetical denial of the established thesis. This is not necessarily borrowed from Marx or Hegel, but from a more ancient dialectic: immemorial to man's attempts to think radically and still count on the benevolence of the most extreme alternative.

It is obvious that in such extreme situations a choice expletive fulfills a very special psychological function. Its physiology is another matter, and in lieu of going farther afield I should like to quote the poet and polymath Robert Graves:

> There is no doubt that swearing has a definite physiological function; for after childhood relief in tears and wailing is rightly discouraged, and groans are also considered a signal of extreme weakness. Silence under suffering is usually impossible. The nervous system demands some expression that does not affect toward cowardice and feebleness, and, as a nervous stimulant in a crisis, swearing is unequaled. It is Saturnalian defiance of Destiny. Where rhetorical appeals to Fatherland, Duty, Honor, Self-respect, and similar idealistic abstractions fail, the well-chosen oath will often save the situation....[4]

Robert Graves once reminded us that in his projection of the "future of swearing" that its past had its ups-and-downs, its meager periods and its rich flowerings. For him, as an ethnocentric poetic Englishman, Tristram Shandy was "at the beginning of the best period of English profanity (1760-1820)," and therefore "culture" was spread downwardly. "Poor man's poetry," as swearing was sometimes called, became thinner, less inventive. It is good to be reminded of the history of the English language when, in our day, a simple-minded threat of "four-letterization" looms ahead. As Graves writes:

> ...The Elizabethan age may have been richer in far-fetched profanities and wild conceits than the Augustan Age, but swearing is an art that cannot trust to mere adventure for its success: it must have a controlled purpose, and always flourishes most strongly in a pure aristocracy. The Elizabethan age swore, it hardly knew how or why: and it was an excitable age with few settled convictions. The Augustan age swore with deliberation and method.... (p.30)

New forms displaced the old which had only antiquity to make them respectable. There were "referential" and "sentimental" swear-words, and according to Sheridan's *The Rivals* (1775): "Ay, ay, the best terms will grow obsolete–*Damns* have had their day" (Graves, p. 32). The best words are always coming and going, and leaving perhaps the future all to the worst, that is, abusive or foul language on parade. Triviality comes to be more impressive than "the thunder and whirlwind" which used to precede it. And where went the wit, and the ingenuity? Tristram Shandy referred to a gentleman, "who sat down and composed, that is, at his leisure, fit forms of swearing suitable to all cases from the lowest to the highest provocation which could happen to him...and he kept them ever by him on the chimney-piece within his reach, ready to use." Coleridge as well mourned the passing of what he called "the least deceptive symptom of deliberate malignity." In his preface to *Fire, Famine, and Slaughter* Coleridge referred to the "…rapid flow of those outrageous and wildly combined execrations which too often with our lower-classes serve for escape-valves to carry off the excess of their passions…." Our century has democratized the "superfluous steam"; and the steaminess is now free for all classes. As a mass phenomenon it is marked (as we have seen) by an adjectival barrenness as well as a distressing sameness.

Although he is one of the few phonetic visionaries of a post-profane future, Graves himself does not set a very good example. Writing in the 1920s, he confesses quite sympathetically,

> …Observe with what delicacy I have avoided and still avoid writing the words x——
> and y—— and dance round a great many others of equally wide popular distribution.
> I have yielded to the society in which I move, which is an obscene society: that is, it
> acquiesces emotionally in the validity of the taboo, while intellectually objecting to it….

Before publishing his little book–and I know the London procedure well, having gone thorugh it innumerable times as editor of *Encounter*–he let "a learned counsel" go through his pages with a blue pencil and it struck through paragraph after paragraph of "perfectly clean writing." Graves admitted that his only "self-justification" was that the original manuscript of *Lars Porsena* "should be kept safe for a more enlightened posterity." And there it presumably lies, by now for us–"in the strong room of one of our greater libraries." It should reveal no great surprises.[5]

31

Counter-Revolution and Utopia

There are in some circles, as I have already detected, a measure of despair at the future of the f-word. Everybody has been saying it, and practically everybody is quoting it. Yesterday, throughout the known world of speech and language, numberless men and women (and precociously conversational children) had been expressing themselves rudely in polite society–and, on the morning after, newspapers have reveled in their entitlement to reproduce a few choice newsworthy examples...or, otherwise, they are not just telling-it-like-it-is.

But when, I venture to ask, will the law of diminishing returns be setting in? When will the f-word, as it must to all phonemes, become a cliché, old hat, a yawn? At what point will all those little hyphens, laid end to end, like hurdles, become a slow cumbersome hundred-yard crawl? When do a cool million asterisks reach fading star status? Enough being enough, would then a new tranquil tedium be displacing our agitated post-modern reading habits? And what, in the end, will be left of "the night words" after so much sexual abuse and verbal harassment? What resources will be available in the new day, in the aftermath of old niceties and current profanities, to rudely shock, to coarsely titillate, and scabrously to suggest?

The coming apocalypse of language, as I venture to foretell, may well arrive when profanity is not merely socialized and domesticated but is politicized, and expletives are openly and officially used at the very highest level of public life. We had a hint of the semantic shape of things to come in the Watergate breakthrough which brought to light the language—albeit still private, secret, off-the-record (if on the tapes)—that President Nixon used in various White House crises of his benighted administration. On the occasion of a European financial disaster the President, with unwonted faecal felicity, said he didn't "give a s—t for the Italian lira." In a similar, straight-talking no-punches-pulled spirit Richard Nixon said of the Japanese, when they were making some commercial-diplomatic difficulties, that he didn't "give a f—k for the Nips." These didn't quite yet make banner headlines.

But there were indeed shocking streamers–in *Le Figaro* (and elsewhere), if not in *Le Monde*–when General de Gaulle expostulated his rude contempt of the revolting students of '68. *Les événements,* as the demos and strikes and riots were called, had almost brought France to "a pre-revolutionary stand-still," as the would-be rebels thought, among them old Sartre and young Cohn-Bendit. But they were all–for the General and the President, in his official and considered judgment–just *chien-lit.* (This was the canine version of *le mot de Cambronne,* i.e., *"Merde!"*) For a Gaullist moment ideology became scatology.

The disenchantment is not, of course, confined to political passions since what was inevitably involved in the "end of ideology" was the language of subversive values. This was especially true (as we have seen) in the USA where old-fashioned vocabularies of alienation and radical action became new-fangled obscenities. After the waning of anger and activism, the essential profanity and its handful of self-repeating four-letter words remained; but the high-minded radical principle went out with the disposable garbage. As one writer has confessed, "We left-wing types popularized rudeness and slangy candor thirty years ago–our language, we thought, would discredit the official hypocrisies–and now everyone is going in for it." But he quickly adds: "With depressing effect." Not only have the ideal purposes of the crudities disap-peared, the coarseness has become, increasingly, the sound of the official hypocrisies themselves: "even those who love profanity may be dismayed to hear a former Mayor of New York calling someone a 'schmuck' on the radio. It is not the words that matter so much as the ravaging lack of dignity. The rout of gentility, which [we] cultural libertarians sparked, has now been followed by the rout of self-respect." This may be only a bit of provincial bitterness over the local Manhattan effects of the semantic revolution of the 1960s; but the era of candid slang and ravaging rudeness may well be only beginning. Real lovers of profanity will be coming in for more than mild dismay.[1]

Could this, one day early in our next century, become the rule of a new uncouth candor in politics and diplomacy? Can one conceive of a philologi-cal revolution, with honestly visceral sentiments taking, at long last, to the offensive?

Should this become a prevailing style in the universe of discourse among the nations and statesmen of the world, I foresee in the stage thereafter a counter-revolution in the entitlements of our newspaper culture.

A utopian prospect beckons. We would be moving out into a time when profanity was itself becoming obscene. Nobody wanted to talk dirty any more. Everybody wanted to write like the writers whom Henry Miller, that scatologi-cal master, hated most: Matthew Arnold, Walter Pater, Ralph Waldo Emerson. Thereupon, a new generation of writers, representing a counter-cultural re-vival of what was once called The New Journalism, gratefully seized upon s-free phrases and f-free sentences to garnish their stories and interviews. Editors were quick to assert in the name of the freedom-of-the-press and the First Amendment their right, indeed their duty, to cut or paraphrase or otherwise rewrite all salty, old-style and boring quotations for the edification and proper instruction of their readers. Desalinization was the "in" style. You might well ask: What manner of cultural catastrophe had befallen our f-word, only yesterday so obligatory and ubiquitous?

I imagine it would be like the first sixteenth-century English Puritans, who reacted in panic and dismay to the threat of the European-wide syphilitic plague, and consigned the sexuality of the day and all its associations (words, songs, plays, clothes) to obloquy and oblivion.*

Now a pendulum was again swinging in an opposite direction. Prose everywhere has been behaving itself, and there is no need any longer for the latter-day Bowdlers. Asterisks and hyphens had become superfluous: as obsolete as Dr. Samuel Johnson's capitalization of nouns. In a counter-cultural twist that Orwell didn't exactly predict, Oldspeak was enjoying a fashionable comeback, and some thought it had saved civilization as they had known it. Journalistic scoops were unfailingly well mannered, and even films faded out the steamiest of scenes to avoid the soporific calisthenics of Hollywood's yesteryears nude bodies writhing on a mattress in a half-light. For the most diligent of students of newspaper culture there were no detectable sly or insinuating nudges or winks to be clipped for the cutting file, even in the trickiest of stories.

The day the effing f-word had to stop was made into an official bank holiday. (O frabjous scabrous day!) Blue jokes were being told whiter-than-white; off-color was restored to its proper on-going hues; raunchy stand-up comics were being requested to sit down (how weary we've become of mixing into their private lives). Literary conversations in our highbrow newspapers would "explode" into delicately-worded witticisms. Forsaken wives would invent other ways for their lipstick to wreak marital revenge in the beachside sun. Characters in street-wise fiction will no more explain themselves in outmoded four-letter words than priests would preach in Latin in your friendly neighborhood church. Obsolescence has come yet again. Sic transit gloria...of the f-Word and so many other related obscenities.

As for "the night words," they will be shrouded as of old in the discretion of darkness; and not even the D.H. Lawrences and James Joyces of the future will be able to summon up the radical verve to strip them again, to uncover them in the light of day, to liberate them in a public outing....

Or perhaps not. Obscenity, crushed to earth, can rise again, and the profane may once more take its turn to making us truly free at last. Old gods have a track-record of failing; utopian dreams disappoint. Revolution, with its semantic and other cycles, has a way of coming full circle.[2]

---

* This is the scholarly thesis of Professor S. Andreski – see his articles on "*The Syphilitic Shock*" in *Encounter* (October 1980 and May 1982); also his book *Syphilis, Puritanism and Witch Hunts* (1989).

Notes

Part 1: Intermezzo:

Robert Burton's Melancholy Dilemma: Journalism without Newspapers

2. The Journalistic Imagination

1. Robert Burton, *The Anatomy of Melancholy*, Everyman edition (1621, ed. Holbrooke Jackson, 1932), p. 17, 97, xi, 22.
2. For a startling analysis of the pedagogical polemics from Plato and Montaigne by way of Comenius to Pestalozzi, to Albert Schweitzer and John Dewey, see Jacques Barzun's essay on "Educational Disputes," in *Encounter*, November 1973, pp. 40-48. It is admirable, as is all his work – especially in his long and masterful *magnum opus: From Dawn to Decadence: 1500 to the Present, 500 Years of Western Cultural Life* (2000) – with its dissection of "*thought-clichés*" and their erratic transmission through the media, especially in the language of journalism. One passage in Barzun's *Encounter* essay is especially pertinent:
    ...[M]odern culture is less and less at first hand. To the normal and natural distortion of ideas as they pass from mind to mind is added the distortion and fragmentation and falsification resulting from our means of diffusion. About every great idea or doctrine or thinker there is now a conventional error, journalistically fixed. I have called these "thought-clichés"; and they serve the mass media as a handy substitute for truth. It saves thinking, it fits the universal wish to know and learn with normal inattention, it serves advertisers when making their highbrow appeals for luxury products. Think of Plato, Dante, Rabelais, Leonardo, Machiavelli, Hobbes, Rousseau, Goethe, Byron, Shelley, Nietzsche, Spengler, and a hundred others about whom something is generally known, and you can without effort summon up in set phrases what that prefabricated knowledge is.
3. Burton, *Melancholy*, I, pp. 85-89, 97-101.

3. Reporting Murder, Observing the World

1. Burton, *Melancholy*, vol. I, pp. 2, 5.)

4. From More to Tyndale to Burton

1. Thomas More, *The Confutation of Tyndale's Answer* (1532), 2:129. On Tyndale, see: Brian Moynihan, *If God Spare My Life: William Tyndale, the English Bible, and Sir Thomas More—a story of martyrdom and betrayal* (2002).
    How much of the King James Bible is William Tyndale?...an average of the King James New Testament of 83.7% to be found in Tyndale 2.8% to be original to the King James. Of the Old Testament books that Tyndale translated, 75.7% of the King James is found in Tyndale...and 8.7% is original to the King James. (pp. 402-3)

For other quotes above, *If God Spare My Life*, pp. 349, 350, 361-2, 377, 378, 350.

A body of fifty-four translators had been appointed by James I to produce a new version, and they completed their work in 1611. Thus, it is "overwhelmingly Tyndale's Bible...."

Edmund Wilson, that sensitive American literary critic, once wrote of (p. 378)

"that old tongue with its clang and its flavor that we have been living with all our lives..." (p.378).

5. Euphuistic Euphoria

1. For a brief sketch of the intellectual climate of Burton's time, see W.R. Mueller, *The Anatomy of Robert Burton's England* (1952). Mueller praises the prose but classifies it "at the opposite pole from the euphuist...." He feels more comfortable with Burton's self-deprecating confession to an "extemporanean style...a rhapsody of rags gathered together from several dung-hills, excrements of authors, tags, and fopperies confusedly tumbled out, without art, invention, judgement, wit, learning..." (Mueller, p. 27; Burton, I, p. 24).

Burton adds, with wonted insouciance: "Go now: censure, criticize, scoff and rail."

See also: Andrew Solomon: *TheNoonday Demon: An Anatomy of Depression* (2001). The use of "depression" in Andrew Solomon's sub-title – and, generally, in everyday speech – presents a semantic problem which, in these concerned and sensitive circles, is severe enough to cause a bout of migraine. There is a whole tribe of victims who appear to be less depressed when they feel that they are having to cope with a disease traditionally known as *melancholia*. Outsiders can hardly comprehend the symptoms and suffering involved; but there is the novelist William Styron, in his moving little book *Darkness Visible: A Memoir of Madness* (1991), expressing nostalgia for the olde Englishe worde which appeared as early as the year 1303 and crops up more than once in Chaucer (who, in his usage, "seemed to be aware of its pathological nuances") –

"Melancholia" would still appear to be a far more apt and evocative word for the blacker forms of the disorder, but it was usurped by a noun with a bland tonality and lacking any magisterial presence, used indifferently to describe an economic decline or a rut in the ground, a true wimp of a word for such a major illness. It may be that the scientist generally held responsible for its currency in modern times, a Johns Hopkins Medical School faculty member justly venerated – the Swiss-born psychiatrist Adolf Meyer – had a tin ear for the finer rhythms of English and therefore was unaware of the semantic damage he had inflicted by offering "depression" as a descriptive noun for such a dreadful and raging disease. Nonetheless, for over seventy-five years the word has slithered innocuously through the language like a slug, leaving little trace of its intrinsic malevolence and preventing, by its very insipidity, a general awareness of the horrible intensity of the disease when out of control...(pp. 36-7).

A cry of anguish; but in our melancholy history of "the language of journalism" the record is crowded with tin ears for the rhythms of prose, with true wimps of words, and bland nouns slithering through the language like slugs.

6. In Dreams Begin Irresponsibilities

1. See, among innumerable books the still noteworthy contributions of Raymond Aron, *Opium of the Intellectuals* (French version, 1955; English translation, 1957); J.L. Talmon, *Origins of Totalitarian Democracy* (1955) and various seminal essays of the late Prof. Edward Shils (1910-1995). Many influential phrases which emerged

as catchwords – *viz.*, "*secular religion*," "*totalitarian democracy*," "*the end of ideology*" – originated in the discussions among Aron, Shils, and Talmon in the 1950s.

2. Lawrence Babb, *Sanity in Bedlam: A Study of Robert Burton's Anatomy of Melancholy* (1959), p. 60. He discusses Robert M. Browne's study of Burton's "cosmology" (especially his "Digression on the Air," at pp. 61-2).

7. Secret Expletives

1. J.B. Bamborough's commentary in the 3-volume Oxford edition of *The Anatomy of Melancholy* (1989, ed. Faulkner *et al.*, pp. xxxx, vi.)
    For "innuendo" quote: see Burton, *The Anatomy of Melancholy* (ed. Floyd Dell & Jordan-Smith, 1927). I have enjoyed reading in this remarkable edition, but have quoted and cited it only rarely. As the Editors announce on the frontispiece: "Now for the first time/With the *Latin* completely given in translation/And embodied in an *All-English* text."

    It is highly readable and should be reprinted. Still, for my purposes – which highlighted the "relevance" of an olde English text – the modernization (of spelling, punctuation, and the like) might have undermined a bit of the authenticity; and it could mislead the reader…who ought to be slowed down by the old orthographical and grammatical complexity…and should sense at once the somewhat "alien" and surprising pertinence of a singular, even uncanny Renaissance masterpiece. It should not be read – which is the basic fault of most efforts of "up-dating" – as if it were written yesterday.

    This "All-English" text, a model of its kind, was first published in the U.S.A. by Farrar & Rinehart in 1927, and was reprinted in 1947 by the Tudor Publishing Company.)

2. In all the scholarly Burton literature I single out for special mention two fairly recent essays: by a historian and a poet, respectively.
    Hugh Trevor-Roper (Lord Dacre), "Anatomist of Melancholy," in *The Listener* (which duly published BBC-Radio-3 broadcasts), 19 February 1977, pp. 187-189. It was reprinted in the author's collection of pieces, entitled *Renaissance Essays* (1985). And Trevor-Roper, who at the time also had rooms in Christ Church, Oxford, could read (and did) some of the same library books that Burton had held in his hands.

    Practically unreadable against this is Geoffrey Hill's long, chaotic theologico-politico explication, replete with felicitous obscurities in *The Times Literary Supplement*, for 23 December 1994. I have read the piece half-a-dozen times, and have rediscovered a dozen original, incisive, and not altogether convincing remarks. But they are worthy of Burton who had, after all, said "…if he would not have his words so be understood, he should not have let them runne…."

3. On Floyd Dell's career, see (on the Internet) the useful biographical sketch at www.spartacus.schoolnet.co.uk/ARTdell.htm); and there is also an informative 14-page piece by William H. Roba, "Floyd Dell in Iowa," Iowa being the state he grew up in and which still cultivates his memory as a – one of the few – "local-boy-who-made-good" in American intellectual life. It is at: www.lib.uiowa.edu/spec-coll/Bai/roba3.htm; and notes that "Dell died in 1969, virtually forgotten, meriting but a few seconds in Warren Beatty's recent movie production of *Reds* (1981)."

    Writing in the *New York Times* in 1933, John Chamberlain – who remains the best, in my opinion, of the random lot of chief book-reviewers I have followed over three-quarters of a century – pointed to the importance of Floyd Dell as among those "who, though not the most talented of their generation, yet seem to sit like spiders at the center of things….They are more symbolic of the time-spirit than many more gifted contemporaries. The currents of an epoch beat against them, pushing them now this way and now that...." The *New York Times* obituary was by Alden Whitman on 30 July 1969 and noted, in a personal, perceptive remark (rare in its columns): "Tall and slender, with a mobile and expressive face that tapered from a broad forehead to a gently pointed chin, he always struck people as 'the model of the romantic aesthete'...."

8. Across the Centuries

1. On Immanuel Kant, see my chapter on "The Sweet Dream" in *Utopia and Revolution*, pp. 576-602 and all the footnote references there (pp. 703-708). The original German in Kant's aphorism is: "*Aus so krummen Holze, als woraus der Mensch gemacht ist, kann nichts Gerades gezimmert werden.*"

9. Mentioning the Unmentionable

1. Burton, *Melancholy* (Everyman's ed.), I, 216.
2. Burton, *Melancholy* (Dell/Jordan Smith), *i*, p. viii, pp. 186, 213-214.
3. Burton, *Melancholy*, Everyman ed., Part II, pp. 134-139.
4. J.B. Bamborough, in the introduction to the Oxford edition of *The Anatomy of Melancholy*, p. xxxxvi. Burton, *Melancholy* (Everyman, ed. Jackson), vol. I, p. 17.

Part 2: The Orgasm That Failed

10. The Swinging Pendulum

1. *Daily Telegraph*, 8 May 1995.
2. Algis Valiunas, "Innocents Abroad," *Commentary*, November 1998, pp. 70-72. This is a review of the Library of America's *Reporting Vietnam* (1998), anthologizing more than 80 writers on 1700 pages. There was also another dissenting review in the *Wall Street Journal* (1999) which made similar points: M.T. Owens, "Blood and Ink."
3. William Safire, "Enter 'Mother Wit,'" *New York Times*, 8 February 1999, p. A23. E.J. Dionne, Jr.,"The Unspoken Art of Cablese," *Washington Post/IHT*, 2 March 1999, p. 9. *The Washington Post's Desk-book on Style* (ed. Thomas W. Lippman, 1989), pp. 170-1. *The Sunday Telegraph*, "MPs foul mouth sparks protest," 14 November 1999, p. 42.
4. H.L. Mencken, *American Language: Supplement One* (1945), pp. 660-661.
5. H.L. Mencken, *The American Language, Supplement I* (1952), pp. 672 *ff*. Robert Graves, *Lars Poena, or The Future of Swearing and Improper Language* (1927, rev. ed. 1936).
6. Graves, *Lars Porsena*, p. 86.
7. *Sunday Telegraph*, "Austin Powers, The Spy Who Shagged Me," 20 June 1999, p. 31. *Sunday Times*, Peter Millar, "Okay...so make with the dialogue," 20 June 1999 (News Review), p. 2. The *Daily Telegraph* (2 August 1999, p. 19) reported from Singapore – that urbane metropolis of hide-bound censorship – that the film would be released as "*Austin Powers, The Spy Who Spoke Well of Me.*"
8. Benedict Nightingale, "Agitprop drama returns to West End," *The Times*, 16 October 1999, p. 21.
9. Nicola Tyrer, "Is vulgarity our common denominator?," *Daily Telegraph*, 5 August 1999, p. 22.
10. Richard Brooks, "Young women see off naked Sophie," *Sunday Times*, 24 december 2000, p.7.

See on Flaubert, the translated edition of *The Dictionary of Received Ideas* (tr. Jacques Barzun, 1954). Flaubert was especially incisive on politically correct notions which were as modish as they were superficial...and as transitory. There are few personal 19th-century letters which are as wise and witty in the approach to words, ideas, and deeply-held convictions than his letter of 18 May 1857 (to Mlle. Leroyer de Chantepie). See: For the original French text, Flaubert: *Correspondance*, volume II (ed. *Pléiade*, 1980), pp. 716-719. It was, alas, omitted in the otherwise useful selection which Francis Steegmuller made: *The Letters of Gustave Flaubert 1830-1857* (1979).

Minette Marin, columnist, *Sunday Telegraph*, 13 January 2001, p. 24.

11. "Advertising Complaints," *Daily Telegraph*, 24 April 2001, p.5
12. "Vodaphone adverts banned," *Daily Telegraph*, 16 October 2002.
13. *Evening Standard* (London), 27 October 2000, p.8.
14. Correspondence, M.J. Lasky and Dr. Walther, March 2001.
15. "Benetton ends partnership with pioneer of shock ads," *Financial Times*, 1 May 2000, p. 1. "Der Shock-Therapeut tritt ab," *Die Welt*, 2 May 2000, p. 34.
16. Dominic Mills (editorial director of *Campaign & Marketing*, a trade journal in London) in the *Daily Telegraph*, 19 March 2002, p. 35.
17. "Row over Tory slogan," *The Times*, 16 September 1999, p.2.
18. "Hague drops Cfuk logo," *The Times* (London), 2 October 1999, p. 19. "Tories drop...," *Daily Telegraph*, 2 October 1999, p. 8. "Whiff of sensation hits New York," *Daily Telegraph*, 2 October 1999, p. 19. "Court Battles, arrests and manure, all over art," Associated Press, in *Athens News*, 2 October 1999, p. 9. James Bone,"Brit-pack confronts New York taboos," *The Times*, 2 October 1999, p. 11.

11. Searching for an Immoral Equivalent

1. David Sexton, "Just words in other people's mouths," *Sunday Telegraph*, 5 May 1996, p. 28.
2. Neil McCormick, "George Michael is back after a five-year silence...the long-awaited album," *Daily Telegraph*, 8 May 1996, p. 16.
3. Carol Midgely, "Taboo row over one woman and her dog," *The Times*, 16 September 1999, p. 5.
4. See also Andrew Swarbrick, *Out of Reach: the Poetry of Philip Larkin* (1995) an Philip Larkin, *All That Jazz* (1993), *This Be The Verse* (1974). 5. Alex Renton, "Squalid, tender, cruel...," *Evening Standard*, 28 August 1997, p. 8.
6. Lorne Manly, "Media Upstart Felix Dennis Serves Many Mistresses, Many Magazines," *New York Observer*, 18 November 1996, pp. 1, 36.
7. William Norwich, "Style Diary," *New York Observer*, 18 November 1996, p. 29.
8. Mark Porter, "Rules to swear by," *Evening Standard*, 17 March 1999, p. 63.
9. "Spirits of the Age," *Sunday Telegraph*, 28 April 1997, p. 36.
10. See Herbert Huncke's own *Journals* and his last book *Guilty of Everything* (1990). A long obituary article appeared in *The Times*, 17 June 1996.
11. George Stephanopoulos, *All Too Human: A Political Education* (1999), pp. 214.
12. Stephanopoulos, *All Too Human: A Political Education* (1999), pp. 328-341. The serialization of the book in one of Rupert Murdoch's London newspapers, *The Sunday Times* (in March 1999), gave his views on the Clinton White House and its political vocabulary wide transatlantic publicity. The obscenities are published unedited in the book and also in my quotations therefrom. In the newspaper excerpts they are touched up. As such these are even more prominent; when camouflaged they stand out with their clusters of flashing asterisks. *The Times*' skill at excerpting always guaranteed the inclusion of the juicier bits: for the scoops. See the London *Times*, 7

March 1999 (News Review), "The Insider: Public smiles and private rage: a close-up view of the Clinton marriage," pp. 1-2, 14 March (News Review), "Clinton's Clone: Inside the White House: Plotting the Perfect Picture," pp. 1-2, 21 March (News Review), "Bedazzled," p. 6.
13. Tony Allen-Mills, "Insider's dealings," *Sunday Times* (Books), 21 March 1999, p.3.
14. See Charles Mee, Jr.'s *Meeting at Potsdam* (1975), p. 263. Also the documentary film history by Dr. Bernhard von Gersdorff, *"Potsdamer Konferenz"* (Chronos, 1995).
15. My excerpts from Christopher Anderson, *Bill & Hillary: The Marriage* (Little, Brown, 2000) are taken from the text as abridged in four installments in the *Daily Mail*, 3 August - 6 August 1999.
16. Bob Woodward, *Shadow: Five Presidents and the Legacy of Watergate* (1999), pp. 439, 364. Woodward, "God Only Knows," *Sunday Times* (News Review), pp. 1-2. The asterisks are, as always, the newspaper's. Peter Millar, "Dialogue," in the same *Times* issue, p. 2.
17. These Clinton quotations are from Bob Woodward's *Shadow*, as serialized in the *Sunday Times* (News Review), 20 June 1999, pp. 1-2, and *Shadow: Five Presidents and the Legacy of Watergate* (1999), pp. 447, 374, 435, 495, 465, where all the profanity is spelled out.
18. The reference to Cromwell is no mere vague or demagogic reminiscence. Since the recent "time of troubles" (beginning with "Bloody Sunday" in 1969) the "Lord Protector of the Commonwealth" (1599-1658) has never been out of the headlines. The faltering Anglo-Irish "peace process" of the 1990s has made the reassessment of the historic heritage of hate and hostility even more pertinent. On one recent occasion (23 May 1999) the *Sunday Times* published a feature on "Essential Cromwell," including recommended popular and academic studies together with the Internet number of the official Oliver Cromwell website (*www.cromwell.argonet*) and the home page of the Cromwell Association. See: Ruth Dudley Edwards, "The Good Soldier," *Sunday Times* (Books), 23 May 1999, pp. 1-2.
The latest volume to be discussed and argued over in the Cromwell Centennial Year is by an amateur historian, Tom Reilly. His *Cromwell: An Honourable Enemy* (1999) represents yet another swing in the pendulum of Anglo-Irish emotion, with its attack on "mythological bunkum."
One English scholar wrote that "up till now" there was general agreement that in 1649 Cromwell committed appalling atrocities in Drogheda and Wexford: "We stood together believing that Cromwell had behaved with exceptional cruelty." But Reilly went back to "basics" (unlike some other historians) and scrutinized the primary sources. As a result he disagreed with almost everybody on the subject. There were indeed massacres – but still Cromwell "kept to the rules of contemporary warfare throughout his campaign." There was "no murder of unarmed citizens in Drogheda," and Cromwell's own correspondence show "how strong was his desire to keep casualties on both sides to a minimum," showing also "a rare compassion" towards non-combatants.
"Slaughter" there was; and the usual excessive looting and pillaging. But the essential understanding – to which the politicians and press propagandists have not contributed – is that the past should not be judged by the standards and fashion of our own times....Tell that to the *IRA* in Ulster, and indeed to the *KLA*, fighting for the liberation of Kosovo from the Serbians (to whom it happens to be "sacred soil"...since their historic defeat on the field of the Battle of Kosovo in 1389 at the hands of the Osmanic/Turkish Empire....
The big news-stories of five or six centuries ago are still topical.

19. Stuart Wavell, "'Charlie's girl' tells of Irish leader's secret 27-year affair," *Sunday Times*, 16 May 1999, p. 3. Mrs. Terry Keane's memoirs were being serialized in the Irish edition of the *Sunday Times*. Also see: Toby Harnden, "Dining out on champagne," *Daily Telegraph*, 22 May 1999, p. 22.

20. John F. Harris, "Kosovo War Bringing Out Clinton's Best," *Washington Post/IHT*, 9 June 1999, pp. 1,4.

21. "Mo's secret book deal…," *Sunday Times*, 12 December 1999, p. 15.

22. Sheridan Morley, "Entertainment," *IHT*, 9 October 1996, p. 12. *The Sun*, "Barely Honest," 8 October 1996, p. 11. *The Sun*'s item is by Ms. Jane Moore who is identified as "*Sun* Woman Editor" with an extra headlined encomium: *"She takes no prisoners."* I recall when a German journalist quoted this tag-line he was accused of "subtly relativizing *Wehrmacht* war crimes…" as well as being oblivious to Fleet Street's "very English sense of humour."

23. *Sunday Times*, Kirsty Lang's "Canned Heat," 19 May 1996, p. 14. *Focus*.

24. *IHT*, "'To Be or Not to Be' Is Asked Less Often," 4-5 May 1996; *IHT/New York Times*, "Same-O, Same-O; Been There," by William Safire, 13 May 1996, p. 9.

25. *Private Eye*, "How They Are Related" (i.e. the *Observer* critic, "by an amazing coincidence,"was married to Ms. Hyman), 24 January 1997, p. 10.
    See also, "Slag," in Green, *Slang Down Through the Ages*, p. 134; and for "shag," Mencken, *The American Language*, p. 367.

26. Quentin Curtis, "A Slice of Gangster Life," *Daily Telegraph*, 3 May 1996, p. 8, reviewing the film *Things To Do in Denver When You're Dead*.

27. Adam Turpin, reviewing *Lady Chatterley's Lover*, at the Cockpit, London, in *The Independent*, 13 April 1996.

28. Peter Kemp on Jilly Cooper's novel, in the *Sunday Times'* "Books," 31 March 1996, pp. 1-2; on the novels of Edwina Currie and Philip Oppenheim,19 May 1996, p. 6.

29. *New York Post*, interview with Divine Brown, 215 April 1996, a "Page Six" column which, curiously, is printed on p. 8.

30. "Reith Lecture," *The Times*, 21 Feb. 1996.

31. *Sunday Telegraph*, 13 August 1995, "Labour Problems grow in Walsall," p. 2.

32. "Head attacks Lady Jay's 'hypocrisy,'" *Daily Telegraph*, 3 June 2000, p. 4. "Blair head denies old school bias," *Sunday Times*, 5 June 2000, pp. 1-2. Petronella Wyatt, "University Challenge," *Spectator*, 3 June 2000, p. 57.
    As Ms. Wyatt, whose father (Woodrow) was once in the Labour cabinet and (as a valiant defender of colonial minority rights) tried to use methods of patronage to get his daughter into Oxford, writes:
    …[I]f I hadn't got into Oxford I would probably be too embarrassed to say so. It certainly wouldn't occur to me to blame the selection panel for discrimination….At any rate, I did get into Oxford and do you know what? I agree with Gordon Brown. The place is disagreeably elitist and intimidating…a terrifying place. As my dear late father said in his diaries, patronage ain't what it used to be. I recall his telephoning a tutor at one of the colleges and being told, to his astonishment, that the applciants had to pass an entrance exam. I ask you. The very idea….

33. Susan Barnes Crosland, *Tony Crosland* (1982). Paul Barker, in *The Times*, 28 March 1996, Education article, p. 20.

34. The anarchist reference is to Mikhail Bakunin's credo: "The passion for destruction is a creative passion."See: E.H. Carr, *Mikhail Bakunin*, 1937, pp. 24-25.

35. Sir Peregrine Worsthorne, "Sacked…explains the original sin that led him to be cast out of *The Sunday Telegraph*'s columns," in the *Sunday Times*, 5 January 1997, p. 27. Worsthorne, "Our Elite," *Daily Telegraph*, 22 March 1997, p. 16.

36. Articles by Susan Crosland and Liz Lightfoot, in the *Daily Telegraph*, 14 February 2001, pp. 1, 12.

37. See Simon Sebag Montefiore, "Comment," in the *Daily Telegraph*, 21 February 2001, p. 28.)

38. "The class warrior," profile of David Blunkett, *Sunday Telegraph*, 18 May 1997, p. 37.

39. Matthew d'Ancona, "There's more to PR...," *Sunday Telegraph*, 27 July 1997, p. 29.

40. *Sunday Telegraph*, "Blunkett's education," 12 March 2000, p. 38.

41. Rachel Sylvester & Andy McSmith, "Brown and Blair...," *Daily Telegraph*, 19 April 2002, p. 5.

42. Col. Edwin E. "Buzz" Aldrin, Jr., with Wayne Warga, *Return to Earth*, pp. 233-234. The Aldrin broadcasts on the BBC were during the week of 31 January-5 February 2000, on the World Service.

43. The Ali quotation is as given in *The Observer*, "Jungle Warfare with the Lion King," *Observer* (Sports), 18 May 1997, p. 9, and Hugh McIlvanney, "Awed by Ali, the One True King," *Sunday Times* (Boxing), 25 May 1997, p. 19. Norman Mailer wrote a book about what the publicists called "the Rumble in the Jungle," entitled simply *The Fight* (1975). The best journalistic account of the "rumble" at the time was Keith Botsford's articles in the *Sunday Times*, soon to be reprinted (as he tells me) in a forthcoming book.

44. Norman Podhoretz, *Ex-Friends: Falling Out With Allen Ginsberg, Lionel and Diana Trilling, Lillian Hellman, Hannah Arendt and Norman Mailer* (1999), pp. 207-8.

45. Andrew Neil, *Full Disclosure* (Macmillan, London, 1996), p. 162.

46. *Sunday Times*, "Nixon's politics of revenge," p. 27. Andrew Neil, *Full Disclosure*, (London, 1996), pp. 425-7, 438-9. Dominic Lawson, "A Tale of Two Mohameds," *Sunday Telegraph*, 20 October 1996, p. 41.

47. *Sunday Times* (Books), 25 October 1998, p. 18.

48. Bruce Wilson, "All men are bastards Down Under – and proud of it," *Sunday Telegraph*, 28 September 1997, p. 31. Also the dispatch from Sydney, "Feminists deal blow to Aussie manhood," same paper, same day, same page.

49. In mentioning the present ownership of this pre-eminent Sunday newspaper by the liberal-left *Guardian*, I should add that it is by no means the same distinguished liberal newspaper it was when it was owned by the Hon. David Astor.

    Astor built up a staff of writers – among them: George Orwell, Sebastian Haffner, Richard Loewenthal, Kenneth Tynan, Anthony Sampson, Andrew Shonfield, Arthur Koestler, *et al.* – which electrified a whole generation of European readers in the early post-War decades. (And not merely in London; I can remember in the 1950s and '60s, in Paris and Rome and elsewhere, how I rushed with my friends to find an edition of the paper at some railway *kiosque* or airport newsstand.)

    Subsequently it passed into the disastrous ownership of Global Tycoons (first, Robert Anderson of Atlantic-Richfield Oil and then Tiny Rowland of Rio Tinto), whose very presence – not to mention their peculiar interventionist prejudices and world-wide conflicts-of-interest as publishers – negated *The Observer*'s classic traditions of high journalism.

50. Andrew Marr and Germaine Greer, "Viagra: a harder choice...or a soft option," *The Observer*, 24 January 1999, p. 26. Leszek Kolakowski, "How To Be a Conservative Liberal-Socialist," *Encounter*, October 1978, pp. 46-49.

Part 3: Perception of American Words

12. Feisty to Funky to Flaky

1. C.S. Lewis, *Studies in Words* (1960), pp. 324-5. H.L. Mencken, *The American Mercury* (July 1925), in Mencken, *A Gang of Pecksniffs* (ed. Lippmann, 1975), pp. 114-115.

2. *Washington Post/IHT*, 25 September 1995.
3. *Newsweek*, 10 November 1980, p. 15.
4. On the Inman affair, see Stephanopoulos, p. 233-7.
5. One of François Bondy's criticisms – especially the panning (with examples) of the edition of Albert Camus – was so devastating that the publisher Rowohlt withdrew the exisiting edition. Marcel Reich-Ranicki's criticism appeared in the *Frankfurter Allgemeine Zeitung* and were collected in his *Lauter Verrisse* (1970).
6. Jay Parini, "Tourist tale (Sebastian Faulks goes to the U.S.)…," *The Guardian*, 28 April 2001, p. 14.

14. Perception Uncleansed

1. *New York Times*, 1 December 1980, p. B14.
2. See the thoughtful article by Samuel Francis, "Race to a White Minority," *The Spectator*, 28 June 1997, pp. 17-18.
3. James Langton, "Church arson conspiracy is debunked," *Daily Telegraph*, 15 June 1997, p. 24.
4. *IHT*, 14 July 1995.
5. *IHT*, 28 July 1995.
6. Pravin Banker, in the *IHT*, 28 July 1995, pp. 1, 15.
7. (Anne Applebaum, "A triumph, if you say so," *Sunday Telegraph*, 22 June 1997, p. 32.)
8. BBC World Service, 30 May 2002, 9:32 a.m.
9. *New York Times/IHT*, 24-25 August 1996, pp. 1, 5.
10. *New York Times/IHT*, "Let the Advertising Begin," 7 July 1996, p. 15, 20.)
11. Gabriel Escobar, "Life of Anxiety for Argentina's Jews," 5 August 1996, pp. 1, 8.
12. *Evening Standard*, 5 August 1996, p. 21.
13. Edward Gargan, "Chinese Power in Hong Kong," *NYT/IHT*, 6 December 1996, pp. 1, 8.
14. Margaret Miner and Hugh Rawson, "The Talk of the Year," *New York Times*, 26 December 1997, p. A 39.
15. *Telegraph Magazine*, 30 March 1996, p. 24.
16. Amiri Baraka (LeRoi Jones), *New York Times*, 27 November 1980.
17. In addition to Peter Kornbluh's critique in the *CJR*, there was also a good resumé of the errors in Gary Webb's "investigative reporting" and "provocative findings" in the *New York Times*, "Repercussions From Flawed News Articles," 3 June 1997, p. A12.
18. "Diversity Is Good for Business," *New York Times*, 16 November 1996, p. 23.
19. "Splat," quoted in Safire, *In Love with Norma Loquendi*, a collection of his *New York Times* "language" columns, p. 144.
20. Michael Fumento, "Politics and Church Burnings," *Commentary*, October 1996, pp. 57*ff*.
21. Kingsley Amis, *The King's English: A Guide to Modern English* (1997), pp. 154-5. "From Ex-Clinton Aide, Just 'My Perceptions,'" *Washington Post/IHT*, 30 May 1997, p.3.
    A Washington journalist, Fred Barnes, has done an acid sketch of Robert Reich as "The Great Pretender" in the *Wall Street Journal*, 7 July 1997, p. 8 (Int. ed.). According to Barnes, "books by government officials are notorious for self-serving exaggeration and contrived melodrama." He quotes Lane Kirkland who, as the AFL-CIO President, figures strongly in the book, as having called it disparagingly "a novel" – for Reich had Kirkland: "pontificating about philosophers he'd never read and uttering opinions he didn't hold, often in direct quotations that the labor boss denied having ever made. Six of the people Mr. Reich claims to have met at the Kirkland home Mr. Kirkland says he had never heard of, met or invited to his house." Evidently the idea of *perception* has been broadened out here to include *reception* and *conception* and *consumption*, none of which are to be taken literally.)

The Language of Journalism

15. Hillary, and Getting the Perception Right

1. Jim Hoagland, "Even for Foreign Policy, Clinton Has a Lawyer," *Washington Post/IHT*, 11 December 1998, p. 9.

Part 4: A Journalist Gets Serious: In P.G. Wodehouse's "Noo Yawk"

16. The Birth of a Crusader

1. H.L. Mencken in the *Chicago Tribune*, 2 May 1926, reprinted in *A Gang of Pecksniffs* (ed. Lippmann, 1975), pp. 116-117.

17. Facts, From Homer to Kafka (Elmore Leonard)

1. Hervé Duchêne, *The Golden Treasures of Troy: the Dream of Heinrich Schliemann* (1995), pp. 38, 47.
2. Duchêne, *Schliemann* (1995), pp. 57, 92.
3. See, also, M.I. Finley, *The Ancient Greeks* (1963) and his *Democracy, Ancient & Modern* (1973); W.B. Stanford, *The Ulysses Theme* (1963); and Wilhelm Dörpfeld, *Troja und Ilion* (1902).
4. I have been reminded of the Berenson/Finley matter by a letter included in the Berenson collection of *Selected Letters* (ed. A.K. McComb, 1964, p. 294).
5. Robert Fitzgerald, "Postscript," p. 468, and Seamus Heaney, "Introduction," p. xiv, to the Everyman Edition of *The Odyssey* (tr. Fitzgerald, 1992).
6. David James Smith, "The Mersey Killers," *Sunday Times*, 14 July 1996 (Magazine), pp. 35-40.
7. Frank J. Prial, "Elmore Leonard: Saving the Sleaze for His Books," *New York Times/IHT*, 16 February 1996, p. 20.
8. Mark Franchetti's dispatch from Moscow, "Russia's gangs go to war," *Sunday Times*, 30 November 1997, p. 15.
9. Markus Wolf, *Spionage Chef im Kalten Krieg* (1997). The English edition was translated by a young and talented British journalist who objected to the author's "undeveloped sense of morality" and she edited it and shortened it accordingly; Anne McElvoy, later the deputy-editor of the London *Spectator*, was a *Times* reporter in Berlin and Moscow.
10. Paul McCann, "A 'family' drama for grown-ups" (*The Sopranos*), *The Times*, 9 October 2000, Section 2, p. 8.
11. Quentin Curtis, "The very model of a modern mobster family," *Daily Telegraph*, 21 August 1999, p. A5.
12. Mel Gussow, obituary of Mario Puzo in *NYT/IHT*, 5 July 1999, p. 5.
13. On Luigi Barzini, see his classic book on *The Italians* (1964, written in English and later translated into Italian). The two editions were at the center of stormy controversies in both Rome and New York – for ethnicity, or a people's perception of its own culture, is challenged by any kind of self-criticism, whether at home or abroad. See also Barzini's anthology, *From Caesar to the Mafia* (1971; repr. 2000).
14. Fuhrman, *Murder at Brentwood*, p. 279. H.L. Mencken, *The American Language* (1-vol. ed., 1963, 4th ed.), p. 268. Salvatore Gravano, *Underboss* (1997). Blaine Harden, "Mob Meets Media," *Washington Post/IHT*, 16 July 1997, p. 2. Peter Maas, *The Valachi Papers, as told to Peter Maas* (1969). Peter Maas, *Serpico* (1973). Gay Talese, *Honor Thy Father* (1971).

18. Jewish Gangsters and the East Side Story

1. *Greek and Latin Authors on the Jews and Judaism* (ed. Menahem Stern, 3 vols., 1974-1984). See also the discussion of this by Prof. Jasper Griffin (of Oxford), "Their Jewish Problem," *New York Review of Books*, 18 December 1997, pp. 57-59.
2. Michael Gold, *Jews Without Money* (1930). Irving Howe, *World of Our Fathers* (1976); in Britain published as *The Immigrant Jews of New York* (1976), p. 101. Albert Fried, *The Rise and Fall of the Jewish Gangster in America* (1980, rev. ed. 1993), pp. 1-7, 78-80. Fried focuses on New York, but contends that a similar underworld "crime culture" obtained in a number of other American cities where Jewish immigrants established themselves – Chicago, Boston, Detroit, Cleveland, and Newark.
3. Albert Fried's new chapter to the 1993 Columbia University edition of his *Rise and Fall of the Jewish Gangster in America*, pp. 287-294. Daniel Bell, "At the Vecherinka," *Encounter,* July 1956. Morris Raphael Cohen, *A Dreamer's Journey* (1949). Morris Hillquit, *Loose Leaves from a Busy Life* (1934).
4. Maas, *Underboss* (1997), pp. 381, 472, 469.
5. Fried, *Gangster*, pp. 195-196.
6. Fried, *Gangster*, pp. 173-174.

Part 5: In the Cross-Fire of the Media Wars

20. Spin Doctors and Other Quacks

1. Lucian (a Greek writer of the Roman Empire), in the Oxford edition of *Longinus on the Sublime* (1906), appendix, pp. 95-6.C.S. Lewis, *Studies in Words* (1960), pp. 151-2.
2. *IHT*, 10 November 1994.
3. *New York Times*, 5 November 1994; *IHT*, 5-6 November 1994.
4. Bernard Weinraub, "Sony Aims for a Hollywood Ending," *New York Times/IHT*, 10 October 1996, p. 19.
5. *Washington Post/IHT*, 14 November 1994.

21. Images of Violence, Words of War

1. The *New York Post*'s columnist was David Gelernter, writing about "Another Big Lie from CNN," in 1999. Mark Steyn, "Persecution Mania," *The Spectator*, 6 March 1999, pp. 13-14. Bernard Weinraub, "Book Reveals Kazan's Thoughts on Naming Names," *New York Times*, 4 March 1999, pp. E-1, 6 .

    Weinraub's dispatch of 4 March offers many illuminating quotations from an old Kazan interview, only recently published, which suggest that in informing on his Party-line friends, now his enemies, he was behaving as all old Bolsheviks were pledged to do (and in a dozen countries, from Stalin to Browder, from Brezhnev and Slansky to Gomulka and Janos Kadar):

    Despite the fact [Kazan told his interviewer Jeff Young] that I had gone through a violent break with the party, I still found myself thinking like a Communist....It's hard to anybody who wasn't a Communist to understand how strong a hold those beliefs had on you. Your emotional commitment keeps overriding everything your intellect and common sense tell you. It's akin to a kind of religious faith....

2. James C. McKinley, Jr., "In Burundi, Massacres Go On as Hutu and Tutsi Squabble Over Peace Troops," *New York Times/IHT*, 9 July 1996, p. 9.

22. How Not to Report a War (Lebanon 1982)

1.   For one example, see Professor Edward Alexander's article in *Encounter*, September-October 1982, "The Journalist's War against Israel," pp. 87-97.

See also the article "Lebanese Eye-Witness" in the liberal-left Washington weekly, the *New Republic* (2 August 1982) by its editor-in-chief, Martin Peretz – "Much of what you have read in the [US] newspapers and news magazines about the war in Lebanon and even more of what you have seen and heard on [American] television – is simply not true. At best the routine reportorial fare, to say nothing of editorial or columnists' commentary, has been wrenched out of context, detached from history, exaggerated, distorted. Then there are the deliberate and systematic falsifications...." On his return from Beirut and Jerusalem, Peretz was especially struck by the "obscenity" of warped language about "Nazi Jews" and "genocidal" Israel's "final solution of the Palestinian problem.": "It is possible that some use these words sloppily, the way people once talked about American genocide in Vietnam – or Harlem. Others use them knowingly, which is to say, knowing well how inappropriate they are...."

He also noted: "...So try and figure out why you've heard so much about the Israeli occupation of the West Bank and so little about the Palestinian (and Syrian) occupations of southern Lebanon....Not eyeless in Gaza, but eyeless in Lebanon." The *New Republic* critique, be it noted, is even sharper than Professor Alexander's. Peretz's indicts his country's media, and indeed his own colleagues, in the bitterest terms:

...correspondents armed with a peculiarly American mixture of ignorance, cynicism, and brashness, who jet from crisis to crisis – looking for Vietnam, for Watergate, too...a cohort of journalists specializing in the Middle East – the *Washington Post* leads the pack – with a record to defend. The events in Lebanon proved them wrong, some of them deceitfully so, and they shape the facts – as they want to shape the future – to disguise the disservice they've done their readers, which is to say the disservice they've done the truth and, therefore, the foreign policy of our country as well.

2.   What would "move" one London journalist at the quality-paper extreme, would "chill" another at the tough populistic edge of Fleet Street reporting. Here is a snapshot from Shaun Usher's dispatch from Beirut on the expulsion of "the army that had hijacked a country" (*The Mail* on Sunday, 22 August):

They gathered at sunrise in West Beirut's municipal soccer stadium, a dusty, warbattered arena stinking of rancid garbage and human waste. Though the setting was squalidly inglorious they were high on the Arafat version....Nobody mentioned that helpless civilians had been the new super armor making 'victory' possible. Some soldiers arrived by Mercedes Benz. Beirut is lousy with Mercs, many stolen in Europe and selling for as little as £500. Deafening martial music blared from loudspeakers while wavering, badly aligned ranks were formed....
A wife in flowing robes captured the loudspeakers and half chanted, half sang a message of pride and grief soaring up into that chilling, ululating Arab cry, a fiendish yodel that was answered by the men's svagae approval.
One man hears Wagner, another fiendish yodels; nobody clears their ears and listens.

23. Interchangeable Tragedy

1.   On the career of Hanns Joachim Friedrichs, see the obituaries in *Der Tagesspiegel* (Berlin) and *Frankfurter Allgemeine Zeitung* on 30 March 1995.

2.   Charles Trueheart, "200 Victims in Latest Algeria Raid," *Washington Post/IHT*, 24 September 1997, p. 1.
3.   *New York Times/IHT*, 28 March 1995.
4.   "Zaire's War," *NYT/IHT*, 13 February 1997, p. 1.
5.   Two dispatches in the *New York Times*, reprinted in the *International Herald Tribune*, 6 and 7 March 1996.
6.   Alistair Cooke, BBC World Service broadcast, 21 September 1997. Mencken's "Valentino" appeared first in *The Baltimore Evening Sun* for 30 August 1926 and in H.L. Mencken's *Prejudices: Sixth Series* (1927); it is included in *A Mencken Chrestomathy* (1949), pp. 281-284.
7.   "*Media Coverage: Help or Hindrance on Conflict Prevention*," Report by Nik Gowing for the Carnegie Commission (1997), and the comment by Brenda Maddox, in *The Times*, 23 July 1997, p. 22.
8.   On the Holocaust, see Martin Gilbert, *Auschwitz and the Allies* (1981), and Walter Laqueur's masterly little book on *The Terrible Secret* (1980).
9.   *The Penguin Herodotus* (ed. Evans, 1942), vol. II, ch. 1, p. 18.
10. John Simpson, "You've all gone quiet over there," a dispatch from Somalia, in the *Sunday Telegraph*, 22 June 1997, p. 29.
11. Peter Finn, "Survivors of a Kosovo 'Cleansing,'" Steven Erlanger, "Dodging the Inferno," *Washington Post/IHT*, 5 April 1999, pp. 1, 8.
12. Carlotta Gall, "Deported by Train, Dazed Kosovars Stream into Macedonian Camp," *NYT/IHT*, 3-4 April 1999, p. 3.
13. *Sunday Times*, "A Pitiless War: Slaughter of the Innocent," 4 April 1999, p. 15.
14. *Sunday Times*, "Pitiless War," 4 April 1999, pp. 14-18.
15. Elizabeth Becker, "Discovery Gave Clark a Personal Reason to Fight 'Cleansing,'" *NYT/IHT*, 4 May 1999, p. 4.
16. David Finkel, "Spent but Still Standing Outside the Refugee Fences, Weeping and Hoping," *Washington Post/IHT*, 10-11 April 1999, p. 4.
17. Michael Nicholson, ITN's senior foreign correspondent, "TV 'should not sanitise war,'" in the *Times*, 9 October 1998, p. 44. His "True Terror" film on the bombing disaster in Nairobi was televised in the fall of 1998.
18. The lines of verse by Dannie Abse were from "Refugee" in *Arcadia, One Mile* (1989), excerpted in *The Times*, 31 October 1998, p. 20. John Strachey's "*Strangled Cry*," a study in political disillusionment (Whittaker Chambers, Arthur Koestler, *et al.*) was published as an *Encounter* pamphlet in 1963.
19. The poet I refer to was Thomas Wyatt (1503-1542), and the phrases are from his lyric entitled "Remembrance." Thomas Hobbes, *Leviathan* (1651; ed. Oakeshott, 1946), pp. 29-30. See my chapter on "The Noose of Words," in Lasky, *Utopia and Revolution*, pp. 155-165.

24. Of Realities and *Realpolitik*

1.   Jan Ross, "Europas Selbstverachtung: Bosnien und die Moral," *Frankfurter Allgemeine Zeitung*, 20 July 1995.
2.   *FAZ*, 25 February 1995.
3.   Fritz Pleitgen, "*Das Publikum wird kräftig geleimt,*" in *Der Tagesspiegel*, Berlin, 20 September 1995, p. 8.
4.   *Guardian*, 28 February 1995.
5.   *Newsweek*, interview with Nicholas Negroponte, founding director of the Media Lab at M.I.T., 8 January 1996, p. 52.
6.   Matthew Parris, "Visions vie with values," *Times*, 24 February 1999, pp. 1, 2.
7.   "Weasel Words of War," *Sunday Times*, 13 June 1999, p. 21.

8. For the Truman incident and Greek public opinion generally, in the spring of 1999 I followed the daily English-edition of *Katheremini*, published in Athens in partnership with the *International Herald-Tribune*. It is considered a useful supplement, even though it usually reads, in the mediocre translation, like a school-boy "pony." See also the A.P. dispatch, "U.S. Moves to Mend Greek Relations," *IHT*, 15 July 1999, p. 6.

9. Christoph Amend, "Welt ohne Bilder [World without Pictures]," *Der Tagesspiegel* (Berlin), 3 June 1999, p. 30. John F. Harris, "Kosovo War Bringing Out Clinton's Best...," *Washington Post/IHT*, 9 June 1999, pp. 1, 4.

On the Herbert Wehner incident, I am indebted to the extraordinary documentary film on Wehner's life made by the highly talented TV producer, Heinrich Breloer, in 1997. Although he "reconstructs" historical scenes – in this case: Wehner in the Moscow hotel lobby, simmering with resentment at the "ritzy image" of Chancellor Willy Brandt – he tries to conform (which is very rare indeed) to the most rigorous historiographical standards of accurate detail and truthfulness. In the first place, Breloer deliberately chooses his actors *not* to be "look-alikes." The general resemblance is there, but not so striking as to cultivate illusions that the screenplay and its reconstructed scenes are the real thing. Secondly, not a line of conversation in the film-script is invented: every spoken word is directly excerpted from the historical record.

Breloer has done half-a-dozen of such films for German television, all remarkable in these respects. Given such dramatic truthfulness, I find no other form of biography – certainly in the case of Wehner whose complexities can often be explained only by a film's dark scene with deafening silences – coming up with such unprecedented insights.

Much depends on the heights of aspiration, or the qualities of ambition, on the part of the respective filmmakers. Breloer took years to develop and complete his adventurous projects. A younger journalistic entrepreneur, named Romuald Karmakar, took a single day to do his so-called "*Himmler Projekt*." It didn't make it into the German cinemas but won a prize after its TV-premiere in the fall of 2001. Karmakar simply hired a good actor, in this case, not a famous one but with a vaguely face and with no resemblance whatsoever to the repellent features of the unholy Heinrich. He was filmed all morning long, mostly full facial frontal; he did nothing but read that much-hated, much-neglected Nazi document – Heinrich Himmler's cynical, incredible speech to his 90 faithful *SS*-officers on 4 October 1943. On the day it was preserved on the wartime wax records *in toto*...which amounted to 3 ½ hours. The actor (Manfred Zapatka) was not allowed to "act out" the role, and thus the producer saved a full half-hour as against the original speech which, of course, included meaningful pauses and drawn-out shouts and even screams. The "documentary" film thus avoided "counterfeiting" the facial melodrama of the *SS-Reichsführer*; Zapatka's expressions were impassive; but he repeated certain phrases when Himmler, in the original, had also missed his cue and lost his place or train of thought, once or twice.

The whole "projekt" was problematical. Enlightened public opinion couldn't make up its mind about the point of it all. Some critics feared that the neo-Nazis, small in number but susceptible, would be convinced (half-a-century later!) by the public presentation of the Hitlero-Himmlerian defense of the Nazi Concentration Camp State. Others – also flawless anti-Nazis – were worried that, in the full three hours, only a few minutes had been devoted to the matter of the Jews and their ongoing systematic destruction. The monstrous crime – if one has to listen to the pseudo-Himmler at such length – should really have taken up a bit more time...if it would be effective today with a younger generation, coming to grips with the *Erinnerungskultur* ("the culture of remembrance"). Why was Himmler so casual about the Holocaust? Wasn't anti-Semitism central to the Nazi concerns?

I am afraid that the film raised more questions than it could ever solve. The "documentation" character of a proper film that only wanted to put the truth on film was not self-sufficient. It needed explanation, and explication from experts in the press and scholars in the academy. In one of the "round-table discussions" that were tacked on to the *Himmler Projekt*, the historian Eberhard Jaeckel clarified much, and academic Himmler experts went on to make good points about Himmler's vocabulary, pronunciation, rhetorical techniques (as different from *Der Führer*'s or Dr. Goebbels'). But, in the end, I considered the project a failure. I would want my grandchildren or my students to *read* the full text and to compare by arguing out loud the various interpretations put on it by any half-dozen of the innumerable historians of the Third Reich and the murder of European Jewry – say, for starters, Joachim Fest, Ian Kershaw, J.P.Stern, Walter Laqueur, Hannah Arendt, Daniel Goldhagen (or, even better, Christopher Browning)…and, last but not least, George Steiner.

10. Saul Bellow, *Ravelstein* (2000), p. 136. The "gemlike" phrase from Pater is in his conclusion to his *History of the Renaissance* (1873).

11. Tony Allen-Mills, "Pentagon plays by the good ol' Rumsfield rules," *Sunday Times*, 18 March 2001, p. 26.

12. Such "Kremlinological" speculations were often wayward and fanciful, but there were spectacular instances of uncanny insight – especially in the writings of the unjustly forgotten Franz Borkenau. Among the other serious students of Soviet affairs who – in the absence of the kind of evidence that is freely available in democratic societies but not in totalitarian – went in for this sort of imaginative analysis were: Leopold Labedz, Bertram D. Wolfe, Robert Conquest, Leonard Schapiro, Richard Pipes, Wolfgang Leonhard, Hugh Seton-Watson, George Urban, among others.

13. "Interview with Madeleine Albright," *Welt am Sonntag*, 16 October 2000, p. 9.

14. Hilary Alexander, "Clare Short's Feminism…," *Daily Telegraph*, 14 June 1999, p.6.

15. While I am maing national distinctions and comparing differences, I might as well note that the traditional ambiguity of this phrase misleads in German as well as in English. Perhaps even more.

In German it is, in my view, patently absurd, for no exception proved (*"prüfen,"* in German) any kind of rule. It tests it; it challenges it. It troubles the rulemaker to think the matter through: whether, or not, an exception or a chunk of contrary evidence or experience invalidates the whole generalization. It might, or it might not. But it is surely not the rule that *Die Ausnahme bestätigt die Regel* (the exception proves [or confirms] the rule). It does no such thing. Only in the sense that some (if certainly not all) exceptions are so small and unimportant as to leave the general rule intact and unassailably valid.

Language often builds its aphorisms into such tropes and traps that will keep irony and paradox alive. How rules deal with exceptions – which can be controversial, unsettling, invalidating – is a tricky business. One-liners can also use weasel-words.

16. Ben Fenton, "Rice strikes a different chord for Leibovitz," *Daily Telegraph*, 29 October 2001, p. 3. On Carlyle, *The Oxford Companion to English Literature* (ed. Drabble, 5th ed., 1992), pp. 170-1, 866-67.

17. My quotations are from Michael Frayn's adventurous play about Werner Heisenberg and Niels Bohr, *"Copenhagen,"* which had its successful premier at the Royal National Theater in London (21 May 1998); and subsequently had a long run.

In the Methuen edition of the play, Frayn's explanations are in the *Postscript*, pp. 97-115.

My acceptance of the credo I have quoted does not mean that I also am finally convinced that Frayn's imaginative reconstruction is actually "the way it really was."

The Anglo-American press has been replete with "Heisenberg explanations" which range from imputations of Nazism and unconscionable loyalty to Hitler all the way to his secret anti-Nazism which "sabotaged" the German Bomb Project. And even, as in Frayn's play, when he made an important mistake – *e.g.* the amount of enriched Uranium he would need for success – it was (in Mrs. Bohr's ironic aside) supposedly his unconscious making an error in a good cause.

See: Samuel A. Goudsmit, *Alsos: The Search for the German Atom Bomb* (1947); Elisabeth Heisenberg, *Das politische Leben eines Unpolitischen: Erinnerungen an Werner Heisenberg* (1991); Thomas Powers, *Heisenberg's War: The Secret History of the German Bomb*. I am indebted to Simon Bourgin for calling my attention to Arnold Kramish: *The Griffin: The Greatest Untold Espionage Story of World War II* (1986).

18.   I base my account of the Milan Nobel-Prize-Winners conference on the report in the *Frankfurter Allgemeine Zeitung*, 8 December 1995, p. 43.

25. Spielberg, Or the Hollywood Scapegoat

1.   Bryan Appleyard, in the *Sunday Times* ("Culture"), 2 November 1997, p. 2.
2.   "Profile: Steven Spielberg. Smaller than life," *Sunday Telegraph*, 13 June 1997, p. 35.

26. Journalism and Jewry

1.   Katharine Graham, *Personal History* (1997), ch. I, pp. 6, 17.
2.   My quotations are from Katharine Graham, *Personal History* (1997), pp. 51-2, 6, 17. See also David Halberstam, *The Powers That Be* (1979). On the Shylock reference in the history of anti-Semitism, see John Gross, *Shylock: A Legend and Its Legacy* (1994), a brilliant and sensitive study.
3.   George Vecsey, "The ripples of visible racism spread outward," *NYT/IHT*, 3 February 2003, p. 18.
4.   Frederic Raphael (b. 1931) is the author of nineteen novels, four books of short stories, among the most recent and notable: *A Double Life* (1994), *Coast to Coast* (1998). His latest book of essays was *The Benefit of Doubt* (2000).

    The *Sunday Times* account of the "outcast" was its its "News Review" section, 9 March 2003, p. 9. Raphael's memoir of *A Spoilt Boy* (2003) was published by Orion in London.
5.   On Stanley Walker, see his *City Editor* (1934/1999). The John Hopkins University Press has also reprinted *The Night Club Era* (1933/1999). The "ethnic passage" I have quoted is from *City Editor*, p. 328. The Mencken remark on *PM* is in H.L. Mencken: *Mencken's Diary* (1989), p. 422, 198 On Walter Lippmann, see Ronald Steel's informative biography *Walter Lippmann and the American Century* (1980), wherein Lippmann's dissembling is recorded.

    On a related theme, see Alfred Kazin's vivid memories of New York City in the 1930s entitled *Starting Out in the Thirties* (1965) and for the years from the Hitler-Stalin pact (1939) until the 1970s, *New York Jew* (1978).
6.   *Sunday Times*, "Legover Lennie Caught On the Hop," 20 December 1998, p. 11.
7.   A.N. Wilson's column in the *Evening Standard*, 21 December 1998, p. 15.
8.   On the Lawson case, see Dominic Lawson's own account (with an absolute denial) in the newspaper he edits, *Sunday Telegraph*, 20 December 1998, p.24. Also, in the

Sunday Times, "MI-6 used Spectator as cover story," 20 December 1998, p. 5. Sarah Lyall's dispatch from London to the *New York Times*, "British Press Uncovers Spy Scandal of Its Own," *NYT/IHT*, 21 December 1998, p. 4.

9. Toshio Welchel, *From Pearl Harbor to Saigon: Japanese American Soldiers & the Vietnam War* (1999); Arnold Isaacs, *Washington Post/IHT*, 31 August 1999, p. 10.
10. Mark Garrod, "Eight-shot victory pits edgy Goosen back on the top of Europe," *The Independent*, 20 January 2002.
11. Robert Wistrich refers in his history of anti-Semitism as the "longest hatred in history." Wistrich, *Anti-Semitism: The Longest Hatred* (1991). See George Steiner, *In Bluebeard's Castle: Some Notes Toward a Redefinition of Culture* (1971, London).
12. I repeat here the references from vol. I, "The N-Word and the J-Word," pp. 199-266. See Flavius Josephus, *The Life Against Apion* (Loeb Classical Library, 1926). Peter Schaefer, *Judeophobia: Attitudes toward the Jews in the Ancient World* (Cambridge, 1997). See also: Jasper Griffin, "Their Jewish Problem," *New York Review of Books*, 18 December 1997; and Michael Grant, *The Jews in the Roman World* (1973), pp. 126-132.
13. I follow here, generally, the data assembled by the invaluable work by David Goodman and Masanori Miyazawa on *Jews in the Japanese Mind: the History and Uses of a Cultural Stereotype* (1995). My quotes are from pp. 12, 15, 59-60.

    Arthur Koestler's essay, "A Guide to Political Neuroses," first appeared in *Encounter*, November 1953, pp. 25-32. It was reprinted in Koestler's *The Trail of the Dinosaur* (1970).

    See also David Goodman's review article of Masani Uno's *If You Understand the Jews, You Will Understand the World* (1986) and *If You Understand the Jews, You Will Understand Japan* (1986) in *The World and I*, November 1987, pp. 401-9.
14. See Melvin J. Lasky, "A Sentimental Traveller in Japan" (I, II) in *Encounter*, November 1953, pp. 5-12, December 1953, pp. 57-64.
15. I add several other names to whom I owe personal debts of gratitude for their wit and wisdom about foreign experience in Japan: Frank Gibney; Edward G. Seidensticker; Ivan Morris.

    Gibney, who later organized a formidable Japanese edition of the *Encyclopedia Brittanica*, wrote *Five Gentlemen of Japan* (1953); Seidensticker and Morris were admirable translators, the latter producing an edition of the classic *As I Crossed a Bridge of Dreams: Recollections of a Woman in Eleventh-Century Japan* (1971). I might also mention two U.S.A. Ambassadors to Japan; the Harvard historian Edwin O. Reischauer whose *Japan: Past and Present* (1953) and *The Japanese* (1977) were standard works; and the late Robert Murphy, whom I knew as General Clay's diplomatic advisor in the military occupation of Germany.

    Ambassador Murphy encouraged me "to abandon Berlin (for a while)" and invited me to "spend some time in Tokyo"; thus, he is the "onlie begetter" of these impressionist pages on Japan's "Jewish problem." When I returned to Berlin, I published a long travelogue entitled "*Reise nach Japan*" in *Der Monat* (June 1953, pp. 249-267, and July 1953, pp. 358-376).

    Last but not least, there is the instructive memoir of Herbert Passin, *Encounter with Japan* (1982).
16. Goodman and Miyazawa, *Jews in the Japanese Mind*, p. 19.
17. I follow here Goodman/Miyazawa, *Jews in the Japanese Mind*, p. 157, and their sources on p. 286.
18. See, among his other writings, Ian Buruma, "A New Japanese Nationalism," *New York Times Magazine*, 12 April 1987.

27. White House Storm, or "Hurricane Monica"

1. Mary McGrory, "How Scandal Changed Our Lives," *Washington Post/IHT*, 6 March 1998, p. 8.
2. Russell Baker, "Media Meltdown," *NYT/IHT*, 4 February 1998, p. 24. Janny Scott, "A Different Kind of Journalism," *NYT/IHT*, 2 February 1998, p. 3. Art Buchwald, "Press Five for Love," *Washington Post/IHT*, 5 February 1998, p. 22. Associated Press dispatch, "Newspapers Curb 'Doonsbury,' *IHT*, 11 February 1998, p. 22.
3. Hugh Hefner, "HEF on Clinton," on the Internet, *What's Happening at www.playboy.com*, March 1998.
4. *Newsweek*, 9 March 1998, p. 28.
5. *Newsweek*, "Race to the Bottom," 9 March 1998, p. 28. Maureen Dowd, "An Armageddon of Dirty Linen," *NYT/IHT*, 12 February 1998, p.9.
6. Richard Cohen, writing from Davos (Switzerland), "Sorry the Real Scandal Here Is Not About Sex but the Law," *Washington Post/IHT*, 4 February 1998, p. 9. *New York Times*, editorial, "The Press Does Its Job," *NYT/IHT*, 5 February 1998, p. 8. *New York Times* editorial, "New Phase for Clinton: Character at Issue," *Newsweek*, "The Eye of the Storm," 16 February 1998, p. 31. *NYT/IHT*, 18 March 1998, p. 8.
7. David Maraniss, "What Makes First Lady Stand By Her Man," *Washington Post/ IHT*, 2 February 1998, p. 2.
8. Richard Cohen, *Washington Post/IHT*, 4 February 1998, p. 9.
9. Maureen Dowd, "Washington Gives a Beating to 'Everybody's Best Aunt,'" *NYT/ IHT*, 10 February 1998, p. 9.
10. Whoopi Goldberg, *IHT*, 10 February 1998, p. 24.
11. *Newsweek*, "Clinton in Crisis," 2 February 1998, pp. 10-31; the Jordan quotes are at p. 27; the tapes on pp. 18-19 of the International Edition. *Time* Magazine, 2 February 1998, "Monica and Bill: the Sordid Tale...," pp. 43-44.
12. *F.A.Z.*, "Having a Good Time," 13 February 1998, p. 12.
13. "Monica's World," *Time* (International Edition), p. 36.
14. "Collective Shrug Over Clinton Case: It's Understandable to Lie About Sex, U.S. Public Says," *New York Times/IHT*, 25 February 1998, pp. 1, 10.
15. The Koestler reference by President Clinton is in "the Starr Report" as reported in a special issue of *Newsweek*, 21 September 1998, p. 26C, 46 B. The article by Jonathan Alter emphasizes Clinton's "way with words" – "Spinning Out of Sinning: Shameless yet compelling, Bill Clinton talked his way into trouble. Can he talk his way out?" The short answer is that he did...presumably by means of what *Newsweek* referred to as "breathtaking rhetorical jiujitsu.")
16. Andrew Morton, *Monica's Story* (1999), pp. 139-40. The references to Hitler and Stalin are at pp. 210, 216. Among the best of the pieces written about the Lewinsky affair, the Clinton impeachment, and the media's "feeding frenzy" remains Geoffrey Wheatcroft, "Monica's Year – 1998," in *Prospect*, January 1999, pp. 28-32.

    "*Butthead*" is, of course, a "new word" for a stupid and obnoxious person. Jonathon Green – in his *Dictionary of Slang* (1998), p. 182 – notes that is "a term immortalized since the 1990s in MTV's semi-animated series *Beavis and Butthead*." Doubtless contributing to the "immortality" was Monica's usage as a jocular term of endearment. She probably knew that "*butt buddy*" meant a very good friend, and possibly that "*butt boy*" is a homosexual and "*butt fuck*" refers to anal intercourse. For additional associations, see the various entries in Lighter, *Historical Dictionary of American Slang*, vol. 1, pp. 333-334.

    I mention these because in Monica's immortal enrichment of White House vocabulary it must be the first time in U.S. history that a sitting President was called a "*Butthead!*" to his face.

17. My quotations are from the breathtaking text entitled, "Monica Dreyfus," which was published in June 1999 in a periodical entitled *Bad Subjects: Political Education for Everyday Life* (Issue #44). The three authors are identified as Tomasz Kitlinski and Pawel Leskowicz, both Fulbright scholars at the New School University; and Joe Lockard who is a unitary academic narrator, who lives in Berkeley, California.
18. Andrew Morton, *Monica's Story* (1999), p. 266.
19. Walter Kirn, "When Sex...,' *Time*, 2 February 1998, pp. 30-31.

Part 6: Intimations of a Post-Profane Era

28. A Curse on Boyle's Law

1. *The F Word* (ed. Jesse Sheidlower, foreword Roy Blount, Jr., 1995), pp. ix-x, xviii.
2. Robert Graves, *Lars Porsena* (1927, 2nd rev. ed.), pp. 18-19, 22-23, 50.
3. Alexander Walker, "What a criminal way with words," *Evening Standard* (London, 21 November 1996), p. 26.
4. *Independent on Sunday*, "Beauty and the Eye of the Beholder" (*Review*), 11 August 1996, pp. 14-15.
5. Francis Wheen's article, somewhat edited, appeared in the *Sunday Telegraph*; but I am quoting from his letter to me and his enclosed manuscript, 21 May 1996.
6. E. J. Mishan, *Making the World Safe for Pornography, and other Intellectual Fashions* (1973), p. 256.
7. Robert Boyle, *Discourse against Customary Swearing, and a Dissuasive from Cursing* (1695), pp. 111-12.
    On the dream of a perfect, squeaky-clean language, free of the evils of the past (and its sordid usages), see M.J. Lasky, "A Noose of Words," in *Utopia and Revolution*, pp. 155-65, contrasting the traditional conservative tradition (Locke *vs.* the vain attempts at "the perfect reforming of the languages in the world") and the radical principle of utopian hope (1968, Paris): "Old words carry an 'old future' in them. There will be no overthrow until language itself is made new, until speech as we know it and use it ceases...."
    For a detailed history of the quest, its persistence as well as its confusions and contradictions, see Umberto Eco's *The Search for the Perfect Language (The Making of Europe)*, tr. James Fentress (1997).

29. Scholem's Nouns and Verbs

1. Scholem, *Origins of the Kabbalah*, p. 266-7.
2. See A.O. Lovejoy's classic work, *The Great Chain of Being* (1936) and also his *Essays in the History of Ideas* (1948). I have previously – in my *Utopia and Revolution* (1976) – paid tribute to Arthur Lovejoy's seminal originality; and the following passage may illuminate for the reader my own guidelines in the present work. He defines "philosophical semantics" as:
    ...a study of the sacred words and phrases of a period or a movement, with a view to a clearing up of their ambiguities, a listing of their various shades of meaning, and an examination of the way in which confused associations of ideas arising from these ambiguities have influenced the development of doctrines, or accelerated the insensible transformation of one fashion of thought into another, perhaps its very opposite. It is largely because of their ambiguities that mere words are capable of this independent action as forces in history... (Arthur O. Lovejoy, *The Great Chain of Being: A Study in the History of an Idea* [1936], p.14).)

3.   Scholem, *Kabbalah*, p. 408. Scholem, *Sabbatai Sevi: The Mystical Messiah* (tr. 1956, revised 1973). Scholem, *Kabbalah*, p. 410, footnote 105; p. 267; 265, fn. 144.

On Scholem's politics, see his *Messianic Idea in Judaism* (1971) and the various volumes of his published correspondence (with Walter Benjamin, among others). On his life, and the transition from "Gerhard" to "Gershom," that is to say, from his assimilationist German existence in Hohenzollern and Weimar Germany to his Zionist achievement as the savior and protector of a great Mystical Hebrew Tradition, there is "memories of my youth," *From Berlin to Jerusalem* (1980). Harvard University Press has published a critical study: *Gershom Scholem: Kabbalah and Counter-History* by David Biale (1979). I have also found useful the entry by Seymour Cain in *Thinkers of the 20th Century* (eds. Devine, Held, *et al.*, 1985), pp. 506-507.

4.   On the theme of "double challenges," his published correspondence is suggestively rich in biographical details which surely contributed to the great tensions which distinguished his scholarly achievement. See the letters to and from his mother (a recognized masterful prose stylist), available only in German.

Betty Scholem, Gershom Scholem, *Mutter and Sohn in Briefwechsel 1917-1946* (Munich, 1989). His mother was astonished that her young son emigrated from Germany, to which all successful middle-class familites were so devoted, in a romantic Zionist impulse. She herself remained in Germany "to the last minute" (1939) in order to struggle on behalf of another son who, as a Communist, had been arrested (and later was murdered in Buchenwald). All the more astonishing because Scholem had been raised in such an "un-Jewish" family where Prussian values and even Teutonic nationalism (with more than a touch of ironical anti-Semitism) prevailed over ancestral pieties which prayed for the return "next year" to *Yerushalayam*.

Gerhard-Gershom made it to the Hebrew University in Palestine in 1923, and he never saw his mother again. In time after she had realized that the persuasion that her proud and loyal tribe of German Jewry could proclaim that "*Wir sind Deutsche!*" was an illusion. For a National Socialist régime proclaimed that they were no such thing. They were suddenly aliens, and unacceptable. See also the sensitive article by Jürgen Kolbe on the Scholem letters in the *Frankfurter Allgemeine Zeitung*, "Geschichten aus Preussisch-Berlin," 7 July 1990.

30. Robert Graves, Or the Vision of a Post-Profane Era

1.   Robert Graves, *Lars Porsena* (1927), pp. 90-91.
2.   Robert Graves, *Lars Porsena, or the Future of Swearing and Improper Language* (1927, rev. ed.), pp. 89-94.
3.   James Walton, TV review, *Daily Telegraph*, 15 October 1999. The quotations from the South Seas scholars are attributed to "an anonymous ethnologist" in Robert Graves' *Lars Porsena* (1927), pp. 62-66.

When I once asked Graves (in his home on Mallorca) who they were and why they remained "anonymous" in his once popular (with a revised second edition) little book on "the future of swearing," he shrugged the question off and cracked, "I made them up...." (Maybe *this* fib was the sly joke; and in fact he didn't.)

In any case, I haven't been able to identify the sources. I imagine one was Malinowski. Graves hadn't read Margaret Mead (and if he had he wouldn't have found her credible enough to quote her...). Her own fibs have since been exposed.
4.   Graves, *Lars Porsena* (1927), p. 32.
5.   Graves, *Lars Porsena*, pp. 53-54.

31. Counter-Revolution and Utopia

1. David Denby: "Buried Alive in the Annals of Popular Culture," *New Yorker*, 15 July 1996, p. 57.
2. The remark by Henry Miller about "hateable" writers was made to me in a conversation at Formentor (Spain) in the 1960s when we were both serving on the literary jury for the *Prix Formentor*.

Index

Abse, Dannie, 230
Adams, Franklin P., 276
Advertising
    Benetton campaign, 61, 65-66
    global audiences for, 65-66
    Heineken Beer campaign, 63
    Leary political campaign, 61-62
    Mercedes-Chrysler campaign, 63
    "orgasmic collectivism," 63
    Ryvita Crispbread campaign, 64-65
    temptations cashing in, 61
Advertising standards
    authority for, 56-59
    profanity and, 55
    sexual advertising, 56-58
Advertising Standards Authority
    advertising and, 56
    complaints receiving, 58
    Dahl case, 56-57
    French Connection criticizing, 70
    Ryvita's campaign and, 64-65
African Americans
    conspiracy against, 142
    corporate discrimination, 151
    genocide against, 149-150
    killings of, 142
    perception and, 142-143
Albright, Madeleine, 249
Aldrin, Buzz, 111
Ali, Muhammad, 116-117
Ali, Tariq, 197
American. *See* United States
American language
    beau meaning in, 138
    Clinton as feisty, 129
    fast quips use, 131-132
    fate of, 138
    as "homemade," 132
    inventive salesmanship, 133
    military use, 133-134
    new lingo in, 130

    one-liner use, 132
    simple word fate, 139
    word meanings in, 130-131
    world outreach of, 134-135
Amis, Sir Kingsley, 151-152
Anderson, Christopher, 87
Anecdotal evidence, 195
Anti-Semitism
    American institution constrictions, 276-277
    Jewish defending offensive, 278-279
    Jewish differences, 273-274
    media's ethnic correctness, 280
    media's language colorfulness, 280-281
    as rampart, 274
    Raphael case and, 275-276
    as "Semitic problem," 277
    types of, 273
    verbal slurs detecting, 279
    vs. harmless ethnic prejudice, 279
    See also Prejudice
Armstrong, Neil, 112
Australia
    bastard use, 123-124
    f-word use, 123
    illegitimacy rate of, 123
    Knightley's memoirs of, 122-123

Baldwin, Jimmy, 149
Bamborough, J. B., 27
Benetton Company, 65-66
Bennett, Bob, 90
Berenson, Bernard, 167
Berlesconi scandal, 237
Bernstein, Theodore, 43
Bertrand Russell Peace Foundation, 213
Birley, Mark, 80
Blair Administration
    euro terminological dispute, 238
Blair, Cherie, 94